Turning Rocks into Profit

Turning Rocks into Profit

High grade excerpts from 25 years of Gold & General Newsletters

JULIAN BARING AND THE BLACKROCK GOLD AND GENERAL FUND

Edited by

Michael Coulson and Justin Baring

STACEY
INTERNATIONAL

Turning Rocks into Profit
High Grade Excerpts from 25 years of Gold & General Newsletters

STACEY PUBLISHING LTD
19 Catherine Place
London SW1E 6DX
Tel: +44 (0)20 7221 7166; Fax: +44 (0)20 7792 9288
Email: info@stacey-international.co.uk
www.stacey-international.co.uk

ISBN: 978-1-909022-47-8

CIP Data: A catalogue record for this book is available from the British Library.

Printed and bound by TJ International, Cornwall.

Contents

Dedicated to Julian Baring
1936 –2000

*The role of Evy Hambro of BlackRock, who has been associated
with the Gold & General Fund for many years,
has been critical in bringing this project to fruition.*

In Tribute

Julian Baring was an inspirational investor who was fantastically good at generating ideas. He was also extremely adept at making sure that the best ideas were reflected in the Fund as large holdings. As he put it: 'successful investing is all about collecting large amounts of money not large amounts of share certificates'. His philosophy –which continues to this day – has contributed to the long term success of the Gold & General Fund.

 – *Dr. Graham Birch, Former director of BlackRock Commodities Investment Trust Plc and manager of BlackRock's World Mining Trust and Gold & General Unit Trust.*

Not only was Julian Baring logical but he was also persuasive and full of facts and figures to support his argument.

When Mercury bought The Gold & General Fund in 1991 it had a value of £55 million and in the ensuing period fell to about £22 million at which point Julian came over to my desk and told me it was time to buy. Of course I followed his advice. It has been a fabulous investment. I cannot remember his exact words to me but he told me that I would not be sorry.

 – *Stephen Zimmerman, Founding Partner of Newsmith LLP; previously Deputy Chairman of Mercury Asset Management and Joint Chief Operating Officer of Merrill Lynch Investment Managers.*

Julian Baring was every mining CEO's nightmare. Company roadshows, at least in my twelve year experience, normally involved the tired repetition of the company script to ill prepared (and often ill educated) analysts and fund managers. In a discussion with Julian no script helped. He had done his homework. He could not be deflected with corporate spin. He had detected the wealth creating or wealth destroying essentials of the company performance with a terrifying ruthlessness. He was doing his job in ensuring that the funds he invested were rewarded with real wealth creation. The rise of fund manager capitalism has regrettably seen an emphasis on short-term measurement, dubious metrics and often the illusion of both growth and wealth creation. None of these was any part of this man's character. There can be no better tribute to the legacy of this man of real substance than scholarships that give the capacity for real wealth creation to a new generation of Africans.

— Bobby Godsell is Chairman of Business Leadership South Africa, a member of the South African National Planning Commission and co-Chairman of the South African Millennium Labour Council and non-executive director of the South African Industrial Development Corporation. He was previously Chief Executive of AngloGold Ashanti.

Julian Baring's letters were The Gold Standard. For him, it was all about grade, costs, profits and price-earning ratio. To make money as an investor, the company had to make money. It seems that the investors of today agree with him.

— Pierre Lassonde , Chairman and co-founder of Franco-Nevada, Previously Chairman of The World Gold Council.

Julian Baring was the driving force behind the shareholder's rebellion against the management at Randgold & Exploration in the late Nineties. Victory in that battle created Randgold Resources, a FTSE 100 company which for years now has been the world's top-rated gold mining stock, rescued Harmony and DRD Gold from oblivion, and changed South Africa's top-heavy, arms-length mining house culture for good.

Julian's antipathy to traditional mining house structures stemmed from his keen appreciation of value and his dislike of waste. Managers, he believed, were the stewards and not the owners of their shareholders' assets, even though they often behaved as if they were, and should be held fully accountable for the performance (or lack of it) of those assets.

— Dr. Mark Bristow is Chief Executive Officer of Randgold Resources Ltd.

Ode to Julian Baring

From the playing fields of Eton to Sub-Saharan climes
One young Julian ventured forth, and had some high old times,
From car park at Charter (or so he'd have you think)
He worked his way to Capel's, and thus he kept his link
With miners and investors, and optimists for gold,
And how he kept them happy, with stories bright and bold.

As London's foremost broker, with firm and forthright views
And armed with notes and pop charts, he was always in the news.
He talked to Save & Prosper, he schmoozed the M&G,
He made them lots of money – or that's what he tells me!
For longer than a decade he was mining's Number One
Then started Gold & General, with lots of dosh to run.

But then he got fed up, he didn't like Canary Wharf
So he upped and went to Capel's, "sorry lads, I'm orff!"
Capel's lost a treasure, and Mercury got its prize –
The Savoy was very happy as it watched its profits rise.
So from Africa to sovereigns, to vineyards and Chateaux,
He's kept us all in wisdom, we're so sad to see him go.

But we have a strong suspicion, he'll not be losing touch –
How could he lose his contacts, when he loves us all so much?
He'll be lurking in the background, of that we're pretty sure,
With metaphors and similes and probably much more.
But just one thing we beg him, the message of this poem,
Dear Julian, when in London, please leave that wine at home!

*Composed by the mining team at T. Hoare & Company on
the occasion of Julian's retirement.*

The Genesis of the Book

Justin Baring is CEO and co-founder of JB Management, the London-based investment advisor to The Red Fort Partnership Ltd, a natural resources equity fund. Following in his father's footsteps he has spent 17 years immersed in the global natural resources arena, most recently with Citigroup, advising many of the world's largest and best-known mining companies and investment funds. He began his career at Natwest Securities and ING Barings and is a graduate of the University of Cape Town.

When his father Julian passed away in 2000 Justin set up a bursary fund specifically to assist young African individuals from disadvantaged backgrounds in pursuing a career in the mining industry. The fund has awarded scholarships to over forty individuals in mining related faculties at South African Universities with which it is associated. Justin and his fellow trustees have also set up joint ventures with several African-based mining companies which award scholarships to deserving individuals from those companies

When Julian retired just before the millennium to concentrate on his pottery and garden in Provence he was often asked if, like his neighbour Peter Mayle, he had a book in him. Having spent his whole career penning a weekly newsletter, in retirement he was much more enthusiastic about the idea of publishing the letters he had already written rather than starting afresh. It has been Justin's intention ever since his father's death to follow through on the initiative. This year, 2013, as the Gold and General Fund and the World Mining Trust celebrate their 25th and 20th anniversaries respectively there is no better way to celebrate this achievement than with the publication of the best of these weekly letters. The newsletters not only provide a front row seat to the important historical events that occurred in the mining industry during the first decade of the fund's life, but also give a unique insight into the investment techniques and thoughts of one of the world's great mining investors.

This collation of the letters would not have been possible without Michael Coulson who has so generously given his time and experience all for the good of the Scholarship Fund. I am sure Julian would also give credit to all of those that assisted him with these letters over the years, especially those he worked so closely with whilst at James Capel, Mercury Asset Management and Merrill Lynch Asset Management and the team that still remain at BlackRock.

All the proceeds from this book which has kindly been financed by BlackRock (which today is the home of the Gold and General Fund and the World Mining Trust) will be donated to The Julian Baring Scholarship.

About the Editor

After obtaining a BSc in Economics from the University of London Michael Coulson started his career in the City in 1970 as a trainee on the James Capel mining desk headed by Julian Baring. In 1971 he joined Stirling & Co's natural resources team as a mining salesman and analyst. In 1973 he became the gold mining analyst at Fielding Newson Smith and then joined L Messel & Co as senior mining analyst in 1975 and started to produce an annual gold review which he published every subsequent year until 1991. In 1982 he joined Phillips & Drew to establish a mining research desk and during his four years there he was twice voted No 2 gold analyst (behind Julian Baring) in the annual Extel Analysts Survey. He then joined Kitcat & Aitken where he established a highly respected integrated mining team.

During the volatile 1990s he was with a number of broking firms including Credit Lyonnais Laing and in 1998 he was approached by Paribas to head up their global mining research team. Following the merger of Paribas with BNP he became an independent research consultant doing work on mining companies for small UK brokers lacking formal coverage of the sector. He was a non-executive director of Canada's oldest listed mining exploration company, Moneta Porcupine, for a number of years and since 2003 has been a director of City Natural Resources High Yield Trust PLC. He has written two books on mining, *An Insider's Guide to the Mining Sector* (also translated into Chinese) and *The History of Mining*.

Introduction

This book has been put together to mark the 25th anniversary of the birth of the James Capel Gold and General unit trust which is now part of the stable of BlackRock investment funds. The Gold and General trust was the brainchild of Julian Baring, the doyen of mining sector stockbrokers, who in April, 1988 moved from the financial investment sell side to the buy side becoming a Fund Manager. For many years he wrote a weekly fund review which kept investors in his fund abreast of not only his investment actions on their behalf but also the philosophy that drove those actions. This book contains selections from these newsletters and covers issues very close to Julian's heart such as South African Mining House fees, gold hedging and seeking value in the always volatile mining share market. The main text of the book is in Roman typeface and italicised typeface; Roman typeface marks the newsletter selections and italicised typeface marks the editors' guidance comments.

Julian's introduction to mining was with the Anglo American group in southern Africa where he ultimately ended up in the public relations department in Salisbury, Rhodesia (now Harare, Zimbabwe). He returned to London and in 1967 he joined London stockbrokers James Capel and became a partner; his brief being to set up an integrated department researching and selling mining shares. It was the first venture of its kind in the City and came about as a result of Julian's experience with Anglo American in Africa and the rising interest in London in mining as a result of strong metal prices and the boom in Australian mining shares occasioned by what was known as the "Aussie nickel boom", which started in 1966 with the discovery of nickel by Western Mining in Western Australia.

The new department was immediately a success and spawned others in the City, as the nickel boom was closely followed by a ten-year bull market in gold and gold shares. Apart from conventional research notes on individual mining shares by Capel's mining researchers, the department produced a weekly newsletter which contained short pithy reviews of the mining market and individual share recommendations written in a racy style that would horrify today's compliance departments. Needless to say the newsletter was one of the firm's most anticipated weekly publications. Although Julian led the mining sales team, in time he began to pen pieces for the newsletter where he concentrated on gold. Indeed, the Capel's mining team was one of the first groups to put their firm's computer to work on research valuation models – the Capel's one valuing South African gold shares. The first gold programme took a whole weekend to run; later versions reduced the running time to minutes. The fully developed Capel's gold programme was named GoldVaal and was thought to surpass anything that the South African Mining Houses themselves had to value their huge gold share portfolios.

Perhaps spotting that the stockbroking game – driven by the Big Bang and the arrival of large international banks in the London securities business in the late 1980s – was going to change significantly, Julian persuaded James Capel to back the establishment of a specialist mining unit trust enabling him to move from the sell to the buy side. After 20 years selling mining shares to institutional investors Julian had accumulated an enormous amount of knowledge and decided that he would harness this experience of how mining markets work to manage institutional and private money bound for the sector.

There are a number of themes that crop up regularly in the newsletters. Two stand out above all others – the fees charged to South African gold mining companies by the controlling Mining Houses and the price hedging of future gold production, practised with great enthusiasm by many gold mining companies in the 1990s in particular.

The point that Julian made about the fees issue was that gold miners rewarded their general shareholders with dividends but the controlling houses not only received those same dividends, they also received fees from the mines for a range of services they offered the mines. What annoyed Julian was that these fees were paid irrespective of mine profitability and so were part of the operating costs. They were, however, broadly non-negotiable so if the mines were being financially squeezed by a falling gold price the general shareholders' dividends suffered but the houses at least got their fees paid. For Julian this all led to unacceptable conflicts of interest and since the fee structure could not be tested by competitive bidding for providing the required services outside, shareholders never knew if the fee structure was reasonable.

Hedging annoyed Julian even more. It was his view that hedging gold production by selling forward, locking in a fixed price for gold which might suit directors with rewards driven by e.p.s. growth, was not necessarily in his best interests as a shareholder wanting complete exposure to movements in the gold price.

He was also very precise in his views on gold share valuations. He did not think a share cheap if it was unlikely that he could get back, in the form of dividends, the price that he had paid for that share over the remaining life of the mine in question. He had little truck with the concept of retention of free cash by individual mines. Although it should be borne in mind in those days that the structure of the gold mine sector was dominated by the South African mines where single individual mines were listed. He was also often at odds with gold mine analysts who pushed the quality leaders when gold shares were in a bull phase. When the sector was running Julian thought it obvious that the low grade, highly gold-price-leveraged mines were the ones to hold, as it was those that would benefit most at the distributable profit level as a rising gold price led to increasing profit margins.

One of the other value themes that Julian pursued was that he would not buy gold shares just for the sake of it. Over the years he often found the best value in terms of earnings prospects in the base metal sector and, despite the name of the fund and his own reputation as the City's leading gold guru, he would buy these shares in preference to gold shares.

Although Julian favoured the South African gold share sector he was no apologist for the Apartheid political system, a fact which he made absolutely clear to the South African mining industry who did not always appreciate his views. After the rise to power in South Africa of FW de Klerk, the release of Nelson Mandela and the start of negotiations over a new political dispensation, some of the antics on both sides during the three years of talks which led up to the country's first full elections almost drove him to despair. The newsletters carried his thoughts on the volatile negotiation process. But however frustrated he became he never lost hope that a deal would be done, eventually leading to excellent investment opportunities in the post-Apartheid age.

Within these newsletters we also have extracted miscellaneous and entertaining musings of Julian on topics such as his dabbling in horse racing, his love of Provence, his run-ins with compliance – the boys in blue as he called them – and his thoughts on the brokers who serviced him. And no selection of Julian's thoughts on the world of mining would be complete without his famous gold sovereign/Savoy dinner ratio which is still a subject of discussion and analysis today.

Any collection of Julian's writings must be selective but I hope that in the following pages readers who knew Julian will recognise some of the essence of what made him such an iconic figure in the world of mining. I hope also that in these pages, as Julian's thoughts echo down to us, that we might speculate what he would have made of mining today. I suspect that in the current age of Mining House aggrandisement we would have heard Julian thunder against the M and A antics of many of the leading houses as they expanded their empires and kept their heel on dividend payments, and then shamefaced reversed this through writedowns, project cancellations and a belated nod towards shareholder dividends.

For over 25 years first as stockbroker and then Fund Manager Julian Baring dominated the financial sector's coverage of the mining sector, forging the concept of an integrated team providing advice and leadership of what can often be a temptingly lucrative but treacherous sector. It is highly unlikely that the modern world of highly regulated securities would provide the circumstances that would encourage the emergence of another Julian Baring. He was very much a one-off, and I hope this comes through in the following pages.

Michael Coulson, 2013

1. Gold and the Gold Price

When the Gold and General Fund was first set up in 1988 the gold price was wallowing around the $450 level, having been as high as $850 in 1980 and as low as $300 in 1985. Gold shares had staged a strong recovery over the previous three years and in Julian's view were too high, and very poor value compared with leading base metal shares. Since the Fund's remit did not confine it to investing in gold shares, in its early years it was strongly weighted towards base metal shares which Julian thought were cheap. Later, in the 90s, gold shares became cheaper – particularly the South Africans', which Julian favoured – and he became a big buyer of the high cost marginals which gave him the gearing to a rising gold price. One of the Fund's biggest coups was the accumulation of Western Areas at mere pennies.

Julian turns more optimistic on gold but doubts that inflation will be the price driver. He surmises that the key influence will be technical issues relating to forward sale positions. He retains a cautious view of gold shares however.

The recovery in base metals has been going on for the best part of 18 months and is one of the reasons why some commentators have detected a whiff of inflation in the air. The gold price is widely thought to be influenced by inflationary considerations, but judging by the recent price inaction, its proponents seem to have lost their sense of smell. Perhaps those who believe that gold is an inflation hedge have already bought it, but those who disbelieve probably haven't and won't. Personally I think the gold price will go up in the latter part of this year for technical reasons connected with forward sales undertaken earlier this year by the mining industry. The rise will probably be widely interpreted as a response to inflationary pressures, but who cares?

The reason I think that gold (unaided by the forward sellers) could disappoint the inflation hedgers is that it has more than kept pace with inflation already. If it had merely kept pace with inflation since 1914, the price today would be $212. If it had kept pace with inflation since 1934 the price today would be $320. So whichever way you look at it, it seems that gold is probably discounting a measure of future inflation already.

If that is accepted, we must be careful lest the gold price disappoints people again, even when inflation does pick up. I think gold will look after itself for the reasons mentioned above, but I do worry about the level of gold shares. They seem to me to be allowing nothing for accidents. I am investing our money accordingly – carefully! (**6. 10/5/88**) [**The first number is the Newsletter number followed by the date laid out day/month/year. This continues throughout the text.**]

The eternal quandary for Julian – whether or not to sell cheap base metal shares to buy what he sees as fully priced gold shares.

Generally, the market seems to be gradually coming back to life. There is more and more talk about inflation and the fact that Taiwan is an ongoing buyer of gold for its reserves should provide a firm undertone to the gold price in the coming months. Don't forget that the mining industry has already sold forward, in January and February, a significant percentage of the gold it will produce later this year and next. Taiwan has stated that it proposes to spend $5 billion on buying gold this year. This is enough to buy 25 per cent of this year's newly mined production. The mining industry, outside South Africa, is thought to have sold forward some 30–35 per cent of this year's production and this could soon start to cause a squeeze on prices.

All this merely serves to heighten my dilemma as to whether to sell blue chip mining companies on giveaway multiples in order to buy more gold shares which generally look fully valued on foreseeable gold prices. It is, after all, a well-known fact that once people decide they want to buy gold shares, they buy them whatever the multiples! If I do decide to take the plunge, you will be the first to know. (**8. 24/5/88**)

Julian continues to agonise over the prospects for gold and gold shares but admits that Taiwanese government buying looks like powerful support for the price.

The Taiwanese dollar reserves have now reached some U$75 billion. Needless to say they have suffered appalling losses, due to the weakness of the dollar. They would not want to offend the Americans by diversifying out of dollars into gold, but no one could complain if they invested the interest on their dollar holdings into gold. That is just what they are doing. Last week, I pointed out that they were going to spend $5 billion this year on buying gold for their reserves. This amount would enable them to buy about 25 per cent of Western world production this year with their interest cheques and still have change. You can't be bearish of gold this year with that background.

The Taiwanese are great savers too. They save between 30 and 40 per cent of their income every year and unlike Westerners, they love gold. It may therefore not surprise you that they have so far imported 186 tonnes this year. Statistics show that in the East as a whole, approximately 400 tonnes of gold have been imported in the first four months of this year. New mine production in the west is running at some 1,400 tonnes p.a.; statistics that many Westerners choose to ignore. (**9. 31/5/88**)

Julian returns to the issue of the cheapness of base metal miners against gold miners and points out the market implications of a falling gold price and rising gold production.

Here is a chart of the gold price (that's the line that has been rising since February 1985) and the trade weighted US dollar (that's the one that's been falling). You can see that the trend line for gold has just broken downwards. It is easier to see that the dollar has broken upwards out of its trend. Since the dollar has been on a downward trend for three years, there are obviously many well-rehearsed reasons for its continuing decline. It is widely thought that the recent recovery in the dollar is merely a temporary aberration from the overall downward trend to which we have become so accustomed. The gold price may well be signalling that, in fact, the trend for the dollar may have changed and that in future it will require less, not more, dollars to buy an ounce of gold. That is another way of saying that the price of gold is going to fall in terms of US dollars. In case it is, I have drawn in a bear channel within which it might be expected to trade.

Now, if there are widespread expectations that the price of a metal is going to rise, people become very brave and overconfident. They set their sights on the sunny uplands and pay little attention to the ravines. In the case of gold mining shares, many people think they can look forward to a heady mix of rising gold price and expanding production. Take away the rising gold price and the expanding production becomes a threat, instead of a promise. All this could lead to people making a painful reassessment of the price they are prepared to pay for future earnings and that is why I'm into non-ferrous metals, even at the risk of boring you! (**16. 1/8/88**)

Julian ponders the odd situation where massive gold buying by Taiwan and Japan has not stopped the price from falling and also wonders whether gold acts quite differently from other metals.

If I had returned from the East a year ago and told you that I had been reliably informed that Japan and Taiwan were going to buy between them more than half the Western world's gold production in the next 12 months, and I had therefore invested our money in shares which would benefit from a rising gold price I doubt if many of you would have sold your units in disagreement. The fact that, 12 months later, those two countries have indeed done exactly that, and the price of gold has actually fallen, must provide food for thought, even for the most avid "gold bug".

I have certainly been among those who have expressed concern at the relentless increase in gold production which has resulted from the price of gold remaining at levels which encourages ever-increasing expenditure on prospecting for gold. I frequently enquire whether, in the case of gold, the laws of supply and demand have been suspended!

According to the annual gold survey by Consolidated Gold Fields, Western world gold production has been rising at a little less than 6 per cent per annum for the last three years and is expected to continue to do so for the foreseeable future. That indicates an increase in the gold supply of some 80 tonnes a year from 1373 tonnes in 1987 to say 1700 tonnes by 1991. The communist bloc is believed to produce an additional 300–350 tonnes per annum.

So if substantial new buyers of gold, like the Taiwanese and Japanese, have no favourable impact on the gold, why should we be worried about increased mine production, which probably represents about 10 per cent of what was bought by the two great surplus nations?

Perhaps we should be asking, what would the price of gold be now if Japan and Taiwan had not been in the market for such large quantities? Maybe you will deduce that it would have risen!

I am coming round to the view that we should be looking at gold in a quite different way to the way we look at consumable commodities. It would be interesting to know what Consolidated Goldfields thinks about this, since they expend considerable sums of money researching annual supply and demand statistics from which they appear to be increasingly reluctant to forecast even the likely direction of the price. And who can blame them? Certainly not me.

As a diversion, I might mention that, on my travels, I asked my audiences whether any of them knew what the gold price would be tomorrow, in a week's time or in a year's time. None of them seemed to have the faintest idea, or if they did they kept it to themselves. I then tried the same question for copper with no greater degree of success. I couldn't help asking them why, if they were unable to predict metal prices, they were prepared to pay twice the market multiple for a gold share, but only half the market multiple for a base metal share. They couldn't explain that either! (**17. 16/8/88**)

The historic link between the oil and gold price is examined and Julian concludes that there is no longer much connection between the two prices.

The other chart which may interest you is the chart of the relationship between oil and gold. During the 1970s it was widely thought that the prices of oil and gold were linked, since those who were the recipients of oil revenues liked to invest a portion of their new-found wealth in gold.

The relationship was severed in the 1980s when the growth in the oil supply far outpaced the growth in the gold supply. Both fell in value, but oil much more than gold. You can see from the chart that since 1970, when gold was $35 and oil was $25/bbl, it has been possible to buy an average 15.7 barrels with an ounce of gold. Since 1985, the fall in the oil price has resulted in an ounce of gold being able to buy ever-increasing amounts of oil, so that today one ounce enables you to buy 32 barrels, nearly twice the long-term average. If predictions of the oil price turn out to be correct, an ounce of gold will soon be able to buy no less than 43 barrels! An unprecedented quantity. It seems to me therefore, that the price of gold no longer has much to do with the price of oil.

You may, of course, come to the conclusion that a fall in inflation may cause the gold price to decline, thus correcting the unprecedented situation highlighted above. If the historical relationship between oil and gold were to return, then, with oil at $13 a barrel, the gold price would have to fall to $204 per ounce, a similar percentage fall from its peak as oil has already suffered. I remember in 1980, people used to think oil was going to rise at 2 per cent in real terms until the end of this century. It was unthinkable at the time that it might decline to one quarter of its 1980 value or even less if you express it in terms of money of the day.

Please don't go away with the impression that I think the gold price will fall to the levels indicated by this discussion. Those who have been supporting the price of gold at the $425 level since March, regardless of the changing outlook for inflation and recession, and regardless of the oil/gold ratio, or the level of the dollar for that matter; are just as well aware as you and I of the factors which are perceived to effect the price of gold. It seems to me that whatever factors influenced the gold price in the past, they are clearly not doing so now. If they were, gold shares would be very much lower than they are, balancing more equally than they do, the potential risks and rewards. (**21. 13/9/88**)

Despite the attraction of gold to people when living standards are rising Julian continues to be puzzled by the ability of gold shares to trade, in value terms, at a material premium to base metal companies.

I wonder if it has ever occurred to you that the price of gold may have more to do with people's standard of living than with their cost of living. Gold, after all, is the only commodity everybody wants, so it is hardly surprising that as people get richer, more "savings" become available to purchase gold. In the last year or so, it has been people in the Far East who have been buying into weakness.

When I applied for my first job in 1955, I was offered £360 a year by a bank in the City. At that time gold was £12.50/oz, so had I taken that job I would have earned 29 oz of gold a year. Today, first jobs are advertised at £7,000–£7,500 per annum and gold is £251/oz; so people still start work for about 29 ounces a year.

I was discussing this with the mining people at Kleinwort Grieveson, because it obviously has some bearing on one's prognostications about the gold price. They published the following chart in their Weekly Mining World. It shows the number of hours the average American breadwinner (as opposed to a starter in the UK) has had to work to earn an ounce of gold, since 1974. They conclude that, "while the gold price may well come under pressure in the coming months, it is certainly not on the brink of collapse". They predict a minimum price for gold in 1989 of $375/oz, only 12 per cent below current levels. I wish I could share their confidence. Experience tells me that once the rot sets in, metal prices never seem to bottom at levels which are conveniently, but not too painfully, below current levels.

Their prediction of $375 an ounce is 25 per cent below this year's high of $500/oz. In the previous three bear markets for gold, the price has fallen by an average of 47 per cent over approximately a two year period. This bear market started nine months ago.

Capels are now officially forecasting that gold will average $400 next year, but their mining department's gold expert believes that the price will be $320 by the end of next year. I find this most interesting since people are normally reluctant to forecast that the price of anything will change by more than 10 per cent from the price they last saw on the screen. The result is that we all have a tendency to sell too little and too late.

As you know, I have been taking the view that so long as the trend of the gold price is down, I would rather be in base metal shares. They are "given away" because people think that base metal prices have passed their peak. I can't help asking this question: If North American base metal shares ought to sell on half the multiple of the market, because base metal prices are perceived to be past their peak, why should gold shares sell on twice the multiple of the market when gold is already 20 per cent below its peak, and widely predicted to fall further? (**22. 20/9/88**)

Julian is sceptical about the October 1988 rally in gold.

You may have noticed that there is a rally in progress in the gold price, encouraged in part by the strength of oil and base metal prices. There are always rallies in bear markets and you can't go after them all. This is far too dangerous.

Once, or sometimes twice, in the course of a bear market you get a jumbo rally of 40 to 50 per cent. I don't think this particular one is going to turn into a jumbo, (they are usually preceded by a state of near panic and that was not the situation before this one started). I have therefore ignored it in the expectation it will blow itself out before long. The market does not seem to believe it either, otherwise gold shares would have been responding more positively by now. (**24. 18/10/88**)

I drew your attention to the start of this rally in my letter of 18th October and mentioned that once or twice in the course of a bear market you get jumbo rallies in gold shares which are worth going for, but more often, the rallies are simply bull traps which are far too dangerous to try and catch. It was my opinion that the rally that is now in progress would not develop into a jumbo because I did not think there was overwhelming bearish sentiment for the shares before it started. I may have been wrong and we may already have seen the worst of the gold price when it hit $387 recently. Who knows? All I know is that markets tend to move in trends or channels. They go up until they stop going up and then they go down until they stop going down!

As far as I can see, the overall direction of the gold price is still down but there is a rally going on which may or may not have enough strength in it to penetrate the downtrend and thus reverse it. If you think it has the strength to reverse the trend, it is not too late to sell this fund and buy one which is more heavily committed to gold shares. Because I am not yet convinced personally that the overall trend is about to change, I am not going to move wholesale from the base metal shares, which have served us so well and which are still cheap, into gold shares on multiples three, four and five times as great. I have made a move in the direction of gold, but not a big one. Certainly not big enough, I suspect, to fully satisfy the fundamentalists! (**27. 8/11/88**)

The shooting down of two Libyan jets fails to move the gold price.

The final straw came when the shooting down of the two Libyan jets resulted in the gold price going down! A few years ago such an incident would have put five dollars on the gold price. No – gold's time has not yet come, but I keep the situation under constant review and expect, in a year's time, to be much more positive. Meanwhile any new money you give me will go into the American leaders which have served us so well and still look outstandingly cheap.

It is gratifying to see how many of you persevere all the way to the end of these missives. The telephone lines were blocked just before Christmas as the classical scholars among you rang in with your translation of the inscription on the chamber pot. Bad luck for the director of Kleinwort Benson Investment Management who won the champagne. In terms of the Financial Services Act he was of course bound to pass on the benefit to his underlying clients! (**34. 4/1/89**)

Julian continues to be cautious over gold's prospects.

All along I have said that the purpose of this fund is to enable its holders to buy more and more gold with the sales proceeds of their units, so if you feel that gold's time has come, that option is very much open to you. All I can do is keep the fund invested in shares which offer good value increasing our liquidity from time to time to help ride out the squalls. Personally I am still not convinced that gold's time has come because it is only going up in dollars and not in the stronger currencies. In a strong bull market gold goes up against all currencies.

If you look at the charts overleaf you will see that these setbacks in the past have been buying opportunities. The trouble is that, having suffered the pain of the declines, most people in the past were too shell-shocked to take advantage of them. It looks to me as if the units are heading back down to the main support line somewhere between 711 2p and 74p offered. If they fall to 71112p and the gold price stays where it is now, 1,000 units of the fund will be able to buy 3.1 ounces of gold. I have marked these two levels on the charts so you can see for yourselves what I am talking about. (**65. 29/9/89**)

Julian acknowledges that gold is once more in a bull trend.

Now that the gold price is firmly in a bull trend, everyone is asking how far it will go. I think the only thing you can say with any certainty is that the trend has changed. The distance it will travel obviously depends on the speed of the rise. If it goes up too far too fast it will sorely tempt those who bought it when no one wanted to know to take their profits quickly. If, on the other hand, the speed of the rise is moderated then it might in fact go further and last longer. (**71. 23/11/89**)

Unable to buy "safe" paper gold because of regulatory restrictions, Julian buys high yielding Escom bonds instead.

I expect you would like to know what I have done with the £4.5 million of your money I had allocated to paper gold when the guillotine fell. About £2½ million has been reinvested in Escom bonds which now total nearly 12 per cent of the portfolio, £1 million is being held in rands awaiting investment. The remainder has been invested in Canadian and South African gold shares in equal proportions.

Although Escom bonds can hardly be described as "gold backed", there is no doubt that an improving gold price has a favourable influence on their value. First of all, when the gold price goes up, the rand tends to appreciate. A rising rand is bad for gold shares but good for bonds since it depresses the gold price in rand terms and enhances the value of the coupons received by foreign holders of the bonds.

Secondly, when the gold price goes up people forget their prejudices and buy South African gold shares. In order to do so investors have to buy financial rands. An improving financial rand enhances the price of Escom bonds and of gold shares equally.

Third, an improving gold price enhances the Government's revenues and tends to reduce its borrowings. This tends to bring down interest rates and does no harm to capital values in the bond market.

Recently these factors, together with an improving political background, have led to a 20 per cent gain in the value of Escom bonds. Not as good as the gains achieved by gold shares but better than the gain on gold itself which has risen about 12 per cent from its low. The yield on the bonds of 23.5 per cent per annum is some consolation if the above mentioned factors don't come up to scratch.

So, now that we no longer hold paper gold in the "safe" part of our portfolio, that portion is now going to contain these high yielding bonds instead. They are safer than gold shares but not as safe as gold itself. I would have preferred the metal, even if holding it resulted in our fund underperforming those funds which only hold gold shares. (75. 19/12/89)

Julian reminds investors that gold shares are simply equities and often follow equity market trends.

It is disappointing that gold itself is not for the moment behaving in its usual contracyclical manner. Hardly surprising perhaps, since some people must have lost a packet in the Japanese market in the last week or so and may well have had to sell their gold to pay their losses.

I have frequently reminded you that one of the lessons people learned after the 1987 crash was that gold shares are equities and that there is not much mileage in buying equities, even gold ones, to protect oneself against a fall in equities.

Conscious of this lesson and of the fact that most gold shares are already discounting higher gold prices, I have refrained from committing 100 per cent of this fund to gold shares, preferring rather to hold a mixture of gold and other mining shares. I explained the rationale in last week's newsletter. (84. 28/2/90)

Julian turns to the desirability of gold and the tendency for those who are already owners to be the most enthusiastic buyers when gold rises.

The other story relates to the demand for gold jewellery in the Eastern bloc. The political upheavals have lead to a massive surge in demand for gold as a hedge against currency and inflation. With jewellery stores reported to be out of stock, the USSR increased the price of gold by 50 per cent in mid

January and this is expected to put gold in Russia at a considerable premium to international prices.

The second story is probably good news for consumers of caviare. If gold is too high in Russia it won't be long before some gentlemen dressed up as fishmongers will be seen toing and froing between London and Moscow delivering "expensive" gold and collecting "cheap" caviare. Many people in authority think of gold as a rather primitive medium. Being so sophisticated, they cannot believe that there are others, less erudite than themselves, who find that gold serves their purposes perfectly well. It is to be trusted more than the financial instruments which seem to enrich their creators more than their recipients.

Finally, the Gold Council has made a startling discovery which some of us knew already, namely ... "the more gold jewellery women own, the more they wish to own". Those who have more than five articles of gold jewellery own 11.4 pieces on average and have the highest intention of purchasing more. Watch out boys – you have been warned! (**87. 22/3/90**)

High volatility in the gold market caused by a Middle East seller increases Julian's caution, but he remains a bull.

The only funny thing that happened last week was a remark by a wag who rang up to say that if I had really been led to believe that everything was coming up roses, I ought to change my gardener! Yes I know perfectly well that as soon as things start to look nosey, it is tempting providence to open one's garden to the public. Put not your trust in experts! This week's events prove conclusively that there are few experts in the gold market and I am certainly not one of them. If there are any they didn't ring me. If they had, I'm sure I wouldn't have believed them!

So here we are, poorer but little wiser. You have no doubt read the explanations of why the gold price plunged $20 in a day. I always say that if people were as good at predicting a move as they are at explaining one, we would all be rich.

For the record it is said that the forced seller of gold was of Middle Eastern origin. Estimates of the quantity of gold sold ranged between 70 and 120 tonnes worth between $830 million and $1.4 billion. That is a sizeable amount of money in anybody's language. No wonder its sudden unleashing caused the various support levels for gold to be breached; levels which might have held in a more orderly market. You can't rally buyers for that quantity of gold at such short notice. They need time to collect their thoughts and look for their cheque books.

What was impressive, was that sufficient buyers did come forward at the $360/oz level to halt the plunge. It was that level which held throughout last year and it was from that level that the rally started which got us all so excited round the year end. Until that level is breached, as far as I am concerned, I shall continue to act as if we are still in a bull market. However, as I have told you on numerous occasions, I am not so confident of being right that I am prepared to hold all your eggs in one basket. Despite my caution you will be aware that if gold fails us, the portion of the portfolio which is gold related will drag the rest down for a time. (**88. 29/3/90**)

The effect of a falling or static gold price on jewellery demand and marginal production suggests a higher gold price long term.

What is important is that the gold price has fallen so far that it forces the marginal producers to take action and this is happening in South Africa where production is forecast to fall slightly this year. In Australia the industry is being cushioned by the forward sales which have been made at higher prices, but these only serve to disguise the fundamental problem. Gold tax is due to come in next year and that could well sound the death knell for some 40 per cent of the current Australian gold production of 200 tonnes. This is not my statistic. It comes from no less a figure than Mr. Hugh Morgan, M.D. of Western Mining, Australia's largest gold producer, who was quoted in the *Financial Times* this week as saying that this percentage was now unprofitable at present gold prices. All in all therefore, there are grounds for believing that the gold price itself has not got much downside.

The other encouraging feature is that the "cheapness" of gold is gradually entering the consciousness of people other than those, like your Fund Manager, whose livelihood depends upon it! This should in due course encourage jewellery demand in the West as well as in the East where it is already booming. Now we have to encourage the jewellery industry not to use the weak gold price simply to increase their profit margins, but rather to pass on the benefit to the public, thus increasing the demand. The gold industry could also do its bit by emulating DeBeers and spending 3.5 per cent of its revenues on promotional activities – but they won't.

It is obviously through a combination of decreasing supply and increasing demand that the gold price will eventually recover to more sustainable long-term prices. I am still using $400/oz as my long-term gold price for share evaluation and am beginning to think that, if anything, such a price is probably a bit on the low side. The logic of what I have been saying is that the longer the price stays below $350/oz, the higher it is likely to bounce once the marginal production has been removed. You know as well as I do that people have a tendency to assume that the price of a commodity will forever be the last price they saw on the screen. (**98. 20/6/90**)

Julian continues to ponder on why gold shares should still command a premium over base metal shares despite a poor gold price, and also wonders why gold miners do not curtail production in such a poor market.

What the charts tell me is that gold is becoming more and more like any other commodity. Certainly it no longer has as much appeal to investors as it used to, and even Central Banks seem content to see the percentage that gold represents of their reserves, diminish. If that were not true they would surely be topping up their gold reserves at current prices. Instead, a number of them are reported to be selling!

So it is left to the jewellery industry to absorb all the gold and this is what they are bravely trying to do. It is becoming increasingly hard to argue that gold is unlike those other metals which have to depend on fabrication demand to keep the mining industry going. If other miners have to rein back production from time to time to bring supply and demand into line, why should not the gold industry have to do the same? Being seen to do so would appear to me to be the most effective way of rekindling the investor demand which is so desparately lacking. Meanwhile, it is hard to fathom why the market continues to pay a premium for gold shares over base metal producers. It certainly explains why the fund remains heavily overweighted in base metal producers. (**99. 27/6/90**)

The Iraqis invade Kuwait.

Past experience teaches us that people who fight wars use up great quantities of base metals. People who try to escape from war zones tend to buy gold to take with them. After all, who can be sure that he will be able to exchange his paper money outside his country's borders. It is therefore not surprising that metals have been firm recently and the Gold and General Fund has been behaving well relative to shares generally, fulfilling one of its roles, namely as a hedge against financial uncertainties. A sort of financial umbrella you might say.

It is said that people buy gold when they are scared. It must be scary to be living in the Middle East today, but not as scary as it may yet become if the Americans are to succeed in their endeavours. Few people believe that everything will return to normal in a short space of time, so the initial upward move in the gold price could well be sustained for quite some time yet. (**16/8/90**)

Gold gets the thumbs up as a hedge during times of uncertainty but again Julian is puzzled that gold has not performed more strongly in the wake of the Iraqi invasion.

The alarming turn of events in the Middle East has underlined the merits of holding a portion of one's portfolio in gold and gold related assets. (At least they have not gone down!) What is rather surprising is that they have not gone up more.

If it is true that the Russians, who are pushed for readies, have been taking advantage of the current demand for gold to off-load 75 tonnes of the stuff to raise US$1 billion, that would help to explain why the price has not risen further.

As far as gold shares are concerned, they are having to compete with the falling markets everywhere. They are more than holding their own, but they are not exactly steaming away yet. Of course, if you have to pay 30–50 times earnings for the protection that North American gold shares offer, that too may contribute to their somewhat lacklustre performance.

In South Africa the background news would surely be hitting the headlines were it not for Kuwait. If the gold price was falling, not rising, the news from that unhappy country would be depressing share prices yet further.

The problem facing your Fund Manager is to strike the right balance between the bullish scenario for the metal price and the vulnerability of the shares should peace break out or the gold price fail to rise further.

This is another of those occasions where one wishes that the Authorities would allow funds like this one to hold the metal itself. After all, with the metal, the costs of producing it have already been paid and the political risk has been taken out. Why it should be thought less desirable for the public to be allowed to hold the metal than the shares which produce it, remains one of the mysteries of the modern world. (**107. 20/8/90**)

Julian, way before GATA's formation, suspects that governments may be manipulating the gold price and also anticipates the hedging problems of companies such as Ashanti Goldfields eight years ahead of events!

My guess is that the Authorities are doing their best to keep the markets calm. There was a rumour late last week that the Bank of Jeddah has again been active in the market. They have reputedly sold a further 500,000 ounces of gold which has had the effect of keeping a lid on the price. Some people think that the Bank of Jeddah is acting for a third party.

The Americans have enough on their plate already with the Gulf and the banking crisis, not to mention the recession. The last thing they need is a soaring gold price to highlight a worldwide loss of confidence in the financial system. It would therefore not be in the least surprising if they were taking steps to nip any rise in the gold price in the bud.

Those of us who have been in the gold market for a few years know that you can control the gold price for a time but you cannot do it for all of the time. Governments can decide what is currency; in the end it is the people who decide what is money.

Current high real interest rates provide a disincentive for investors to buy gold. The prospect of lower interest rates is stimulating the gilt market at the moment, so gold may yet have its day. Furthermore, as I pointed out last week, the current craze for gold loans and forward sales by the gold mining industry could so easily backfire on them causing a shortage of physical metal. It is by no means easy to manage a successful gold hedging programme, but it is certainly easier when the gold price is falling than when it is rising. Ironically the problems may only come to light when the gold price starts rising and the margin calls start arriving. I think insufficient notice is being taken by the investment community of this aspect of the gold mining industry. The problem is not widely understood at the moment but it will have to be when someone gets into difficulties. By then it will be too late. Most of the shares we own do not have massive forward sales and gold loans so hopefully we will not be hurt too much if there is a problem. (**123. 10/1/91**)

A gentle poke at gold price forecasters.

I do not know whether you have noticed how much better people are at explaining a price movement once it has taken place than they are at forecasting one.

I have read page after page of predictions about the gold price, but it is usually the unexpected that alters the equation so one wonders why they bother! One of the major factors which is thought to have a depressing influence on the gold price is forward sales and gold loans undertaken by producers. A few years ago such sales were virtually unheard of and those that had heard of them usually lost money by participating in them. Gold forecasters did not take them into account because they did not know about them.

People like to predict the continuation of a trend. There is the wellknown example concerning the pollution of the streets of New York at the turn of the century expected to be caused by the predicted growth in the volume of horse drawn carriages. No one predicted that horseless carriages would remove the problem completely within a few years, nor did they predict that the horseless carnage would in turn create unacceptable levels of pollution a couple of generations later. (**132. 11/4/91**)

As Japanese buyers gobble up an anniversary gold coin issue commemorating the Emperor's wedding anniversary, the FT writes off gold as just another commodity – much to Julian's puzzlement.

At a time when many commentators, including the Lex column of the FT, are writing gold off as just another industrial commodity, and certainly not a metal which should form part of an investment portfolio, comes news of a different nature. I pass it on to you since I have always believed that one is better advised to watch what people do and not take too much notice of what they say.

In the same edition of the Financial Times as Lex was writing off gold, it was reported that the Japanese public had gobbled up the entire issue of gold coins which had been minted to coincide with the first wedding anniversary of the new Emperor. The interesting thing about these gold coins is that they have a face value of 100,000 yen but they only contain 48,000 yen's worth of gold. In other words, these unsophisticated people – you could hardly call them investors – have seen fit to exchange 100,000 yen notes with no gold backing for 100,000 yen coins with 48,000 yen of gold backing.

Both are legal tender so the owner of a 100,000 yen note or a 100,000 yen coin could go into a shop and buy 100,000 yen's worth of goods. But believe it or not, they have chosen to exchange pieces of paper with 100,000 yen printed on them for gold coins with 100,000 yen stamped on them. A perfect example of Gresham's Law which states that bad money drives good money out of circulation – people hoard good money. It becomes a store of value.

It seems to me that there might be a lesson here for HM Treasury. Why don't they buy a few tons of gold, mint them into £100 legal tender coins containing £50 worth of gold and then sell them to the public for £100. In that way they will make £50 profit on every coin, which could go towards the cost of reducing the Poll Tax.

Now the question I ask you is this. Would you rather own a £100 note containing no gold or a £100 coin containing £50 worth of gold, but which could be used for shopping in exactly the same way as you could use a £100 note, if there was such a thing?

I think I know the answer. Given the choice you would probably rather own the coin. Now I ask you another question. Are those Japanese who bought the new coin investors or potential shoppers? When you read that gold is no longer thought of as a store of value and will never again be of interest to investors just remember what the Japanese are doing and don't take too much notice of what the commentators are saying. (**133. 19/4/91**)

Julian challenges the experts again, suggesting that they and their opinions might act as lead indicators, albeit of the "contra" variety.

Those of you who regularly struggle through this weekly addition to your junk mail will know by now that I distrust the conventional wisdom dispensed by so called "experts". If experts were so often right they would surely make a better living taking their own advice rather than proffering it to us.

But perhaps that is too irreverent. Experts serve a useful purpose in that they provide a distillation of the views of those they have consulted in order to become expert. Unfortunately by the time this knowledge has been passed down to us it has usually been acted upon by those who provided it in the first place, leaving only us to act upon it. For that reason it is frequently more profitable to do the opposite to what the experts recommend. That is why I try to watch what people are doing rather than take too much notice of what they are saying.

Let me give you an example. Last week the *Financial Times* reported on this year's annual gold survey of Gold Fields Mineral Services. The article contained a chart rather like the one I showed you in Newsletter 130, but prettier. It showed what we suspected all along, namely that the lower the gold price falls the more people buy it. Since almost everyone would like to own some gold and those who already own it would like to own more, it is hardly surprising that the public, who could not care less what gold price the experts are forecasting, buy more of it when it is cheap than they do when it is expensive. A phenomenon that has made Mr Gerald Ratner, the eloquent jeweller, very rich indeed.

In the above example, as so often happens, painstaking research into a subject still leaves the researcher, despite his superior knowledge, at a loss to know what to recommend. Faced with this dilemma he usually falls back on the well-worn practice of projecting forward the direction, or lack of it, of the last few months and forecasting that the trend, or lack of it, will continue within a range not exceeding 10 per cent of the price last seen on the screen. (**136. 29/5/91**)

The issue of the gold price, GDP growth and its interaction with demand is considered.

The following chart, shown by Dr Stewart Murray of Gold Fields Mineral Services Limited, demonstrates how the demand for gold increases in line with GDP. I would remind you that jewellery demand is choked off by very high real prices for gold. No prizes for guessing in which two years the price of gold was very high in real terms. I told you last week that in 1980 the owner of a quarter of an ounce of gold could take 5.4 people to dinner at the Savoy, whereas now he can only take 1.48 people. In 1974 he could dine three people.

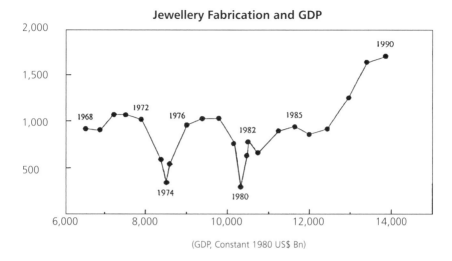

Jewellery Fabrication and GDP

(GDP, Constant 1980 US$ Bn)

It is worth noting that the gold price has varied little in real terms since 1985, but the chart shows clearly how the increase in world Gross Domestic Product has led to a remarkable increase in demand for jewellery which has just about doubled in the last five years. (**140. 2/7/91**)

Highly pertinent today, Julian measures the benefits of holding assets in banks such as BCCI as opposed to buying physical gold.

Last time I wrote to you I made the point – much pored over by the boys in blue – that those who deposited their cash with BCCI, would have avoided a lot of hassle if they had used it instead to buy gold bullion.

The BCCI affair will, in my opinion, cause a lot of people to consider the safety of the institutions they entrust with their savings.

As unitholders you can sleep soundly in the knowledge that, notwithstanding the financial might of the Hongkong Bank, the regulations ensure that share certificates bought on your behalf are held by independent trustees in the form of the Bank of Scotland. The wisdom of this "belt and braces" approach is every day becoming more apparent. People with money in the bank may well wish they felt equally secure. It is said that it is an ill wind that blows no one any good. The current bout of weakness in the gold price may not be unconnected with the misfortunes of those who have seen their savings with BCCI go up in smoke, since many of the bank's Asian customers have a tradition of holding some of their wealth in gold. If the bulk of your cash had disappeared overnight, I would not be at all surprised if you decided to dispose of some of your gold to pay the most pressing bills. That could explain the current softness in the gold price since very large sums have been lost.

So I am by no means despondent about the current weakness in the gold price which if I am right, should prove temporary. Indeed my contention is that the worse the ripple effect of the BCCI debacle becomes, the more people may decide that the "barbarous relic" is not so barbarous after all. Don't forget a lump of gold is no one else's I.O.U. It is more like an I.O.U. NOTHING. Unless you have stolen it, you either own it or you don't. If you wait until disaster strikes, you may not have the wherewithal to buy it.

That is why I think it is so inequitable that gold funds such as this one are not allowed to own gold bullion. Just as the regulations make it impossible for me to run off to Provence with your share certificates, so it should not be beyond the wit of man to devise a way of ensuring that I cannot run off with your gold either!

There are times to own gold and there are times to own gold shares. We have done well until recently by holding mainly South African gold shares which are still some 40 per cent above their lows compared with a rise in the gold price of 16 per cent in sterling terms (1 per cent in dollars). If I was allowed to do so, this would seem to be a good moment to hold our spare cash in the form of bullion.

One final point. The fact that so many commentators in the investment community are dependent in one way or another on the banks for their livelihood, may result in rather less comment about the likely ripple effect of the BCCI debacle than would otherwise be the case. Fear of eroding confidence in the system which pays one's wages is a powerful incentive for trying to emulate an ostrich. If you see a lot of ostriches with their heads in the sand, you may however reasonably suspect that there is danger about. (**144. 6/8/91**)

The Soviet upheaval failed to stimulate gold but Julian remains convinced that in due course low gold prices will re-ignite gold through collapsing supply.

When Murphy invented the law which stipulates that if anything can go wrong, it will, he must have been thinking of events such as the overthrow of Mr Mikhail Gorbachev. It's a shame that happened just as world stock markets were reaching new highs, thus providing one of the few silver linings to the dark clouds of recession. It's a shame those who sold on the news were whipsawed. Such is life. Just like Murphy said.

Some of us know from experience that gold and gold shares sometimes provide protection against the storms which Murphy's Law predicate. But not always. Why should they after all? The gold price is greatly influenced by the attitude of investors. Investors are fickle creatures. They react one way on one occasion and they react differently on another occasion. They also have "big boots". What they do can easily disturb the equilibrium of traditional supply and demand for a metal, the demand for which is very price sensitive.

In 1980, for instance, investor demand for gold was so great that it virtually put a stop to jewellery demand by forcing the price up to the unprecedented level of $850/oz. Ten years earlier, when gold was $35/oz, investment demand was almost non-existent even though it was clear to some far sighted people that jewellery demand was not going to be met at that price for much longer. Unfortunately, when it comes to gold, investors have a terrible track record!

It has taken 11 years for these excesses to be unwound. In the process these self same investors have become excessively and almost universally bearish. In such circumstances it is not surprising that they are in no mood to buy it. When gold does not react to Murphy's Law, they then tend to say "told you so, gold is no longer a store of value!" But it was investment buying that used to push the price up whenever there was trouble. If investors always reacted the same way to a given bit of news, investment would be a science not an art!

So if wars and rumours of wars and banking scandals and falling interest rates etc. etc. do not cause investors to buy gold, why should you and I invest in gold shares through this Fund? The answer is that low gold prices tend to choke off supply just as high prices tend to stifle demand. Low prices encourage demand. The outlook for supply and demand for jewellery purposes is the basis of my bullishness for the price. The chart in Newsletter 143 says it all. If I am wrong about that, you have backed the wrong horse! (**146. 21/8/91**)

Rumours abound of possible Russian gold sales and the downgrading of gold in Swiss bank clients' investment accounts.

It becomes pretty obvious when people stop thinking what they are doing. Look at all the scare stories about the threatened Russian sales of gold! The Russians had been selling all along without telling anyone and this had already depressed the price. As soon as people heard that they had not got much gold left to sell, the price started rising.

Those of you who have discretionary investment accounts in Swiss Banks will know that it has been their normal practice to hold between 5-10 per cent of discretionary portfolios in bullion. Rumour has it that this policy has been changed and the Swiss have been disposing of their clients' bullion in recent months. Market sources suggest that this selling is now starting to dry up but while it was going on it was obviously going to be a depressant for the gold price. If the Swiss had told us that they were selling the gold held in private portfolios, we would have been even more depressed than we were without that knowledge.

Everyone has become totally bearish and dispirited. Those few of us who remain bullish are rendered powerless to act by the continuing stream of redemptions which force us to go on selling at very depressed levels when we know we should be buying. No wonder falls get overdone and rises too! You know me, I refuse to sell when the market is flat on its back and I am not going to give you any encouragement to do so either. (**152. 4/10/91**)

Jewellery demand for gold exceeds newly mined production.

Worldwide jewellery demand already exceeds newly mined production by 250 tonnes but, if the gold price remains depressed, we will not see the increases in production which were the feature of the 1980's. The exploration dollar is always the first to be sacrificed when times are bad. The following chart shows the build-up of annual consumption of gold for jewellery purposes since 1972. I have added the gold price (inverted) and expressed it in constant 1991 US dollars. The message – high gold price chokes off jewellery demand and vice versa. But why then is jewellery consumption now nearly twice what it was in 1972 while the gold price is ten times higher? The bottom line shows the real purchasing power of the Japanese yen (which I use as a proxy for growing Far East prosperity) versus the US dollar. People in the East enjoy increasing disposable income and it is they who buy the gold jewellery. They like to wear their savings and why not? (**160. 6/2/92**)

Julian speculates on the effect that a De Beers-sized advertising effort on behalf of gold might have on the price.

Now that we have seen a marked degree of leadership demonstrated by one of the foremost players in the gold market, is it too much to hope that others in a position to influence events will reconsider their own policies? I doubt if they will, but they might and if they do they could find that their actions have a profound effect on sentiment. If the producers themselves show no confidence, how can they expect investors to have any?

This week saw another leader in his field taking bold action in difficult circumstances to bolster the fortunes of his industry. Julian Ogilvie Thompson, Chairman of De Beers, announced that they were increasing their advertising budget this year by 9 per cent to revive the flagging sales of diamonds caused by the recession. De Beers is now spending US$164 million a year on diamond advertising, or about 4.2 per cent of last year's revenue.

If gold has ceased to be money, is no longer considered a store of value and is now reduced in people's minds to the status of a mere commodity, the least the producers of that commodity should do is to spend a significant portion of their revenue promoting the use of that commodity. Some gold companies contribute nothing at all which those with less finesse than the writer might describe as pathetic. What if the gold industry, which is five times larger than the diamond industry – but much less profitable – were to follow the diamond industry's example? 4.2 per cent of the gold mining industry's revenue of about US$20 billion is US$840 million, equivalent to about US$14 an ounce, whereas the World Gold Council, through which the gold industry's promotional budget is channelled, last year received the equivalent of US$2.5/oz. (**173. 6/5/92**)

Julian reiterates his support for high cost gold mines with large but low profit margin reserves.

That is why I like to fly in the face of conventional wisdom and buy gold shares which value gold in the ground at a low figure. Conventional wisdom has it that you should buy gold mines with low costs per ounce and not worry how much you pay for those ounces. At least, in that way, you know that the company itself will survive a period of low gold prices. Normally, but by no means exclusively, it is the low profit margin mines whose reserves can be bought most cheaply because it is these low margin mines which are most vulnerable if the gold price falls.

However, in my experience, people who buy gold funds don't expect the gold price to fall. They are (in a triumph of hope over recent experience) usually of the opinion that nothing goes down forever and that it is only a matter of time – and a short time at that – before gold will come good. (**178. 12/6/92**)

In lighter mood Julian describes how an expensive krugerrand was turned into a 21st birthday present and speculates on adding value to precious metal bars.

When my son recently became 21, as you might expect we wanted to give him something made of gold. My wife had a krugerrand containing one fine ounce which she had bought some years ago at the wrong price. I have a friend who is a jewellery designer, so my wife contributed the krugerrand and I paid for the workmanship. This conjugation gave birth to a pair of gold cufflinks, the price of which was as follows:–

Gold value:	£200
Workmanship:	£260
	£460

Having established the price, what can we say about the value? It occurred to me that gold in the form of cufflinks might have more value, certainly to the recipient, than gold in the form of krugerrands. How much more, I leave to you to decide.

Without the workmanship the value of the gold was £200. With the workmanship the gold seems to be worth 135 per cent more. This led me to think that if bullion could be made to double for something more useful, its value, or at least the demand for it, would tend to increase.

That led me to wonder why bullion dealers chose to keep their stock in trade in a form which is useless, namely in ingots, when they could just as well keep it in shapes which were useful. Obviously the shapes have to stack easily in order to save storage space.

My colleague, Trevor Steel, with the aid of some clever computer graphics, has come up with a design which would enable bullion dealers to store silver kilobars, which cost about £72, in a form which could also "double' as candlesticks. You can buy candlesticks cheaper than that, but they won't be in solid silver, although as such they would make the perfect Christmas present for the man who has everything.

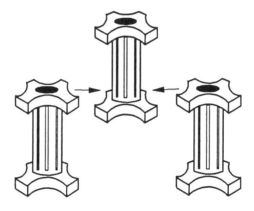

Copyright: Mercury Asset Management

With precious metals languishing at rock bottom prices, any ideas designed to stimulate demand can surely do no harm to the value of your units.

Just a bit of fun to cheer you up during these depressing times. (**192. 16/10/92**)

Although Julian's favourite yardstick for gold's long-term value was the "sovereign to Savoy dinners" ratio, here he measures it in terms of the amount of base metals an ounce could purchase.

When people say that gold is losing purchasing power, it is only partly true. Admittedly commodities generally are getting cheaper as technology improves but gold is holding its value relative to base metals.

We like to think that gold "money" is likely, over a long period, to be able to buy a constant amount of other commodities. After all, gold miners are subject to the same cost pressures as the miners of base metals, so it would be logical for the price of their product to move broadly in line with the price of base metals over a long period.

What has actually happened can be seen from the following chart. It shows that on average since 1975, the owner of an ounce of gold could have purchased a basket of 674/lbs of base metals. Believe it or not, the amount of base metals which can be bought with an ounce of gold today is almost exactly the same as the average of the last 18 years! We have chosen to start in 1975 because before that date gold was catching up with the other metals having been held down artificially at US$35/oz by Central Bank intervention for many years up to 1970.

We go along with those who say that base metal prices are likely to rise as the world comes out of recession and we think that if base metals rise, the chances are that gold will rise too. Using Ord Minnett's metal price forecasts for 1994, shown in the box at the bottom right-hand corner of the chart, we can come to the following conclusion. (**202. 14/1/93**)

Dutch Central Bank selling and a bearish broadside from The Economist causes Julian to speculate whether gold's bottom has been reached.

Having been sent reeling against the ropes by the body blow of the sale of 400 tonnes of gold by the Dutch, our knees nearly buckled from the uppercut delivered by no less a protagonist than Mr Rupert Pennant-Rea, the new Deputy Governor of the Bank of England.

The Economist, of which he was chief editor, told its readers this week that since gold was losing favour with Central Bankers, the public should get out while they still could.

It makes us wonder whether we have just experienced the crescendo of bearishness which is normally associated with great buying opportunities, or whether we are about to be knocked senseless by a further torrent of blows to the head!

Despite the awful background noises, I have tried to encourage you week by week not to sell your units when the FT Gold Mines Index has already fallen more than 80 per cent. Those of you who remain loyal will have noticed that the units have been creeping up recently despite all the bad news. When bad news no longer depresses share prices, that is normally a telling sign that the bear case has already been discounted. (**204. 29/1/93**)

A review of those bodies Julian thinks have a vested interest in a rising gold price including governments, Central Banks and the gold mining industry itself.

If you have time to think about it – not many people do – there are quite a few bodies who have a vested interest in seeing a rising gold price. I'll mention some of them and tell you what they are doing about it.

First, of course, there are those Central Bankers who appear to have decided, in stark contrast to their wisdom of 13 years ago when the gold price was US$850/oz, that the wise thing to do now is to exchange their gold for currencies. After all, the gold price has fallen 61 per cent to below US$330/oz and proved to their entire satisfaction that it is a far less good reserve currency than paper money. To add justification for their decision to sell, they argue that gold pays no interest whereas currencies do. It was ever thus!

You would think that having decided they want to off-load some of their gold reserves, governments would be doing all in their power to achieve the best possible price. You would be wrong however. Not only are some of them selling their gold reserves, they are putting additional downward pressure on the price by lending gold to the bullion market which in turn facilitates forward selling by the mining industry. As I have complained many times in the past, the practice of forward selling keeps the gold price at a lower level than would otherwise be the case. If Central Banks stopped lending their gold, the miners could no longer use that gold to depress the price. The miserly interest rate that Central Banks receive for lending their gold to the bullion market is inadequate compensation for the damage their lending does to the gold price. If Central Banks want to get a good price for their gold, they should stop lending it.

Furthermore, the general public has shown an appetite to buy some 600 tonnes of gold a year more than the gold industry is producing. If governments really want to get a good price for their gold it would not be difficult to give further encouragement to their citizens to buy it. After all, governments hold gold on behalf of their citizens. What difference does it make if the people themselves hold it? The trouble is that even coin of the realm such as sovereigns, are subjected to 17.5 per cent VAT. Who would want to pay a premium like that? The UK Government is adept at selling publicly owned businesses to the public, but they don't charge them VAT for the pleasure. If they really want to sell our gold it is hard to see why they charge us VAT for buying it.

So in a nutshell governments and their Central Bankers seem to be doing exactly the opposite to what they should be doing if they want to realise the best possible price for their gold.

Now let's look at what the mining industry is doing to get the best price. Most of them use every spike in the gold price to sell not only what they are currently producing but also some of what they will be producing in future, so little confidence do they seem to have that gold will hold its value. Their actions are self-fulfilling since they result in the industry getting a lower price for its gold! Only gold mining companies that really are on the breadline should resort to such practices. What is so serious is that gold mining analysts always base their valuations of gold shares on a gold price which is within 10 per cent of the price they last saw on the screen. At today's gold price the great majority of non-South African gold shares look over-valued and makes it difficult for the analysts to recommend them. Someone always has to pay for other people's mistakes. Usually it is the taxpayer. In the case of the gold mining industry, it is the shareholder.

It is argued that Central Bankers are selling gold partly to reduce the weighting of gold in their reserves. There are two ways of achieving this. Either gold surplus to requirements can be sold or the required weighting can be achieved automatically by waiting until the price has fallen! By doing the former you can expedite the latter.

Finally, of course, you and I as shareholders of this Fund have a vested interest in seeing the gold price rise in US dollars because the investing public watches the US dollar price of gold, rather than its price in the currencies in which the individual mining companies operate. Until they see the gold price rising in US dollar terms, they are unlikely to pay much attention to the improving fortunes of the gold mining industry in local currency terms. There is one ray of hope however. The soaring price of our units may be enough, with your help, to alert them to the realities of life. (**205. 4/2/93**)

Julian muses on the potential for gold if China was to become a buyer.

Returning to the supply/demand fundamentals for gold, you may have seen an article in last weekend's Sunday Telegraph entitled "Riding the China boom". It highlights several trusts that can be bought by the small investor in order to gain an exposure to the exciting growth prospects of this huge market. Whilst we echo the optimistic sentiments expressed in the article, experience would suggest that by the time this sort of investment is featured in the Sunday press, its attractions are normally well and truly reflected in the price! Indeed, one large investor in China, GT's Oscar Wong, was quoted as saying "The fashion for labelling almost every firm as a China play has pushed prices to levels that seem certain to fall". The real trick is to find an investment which would benefit from the China boom, but where the growth potential is not already discounted in the share price. By now you will have guessed that gold shares are just such an investment bearing in mind the well known affinity of Chinese people to gold and their increasing capacity to buy it.

China has experienced double-digit growth over the past 12 years. By 1994, China's economy is expected to be four times bigger than it was in 1978. This year Chinese output will be equivalent to a quarter that of America's. China has a population of around 1.2 billion people. These people have a reputation of being industrious and innately capitalist. Indeed, the recent economic history of Taiwan is testimony to the Chinese ability to create wealth. Taiwanese income per capita has grown (in 1992 dollars) from US$2,000 in 1980 to US$10,000 today (there are 21 million "Chinese" people in Taiwan). China is thought to be about 25 years behind Taiwan in terms of its economic development. In addition to their success at creating wealth the Taiwanese have been adept at saving it. In 1992, each Taiwanese saved, on average, 29 per cent of his/her income, one of the highest saving ratios in the world. Their growing appetite for gold demonstrates one of their preferences as to how that newly created wealth should be spent, or "saved". Taiwanese demand for gold jewellery has risen from 7 tonnes in 1982 to 111 tonnes in 1991, or over 15 times. Such an affinity for gold is not the exclusive preserve of the Taiwanese. Demand for gold jewellery in the whole of the Far East, including Japan, has grown by an average 16 per cent per year since 1982, to reach 603 tonnes in 1992, according to Goldfields Mineral Services, a leading authority on the gold market.

With these statistics in mind we allowed ourselves the indulgence of reflecting on the "blue sky" in the gold market. Why shouldn't we? After all, if share prices in many markets of the world are anything to go by, everyone else seems to be taking the "blue sky" for granted. In 1991, each Taiwanese spent US$59 buying gold jewellery (a total of 111 tonnes). It is estimated that in China each person spent US$3.75 buying gold (a total of 400 tonnes). If ever the Chinese caught up with current Taiwanese expenditure on gold per head, China would consume over 6,000 tonnes annually, or over 3 times current world mined production. Total world Central Bank reserves of gold are estimated to be 35,000 tonnes. With the Chinese devouring gold at 6,000 tonnes per year, the cupboards would be bare in under six years. Interestingly, and perhaps unsurprisingly, the Chinese authorities were rumoured to be buyers of the gold recently sold by the Dutch Central Bank! **(206. 11/2/93)**

Julian points out that though gold has been falling in US dollar terms it has actually been rising in terms of sterling, the currency of the Fund's units.

Look what people are saying about gold. The downward trend is very well established as you can see from the chart. The trend is people's friend. But if trends went on forever, trees would grow to the sky or their roots would go to hell. Anyone can see that gold is going down. But is it? Only in US dollars, certainly not in sterling. In sterling it is up 30 per cent since 1st September 1992!

US Dollar Gold Price

Source: Datastream

What they are saying is that gold is no longer a currency; the Central Banks are selling it so it can't be. Gold is thought not to do well when inflation is low; and inflation is certainly low. Gold no longer responds to wars or rumours of wars; how true. Gold is thought no longer to be a useful investment; it underperforms. Gold is going out of fashion; there are so many burglaries so why risk being fashionable? The Russians are forced sellers ... You can add to the list if you feel like it.

This sort of talk has reduced the price of gold in 13 years from US$850/oz to US$326/oz. By now the bad news is in the price, surely? Taking inflation into account, the fall has been much worse – nearer 75 per cent! Gold shares have been slaughtered. If there is anyone left who does not know that gold and gold shares have been rotten investments, they must be blind or deaf – or both.

But those of you who still own units in this Fund know better. For all its faults, the FT Gold Mines Index has risen 76 per cent in the last six months! Hardly the sort of performance expected by the great majority of investors. It certainly has not yet attracted the attention of those who inform the public about investment matters. Each Sunday I look to see if the newspapers have noticed it, but so far no one has made mention of it – but they will. Any sector that rises more than 70 per cent in such a short time becomes newsworthy. Explanations have to be obtained. A 25 per cent rise can be ignored as an insignificant blip. A 50 per cent rise can be discarded as a rally in a bear market, but once you get above 70 per cent, explanations have to be sought and as you know, people are far cuter at

45

explaining why a rise has taken place than they are at predicting the rise in the first place.

But in the case of gold shares, there is a case for ignoring them on the grounds that so few readers own them. That, in my opinion, is one of the best reasons for paying particular attention to them. They are very under-owned. Nobody wanted to own paintings by Van Gogh – he had to give them away – but that does not mean that Van Gogh's have been given away ever since. (**211. 24/3/93**)

Julian continues with the theme of the conflicting US dollar and UK sterling experience of holders of gold.

Enough of the past! What you will be much more interested in is how you are likely to fare in the future. As we never cease to remind you, markets are affected by sentiment and perceptions far more than financial analysts would care to admit. An ex-colleague of mine, Vahid Fathi, who now works for Kemper Securities, couldn't have put it better in a recent circular. He said, "If the eyes see something that the brain cannot comprehend, the brain instinctively compensates, or falsely corrects (perceives) the image according to its experience, so that the image can be understood."

Look, for instance, at the following advertising poster, partially concealed by a passing lorry. As Fathi points out, just a glance is enough for the brain to interpret the word on the poster.

When the lorry passed, this is what the poster said.

No prizes are offered for the correct interpretation – just make a mental note of it for your own satisfaction.

Facts and perceptions are very often different, as all of you who read these missives should know by now. The perceptions of the majority of investors is that the gold price is going down, whereas the reality is that it all depends where you live. There follows the parable of the two brothers.

There were two penniless brothers. One lived in America, one in Britain. Their father died on 1st September last year leaving the American brother US$343 with which he bought a krugerrand. He left the English brother £173 with which he also bought a krugerrand. Seven months later, the brothers received a visitation from a man from the planet Mars who asked them who was richer. The American brother looked in the paper and saw that his krugerrand was worth 2 per cent less than he had paid for it. The English brother looked in his paper and found that he was 29 per cent richer, as measured by the price of krugerrands in sterling.

I cannot tell you whether the man from Mars concluded that the price of gold was going up or down, but no doubt you will have your own views about that. All I know is that if both brothers had used a multiple of their inheritance to buy a local gold mine, the brother in the UK would now be richer – much richer. (212. 1/4/93)

Gold as the family silver, and the potential for Chinese buying of the yellow metal.

Have you noticed that countries with trade deficits tend to be sellers of gold and countries with trade surpluses tend to be buyers?

No one finds it strange that when times get hard in a family they resort to selling the family silver. Families in this position are usually only too pleased they had some to sell. It certainly seems unfair to me that when Central Banks sell the family gold, the metal gets the blame for being a useless, if not barbaric, metal. No one blames the economic policies of the countries which have to sell it. The gold, of course, knows nothing of all this and ends up in the hands of those who can afford to buy it and they, on the whole, tend to live in surplus countries.

A couple of sentences in a paragraph on gold in Burns Fry's latest weekly gold mining newsletter caught my eye. In case you missed it this is what they said:–

"Brian Fullerton, our man in Hong Kong, points out that while many pessimists on gold say that it cannot rise because there is no inflation, in the coastal cities of China inflation is running at 12 per cent – and gold is probably the only readily available hedge. How much this factor is influencing the staggering growth in physical demand from mainland China is debatable, but jewellery demand in these cities is up 74 per cent January-over-January!"

With gold, I find, it all depends on where you live. We sometimes cannot stop being little Englanders who think the World's End is either on Kings Road Chelsea or one of the Cinque Ports. We may not find gold as attractive as the Chinese do, but they are different from us in many ways. There are more of them, their economy is growing faster and their inflation rate is considerably higher. They cannot invest in futures or index-linked bonds to protect themselves against its ravages. Nor could we, before these instruments were invented. We used to buy gold – remember? (**214. 22/4/93**)

Julian sees gold in a new bull market.

Gold is not expensive as a long-term store of value either. If gold had held its purchasing power since 1935, it would now be about US$407/oz and is therefore still trading below its long-term value. The recent setback provides a buying opportunity as all setbacks do in bull markets. Setbacks in bull markets are used by the uninitiated to sell. The last setback of a bull market marks the start of the next bear market and that knowledge causes investors to climb their wall of fear. Investors who get scared too easily should not be playing in this playground. They would probably be more comfortable in Bonds. But for a small proportion of investors' portfolios a holding in gold related assets at this time of wild fluctuations in currency markets, seems to me to be a perfectly sensible diversification, provided you don't feel you have to look at the price of your units every day.

So let me try to review dispassionately the situation as I see it.

1. Gold is in the early stages of a new bull market.
2. Gold bullion is the engine which drives gold shares. Investors recognise that gold shares give them a bigger bang for their buck than buying the metal itself. As long as the gold price is in a generally rising trend, gold shares will tend to discount yet higher gold prices. As such, from time to time they get ahead of themselves. Something then happens to cause a setback in the gold price and suddenly all the speculative froth is blown away. The market is healthier for that.
3. The long-term price of gold is US$407/oz. Gold is still below its term value.
4. At the beginning of the year gold was trading US$70 below its long-term value. It is still US$30 below. A good bull market could easily take the gold price above its long-term value by the same amount as it fell below that value. In the next two or three years there would seem to be no reason why it should not achieve the US$500/oz level last seen in 1983 and 1987 (see chart).
5. In bull markets, bad news does not put prices down. The recent unfavourable reports of violence in South Africa, which were widely used as an excuse for not buying South African gold shares last year, have not prevented the South African gold shares from being the best performers this year. Favourable news, even after the recent setback, can still produce

excellent rises for shares like Bakyrchik and Niugini Mining.

6. If a study of the gold price convinces you that we are still in the early stages of a bull market for bullion, the only way you will be able to acquire units at favourable prices is to grit your teeth and buy them on a setback such as we are currently experiencing.

7. If you cannot make up your mind what to do, ask yourself this question. If you woke up tomorrow morning to find the gold price 5 per cent higher would you want to buy more units or sell those you have? If you think you would be happy to sell, get out now and stop worrying.

8. Be your own man and don't listen to those who tell you it must be right to sell any market just because it has gone up as much as the gold market has. If I am right, an investment in the Fund could still be enormously rewarding. Experience would suggest that when it is entirely conventional to own gold, as it was in 1980, then you will have the boom conditions in the gold market that we used to enjoy in the good old days when mining stockbrokers became order clerks. When it becomes unconventional NOT to hold gold or gold shares, that will be the time to say goodbye and slip away quietly. (**226. 11/8/93**)

Julian chastises himself for underestimating the degree of speculation in the gold market.

I have often pointed out that the traditional buyers of gold have never been known to force the price up. They serve a much more important function. Their buying has historically stopped the price falling much below the equivalent of US$350/oz in today's money. All previous peaks in the gold price have been caused by investment and speculative buying. Investors and speculators often buy gold just because it is going up without realising just how much they themselves are contributing to its rise. Traditional buyers stop buying it when it goes up too far. They prefer to buy it in increasing quantities when the price is going down. In that way they can acquire more of it.

So we must hope that once again the traditional buyers will provide the sponge which mops up the gold which was spilt by the "investment" community when their computers told them to bail out.

With the advantage of hindsight I should have been more alert to the degree of speculation in bullion, however turnover figures in the gold market are notoriously hard to come by. It is therefore particularly hard to decipher exactly who is doing what in the market. As any Finance Minister will tell you, such are the flows of hot money these days that countries can be forced by speculators to devalue their currencies even if they have not already devalued them themselves in order to remain competitive.

The bullion market is relatively illiquid compared to international currencies, just as the stock markets of what are known as emerging markets are relatively illiquid compared with the liquidity of the major stock markets of the world. It does not need a lot of international money to be invested in the emerging markets to make them perform particularly well. Nor does it take much international money to be invested in bullion to make the price rise strongly, as we have just seen.

Since investors find it particularly difficult to ascribe value to a non-income producing asset like gold, they rely heavily on the chartists to tell them what to do. Have you ever met a rich chartist? Nor have I. (**230. 9/9/93**)

Julian admits to having taken his eye off the ball as the gold price stormed above the levels that traditional bullion investors saw as still offering value.

We do not usually pass on gossip to you but that does not mean we never hear any. Nine times out of ten, gossip is someone talking his book so it is not worth passing on. But every now and then gossip can serve as a bit of a morale booster so here goes.

Speaking the other night to a friend in New York, I asked the question "Do you think the speculative selling of bullion which has caused such havoc to the price in recent weeks has now runs its course?" "Yes," he replied, "most of it has gone now and some traders are actually short – watch the rally!"

The misfortunes which have overtaken gold traders in the last few weeks are reminiscent of what I call the Donald Duck syndrome. You will remember that Donald Duck had a habit of speeding over the edge of the cliff without noticing that his feet were no longer touching the ground. He continued to walk on air until he made the near fatal mistake of looking down. Investors in bull markets, including me, do not spend enough time making sure that their feet are firmly on the ground. And so it was in the gold market. We all failed to notice how far we had left behind the price levels at which the traditional gold investors had shown themselves prepared to absorb whatever gold was thrown at them.

The gold speculators looked down when someone pointed out that Far East demand had been choked off by the rising price and that altitude was being sustained by self levitation. Like Donald Duck, they encountered little or no support on the way down, as stop losses were triggered and margin calls had to be met. Even though we have now reached sea level, so to speak, the speculators may have further to sink before buoyancy reverses their descent, however investors in the Fund who chose this moment to sell should pause to consider how far the unit price has fallen already.

Fortunately, most of our unitholders are made of sterner stuff. Many of the early birds who took their profits when the units were going from strength to strength have actually been buying back their units, believing that the falls have been overdone. This fund has experienced net inflows in the last three weeks! One can never judge the bottom but your courage has enabled us to buy a few bargains rather like we did this time last year when so many were available. Look what happened after that! (**231. 17/9/93**)

Julian once more returns to the subject of gold's long-term value inspired by a diamond necklace offered for sale by Christies.

As you know, we set great store on the long-term purchasing power of gold. This week we received a letter from the director of Christie's jewellery department enclosing a catalogue for a forthcoming sale of jewels. He highlighted lot 265, a particularly beautiful diamond necklace which has an interesting provenance:

> "The necklace was given to Anastasia (Anne) wife of Luke 2nd Lord Clonbrock, by her great uncle Lord Kerry and is being sold with the original receipt from Rundell Bridge and Rundell, Ludgate Hill, London dated May 1806 showing the cost of the diamonds as £450.00 and the charge for setting was £16.16.0 ... Estimate £25,000–30,000."

A photograph of the necklace in all its glory accompanied the description and led me to ask myself which I would rather own, this magnificent jewel or 16,272 units of Mercury Gold and General Fund. It remains a difficult decision.

Although De Beers always discourage buyers of diamond jewellery from looking upon diamonds as an investment, many buyers cannot help themselves thinking that their purchase may have some merit not just as an adornment but also as a long-term investment. Christie's example is particularly interesting since we know what it cost in 1806 (£450) and will soon know what it will fetch in 1993. While waiting for the result of the auction we will use the mid point of Christie's suggested valuation. Using these figures it is possible to calculate whether Lord Kerry gave his great-niece a present which not only retained its beauty but also its value.

We know that the price of gold in 1806 was £4/oz and we know that today an ounce of gold costs £254/oz. If instead of buying the necklace Lord Kerry had given his great-niece £450 worth of gold she would have then received an ingot weighing 112.5 ounces. That ingot would today be worth £28,575, a rise of 6,250 per cent. A quick call to the Bank of England told us that in the same period the retail price index has risen by a mere 2,727 per cent.

The above statistic suggests that over a long period of time both diamonds and gold have increased in value by about half of one per cent a year in real terms. There are those who say that the price of gold is a truer reflection of people's standard of living rather than of their cost of living. As time passes and the world gets richer, more people can afford to buy gold. When the price falls well below its long-term purchasing price as it did earlier this year, they buy lots of it. Don't forget the demand for gold last year exceeded the supply by more than 800 tonnes. Finally it is interesting to note that renewed investor interest in gold is showing itself to be much more restrained than it was earlier in August and this gives the metal a more stable appearance even at the higher levels which no longer seem to put off the traditional purchasers. (**238. 29/11/93**)

A good lunch with one of the Fund's larger holders and a toast to a bumper year for the gold price, gold shares and the Fund.

When lunching last week at La Truffe, an underrated restaurant on the "wrong side of the Thames", the conversation with one of our larger unitholders soon turned to the merits of owning gold at a time of high stock markets and low nominal interest rates.

My companion had just spent the morning with his investment advisors. They had been bemoaning the fact that choice seemed to be limited as to where to invest the not inconsiderable gains they had made for him during 1993, a most satisfactory year for investors.

I mentioned that a leading personality in the investment world had recently suggested that those who felt that stock markets were dangerously high should consider buying a house, since houses in this country are certainly not selling at record levels. Furthermore, with interest rates so low, they are rather "affordable".

My friend replied that he had enough houses already and could only live in one, or at most two, at a time and that he preferred gold.

After all, he argued, with interest rates at these levels, gold only had to go up by about US$15 per ounce over the next twelve months for a dollar investor to cover his borrowing costs. He did not find it difficult to envisage that the gold price might achieve a price of US$405 by the end of this year. If the price by the year-end were to reach US$450 per ounce, then a perfectly acceptable return of 15 per cent would be achieved on a non-income producing asset. This could then be added to last year's returns, the size of which modesty prevented him from revealing!

One of the reasons for the lunch was to celebrate the fact that Mercury Gold and General Fund had risen fourfold in price and tenfold in size over the past twelve months and in so doing had enhanced the overall performance of his portfolio. Obviously his fertile mind was contemplating the possibility of selling his Mercury Gold and General Fund units and reinvesting the proceeds in bullion.

Whilst one of the aims and objects of the Fund is to enable its owners to buy an increasing amount of bullion for every 1,000 units (the accompanying chart shows you how we are faring in this respect), it would be a shame if the urge to switch turned out to be premature. Gold shares after all, are in a sense, options on the gold price. They are certainly highly geared to it. As a consequence of their "operational gearing", par for the course is that gold shares rise or fall by about three times as much as the gold price itself. So all other things being equal, a 15 per cent rise in bullion to US$450 per ounce by the year-end, could well give rise to a 45 per cent improvement in the price of gold shares. If current boom conditions continue that could well be something of an under-estimate. (**241. 6/1/94**)

More bearish chatter from the financial press drives Julian to the World Gold Council's Christmas gold sale to select an item or two for Mrs Baring!

Two of the great contrary indicators for the gold market are when Central Banks announce they are selling part of their gold reserves and when journalists choose a moment of weakness in the gold price to pronounce that the final nail has been driven into gold's coffin and that no one in his right mind would think of investing in it. The arrogance of it! How can anyone be so certain that December 1994 is the date from which a metal, which has appealed to one of man's most basic instincts for the last 5,000 years, will suddenly cease to do so.

Fortunately the people who most like to buy gold, live in countries where they have little opportunity of hearing the "words of wisdom of those Western commentators who pontificate about a metal for which they have very little "feel". Luckily for us there are many people in the world who know from personal experience that gold is good for them and more importantly, that their wives enjoy wearing it. In those respects they are no different from me!

The recent article in a leading financial journal which suggested that it's all over for gold, prompted your Fund Manager to accept the World Gold Council's invitation to attend an exclusive Christmas Gold sale next Wednesday. The sale is purported to provide an opportunity to buy real gold jewellery at trade prices! Call me primitive if you will, but it's Christmas time – the season of goodwill – and my instinct tells me that I will earn some of that elixir if Santa brings my wife a gold bauble, even if it does not turn out to be a good investment. Like scent, diamonds, Veuve Cliquot and van Goghs, the little luxuries of life bring a ray of sunshine to those who otherwise have very little pleasure!

Even if its detractors can't see the point, the ownership of gold gives pleasure to millions of people both rich and poor, but mainly those whose standard of living is improving. If you think about it gold, like the family silver, tends to move from rich people who are getting poorer, to poor people who are getting richer.

I do not wish to give you the impression that I am always a bull of gold, or gold shares for that matter. There are times when they lose touch with reality as gold did in 1980 and as gold shares did a couple of months ago. At that time we reminded you that trees didn't grow to the sky and told you that we had already reduced the gold share exposure in the portfolio and increased the exposure to bonds and base metals. The effect of so doing can be seen clearly in the following charts which show the performance of the fund against the FT Gold Mines Index from the beginning of last year to the peak of the market in September and from the peak in September to the present day. (277. **9/12/94**)

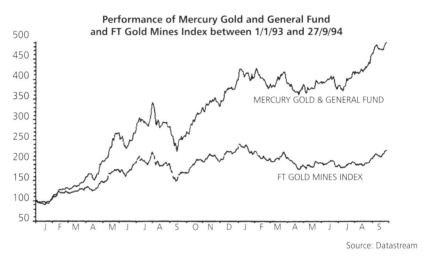

Performance of Mercury Gold and General Fund and FT Gold Mines Index between 1/1/93 and 27/9/94

MERCURY GOLD & GENERAL FUND

FT GOLD MINES INDEX

Source: Datastream

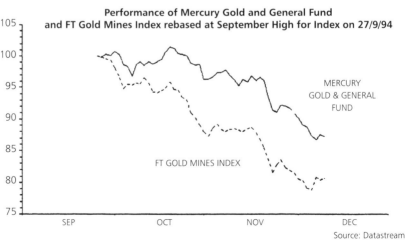

Performance of Mercury Gold and General Fund and FT Gold Mines Index rebased at September High for Index on 27/9/94

MERCURY GOLD & GENERAL FUND

FT GOLD MINES INDEX

Source: Datastream

Julian has another go at chartists and also suggests that gold can hold its own when interest rates are rising.

Gold is a rather different animal. It is not just a commodity, it is also money. It too is not behaving according to many people's expectations. People tell us that gold cannot prosper in a high real interest rate environment. We see no reason why it should not. After all, those who hold it can use the futures market to secure the same real return on gold as is available on Bonds and those who buy it to adorn themselves could not care less about real interest rates. Once base metal shares start to behave better, it probably won't be long before gold shares join in.

Finally, the contrarian among you may like to study the following chart of "bullish consensus" which highlights bullish or bearish sentiment in the gold market. When the chart shows the consensus to be at an extreme level, it is usually the moment to take the opposite view. Needless to say, the chart now shows extreme pessimism. Professional chartists, who make their living from the study of past performance in order to predict future trends, have recently been frightening us to death by their talk of a "Dead Cross" on their charts of the gold price. This constellation apparently heralds a substantial and unusually long-term decline. Fortunately for us, you seldom meet a rich chartist, and certainly not one who has made his money from following his own advice. They are no less subject to human fallibility than we are, so most of them wisely earn a crust by advising others. Like soothsayers, they do, however, come into their own at moments of maximum uncertainty. When no one knows what to do, their predictions can often be particularly influential, as seems to be the case at present. (**281. 24/1/95**)

The story of "Chickin Lickin" provides a backdrop to a burst of panic selling by gold shareholders.

Some of you may know the children's story about "Chickin Lickin"? She was a hen who when bumped on the head by an acorn falling from an oak tree, worked herself up into such a frenzy that she took it as evidence that the sky was about to fall on her head. She was wrong of course, but she told so many people and was so sure of herself that eventually a good few began to believe her. They, in turn, told their friends and before long it became conventional wisdom that the sky would indeed fall. Those who thought otherwise either kept very quiet or came to be regarded with deep suspicion by everyone else. After a while, even the sceptics thought it better to be safe than sorry and cowered in bunkers with the others. It was quite a while before a few brave souls ventured back outside. When they found the sky was still intact, a large number of people felt rather foolish.

We feel as if we have turned into characters in just such a story. Gold's failure to keep pace with the upward spiral of base metals prices has led many investors to give up hope of it ever breaching US$400/oz again. They seem to be thinking that if it can't go up, then it must come crashing down around their ears. The logical next step is to form the view that if gold is either going to stay the same or fall, then gold shares are at best dead money and at worst a dreadful investment. You can see the overall result of this type of thinking in the following table; a fall of 3 per cent in the gold price since the beginning of the fourth quarter last year has translated into a market move about 10 times greater!

	1st October 1994	26th January 1995	% Change Local	% Change Sterling
JSE Gold Index	2441	1597	-35 %(R)	-33 %
Toronto Gold Index	10957	8900	-19 %(C$)	-24 %
Aussie Gold Index	2387.7	1743	-27 %(A$)	-25 %
MSCI Gold Index	846	639	-24 % (S$)	-25 %
Mercury Gold & General Fund	259	209	-18 % (S$)	-19 %
Gold Bullion	US$393 (£250)	US$381 (£239)	-3 %(US$)	-4 %

(282. 26/1/95)

The jottings of yet another FT gold bear (they must take a vow when they join the paper), Barry Riley, catches Julian's eye. The old mantra that gold is simply a commodity is trotted out again, but although troubled by gold's weak performance Julian sees hope.

Many of our readers will be familiar with the much respected writings of Mr. Barry Riley who takes "the long view" in his twice weekly column in the Financial Times. You may have noticed a piece he wrote on the Wednesday following "Baring Crisis Week", saying that gold has finally been consigned to the sidelines by global investors in their flight to quality. "Why buy useless slabs of metal when you can convert your money into deutschmarks and yen?"

As one who had money deposited with the family bank I had, until I read Mr. Riley's article, been kicking myself for not having had the foresight to give Barings standing instructions to invest any uninvested cash in gold because it is a form of liquidity that is no one else's liability. Since things turned out all right for us depositors in the end, I suppose Mr. Riley was right. He usually is!

Since in Mr. Riley's view Western Central Banks seems to be coming to the conclusion that there is not much point in holding gold as a reserve asset, investors too should get the message that gold has been demonetised and has simply become a commodity. In other words, they should stop kidding themselves that gold has mystical qualities which could protect them from the slings and arrows of outrageous fortune.

For my part I don't intend to give up on gold so long as governments persist in making it unattractive for their citizens to acquire it. For instance, VAT at 17.5 per cent is levied on the purchase of new sovereigns, despite the fact that they are officially designated "coin of the realm". No wonder most people in this country no longer think of gold as money! What is really surprising about such a friendless metal is not how badly, but how well, it has held its purchasing power compared with currencies, over the long term as the chart overleaf shows. People prefer to point out how badly it has done since 1980 when it was ridiculously overvalued. It has certainly done no favours to people who bought it then.

Whatever way you look at it, the week before last was not one during which anyone called Baring expected any favours. On top of everything else, the gold price was indeed behaving very disappointingly against a weak dollar. Mr. Riley's article came close to fulfilling the role of the proverbial straw.

But as so often happens when the scribes sign gold's death warrant (as they tend to do whenever it is looking sick) the barbarous relic started to recover almost before the ink had dried. It was as if someone had at last noticed that gold was looking cheap even against a weak dollar. That "someone" may have been a German or a Japanese, because to them it must seem as if gold is being given away.

Last Saturday, Mr. Riley was pointing out, in an article about the currency crisis, that "... by most counts the dollar is currently very cheap". He then made the point that the Americans are demonstrating their unwillingness to manage the dollar in a way that will provide a reliable store of value. "International holders of the US currency are therefore engaged in a periodic urge to diversify risk into deutschmarks, yen and Swiss francs, but not yet into gold."

We share the surprise that investors have not responded more favourably towards gold. If gold had held its value in dollar terms during the recent bout of dollar weakness, the price today would be about US$410/oz instead of US$385/oz. Normally investors would be quick to take advantage of such divergence, but investors for the most part are simply not interested in gold. If they don't own any, it should not surprise anyone if they fail to respond to the advice of those who opine that it should be sold. (**287. 15/3/95**)

Currency volatility fails to attract buyers to gold, and despite gold selling below its long-term purchasing power level mines continue to sell production forward.

The gold price is getting up to its old tricks again, playing cat and mouse with its supporters. You would be forgiven for thinking that the bout of currency unrest which we have been experiencing in recent weeks would have attracted a few investors into gold, but so far they have been conspicuous by their absence.

Of course the fact that gold has fallen nearly as much as the US dollar has made it look very cheap in terms of the stronger currencies like the yen and the deutchmark and there has in fact been an upsurge in demand from Japan in particular. It is said that in order to meet this demand, the bullion houses are having to borrow gold from the Central Banks who, for the most part, seem happy to go on lending it.

Investors continue for the time being, to prefer the yen and the deutchmark as a safe haven from the tabulations of the dollar (that is everyone except the Japanese and the Germans who seem to prefer gold) but who is to say that if investors push their two favourites much further, they too may feel the need to find an alternative bolt hole.

Gold is selling below its long-term purchasing power and it tends not to do that forever, even though it may seem like an eternity at the time. The last time gold found favour with investors was a couple of years ago when Messrs. Soros and Goldsmith drew the attention of a wider audience to its attractions. The subsequent flurry was a constant reminder of just how responsive gold and gold shares can be to even quite modest investment demand.

How have the gold miners responded to the appetite for gold of those who live in the strong currency countries? I don't have to tell you! True to form they are selling gold they have not yet produced, thereby increasing the supply and helping to prevent the price from rising. Best estimates indicate that 1200 tonnes of gold have been sold forward, or about six months production. To add insult to injury, they are selling paper gold but at the same time they are effectively taking on a liability to repay the real thing. I hope they know what they are doing! They tell us that if the gold price rises above the agreed forward sales price they will simply roll over their forward sales, thereby postponing the evil day when they have to crystalise their opportunity loss. (**291. 11/4/95**)

Julian sees both mole and lemming in action in the gold share market and decides that more higher quality mines are needed in the Fund.

The gold mining industry has now come to believe its own propaganda. "We mine a metal", they seem to be saying, "that can be produced in any quantity without harming the price. It's a shame it does not go up, but since it does not go down much either, let's produce as much of it as possible."

When Central Bankers did that with currencies in the 1970s, look what happened to the relative value of gold. If gold miners do the same thing in the late 1990s, they should not be surprised if the value of their currency, gold, behaves badly relative to paper money. I often think that miners have mole-like qualities. They just love digging. You can't stop them, it is in their nature. But unlike miners, moles can't see where they are going and are not motivated by profit. Miners are like moles, but they have a lemming-like quality about them as well. Every few years they have an overwhelming instinct to hurl themselves over the cliff. Of course, some have the even more powerful instinct of self-preservation, otherwise lemmings would be extinct! The message for us from Denver was that we must ensure that we have sufficient low cost quality mines in the portfolio as opposed to high cost quantity and we have taken steps to achieve this. **(360. 8/10/96)**

Julian takes a swipe at the Swiss for planning gold sales but muses that a successful run of sales may signal that the oversupply of gold to the market is just a short-term phenomenon.

A complicating factor in deciding whether the market it likely to head higher or lower is the adverse sentiment caused by the intention of the Swiss, of all people, to dispose of some of their official reserves. This sets a bad example to other Central Bankers who may have nearly convinced themselves that their skills at successfully running the world economy, make gold redundant as a monetary asset. We think that the sooner the gold gets out of the hands of those who don't want to own it, into the hands of those who do, the quicker the laws of supply and demand will once again prevail. We take the view that if a government does decide to sell an asset to the people who already own it, they will get a better price in the end by being open about their intentions, like the Swiss, rather than by selling it surreptitiously and announcing their sale on completion.

It may seem contrary to you but the announcement of a potentially large piece of business by the Swiss Central Bank must be causing a number of Swiss and other financial institutions to decide what their attitude to this sale should be. Since fees charged for financial services rendered are what enables financiers to pay their own school fees, it would not be in the least bit surprising if the best brains in the Swiss financial community were being applied to the problem of how to place large quantities of such an unfashionable financial asset.

In Switzerland this week we were pointing out just how cheap gold had become as a financial asset and how just a small percentage of gold in a portfolio was a good risk diversifier. Is it entirely fanciful to suggest that the fee payable by the

Swiss Central Bank to the financial institutions placing their gold might just be enough to convince them that there is a place for gold in their clients' portfolios after all. It would be all part of the process of getting the gold out of the hands of those who don't want it into the hands of those who did not know they did! If relief in the market place that the gold had been successfully placed caused the price to rise the next Central Bank wishing to sell its gold might find it easier than they thought. Perhaps the gold share market's relative strength is telling us that in a year or two's time our current worries about the oversupply of gold to the market will have evaporated, after all the market is very seldom wrong. (**375. 13/3/97**)

Here, in full, is one of Julian's last public presentations on gold and gold shares at the European Gold Mine Investment Forum in Geneva in June 1997. Often with tongue-in-cheek, he gently chides the whole gold industry for tactics that have guaranteed a lower gold price over the years since the 1980 peak.

I was a bit shocked when Michele asked me to speak at this conference. Shock turned to horror when I realised that my audience had been given Hobson's choice – listen, or no lunch! I hope the invitation did not deter too many potential attendees because my views on certain aspects of the gold industry are well known and not much loved by many of you. Furthermore I run the risk that if I speak my mind, I may be accused of biting the hand that has just fed me. I can't believe there are many people here who can stomach the thought of sitting through even a variation of my usual theme. I therefore promise to be brief – the greatest quality in any speaker.

So here we are, yet again, going through one of those seemingly endless periods of penury which have been the lot of gold miners since time immemorial. Before we can once again enjoy the fruits of our labours on a sustainable basis, we have got to move heaven and earth to get gold out of the hands of those who do not want to own it and into the hands of those that do. I hope it won't spoil your lunch when I tell you that in order to achieve this, we need a lower gold price!

Last year I visited India for the first time and I asked my taxi driver how much gold Indians gave as a dowry. His reply was as interesting as it was unexpected. "As much as we can afford." Obviously, the lower the price, the more gold they can afford. Since India is already the largest consumer of gold in the world, we must all pray for that country's continued and growing prosperity, because if our prayers are answered, they will be able to afford more of it. We, in this room, must continue to play our part in encouraging consumption by doing all we can to depress the gold price. No one should under-estimate what we have already achieved in this regard. We have done much already, but we must do more!

Our efforts to make gold more affordable have already born fruit. The low price has resulted in some 800 tonnes more gold being consumed than the gold miners can produce each year. The trouble is that if we go on as we are, it will still take more than a generation for the Central Bank's stocks to be depleted and for the laws of supply and demand to reassert themselves. Most of us cannot wait that long! We have got to try harder!

If we want to encourage the transfer of gold from those who wish to dispose of it to those who wish to acquire it, we must at all costs avoid a repeat of the state of affairs which existed in the late 1970s and early 1980s. In those days, when the purchasing power of gold reached unprecedented levels, we never read about Central Banks lending or selling their gold. Mining companies did not sell forward for fear of the price going higher. Now they are selling forward for fear of the price going lower! A self-fulfilling policy if ever there was one. But what really helps to keep the gold price affordable is the powerful message that the producers broadcast about their own perceptions as to the direction of the price. No one in his right mind would sell gold forward if he thought the gold price was going to rise. Investors in gold and gold shares have received that message, loud and clear, and have acted accordingly.

If we want to keep the gold price low, the last thing we must do is to encourage investors to buy it. Investors, as we all know, are nervous creatures who hate buying things that are freely offered; they much prefer to buy into a shortage. At the risk of seeming sexist I should point out that this preference is largely a male preserve. Men seem to think that if something is cheap, there must be something wrong with it. Women, on the other hand, think if something is cheap it might be a bargain. In the late 1970s, when gold was expensive, it was hard to find an investor who did not have some gold in his portfolio. Nowadays it is hard to find one who admits to having any. But women can't get enough of it. The World Gold Council did a survey once and what do you think they found? The women who want more gold most are the women who have most gold!

One of the best ways of discouraging people from investing in gold is to hold conferences like this. These conferences give the gold industry an excellent platform from which to blazon to the world their aggressive expansion plans. The raison d'être for these conferences is that they give the producers an opportunity – which they are actually willing to pay for – to impart the message to prospective investors that gold mining is a growth industry whose glittering prospects are based on a massive expansion of reserves, resources and production, past and future. Needless to say past performance is made to pale into insignificance, compared with what lies ahead. We Fund Managers are obliged to point out that past performance is no guide to the future. In the interests of fair play miners should be required to do the same! The fact that growth in reserves and production have not, in the main, been accompanied by a commensurate growth in earnings per share, is of no greater relevance than the fact that the Emperor wore no clothes.

As you know, almost nobody noticed that the Emperor was as naked as the day that he was born. But there is now reason to believe that one or two eagle-eyed investors have spotted something which frightens them. Rather than buying the shares of the producers every time they hear about a company's growth potential, investors now seem to be selling them. In other words the message has not changed but the reaction to it has. The industry now finds itself in something of a hole. The best advice for someone who finds himself in a hole is to stop digging.

If we really believe that it is in the long-term interests of the gold mining industry to have the lowest possible gold price in the short term, it obviously makes sense to tell everyone that your mission is to produce more and more of a product which, judging from the price, is already in oversupply.

You must keep telling the world how much you are spending on exploration and then that your finding costs are less than US$15/oz. They can work out for themselves how many extra ounces the market is going to have to absorb in the future. No one ever asks why, if it costs so little to find an ounce of gold, gold is not a base metal like copper? All we know is that exploration expenditure has resulted in an exponential growth of the four categories of ounces, some of which are for real, others imagined. The categories are as follows: Proven and Probable ounces, Possible ounces, Blah-blah ounces and Yet-To-Be-Discovered ounces. Strange to relate, Blah-BlaH and Yet-To-Be Discovered ounces are often valued more highly by the market than Proven and Probable ounces! If you doubt me, ask the shareholders of BRE-X.

So to the producers I say, don't be shy about publicising the sacrifices your shareholders are making in order to achieve the speedier transfer of gold from those who have it to those who want it. At the last gold conference I attended, I could not restrain myself from asking one of the presenters whether he had perhaps omitted one of his slides by mistake. He had shown a number of charts going from the bottom left hand corner of the page to the top right, demonstrating the growth of his company's reserves and production. What was lacking was a chart showing the corresponding growth in profitability and it was that chart that I thought might have been mislaid. I think it is right that a wider audience should be told how painful it is to be a shareholder in this industry and how much they are suffering for the cause of lower gold prices. Shareholders themselves are only too well aware of this.

I speak from the heart since it is mainly my fault that Mercury Asset Management, on behalf of clients, is one of the world's largest owners of gold mining shares. We call shareholders, shearholders at Mercury because we are fond of the saying that if God had not intended shareholders to be sheared, he would not have made them behave like sheep!

We have watched with interest how shareholders have reacted to the announcement of forward sales by mining companies. You would have thought that if such sales were as beneficial to shareholders as the mining companies say they are, their shares would go up every time a forward sale was announced. But that has not been the case. Shareholders are clearly taking the view that in order to keep the gold price down, forward sales are a necessary evil which must be born with fortitude.

The same can be said about the reaction of shareholders to mining company presentations. Presumably the presentations are designed to achieve the expansion of the shareholder base and thus the share price. They certainly used to achieve that end, but now for some reason the same type of presentation seems to be having exactly the opposite effect. I wonder whether those of you who are responsible for investor relations have noticed this.

People keep asking me when they should start buying gold shares again. Of course I don't know, but I have a pretty good idea. We at Mercury have battled for reform in various parts of the mining industry over a number of years, sometimes with a fair measure of success. The one battle which we have fought and decisively lost has been our battle with the gold miners against forward sales. Not only have we been seen off with our tails between our legs, but with the advantage of hindsight it is now clear to us that the mining industry has been far more skilful at predicting the trend of the gold price than we have, and to prove it they tell us how much they have saved their shareholders by their actions.

In my experience, people buy gold shares with a view to making as much money as possible rather than losing as little as possible. In other words they buy gold shares when they think the gold price is going up. Since the miners have shown themselves to be so adept at predicting the direction of the gold price, I simply advise people not to buy gold shares until they see the gold mining industry unwinding their forward positions. That will be as good a sign as any I can think of that the pain we are suffering is nearly over.

Having paid tribute to the gold miners for their efforts to keep the gold price affordable, it would be churlish not to acknowledge the contribution of the Central Banks to that cause.

But for the Central Bank's willingness to lend their gold to people who subsequently sell it, the price would probably be a lot higher. Since Central Bank gold is valued in the books at a price which bears no relation to reality, it does not matter to them what effect their actions have on the price. Even if they decide to sell it at today's depressed price, they still make a huge profit.

Personally I have never worried too much about potential Central Bank sales. First, if history is anything to go by, the timing of Central Bank sales of gold is one of the best contrary indicators you will get. Secondly Mrs Thatcher taught us that people are quite prepared to buy what they already own if the price is attractive enough. The prospect of a large seller is always conducive to achieving that. Furthermore the disposal of State assets gives rise to juicy commissions which are the life-blood of the larger financial institutions. Would it surprise you to hear that the major Swiss Banks have already been in touch with the Governor of the Swiss Central Bank to ask if they could be helpful over the proposed sale of the Swiss gold. It certainly would not surprise me! It was not so many years ago that as a matter of policy, every Swiss-run portfolio contained 10 per cent in gold. Faced with having to find a home for Central Bank gold, don't be surprised if that policy is revived. Once large institutions which have not previously been actively involved in a market, become involved, that in itself enlarges the size and depth of the market.

There was a nasty moment a week or two ago when the German Government was talking about valuing its gold at a price which bore a more realistic relationship to the market price. This is the last thing we want to see!

If Central Bank gold was valued at the market price it would discourage Central Bankers from doing things which might adversely affect its value. We can now heave a sigh of relief that the uproar which was caused by the proposed revaluation of the German Gold reserves, will probably deter other governments from tinkering with theirs. No one seems to have noticed that gold has been demonetised for over 20 years. What on earth is all the fuss about! In fact the public's interest in gold reserves has suddenly been aroused in a way that even the World Gold Council could never have engineered.

And speaking of the World Gold Council, I can't refrain from pointing out that the industry is paying more than $2/oz to support an organisation, the sole purpose of which is to increase the demand for gold. I thought we had decided that what was required was a lower gold price, not a higher one! Perhaps this is why there are a number of major producers which have decided not to belong to the World Gold Council nor to support its efforts. But surely it is only fair that those who receive more than the market price by selling gold they have not yet produced, should finance the organisation which has to find a buyer for it. Those who do not depress the gold price by selling forward have already done their bit and should therefore not be required to pay twice.

Sitting between the miners and the Central Bankers are the Investment Banks. They facilitate the process of lending gold from the Central Banks to the mines so that the latter can sell it at lower and lower prices. It is, of course, in the interests of the middle men to talk the price down. It encourages both the lenders and the sellers to act quickly before the price goes lower. They know full well that a commission today is worth more than one tomorrow. There is no contango on commissions!

Mining is a relatively harmless activity, which gives gainful employment to a lot of people, often in remote areas. Whether or not it is a profitable occupation does not seem to matter. Miners are like moles – they are not motivated by profit.

They just like digging. You can't stop them even though they may be approaching a mole trap.

Central Bankers may consider themselves more sophisticated than miners. But by seeking to earn a return, however small, on their gold reserves they are helping to make gold more affordable. It makes you wonder whether they ever consider foregoing the income on a small portion of their reserves in the interests of enhancing the capital value of the whole.

So speaking on behalf of those billions of people who live east of Suez it remains for me to thank each and every one of you who have contributed, to a greater or lesser extent, to making gold more affordable. Speaking selfishly as a shareholder, I wish you would stop. If you will, I will.

Thank you for your attention. (**384. 13/6/97**)

In his valedictory piece for the Newsletter, Julian launches a final assault on those whose tactics over the years have led to the decimation of the gold price and the chronic weakening of the industry's finances.

They say that the Scots are good Fund Managers because they are situated far enough away from the hurly burly of the market place to be able to see the wood from the trees. Perhaps this is also one of the advantages of living in Geneva, because from there it seems to me that people in the gold market have lost all sense of proportion and are allowing themselves to be carried away on a wave of conventional wisdom which is working to the detriment of all those concerned with this once precious metal.

Conventional wisdom has it that the price of gold is going down and that rational people will therefore sell it before the price falls further. It is tragic that the gold mining industry itself is the mother of this invention. Their own lack of confidence in the outlook for the metal has persuaded them to sell it forward. If the Central Bankers had not been persuaded that the miners had a point, they would not be selling it themselves. After all the same bullion dealers advise them both. Does no one stop to think whether what they are selling might be extraordinarily cheap? Especially as demand far exceeds newly mined supply and the industry as a whole is barely breaking even. Can the sellers of gold at the current price really believe that what they are doing is still in the best interest of their citizens or their shareholders?

It is one thing to lock in profits when the price of gold is above rational expectations of its long-term value, but where is the sense of locking in prices at which half the gold producers are making losses and at which total demand for gold exceeds newly mined supply by some 1144 tonnes annually? (GFMS 1997) Is there really no price at which those who are trashing the price of gold will stop to ask themselves whether they are now positioning themselves to lose far more than they can expect to gain?

What is clear to those of us who are closely associated with this industry is that we can't go on like this indefinitely. Maybe the gods really want to destroy the gold mining industry. They have certainly made those involved in it do some mad things recently. However, human instinct for survival is very strong and all miners and Central Bankers are human, but not all of them are mad – sanity must surely prevail. There has to be a better way. What is needed now is the will to find it! (**388. 25/7/97**)

2. Gold Hedging – a Cause Célèbre

Over the years Julian Baring made a name for himself and was a thorn in the side of the gold mining industry with his now prophetic comments and warnings about the merit (or lack of) in the developing trend in the 1980s for many gold miners to hedge their gold production, using the natural market arbitrage to reap higher prices for their future production. The whole edifice began to crumble in the early years of the new millennium, but by then Julian had passed on. The newsletter issued an early warning on the associated subject of gold loans in May 1988.

Last week, Consolidated Gold Fields launched their latest gold survey, which gave rise to a certain amount of discussion about the recent spate of gold loans arranged by the industry. It seemed to me that Gold Fields were somewhat coy about the effect these gold loans would have on the market. It is interesting to note that this convenient method of financing future gold mining operations has been used in all the major gold mining areas of the world this year, except South Africa. The reason why the South Africans have not resorted to this method may have something to do with the fact that the last time they tried hedging, the gold price did not go down as expected and significant sums of money were lost, as were the jobs of some of those responsible, "pour encourager les autres". **(9. 31/5/88)**

After an extended period of weakness the gold price started to recover in 1989 and Julian returned to the subject of gold hedging in November.

On the gold front, the directors of gold mining companies have been telling us for the last 18 months how clever they were to think of selling part of their production forward. That was true when the gold price was falling. Now it is rising and those who have sold their production forward are not benefiting from the increase. I know the feeling only too well! When the gold price changed direction, this fund was less than 20 per cent in gold shares. The proportion was immediately increased to nearly 50 per cent the moment the trend was broken. No one is going to buy a gold fund with no gold shares any more than they will buy a gold share which cannot benefit from the improving gold price.

It was forward selling by the gold mining industry which helped to bring the gold price down in the last year or two. Reversing the procedure will have the opposite effect. None of us who run UK gold funds have come within a mile of beating the FT gold mines index in the last three months, least of all me. I venture to suggest that few mines outside South Africa will reap the full benefit of the recent increase in the gold price. Too few of us are genii! (71. 23/11/89)

With the gold price improving Julian vents his frustration with the gold mining industry as forward selling continues despite a bright outlook for gold.

Perhaps it is because of a surfeit of mince pies or an excess of Christmas pud, but everyone seems to be liverish when it comes to assessing the outlook for 1991. And who can blame them when the Chairman of Barclays Bank says the clearers will have to find £2 billion for bad debts this year and the Rhode Island Governor orders the closure of half the state banks – and all that before the new year is more than three days old!

What strikes me is that gold could turn out to be a relatively good investment this year, even though at this stage few investors seem prepared to consider it. The gold mining industry, having had a good party for most of the 1980s, is now suffering from a nasty hangover and much of it is struggling to make ends meet. They have been making a virtue of necessity by selling their gold forward, taking advantage of the fact that gold always fetches more on the futures market than it does spot.

In a nutshell, this means that the gold mining industry has already sold a lot of gold which it has not yet produced and it has become increasingly fashionable to be seen to be doing so. Sooner or later this policy may backfire on those who adopt it. For if their policies, for whatever reason, start to cause a shortage of physical gold they could be squeezed painfully and the gold price could shoot up. The Governor of the Bank of England warned us over a year ago that something like this could happen, so it is not just me being alarmist.

Once gold starts going up, investors may suddenly wake up to its attractions, one of which is that bullion is no one else's liability. Either you own it or you don't. Better have some gold under the bed than a dollar bill under the counter of a bank that cannot open for business. (122. 3/1/91)

Whilst selling forward can lock in a mining profit, it locks out "blue sky" which Julian points out is what most people buy gold shares for.

That is the aggressive side of gold investment. The defensive strategy is to buy gold shares whose future earnings are protected by forward sales. Many gold companies have sold their production forward for the next few years at rising prices like only gold companies can. The question is whether they are worth the price we have to pay for the protection they offer. I am of the old fashioned opinion that a gold mining company cannot be worth more than the total profits it can generate from mining each ounce of gold it owns. The trouble with forward selling is that although you lock in the profit, you lock out the "blue sky" provided by a rising gold price. In other words, you lock out the very thing which makes people most want to hold gold shares. Conversely, with a company which has sold forward, you know exactly how much profit it is going to make which may be safe but is not very sexy. Investments which provide a certain stream of income are called gilts. They do not enjoy very flattering ratings. Why should gold shares which have locked in their future profits be any different? (**124. 16/1/91**)

Here Julian delivers a backhanded compliment to forward sellers when comparing them favourably with miners who take out gold loans.

Gold mining companies which have sold their production forward may occasionally miss out on some super profits when the gold price goes up, but at least they will be better off than the companies which have taken out gold loans. Those companies have already sold their gold and received the money for it. The only decision they have to make is the one I have just had to make with our Transnet Bear Bond, namely whether to cover what is basically a bear position. Gold loans are wonderful inventions when the gold price is falling, but there is no such thing as a free lunch, even if you are a gold miner. It is how to structure the gold portion of the portfolio that causes me the most headaches. What we have discussed so far, namely the gilts and golds, represent two thirds of the portfolio. The remaining third is undeniably vulnerable to a prolonged recession. The brokers are now reducing their metal price forecasts to levels closer to those we have been using since we started this Fund. Lower metal prices mean lower earnings projections and these are debilitating to share prices. We must not complain however. It is share price weakness which provides us longer-term investors with buying opportunities. (**124. 16/1/91**)

Gold shares backed by forward sold gold are very like bonds but with little or no yield.

There seems to be a growing trend for South African gold mining companies to follow the example of their overseas counterparts by selling their production forward. I have mixed feelings about this as you know. A gold mine that has sold all its production forward looks awfully like a bond to me – but a bond without a yield. Very few gold mines yield anything worthwhile these days. They are rated more like growth stocks but if Tony Henfrey's chart is anything to go by there is not going to be much growth. **(125. 24/1/91)**

Forward sales protect some miners margins as currencies go against them.

Last week I was trying to show you how the gold price was rising in rand terms due to the weakness of the rand versus the dollar. If you were a South African mine manager you would not exactly be jumping for joy about the recent behaviour of the gold price but you would be a good deal happier than your Australian and North American counterparts who have seen the gold price fall in terms of their own currencies.

Of course many of them could not care less since they have sold so much of their gold forward, so that the lower the gold price goes, the more their forward sales are worth should they wish to cover them, as well they may one day! **(131. 27/3/91)**

As forward selling continued Julian piled on the pressure on gold miners beating a path to his door, hoping to attract his support.

Little wonder then that there has not been much to say for the last week or two. Gold in fact has been behaving surprisingly well bearing in mind the general air of doom and gloom. Predictions of $300/oz–$320/oz have so far been confounded, but the miners, with one or two notable exceptions, lack sufficient confidence in the gold price to dare to close out their hedged positions. I ask visiting miners whether or not their Board of Directors are agonising over whether to close out their forward sales. About half of those I speak to admit to agonising a bit. All say that they would close their forwards if someone could give them a cast iron guarantee that the gold price was not going to fall further. In other words, they openly tell you what they are likely to do once they have regained their collective nerve. Nothing could be more beneficial for the gold price than the closing of forward sales, but they will not do so at these low prices, only when they have convinced themselves the gold price won't go lower.

I chide them further, what if the leaders of the gold mining industry happened to meet by chance and pledge each other not to sell gold forward for 30 days? They all know the answer to that one. The gold price would shoot up! But none of them trusts the others not to sell forward when it does, even if the 30-day embargo was still in force! Talk about shooting oneself in the foot. The mining industry sometimes deserves what it gets from its actions, namely cutbacks and closures. The only comfort we have is that the survivors will make a great deal of money when the turn-round comes. More so if investors join the bandwagon by buying gold for the first time in years. (**151. 25/9/91**)

Canadian gold miner Royal Oak closes its forwards, but much to Julian's frustration the industry appeared to be building more forward selling positions as the gold price rose.

Don't tell anyone but contrary to widespread expectations the gold price is actually going up not down! No one believes it because they have been caught too many times before trying to capitalise on an improving gold price by buying gold shares.

To make matters worse the mining industry, which I am sorry to say can at times be its own worst enemy, has been congratulating itself on the quantity of gold it has been able to sell forward this year.

That is fine so long as the gold price is falling, but it does not look so smart when the opposite is true. There are fewer and fewer gold shares that you can buy where no gold has been sold forward and where the shareholder will receive the full benefit of any improvement in the gold price.

The other reason why the improved gold price has left investors nonplussed is that most commentators have now got it firmly into their heads that as soon as the gold price goes up a few dollars, the industry will once again shoot itself in the foot by selling forward, thus bringing the price right down again.

Just imagine the effect on the gold market if an American Barrick or Newmont Gold were to announce that they had closed out their forward positions like Royal Oak has recently done.

The directors of Royal Oak came to see me about a month ago. We discussed by how many dollars they would be able to reduce their costs per ounce from then on by closing out their forwards. The answer was close to $10 per ounce. When I asked them why on earth they didn't do it, they told me they had given instructions to do so that very afternoon. On hearing that I bought 100,000 shares. I wish it had been a million but the price shot up before I could raise the money. (**152. 4/10/91**)

Not for the first time Julian points out that investors buy gold shares because they think the gold price is going up, not because they like the structure of a miner's forward book.

The mining industry's attitude to forward sales is reminiscent of a gambler who has a big win at the tables when he first starts playing. Instead of "banking" profits, most gamblers pretend they are gambling with the casino's money and go on until they lose it all. The miners complain that the market gives them very little credit for the "value" of their forward sales. All the more reason to close them out! They should use the proceeds to pay down debt. That in turn will reduce costs. The market will willingly pay for that just as they did when Royal Oak closed out its forwards recently.

In this game everyone tries to out-guess each other. I believe miners should get on with what they do best, mining. Fund Managers should buy those shares which will do best if the gold price goes up – why else do people buy gold funds? You have already shown by your actions what you do, you sell this Fund when it is underperforming the UK market and you buy it when it is outperforming the UK market. Whether the gold price is going up or down seems not to interest you. That is fine. As long as you are consistent in your behaviour I can cope with your proclivities. What I cannot cope with is gold mining companies who try to combine mining the stuff, trading the metal and playing the stock market all at the same time. When something looks wrong, it is described in the vernacular as "a lot of old cobblers" perhaps that is because old cobblers forget to stick to their last. (**153. 16/10/91**)

Julian predicts that, like a casino gambler, gold mines will only cover forward sales when it's too late …

I am told that the gold mining industry has sold forward some 40 per cent of this year's production and some 30 per cent of next years. If they were to cut production by the same amount as the aluminium producers, or equivalent to roughly 70 tonnes of gold, Ord Minnett have calculated that the gold price would likely rise by some $47 to about $405/oz. So the whole industry would be selling less; 1660 tonnes instead of 1730 tonnes, but what they would get for it would be more; nearer $21.3 billion than the $19.8 billion they are receiving at the moment.

Miners hate cutting production unless they absolutely have to and in the case of the gold mining industry they do not have to. All they have to do is to close out some of their forward sales instead.

But will they be so farsighted? I think you know the answer. My guess is they will forget that the "profits" they could now take from their well-timed forward sales of two or three years ago, belong to the shareholders. Instead they will wait like a gambler in a casino until their windfall gain is frittered away by a rising gold price. They will eventually cover their forwards when they see them starting to go too far "out of the money". I cannot help thinking that the poor gold miners are being legged over by those clever bankers who have found a lucrative line of business in providing them with so called "protection" which seems to me to better serve the interests of the bankers than the miners. How do I know? A banker told me so! **(154. 23/10/91)**

As you are aware, I take a jaundiced view of gold mining companies who help to depress the gold price by selling their production forward.

My trouble is that I am not sure how much value I should be placing on a board of directors' ability to successfully speculate on the future direction of the gold price. Just because they got it right two years ago when the gold price was relatively high, doesn't seem to me to provide any proof that they will be proved right, in two years' time, to have sold gold forward at today's depressed prices.

What has happened is that whereas two years ago it seemed perfectly sensible to lock in an extremely satisfactory level of profit by selling forward, today's forward sellers are doing no more than using forward sales to keep their heads above water.

… and indeed some may simply leave them well alone or even open up new positions despite the gold price being low.

Now the question I want to put to you is this. If you were a director of a gold mining company which had sold a proportion of its production forward two years ago and if you had an unrealised profit of say $30 million, would you cover your forwards and bank your profit or leave them intact? The mining companies are leaving them intact which implies that they can find no more profitable use for the theoretical $30 million than to sell gold forward even at these low prices!

I find such lack of confidence, particularly in the case of the South Africans who persist in selling forward even at these low prices, rather worrying. What have they heard I wonder? Perhaps they have come to the conclusion that the jewellery industry is not as robust as we think it is. Let me put it this way. New mine production is about 1750 tonnes. If, as I think to be the case, about a quarter of newly mined production is currently earmarked for the repayment of forward sales made two years ago, that implies that the jewellery industry is now only having to absorb 1150 tonnes.

After next year, most of the forwards taken out at very high levels will have been utilised, so the industry will then be faced with a decision whether to sell all their newly mined gold in the spot market or whether to embark on yet further forward sales at prices which could make them look awfully silly if the gold price were subsequently to rise. (157. 22/11/91)

Julian has to admit, though, that without forward sales Canadian gold mines would be losing money.

I liked the comment this week from John Lydall, a Canadian broker who has the knack of getting straight to the point.

"Never in the history of gold mining has so much time been spent by so many analysts on so little (profit)."

He is quite right of course. The profits of the Canadian gold mining industry are pitiful. Their reserves are calculated using a gold price of $400/oz (down from $430/oz last year). This is because with gold currently at $353/oz the regulatory authorities would look askance at ore reserve calculations based on a gold price $80 higher than the current price. If the gold price were to remain at current levels, my guess is that the price at which reserves will be calculated this time next year, will be lower than $400. Then there will be more write-downs of gold reserves and consequent write-offs of unrealistic value.

The gravity of the situation is masked by forward sales taken out two or three years ago at much higher gold prices. If these were excluded (and they won't be available forever) the market would see that current wafer-thin profits for the industry would be turned into loss. Burns Fry, the Canadian broker, tells me that last year the leading four Canadian gold companies made a total profit of $170 million equivalent to $41/oz for the 4 million or so ounces they produced. Without forward sales they would have lost $11 million equivalent to $3/oz assuming they had sold their gold at the average spot of $362/oz. Don't worry, we do not own any – the profitable ones are too pricey and the unprofitable ones are unattractive. (164. 20/2/92)

In a further sally into battle against forward selling Julian calls on support from Union Corporation's scholarly Hugh Munro.

It is bad enough increasing gold production to a level that is more than the market can absorb. That's private enterprise. What is not so clever is to sell gold that you have not yet produced. To do something that serves to make a bad situation worse is akin to carelessness, in my opinion.

Last week a learned paper landed on my desk. It was written by Mr. H.C. Monro, a retired director of Union Corporation. He demonstrated by means of higher mathematics that the overall loss of revenue suffered by the mining industry from selling gold forward in 1990 can be calculated using a formula such as 32 151 G (DT-NP) dollars. I will not bore you with the minutiae, but the loss of revenue calculated by this formula came to $2,551 billion in 1990!

Well, as you might expect, the people who had been selling forward dismissed poor Mr. Monro's higher mathematics as being "over-simplistic". I know from personal experience how Mr. Monro must have felt about that. He should be comforted by the fact that some people derive profit from making things seem more complicated than they really are. That enables them to sort them out for you, usually for a fee. I like things kept so simple that even I can understand them. If I can, you certainly will.

Far from being too simplistic, I think Mr. Monro was being too gentlemanly. It seems to me that the damage the directors of gold companies do, by selling gold forward, is rather more serious than Mr. Monro's mathematical formula would suggest. Nobody cares more about the gold price than the shareholders of the companies that produce it. And by that I mean you and me. **(167. 13/3/92)**

And below Julian with one swift thrust demolishes the value of forward selling.

The gold industry may have suffered a $2.5 billion loss of revenue by selling its gold forward in 1990, but the luckless shareholders have seen $14 billion wiped off the capital value of their shares! In their search for short-term advantage, the directors of the companies who are employed by the shareholders to look after their interests have succeeded in diminishing our wealth by a far greater amount than any possible extra revenue that could be earned over the life of the mine by selling forward.

Anyone who has had the task of running a fund for more than a month or two, knows how easy it is to depress the balance of a holding by selling some of it. You have to "feed the ducks when they are quacking", if your own selling is not to damage your own wealth. By selling gold forward, the gold industry has depressed the value placed by the market on all the rest of their production. I will give you one example which is not unrepresentative. The future revenue of one well-known Australian company, if they were able to sell all their gold at $392/oz, is $2.75 billion. Their forward sales of 1.1 m oz at $410 would net them an additional $34 million or 1.2 per cent of revenue. However they and others, by selling forward, have depressed the gold price to $350/oz, dropping their future revenue by 10.5 per cent to $2.460 billion. Their forward sales may now be worth $81m, a gain of $47 million. But compare that with the overall loss of revenue of $249 million and the consequent loss of market capitalization!

Since everybody's doing it, you can take comfort. Sooner or later they will all change their minds and decide that its not worth the candle. Then the situation will be reversed and all the remaining ounces will be valued as if the gold price will forever be $392/oz rather than $350/oz. (**167. 13/3/92**)

Newmont closes out its gold loan and Julian spots the hand of Jimmy Goldsmith, Newmont's largest shareholder, at work ...

Just when the gold market had seemingly given up all hope, the depths of depression were lifted a little this week by an act of leadership by America's largest gold producer, Newmont Mining.

Newmont announced that it had taken advantage of the low current gold price of US$335/oz to buy enough gold in the forward market to repay the outstanding balance of the million ounce gold loan taken out in 1988 at a price of US$449/oz. You may remember the depressing effect that this gold loan had on the gold price at the time.

It reminds me of the action alleged to have been taken by certain leading financial institutions at the bottom of the bear market of 1974 when they decided that UK equities had fallen to ridiculous levels and that they were going to do something about it. Summoning up their courage and a few million pounds they entered the UK equity market and caught the dismal Jimmies short.

I have never met the gentleman, but this time I detect the kind of bold action associated with the persona of another Jimmy who just happens to have a 49 per cent shareholding in Newmont Mining. If rumour is to be believed, he exerts a powerful influence on the Board of that company.

What Sir James Goldsmith seems to be saying to those who have been depressing the price of the product which pays their salaries (by selling it forward) is "Can't you think of anything better to do with the profits you have made from your forward sales than continuing to go 'short' of gold at these depressed levels?" A policy of despair if ever there was one. (**173. 6/5/92**)

... but to no avail as forward sales by others continues unabated.

Any good that might have been done by Newmont Mining's sensible decision to close out its gold loan, which we wrote about a couple of weeks ago, is so far being frustrated by other producers who have added to gold's decline by swamping the market with sales of future production.

First Marathon Securities inform us that one of the main culprits last quarter was the Canadian-based company, Lac Minerals. At 31st December 1991, the company reported forward sales totalling 1,543,000 ounces at an average price of US$398/oz. Then, on 30th April, they announced that their forward sales had increased to 2,420,000 ounces at an average price of US$376/oz. This effectively means that in the first four months of the year Lac has sold forward almost 900,000 ounces of gold in addition to delivering its regular production of approximately 370,000 ounces. Judging by the reduction of US$22/oz in the company's forward pricing schedule, it is evident that the recent forward sales must have been made at an average of US$355/oz.

Lac's sale of 1,270,000 ounces puts Newmont's purchase of 375,000 ounces into perspective and should be seen in the light of the 32 million ounces of future production that Gold Fields Mineral Services' annual survey recently suggested was already committed at the end of 1991.

Forward contango rates in North America are now around 3.5 per cent per annum, suggesting Lac has secured a gold price of US$367/oz next year. Geoff Campbell at Ord Minnett calculates that an investor in Lac requires a gold price of US$378/oz just to get his money back, let alone a return on his investment. Lac Mineral's action of locking in a future gold price below this breakeven level cannot do much to boost the confidence of its shareholders. Last quarter Lac generated profits of US$13 on each of the 278,000 ounces it produced; a fairly meagre amount when one considers that the company reported sharply reduced cash operating costs of US$219/oz. Subtracting the US$13/oz profit from the revenue per ounce of US$396/oz suggests that total costs (including tax) were US$383/oz.

Having locked in its future gold price, Lac will have to reduce its costs even further in order to improve profitability. One way to reduce costs is to raise the head grade of production. Higher head grades produce more ounces of gold for the same or similar costs but tends to reduce the life of the reserves.

If mining companies are forced to "high grade" in order to remain in business, that implies that published proven and probable reserves will probably have to be scaled down in future. That does not bode well for future valuations. (**176. 28/5/92**)

Anglo claims its forward selling is done to keep high cost shafts open and Julian admits his approval of forward selling, in this case based on the fact that the Fund holds many of these Anglo marginals.

This week Warburgs organised a European roadshow for Anglo American Corporation to display its virtues. One of the most interesting comments came from Clem Sunter, who heads their gold division. He explained that Anglo American had sold about 50 per cent of this year's gold production forward to ensure that the highest cost shafts remained profitable. He said that if the gold price rose US$20 or so and stayed there, there would be no need to hedge so much. This is in stark contrast to other gold companies who say that contango rates are now too low to make selling gold forward attractive. They say they prefer to wait for the gold price to recover and take advantage of a spike before opening up new forward sales positions.

Gold mining companies, in my opinion, are in the business of mining gold not speculating in gold futures. It is one thing to sell gold forward to bridge an otherwise unprofitable gap. It is quite another thing to depress the price of the product you produce and thus the value of your company, to the short-term benefit of earnings per share.

It seems to me that Anglo American's hedging policy is being conducted for all the right reasons, but I am biased because we own the sort of mines that benefit from those policies. What I am far less enthusiastic about is the stated willingness of the gold mining industry generally to "tap gold on the head" as soon as it shows some signs of recovery. It was encouraging to hear that one of the larger hedgers has no intention of doing that. (**181. 3/7/92**)

Newmont's closing of its gold loan in 1992 demonstrates the lost opportunity cost of hedging production.

Now let's look at what has happened since Newmont Mining repaid its gold loan in April this year by buying back some 375,000 ounces of gold at around US$351/oz. The price of gold has risen by some US$22/oz since then achieving for Newmont shareholders a "benefit" of over US$8 million which they otherwise would not have enjoyed.

The gold industry as a whole is reputed to have sold some 32,000,000 ounces of gold they have not yet produced, so by failing to follow Newmont's lead, the industry's shareholders have so far said goodbye to US$704 million in lost opportunity cost. By comparison it is interesting to note that last year the industry paid dividends totalling some US$900 million.

It is a pity that the captains of the gold mining industry couldn't think of anything better to do with their shareholders' money than to continue to go "short" gold even at the particularly deep levels of early May ... But you already know my views on that particular subject. I am against forward selling and try not to buy companies which indulge in it. (**182. 30/7/92**)

Julian points out that if gold goes on falling gold miners may only have losses to lock in through forward selling.

Yet again, just as the currency turmoil of last week was starting to have a beneficial effect on the gold price, the rise was capped by forward selling by producers. It makes you want to weep!

One can only conclude that some sections of the gold mining industry are in such dire straits that they are forced to sell forward at these low prices, not because they want to but because they have to.

Logic would dictate that with costs rising and interest rates falling, it is only a matter of time before forward selling at current prices will merely be locking in losses rather than profits. Meanwhile forward selling by the chronically sick is simply reducing the profit margins of those that remain in good health. But that's capitalism for you!

As I said last week, it seems that the gold price will only go up when potential investors can see for themselves that supply and demand is being brought into equilibrium by cutbacks and closure of uneconomic production. (189. 24/9/92)

As the spot gold price begins to rise, shareholders of forward sellers begin to make a "Chinese loss".

The rising gold price must be giving food for thought to the directors of mining companies with regard to their forward sales policy.

Ord Minnett calculate that 818 tonnes of gold have been sold forward, equivalent to some 26 million ounces. Australia accounts for 302 tonnes, North American 299 tonnes and South Africa 175 tonnes. To put this into perspective, annual mine production of gold is approximately 1800 tonnes.

Since the gold price has risen from its low of US\$326/oz to US\$352/oz, the luckless shareholders of those mining companies who have forward sold, have so far made a "Chinese loss" of US\$676 million. For the uninitiated a "Chinese loss" is similar to that which the writer is often accused of making by his wife when, with the advantage of hindsight, she points out ruefully "we should have bought this or we should have sold that".

I have often remarked that the one thing you know about investment is that when all investors are saying the same thing (as they did about gold and gold shares towards the end of last year) they are always proved wrong. By the time they say it, they have usually done it.

The one thing about which the Directors of mining companies were virtually unanimous during the bear market, was that forward sales were in their interests. I say "their", because shareholders had to suffer the loss in the capital value of their shares brought about by the falling gold price, resulting from forward sales.

Now that the gold price has reversed direction, each dollar rise in the gold price reduces by US\$26 million the total benefit which the companies had accrued by selling forward. Once companies have convinced themselves that the gold price is going up rather than down, it is reasonably safe to predict that, sheep-like, they will come to the conclusion that the smartest move they can make is to close out their forward positions.

Of course, just as forward sales helped to depress the gold price, the closing out of forwards will help to make the gold price rise. The last man to cover is the one who will "lose" most. I predict that in one year's time forward sellers will have much in common with the Dodo. (**216. 6/5/93**)

More forward sellers close positions, benefiting the gold price and share prices.

As you know, I have been a vociferous opponent of forward selling by the mining industry which has sent negative messages to the market about the industry's own perceptions of the future direction of the gold price and more seriously, has probably been responsible for the last US$70–US$100/oz fall in the gold price. I have often pointed out that when everyone thinks the same way, they are almost always proved wrong. The fashion for selling gold forward will cost the unfortunate shareholders dear.

Two mining companies took this message on board last week. Lac Minerals covered 500,000 ounces of their forward sales and took a loss of US$17 million by so doing. Dominion Mining was more fortunate. It covered one third only of its forward sales, 300,000 ounces, and booked a profit, though it was a much smaller profit than it would have been if they had acted earlier.

The repurchase of 800,000 ounces by two mining companies was largely responsible, in my opinion, for the US$ 11/oz rise in the gold price last week, yet 800,000 ounces is a mere 2 per cent of the 38 million ounces which the mining companies have sold forward. As I said last week, the last forward seller to cover will be the one that makes the largest loss.

What is particularly interesting is that when the gold price was going down, the forward sellers vowed to increase their forward sales on any worthwhile rally in the gold price. Far from increasing their forwards, it now appears that the mining industry is starting to buy back what it has already sold. The market sniffs a short position. This normally gives rise to a ruthless activity known in the indelicate language of the marketplace as "squeezing the shorts".

How did the market react to Dominion's announcement? It added 16 per cent to the company's share price in a week, a reaction that will not go unnoticed by Dominion's competitors. We added to the Fund's holding of Dominion on the announcement and will buy more when they announce that they have covered the remaining 600,000 ounces sold forward. Who needs crutches when their broken leg is mended? (**218. 20/5/93**)

Julian turns his guns on the hedging policy of the South African mines and bemoans the lack of transparency which keeps most (but not all) shareholders in the dark as to the identity of the hedgers, and he points out the cost of the policy.

We await with some trepidation the publication of the June quarterly reports of the South African gold mines. As you know, a number of Houses have been selling gold forward on behalf of their group mines, but those who have done so will not tell us for which mines they have sold forward or at what price they have sold. We suspect the reason for their reticence is that they have sold forward at prices lower than the current spot price and may find themselves either having to cover at a loss or deliver gold into their forwards at prices which won't look too clever compared with the spot price. If the market knew the extent of these forward sales, the mines could be held to ransom by the bullion dealers, so we shareholders not only have to carry the can but are kept in the dark while so doing. What upsets me is that the mines continue to pursue a policy of forward sales which arguably may be suitable for a bear market but which is entirely inappropriate in a bull market. One important segment of the mines' shareholders is informed of what is going on. The rest of us can only guess. The Boards of the individual mines are often comprised of representatives of Mining Houses who held the original mineral rights. This highly price-sensitive information about forward sales is available not only to the directors of the controlling Mining House but also to the Directors of other Mining Houses through the famous cross-holdings which exist in the South African mining industry.

Whilst I am not suggesting for one moment that such price-sensitive information would ever be used to the advantage of one set of shareholders over another, it would be much better if the mines came clean with their forward sales position. If some rogue happened to get word of the true position and act accordingly, the finger of suspicion would be pointed at the controlling Mining House even though there has never been any reason to suspect that the Houses have ever used inside information for their own benefit.

To give you an example of the misfortunes which can beset shareholders of gold mining companies which sell forward, let me tell you what happened last quarter to the shareholders of Harmony. We have an indirect interest in this mine through our shareholding in its controlling Mining House Randgold.

Harmony announced a working loss of R500,000 for the quarter, based on a gold price received of R1,064/oz. The average gold price for the quarter was 8 per cent higher at R 1,153/oz, but Harmony sold a major proportion of its production forward at the wrong price. If they had received the market price by not selling forward, they would have made a profit of R14.9 million instead of a loss of R500,000!

That is bad enough for Harmony's luckless shareholders who have suffered great pain in recent years in the hope of benefiting when the gold price rose. To add insult to injury, the directors say that a significant proportion of the production to June 1994 has been hedged at prices below the current gold price!

Although it is argued (but not by us) that hedging is an aspect of prudent management when the gold price is clearly in a downward trend, it seems to us not unreasonable to expect management to be sufficiently flexible to adjust its strategies to market circumstances. As ever, when they fail to do so, it is the shareholders who suffer. Let's hope that what has happened to the luckless shareholders of Harmony will be taken as a cautionary tale by the management of other gold companies in a similar situation. If the lesson is learnt, the pain suffered by Harmony shareholders will not have been entirely in vain. Hopefully the shareholders of Doornfontein, of which we own 9.5 per cent, will fare much better. It is the wise policy of the Gold Fields Group, of which Doornfontein forms part, not to sell forward, so we should enjoy the full benefit of last quarter's improving gold price in rands. (**223. 5/7/93**)

Harmony gets hauled over the coals again!

The next thing that needs to be addressed is the question of selling gold forward. Forward sales can certainly be justified in exceptional circumstances to protect capital expenditure which otherwise might not be prudent. But people like us who buy marginal mines like to do so because we recognise that we will gain an exceptional reward if the gold price goes up. If it goes down, we recognise that with marginal mines we are exposed to greater than average risks. The one thing investors do not want to find is that having borne the risk, their upside has been capped by the management selling gold forward. The knowledge that sufficient forward sales are in place to ensure the continued payment of management fees discourages timely action being taken by management to bear down on costs at all levels of the business.

We asked stockbrokers Societe Generale Strauss Turnbull to work out how much it would cost Harmony to buy back the forward sales already made. The answer was US$998,397.

We then asked how much the shareholders of Harmony would fail to make if the company remained hedged as at present and the gold price in rands were to rise as a result of an 11.7 per cent devaluation of the rand. The answer was that the opportunity cost would amount to US$8.6 million!

Investment is about risk and reward. We think Harmony shares would enjoy wider appeal if the new management covered the forwards as we have suggested to them. (**266. 25/8/94**)

Julian names November (1995) as "no hedging month" and challenges the industry to exercise restraint when approached by business-hungry bullion banks, especially as forward selling is not enhancing share valuations.

Every time we see a gold mining company, and we see five or six every week, we give them a piece of our mind about forward selling. As you are aware, we don't believe that hedging is in the shareholders' best interest since we perceive that it helps to put a cap on the gold price.

Gold shares have many of the same characteristics as options on gold. Although forward sales may or may not enhance a company's future cash flow, they diminish the gearing which is one of the main attractions of investing in gold shares.

As we pointed out a couple of weeks ago, if forward sales really enhanced value, a company's shares would rise every time a forward sale was announced. We wonder if the hedgers ever stop to ask themselves why that does not happen.

Obviously the last thing we want is to see the gold mining companies we own, shooting themselves in the foot. That is why we have designated November "QUIT HEDGING MONTH". And that is why we have started to suggest to each of the companies who come to see us that they try exercising voluntary restraint over forward selling during the month of November and let it be known that if their restraint bears fruit in the form of a higher gold price, they will continue to restrain themselves into December and beyond.

What chance is there of the mining industry putting our proposal to the test? Alas very little, since we are up against the big battalions of the bullion banks, who have prospered greatly by persuading the gold mining companies to sell them gold which has not yet been produced. No doubt they know of people who wish to buy it! What hope have we as mere shareholders, the ultimate owners of the companies, of persuading the miners to reconsider the conventional wisdom that forward selling is in their best interests?

We like to think that there is at least a glimmer of hope. By now it must be becoming painfully clear to the directors of gold mining companies, especially those who are also shareholders, that something is going wrong with a strategy that previously looked so water-tight. Although the forward sales entered into a year ago may be looking pretty smart when compared with today's gold price, for some reason the market is now placing a lower value on gold shares than it did a year ago! In other words, the market is now telling them that their actions have become counter-productive. By designating November "QUIT HEDGING MONTH", we hope to reverse that perception. (**303. 6/7/95**)

Admitting that the forward sales drum may have beat a bit too loud, Julian thinks nonetheless that another of his big themes, mine management fees, may be in retreat too.

Some of you understandably felt that if you ever heard our opinion about forward sales again, you would take leave of your senses! That's the bad news. The good news is that the newsletter mysteriously seems to find its way into the hands of some of the directors of the mining companies, who would rather die than admit it, but who actually appear to read it! Some of our long-fought battles for reform seem to be bearing fruit. For instance, Gencor announced last month that it intended to give its mines more autonomy. That could be the thin edge of the wedge which signals the death throes of the dreaded management fees system which does so much to inhibit the natural development of the industry. (**308. 10/8/95**)

Falling profitability forces South African gold mines to hedge.

Brokers, Baring Securities, have been drawing our attention to the fact that the profit of the South African gold industry averaged a mere US$16/oz in the June quarter of this year and only US$20/oz in the September quarter. The bad news is that such a lamentably small industry profit margin is hardly likely to attract capital for new projects. The good news is that the recent US$10 rise in the gold price, drew everyone's attention to the dramatic effect a small rise in the gold price can have on the profit margins. No wonder the market responded by rising 7.6 per cent in one day. Hope, after all, springs eternal in the breasts of gold investors!

These hopes have since been dashed yet again as the meagre rise in the gold price unleashed an avalanche of forward selling by the South Africans who need constant reminding that companies, including gold companies, belong to their shareholders. Shareholders can become so bored waiting for the gold price to rise that they simply sell their shares regardless of whether the companies are earning more than they would have done if they had not sold forward. People forget that a share price has much less to do with its true value than with the number of people who want to buy, rather than sell it. (**322. 25/11/95**)

It is now widely accepted that forward selling has a depressing effect on the gold price. As shareholders of this Fund, we are recipients of what is colloquially known as a "double whammy". It is our gold, as citizens, that the Central Banks are lending, receiving in exchange another piece of paper which is someone else's liability and it is our gold, as shareholders, that the mining companies are borrowing in order to sell forward.

Some people believe that gold acts as a type of financial thermometer of a nation's health, and the last thing a Central Banker wants is for the citizenry to be alerted by the gold price into thinking that the nation's finances are being mismanaged. Keeping the gold price subservient to paper money and at the same time getting a rate of interest on an otherwise non-income producing asset helps to ensure the continuance of the Central Banker's ability to pay the school fees.

The irksome thing about borrowing is that, although the payment of interest is often a doddle, the requirement to repay capital can be most inconvenient. In the case of the gold mining industry, the eventual repayment of gold borrowed from the Central Banks could well result in a shortage for the jewellery manufacturers. This could adversely affect the jewellery manufacturers' ability to pay the school fees.

Of course you will have heard many times from the directors of gold mining companies how much additional cash flow the shareholders have derived from their policy of forward selling. It is undeniable that, if you sell something you don't have, in a falling market, you are likely to be able to buy it back at a profit. Gold has been declining for most of the last 16 years, so of course the forward sellers and the bullion houses who conduct their business have benefited. But when we buy shares, we are taking a view on the future and it seems to us less likely that the gold price will continue to decline since, over the last 16 years, it has fallen from being 128 per cent above our estimate of its long-term purchasing power to being more than 10 per cent below it.

Those of you who own this Fund obviously agree with us. Who would be stupid enough to own a gold unit trust if he thought the gold price was going to decline for a prolonged period? We want the gold price risk! That is exactly why we bought the Fund in the first place. The companies we own do us no favours by trying to remove that risk! From our point of view, the ownership of units of this Fund can, from time to time, help to pay the school fees. The real irony is that often the directors of the South African Mining Houses who are currently the main perpetrators of forward selling, don't even own shares in the individual mines, like we do. They are incentivised with options in the shares of the Mining Houses for which they work. Years ago the Mining Houses earned most of their revenues from the mines they controlled. Nowadays most of their earnings come from their industrial interests into which they have diversified. They are what really pay the school fees. (**345. 13/6/96**)

3. Mining the Markets in Base Metals

For the first few years of Gold and General's life Julian favoured base metals as the backbone of the portfolio. He felt base metal shares offered much better value than gold shares, although many potential buyers of the Fund may well have wanted a higher exposure to gold than they initially would have got. The relatively low PE multiples seemed to suggest that sharp falls in metal prices were expected around every bend, something that Julian's analysis indicated was unlikely from both a macro and a micro point of view.

Julian backs a continuation of high base metal prices following the sector's revival.

Of even greater influence on the price of base metals is the backwardation at which they are all selling. The cognoscenti tell me that players in the metal markets are having the greatest difficulty in getting used to the present level of metal prices, so accustomed have they become to prices which resulted in the mining industry making losses for the last three to four years. Nickel is a good example. Producers have been struggling for years to make a living and are not easily going to be persuaded to expand production until they have repaired their balance sheets. That won't happen overnight. I agree with RTZ that metal prices will stay higher for longer than most people now expect. (**3. 19/4/88**)

Julian pours cold water on those who would sell base metal shares on low PEs, believing that they have not given enough consideration to cost cutting within the industry.

The conventional wisdom, and you hear it all the time, is that you should buy base metal shares on high PE ratios and sell them on low ones, like now. Base metal prices are perceived to be high now, in historical terms. This can be disproved at the press of a button on a desktop computer, so let's not waste ink on it. What the Conventional Wisdomers don't tell us is, what "high multiple" they will think appropriate to pay for the lower future earnings they foresee. They seem to overlook the fact that the mining industry has had to cut costs to the bone in order to survive the low metal prices of the last four years and are now probably as well placed to ride any future economic down-turn as any sector of the market. Investors don't see it that way, they want to apply a belt of low multiples to the braces of increased efficiency which the miners are already wearing. Let them. All it does is to provide buyers with even greater value.

I look at it from the opposite point of view. To my mind the action taken by the mining industry to reduce costs will make their earnings less, not more, volatile and that should result in higher, not lower, multiples being applied in the future. (4. 26/4/88)

Julian continues to pursue the issue of divergent PEs on base metal and gold shares, and points out that if the market believes that base metal and gold prices are going to perform similarly in the future then the low PEs on base metal shares and the high PEs on gold shares make no sense.

What bugs me is that, since no one knows what metal prices will be in a year's time, there is no logic in paying 6.25 times earnings for the base metal producers and 25 times prospective earnings for the gold producers? What have people heard about the prospects for one compared with those of the other? If any of us were any good at predicting metal prices, mining shares would not have their well-deserved reputation for volatility!

Those of you who follow these scribblings will know that I pay a great deal of attention to market perceptions. It is changing perceptions about an industry which alter values more than anything else. Good research can tell you what a company is likely to earn, but what matters is the value that the market will place on those earnings. I am trying hard to get the brokers to focus on the multiples they think mining companies will command, based on next year's earnings, so far with mixed success.

I was particularly interested in a remark made by a broker last week when I asked him what he thought metal prices would be in 12 months' time. He admitted that he hadn't really thought that far ahead (in other words he didn't know) but he did say he expected the current relationship between gold and the base metals to persist, more or less. That comment was much more useful to me than any forecast of metal prices, since it demonstrated a growing perception in the market place that, in order for the mining industry to supply the raw materials required by industry, it is necessary for it to enjoy a sufficient level of profitability with which to finance new mines. This, of course, has been the case with the gold mining industry for well over a decade and you can see for yourselves how quickly gold production is increasing. It has been the case with the base metal miners for only nine months, but our broker's perception implies that current profit margins of the base metal mines will persist, since he is not expecting the gold price to fall much, if at all.

His comment put me in mind of some research we had done here in Capels, the results of which were published in Issue No 1 of this series. You may remember the charts of the long-term prices of gold and copper, which appeared in that first issue. They showed that since 1914, the gold price has averaged $210 per ounce and copper has averaged 108 cents/lb, both expressed in today's money. (Gold is currently $444/oz and copper is 100 cents/lb). You know I think that gold is a kind of money which has (unlike paper money) more than maintained its purchasing power over the years. It is therefore interesting to work out how many pounds of copper could have been bought with an ounce of gold, on average, over the years. The answer of 204 lbs.

At today's prices you can buy 440 lbs of copper with an ounce of gold. So even though copper has risen from a low of 60 cents in the last quarter of 1986 (when virtually the entire industry was loss making) to 100 cents today, it is still well below its long-term average relationship to gold. At its low in 1986, you could buy 652 lbs of copper with an ounce of gold! In the depths of the great depression in the thirties, an ounce of gold could buy 430 lbs of copper, roughly the same as it can today, yet people say copper is expensive? Don't you believe them!

If I have not lost you by now, and it's important that I shouldn't, my broker friend's perception that, whatever happens to metal prices, the relationship between copper and gold will not revert to the disaster levels ruling 18 months ago, has unimportant implications for share ratings, in my opinion. The current disparity between the multiples paid for one type of mining share and another, just does not make sense in the long run, if the metals mined by both are going to rise and fall in sympathy with each other from now on. (**15. 26/7/88**)

We are introduced to the "gnu" investor and the cheapness of base metal shares is again emphasised.

One of the pains and one of the pleasures of returning from a business trip (in this case from Australia and Singapore) is to catch up with what the gnus are saying. You get a better overview when a huge pile of circulars has to be digested all at once, than when they turn up a few at a time, day by day.

This might be the place to acquaint my readers with the gnu-like behaviour of us investors and our advisors. Gnus are animals of a nervous disposition, liable to stampede at the least provocation, who follow one another in long lines across the plains in search of greener pastures. Every now and then they get held up on their migrations by a natural hazard like a river and then they form into huge herds waiting for some brave soul to give them a lead.

You will recall that when I first started writing to you, seven months ago, I kept banging on about the attractions of base metal shares, rather than the gold shares which were much favoured by the gnus at that time. I remember feeling rather brave, having a reputation as a gold man, for weighting our fund very heavily in base metal shares. I'm glad I did, since the Fund Statistics published by Opal Group Ltd reveal that on an offer to offer basis our fund had risen 18.1 per cent between the launch date on 1st April and 24th October 1988. The next best gold and minerals Fund had risen by 3.5 per cent in the same period and most of the other gold Funds have actually lost money.

Now most advisers are saying that base metals are likely to remain higher for longer than they had expected. They are now bringing out their forecasts of earnings for next year based on metal prices which would have been considered impossible of achievement a year ago. I'll take one example at random to show you what they are forecasting for metal prices and earnings for 1989. I have calculated the PE ratios at today's share prices to show you how cheap the producers still are.

Company	EPS	P/E
Asarco	$6.85	3.8
Cyprus Mines	$8.10	4.1
Magma Copper	$ 260	2.7
Phelps Dodge	$ 130	3.5
Alcoa	$8.45	6.5
Amax	$5.80	3.8
Reynolds Metals	$6.95	7.9
Amax Gold	$1.00	17.0

Although most, but not quite all, brokers are now coming round to the attractions of the base metal companies (whose profitability is now equal to that of the gold companies), they don't seem to be having much luck in convincing the Fund Managers of the cheapness of the stocks. If they had, the stocks would be selling at much higher multiples then they are. In my opinion, it's just a matter of time before the re-rating will occur and I am quite happy to be patient, since the rewards will be so great. Many of these stocks are worth double the present price. **(25. 26/10/88)**

Julian spots that under pressure from over supply the aluminium producers have cut production. He points out that a similar move by gold miners would boost, rather than cut, revenues, but comments that the bankers make far more money by persuading the mines to sell gold forward rather than cut output.

Closer to home, I have bored you to distraction by banging on about the gold mining industry's practice of shooting itself in the foot by selling gold that it has not yet produced. Forward selling, as it is called, may or may not improve the price a company will get for its gold in a year's time. It certainly depresses the price they get for it today.

Last week a few of the aluminium producers bit the bullet and announced production cutbacks. Guess what! The price of aluminium rose from 50 to 55 cents per pound and the shares of the aluminium producers jumped for joy – or was it relief? In a blinding flash of enlightenment the miners found that by cutting production by 4 per cent, they improved the price of the remaining 95 per cent of their production by 10 per cent. The question the aluminium producers must now be asking themselves is whether, if they had acted sooner, the price of aluminium would have risen from 60 cents to 65 cents/lb. We shall never know. All I can tell you is that Nick Moore greeted the news with words more suited to a revivalist meeting – something along the lines of "Saints be praised – a real aluminium cutback!!"

Now, what I would like to ascertain is what, if anything, the gold mining industry is going to learn from the experience of the aluminium producers. I think we know the answer. People seldom learn from other people's experience.

I am told that the gold mining industry has sold forward some 40 per cent of this year's production and some 30 per cent of next year's. If they were to cut production by the same amount as the aluminium producers or equivalent to roughly 70 tonnes of gold, Ord Minnett have calculated that the gold price would likely rise by some $47 to about $405/oz. So the whole industry would be selling less; 1660 tonnes instead of 1730 tonnes, but what they would get for it would be more; nearer $21.3 billion than the $19.8 billion they are receiving at the moment.

Miners hate cutting production unless they absolutely have to and in the case of the gold mining industry they do not have to. All they have to do is to close out some of their forward sales instead.

But will they be so farsighted? I think you know the answer. My guess is they will forget that the "profits" they could now take from their well timed forward sales of two or three years ago, belong to the shareholders. Instead they will wait like a gambler in a casino until their windfall gain is frittered away by a rising gold price. They will eventually cover their forwards when they see them starting to go too far "out of the money". I cannot help thinking that the poor gold miners are being legged over by those clever bankers who have found a lucrative line of business in providing them with so called "protection" which seems to me to better serve the interests of the bankers than the miners. How do I know? A banker told me so! (**154. 23/10/91**)

Julian's theory about base metal prices at the turn of the 90s worked out rather well, but rising inventories and sluggish growth became a worry by the end of 1993.

One of our main worries is concerned with who actually owns the metal inventory on the LME. We suspect that much of the inventory is ultimately financed by the banks. In normal markets the forward price is usually higher than the spot price, by an amount which reflects current interest rates. The banks earn "interest" on the metal in LME warehouses by borrowing it and lending it. There is enough evidence to suggest that the banks are no longer happy to keep pumping in new money to finance an ever-increasing stockpile. I say that because it can be seen that the value of the stockpiles of certain metals has not grown despite a continual rise in inventories. Once this point has been reached, prices fall in direct proportion to the rise in inventories. If ever the banks were to try to reduce their risks by lessening their exposure to this type of business, you don't have to be a rocket scientist to work out what would happen to the holders of the base metal inventories. The metals would themselves probably end up being owned by the banks – heaven forbid!

The growing level of base metal stocks must therefore represent an increasing risk unless a sustained uplift in world economic activity starts fairly soon or producers take action to curtail supply. Unlike gold, where low prices stimulate consumption – just like cheap money does – low base metal prices make very little difference to consumption. If you cannot sell cars, it does not matter how cheap the materials are that go into them. Some commentators are suggesting that we are very close to the over valuation condition that occurred in late 1987 when the base metal shares lost nearly 50 per cent of their value. Don't worry, our negative stance towards the base metal shares has ensured that our exposure has been kept to a minimum, although we are very alert to the possibility that a severe setback could provide excellent buying opportunities. (**233. 30/9/93**)

4. South Africa – Opportunity at a Time of Change

Julian's connections with South Africa were life-long and deep. He dubbed himself a liberal in terms of his attitude to Apartheid, but did not believe that he should exclude the South African gold share market from his Fund, even though he opposed the political system – a position and attitude shared by many City brokers and investors active in the Republic. He believed, however, that the political risk attached to South Africa made it obligatory for the shares, which because of the structure of the South African gold industry were classic wasting assets, to provide a regular stream of income in the form of dividends, to mitigate the inherent risk in holding the shares. When FW de Klerk became Leader of the National Party (and then President of the Republic) the way was opened for the release of Nelson Mandela and the start of negotiations with the ANC. The spread of violence which accompanied these negotiations, and the fact that they were long, drawn-out and often extremely bad-tempered, frustrated Julian, but he continued to have a substantial exposure to South African mining shares throughout his stewardship of the Fund. He believed also that when the election threw up a new political dispensation for South Africa foreign capital would pour into the country. He would probably have approved of the restructuring of the mining industry that has taken place since the end of Apartheid, but would have been disappointed at the lack of foreign interest in the mining industry.

The Minorco bid for Consolidated Gold Fields in 1988, the subject of an investigation by the UK Monopolies and Mergers Commission, is further complicated by the broadening of the investigation to include Minorco's South African connections.

Strangely enough I am not entirely downhearted by the move since even if Minorco is not allowed to take over Gold Fields, there are other aspects of my "masterplan" which could still be carried out. Whatever happens, it seems unlikely that Minorco or Gold Fields will ever be the same again. Minorco will cease to be a passive investor and Gold Fields will be "in play".

What I do feel downhearted about is the way Mr. Harry Oppenheimer is being treated by all concerned. Having had liberal tendencies myself when working for Anglo American in Rhodesia in my 20s, I remember being constantly warned by the more conservative members of society that we liberals would get no thanks from either blacks or whites if what we stood for ever came about. How very true!

There can be few South Africans who have done more to promote constructive change in Southern Africa than Mr. Oppenheimer who in many ways, large and small, has contributed his wealth and influence to progressive measures over very many years, perhaps to an even greater extent than the company he is trying to take over.

Yet to my knowledge hardly a voice has been raised in his support against the campaign of vilification which has been mounted in opposition to the bid. It looks as if the reactionaries were right all along. They told us so.

When it comes to the crunch it is still true, as it was in Roman times, that the Authorities can enjoy a quieter life by throwing a few Christians to the lions. Not a pretty sight. I have sold some of our Gold Fields shares. (34. 4/1/89)

In whimsical mood, Julian gives South Africa a make-believe name and makes a rapid journey through the country's social and political attitudes, briefly alludes to its intellectual isolation and ends up poking around the gold industry's Head Office costs.

I spent last week in a beautiful country, a beautiful country of make-believe. I can't resist giving it a make-believe name. Let's call it Lowa Falonga. Few people in that country believe what other people in their own country tell them. They certainly don't believe what people from other countries tell them, so I doubt if they believed me. It was, however, flattering to have been asked.

The currency of this country of make-believe is the Wand. It is so depressed that only the richest citizens can afford to travel abroad and discover for themselves if what they are hearing is true. Those who have travelled, told me that they still found it hard, when they got home, to make up their minds whether Lowa Falonga really was the only country to be marching in step. The economy of Lowa Falonga used to depend heavily on the "barbarous relic". It still does, but not so much as it used to; though it is still the world's largest producer. When I suggested to the Lowa Falongans that the price of gold might well stay lower for longer than most people expected, they certainly did not want to believe that. They are relatively unprepared for that eventuality. Never mind. As they see it, they have already survived a number of catastrophes caused by circumstances beyond their control, which make the tribulations of Job look like a series of summer showers. They cite the drought which ended last year, sanctions, the inability to roll over debt, political unrest requiring the maintenance of a state of emergency, the war in Angola and endemic inflation, to mention but a few. The last thing they want to believe is that the current weakness in the gold price is anything other than a temporary phenomenon.

The Lowa Falongans who are actually mining the stuff have, up to now, enjoyed a privileged and rather cosy existence. The reason for this is that the government of Lowa Falonga has been persuaded to devalue the currency sufficiently to ensure the survival of the unfittest. I have a feeling that this state of affairs is coming to an end, though of course the Mining Houses will be doing their utmost to ensure that it does not.

What is so shocking is that despite the fact that the Wand is now only worth about half an Aussie dollar, the cost of producing the average ounce of gold in Lowa Falonga is the highest in the world. In today's circumstances that fact has got to be addressed.

Unless the gold price comes to their rescue, it looks as if the marginal mines will have to take severe remedial action in order to avoid going bust. The mining people I met told me that costs could certainly be cut to ensure survival, albeit at reduced capacity (shades of British Steel and British Coal), however it was unreasonable to expect all the economies to be made by the mines themselves. Head Office costs, which have to be borne pro-rata by the mines, whether they require their services or not, will also have to be reduced. The Mining House system which has served the mining industry of Lowa Falonga for many years, and is widely taken for granted, is now coming under increasing scrutiny. It was even being questioned in certain circles why, if the system is as beneficial as it is cracked up to be, it has not been widely adopted elsewhere in the world. Whilst I am in no way suggesting that the Lowa Falongans are about to scrap the Mining House system it seems to me that they are looking at it more critically than ever before. It is beginning to dawn on them that Minorco may be planning to administer one of the world's largest mining empires, with a Head Office staff even smaller than that of RTZ! If they succeed, what a good example they will set to the Lowa Falongans! (**40. 22/2/89**)

South African shares had been rising for months on the expectation of major political change, but the release of Nelson Mandela proved that the top of the market, and perhaps the great man's mixed messages – "white man please stay, foreigners don't you dare lift sanctions" – were part of the problem.

Last week, the euphoria surrounding President Mandela's release from prison caused South African shares to skyrocket. The ducks were quacking loudly so I fed them with about £4.5 million worth of our South African investments. A week later investors changed their minds and turned sellers. Some shares fell 25 per cent in less than a week! Since the political risk had not changed I bought them. What else should I be doing to justify my existence? The fund has suffered because I did not sell our South African investments, only about one sixth of them, but at least it cushioned the blow.

In the next few months and years we can expect great volatility in our South African holdings as the tide of opinion ebbs and flows. As a simple Fund Manager I can only marvel at the way the leading players are expected to tell the media which of their principles are negotiable before they start negotiating. Apparently the ANC are expected to eschew violence, drop nationalisation threats, provide white homelands, protect minority rights and in all ways behave like black white men. And all this before they even sit down to discuss the future. If anyone seriously thinks that sensible people enter into negotiations telling the world what they are prepared to concede before they start talking, they shouldn't be trying to read the South African gold share market at a time like this.

President Mandela's courageous words of encouragement to the whites, telling them that there will be a place for them in the sun despite what has gone on in the past, contrast strongly with most people's view that no encouragement should be given to the South Africans by Western governments, only more stick and more sanctions. No one, except perhaps Mrs Thatcher, seems to care that once money has been withdrawn from South Africa it is most unlikely ever to return permanently. (**82. 19/2/90**)

Mandela strikes a hard line on sanctions and Julian rushes for cover as gold shares plummet.

You would be shocked to see how far some of the South African gold shares have fallen in the last month or so, partly as a result of Mr. Mandela's continued hard line on sanctions and partly because of the dispiriting performance of the gold price. Yes – I sold some in time, but, in retrospect, never enough.

The overwhelmingly bullish sentiment of a month ago has been replaced by a widespread feeling of doubt and uncertainty. The marginal South African producers, such as we own, have fallen anywhere between 35–60 per cent in a month! It is just as well that we didn't have all our eggs in that particular basket! After such huge falls I cannot resist adding to our holdings. Surprise, surprise, I find I can buy more shares with a given amount of money now they are out of favour – like buying straw hats in winter.

In spite of the user-unfriendly behaviour of our South African holdings, the fund is only about 7 per cent below its all time high. That is nothing to be proud of, but I am told it is better than some other investments at the moment.

In my experience, funds of this type do quite well at times like this when there is a lot of uncertainty about. I liken this fund to an additional anchor put out when the storm cones are hoisted up the yard arm. Or for you landlubbers, like the extra guy rope attached to ensure your tent remains upright when a gale warning has been issued. (**86. 15/3/90**)

Further post-Mandela release blues.

My second chart is rather more gratifying. I mentioned in my letter to you dated 19th February that the euphoria surrounding Mandela's release from prison had caused the "ducks" to quack loudly. I reported that I had fed them with R26 million of our Escom loan stock, then priced at £13.07 and yielding just over 18 per cent. This week I was able to replace that stock at £9.81 on a yield of nearly 24 per cent (**100. 3/7/90**)

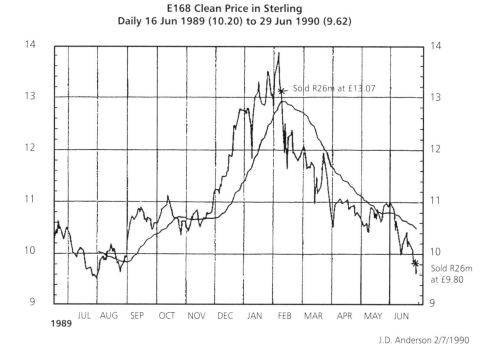

E168 Clean Price in Sterling
Daily 16 Jun 1989 (10.20) to 29 Jun 1990 (9.62)

J.D. Anderson 2/7/1990

Those of you who have been frequent visitors to South Africa will know what I mean when I say that you can sometimes return from a country more confused than you were before you went there!

That is not altogether the fault of the visitor. For many years visitors were berated for not understanding the complexities of the country's problems and assured that separate development was the only realistic way of coping with them. This time I found it impossible to find anyone who had ever supported Apartheid! Having told us they are going to change their spots, white South Africans point to the stupidity and injustice of continuing with sanctions for one moment longer, while in the same breath they tell us that sanctions in fact had very little adverse effect on the economy. Sanctions are certainly not seen in government circles particularly, as having had the slightest influence on the volte-face in policy that has taken place. What are we to believe? Black South Africans who have borne the brunt of sanctions and who have not yet quite convinced themselves that leopards can really change their spots, urged us to keep the sanctions going and at the same time, make our plans to invest. Whatever the rights and wrongs of sanctions, the changes which are taking place are a most interesting demonstration of what strong leadership on both sides of the political spectrum, can achieve.

Whoever would have believed that the party which led the white electorate into the bog of Apartheid, should be the same one to lead them out of it again? The Grand Old Duke of York has been thoroughly upstaged this time.

Whatever the ironies, the concept of what is now known as the New South Africa is becoming the focus of a growing number of people's hopes and aspirations. If the present negotiations were to fail the leaders on both sides would soon find themselves on the political scrap heap. No politician wants that, so the community of interest that binds the opposing leaders to the necessity of finding a workable solution, is gradually permeating down to the community as a whole. South Africans are beginning to believe that self interest may best be served by cooperation rather than by confrontation. For the first time they are not only talking to each other but they are also listening to each other! When that happens some of them even find they like each other. Of course, it will not be a smooth passage and given half a chance there could be some back sliding, which explains the ANC's unwillingness to let up on sanctions, but on the whole it is hard for the visitor not to come away with the impression that against most of the previous conventional wisdom, change is going to be brought about in South Africa without a blood bath. (127. 27/2/91)

While gold shares crash, counter-intuitively the SA foreign investment currency (the financial rand) strengthens, Julian speculates, because of a market belief that foreign investors will head for the Republic in due course.

Think for instance about South Africa. For years conventional wisdom had it that you should not invest there because it was inevitable that change could only be brought about by a bloodbath. Now it is beginning to look as if change will take place without the bloodbath. You should not listen to what people say about South Africa, they are too often wrong-footed. Better by far to look at what they are doing. The financial rand discount which is the bell weather of investment interest in that country, has come down from over 30 per cent to 15 per cent in the last 12 months or so despite the fact that the FT Gold Mines Index has declined by over 60 per cent. You would think that a falling gold price would result in people selling South African shares and that in turn would increase the financial rand discount. This has not happened either. The financial rand discount has narrowed considerably and now people are talking about its eventual abolishment.

Judging by the number of people who turned up at the CBI to listen to President de Klerk, there is no shortage of interest in the potential opportunities which might open up for investment in South Africa once sanctions have been lifted. No one wants to forego competitive advantage, so once people see their competitors showing signs of establishing a foothold in Southern Africa, it will not be long before it is considered not only acceptable but prudent to invest there. (**134. 8/5/91**)

Rumblings of discontent among right-wing Afrikaners threaten the peace process, but Julian remains optimistic that sense will eventually prevail.

It occurred to me recently that the requirement constantly to remind potential investors that "past performance is not a guide to future performance" must be very demoralising to chartists who make their living from predicting future performance from historic share price patterns.

The same dictum is true when considering the future of South Africa, a country where more bad predictions for the country's future have been made than for any country I know. Unitholders will know that I am no exception to this observation. This Fund had nearly half of its entire investments in South Africa before the burghers of Potchefstroom tried to emulate King Canute and turn back the tide of history. Of course King Canute was only trying to make the point that even he couldn't stop the tide coming in, but as you know, he has become saddled with a less favourable interpretation of his actions.

The question we have to ask ourselves is this. Do the Afrikaner people really believe that they can reverse the tide of events in South Africa, or are they merely trying to remind Mr de Klerk that he had better not be too pally with the ANC?

I cannot answer that question, but if the referendum goes against the government we are likely to lose some more money in this Fund as we did last week. If the vote goes in favour of Mr de Klerk, we may well claw some of it back. I have never made any secret of the fact that we have a large exposure to South Africa or that it would be a bumpy ride. As an eternal optimist I am betting that white South Africans will, in the end, be persuaded that their best interests lie in giving "The New South Africa" a chance and that sufficient of them will stay long enough to make a success of it. (**165. 26/2/92**)

Aggressive grandstanding at the CODESA talks unsettles investors.

The gold shares remain pretty lethargic and our South African holdings are not helped by the bad blood being displayed at the CODESA talks. Foreign investors, like us, long to see the talks succeed, but when white Africans and black Africans eye-ball each other it is incredible how obstinate they can become. In other parts of Africa many of the white Africans simply packed up and went home but white South Africans are home already and many of those who think they may want to leave often find it difficult to get foreign passports. With so much at stake, it is not altogether surprising that the talks have got bogged down. It would, however, be helpful if they would compromise soon – as they will have to in the end – since uncertainty is the market's greatest enemy. (**177. 4/6/92**)

The talks break down, and South African gold shares collapse to levels not seen since the Soweto riots of 1976.

South African gold shares, as measured by the *Financial Times* Gold Mines Index, hit a 16-year low this week, reflecting the breakdown of the CODESA talks on South Africa's political future. Trust this to happen just as the gold price was starting to show a flicker of improvement, as I suggested it might in my letter to you a couple of weeks ago!

So what can I now say in order to deflect the slings and arrows of outrageous fortune which are surely winging their way in my direction?

First, I can say that I have never made any secret of our larger than average exposure to South Africa. It will therefore have come as no surprise to you that when things go wrong in that country, it hurts.

Second, I will say that as a general rule it is wrong to sell after a large fall, in a fit of depression. Others more nimble than us are likely to have already gone short and we don't want them covering at our expense.

Instead let us hope that it will not be necessary for the international community to have to prod the South Africans back to the negotiating table by means of the well-tried combination of renewed economic sanctions and bans on international sporting activities. If that has to be done during a period of seasonal strength in the gold price, the main beneficiaries are likely to be the North American and Australian gold mining shares in which we are relatively underweight because they represent less good fundamental value. Ah well, it never rains but it pours – but can things really get much worse? (**180. 26/6/92**)

Julian begins to lose heart as violence in the wake of the CODESA talks breakdown escalates.

As you can imagine, I rue the day that I failed to reduce our South African exposure, hoping against hope that an amicable solution could be found to that country's problems. The breakdown of the CODESA talks in June caused by the Leaders' inability to reach agreement over the percentage vote needed to change the interim constitution was the warning signal to get out. Failure to heed that signal has cost many lives and much money.

As a result of the tragic events which have occurred since that time, sentiment has naturally become exceedingly negative and this has caused gold shares to fall day after day and the buy/sell indicator to fall to levels rarely seen.

Although it is just as hard to see how sentiment could ever recover in the South African market, we should bear in mind that if this level of violence continues, many of the conditions would exist which could give rise to a military coup or at least the re-imposition of a state of emergency. Politicians of all races must realise that if they do not cool it, far from leading South Africans to the promised land, they will find themselves en-route to another Yugoslavia. (**187. 10/9/92**)

Julian and other international Fund Managers visit South Africa and find things at a very low ebb, with deep pessimism about the country at all levels; a time when bargains often abound and contrarian investments are made.

With 38 per cent of our money invested in South Africa, I grasped the opportunity to join 12 international Fund Managers on a week's visit to that country organised by Martin & Co., one of the leading South African brokers. The purpose of the visit was to update the participants about the economic and political outlook of South Africa – no doubt with a view to attracting to that country a larger portion of the US$440 billion managed by their firms. However, as so often happens in South Africa, the advice we received was in most cases exactly the opposite of what might have been expected.

Government representatives sought to reassure us by leaving the impression that whatever the eventual constitutional arrangements, they would under no circumstances hand over power without stringent safeguards. Those close to the Ministry of Finance painted a picture of such unutterable gloom that we gained the impression the only thing we had to remember was to "turn out the lights before leaving"! The political representative of the ANC told us not to invest until given the green light by them. Their financial representative arrived late for our meeting and seemed inadequately briefed to leave us with any clear-cut impression at all. Mining industry representatives were cautiously pessimistic; an emotion brought on no doubt by the threat of being "unbundled".

Students at the University of Cape Town were so concerned about making up for time lost in preparation for their exams as to leave the visitor with the impression that the idealism of youth had completely passed them by! University students live next to one of the worst slums to be found anywhere in the world. Yet, none I spoke to, black or white, had so far lifted a finger to help their less fortunate compatriots in any way whatsoever. They promised to do better next year – but will they?

If South African gold shares had not already lost 80 per cent of their value in the last two and a half years, I would have been tempted to call it a day. Although none of my companions were seen reaching for their cheque books, none of them seemed to be taking the view that sentiment would deteriorate enough to make it worth selling now.

In a nutshell, I have never seen white South Africans so totally demoralised; never seen Black South Africans less inclined to cooperate with each other; and never heard so few positive prognostications about a country's future. Exactly, if I dare say so, the situation in which bargains are likely to abound.

Out of this gloom is coming the realisation that without a speedy political settlement, the economic problems facing the country will never be solved or, if they are, it will be at the expense of the white man's standard of living. There are hints that some kind of Government of Natural Unity may soon be formed to run the country for the next three or four years. This, some observers think, may give time for a realignment of political forces which would give the Nationalist Party a chance of winning the next election after that.

Meanwhile, immense changes are taking place. Downtown Johannesburg has become a city of street vendors. Virtually every meal we had was served by young whites who are turning their hands successfully to jobs previously done by blacks! White servants – fancy that in South Africa! Even our departing aeroplane was cleaned by a team of young white workers called Airport Cleaning Services. Scarcity of jobs is already leading to unexpected changes.

Unemployment among blacks has reached frightening proportions, yet on the roads and in the mines those who were "working" seemed to spend a disproportionate amount of time leaning on their shovels. Man-management and organisational skills do not appear to be thriving in South Africa in the present climate.

Despite what management says in public, there still seems to be plenty of scope for reducing costs in the gold mining industry. Gold mining has never been thought of as a competitive business in South Africa. This has resulted (in three years) in

South African mines becoming the most expensive producers in the world. They now find themselves in the position of having the most marginal mines in the world. Marginal mines are closed first!

Entrenched working practices will have to change. They will not change if the gold price rises. To force them to become competitive, South African gold producers need a further period of low gold prices. The most glaring example of uncompetitiveness is the fact that, unlike their foreign counterparts, the South African mining industry only works a six-day week. The Harmony Gold Mine when faced with closure tried to persuade the white unions to work on Sundays and failed, although a compromise has now been reached which comes to the same thing. Sunday working reduces costs by some US$30/oz to the benefit of the country and the shareholders. If the entire industry were persuaded to work a seven day week, Martin & Co. tell us it would increase the industry's revenue by R4.6bn, the governments' taxation by R1 billion and the shareholders' dividends by approximately 50 per cent.

Further substantial savings are likely to be brought about if the ANC succeeds in its stated policy of tackling the monopolistic nature of the South African businesses through the introduction of anti-trust legislation. In the mining industry, the larger mines are responsible for much of their own technical services, yet they pay their controlling Mining Houses substantial fees for providing just those services. Since the senior mine management are paid by the Mining Houses and not by the mines themselves, there is less incentive for them to bear down on costs than there would be if they were directors, shareholders or employees of the mines themselves, as they would be in other countries. (**194. 3/11/92**)

Julian notes that the continuing nervousness concerning negotiations (or lack of) between de Klerk and Mandela have led to a wide discount on the financial rand, and a steady stream of capital leaving the country via the commercial rand.

A depreciating rand would, of course, lead to a higher gold price in local currency. The double figure yields, now widely available, could be expected to increase substantially, since a 5 per cent increase in the rand price of gold would boost pre-tax industry profits by some 20 per cent so narrow are the existing profit margins. But South African investors clearly believe that the Government of National Unity will be all white on the night, unaffected by the need to cater for the masses in the future any more than they did in the past.

Confused as ever, the foreign investor is voting with his feet, accompanied by some local institutions who are prepared to invest abroad through the financial rand even though it is standing at a discount of 36 per cent to the commercial rand. Hardly a vote of confidence on their part in the future stability of the currency.

Meanwhile, it is no secret in South Africa that the commercial rand is widely used to sidestep exchange controls by sending money out of the country, never to return. You would think that the government would try to discourage this anti-social practice by abolishing exchange controls altogether and letting the rand float in much the same way that the UK Government has let the pound float. Unlike the UK Government, the South Africans have the option of providing buoyancy to their currency, once it had found its natural level, by linking it to gold.

Finally, it is reported that talks between the ANC and President de Klerk will start again on 29th November to get constitutional negotiations restarted. The meeting is reportedly going to be held in a remote bush resort.

My suggestion that the parties discussing the political future of South Africa should meet on neutral territory such as Sarajevo (where they could see for themselves the consequences of failure) and remain there until they reached a settlement, was thought less than helpful, the main worry being that they might never return. (**196. 17/11/92**)

Julian wonders whether South Africa might consider minting a gold "Mandelarand".

Until some unsung genius discovered that governments could get a premium for their gold by minting it into one ounce blanks and stamping the face of the Father of the Nation upon them, few people outside the borders of South Africa had ever heard of President Kruger. Most have forgotten, if ever they knew, what role he played in the turbulent history of that country. Such ignorance did not prevent thousands upon thousands of krugerrands being sold to the public at a premium to the gold price in the late 1970s.

Subsequently, as the price of gold fell and the policies of Kruger's successors met with mounting international disapproval, many krugerrands were melted down and probably ended up as "chuk kam" jewellery for the Chinese mass market.

Now that it has been agreed that the first "one man one vote" election will be held before April 1994 and that the actual date will be announced within a month, it can be expected that Mr. Mandela will soon mark the final meltdown of Apartheid by asking the international community to lift sanctions and start investing in South Africa. He desperately needs all the international help he can get in the urgent task of rebuilding the economy, failing which many of his increasingly frustrated followers will continue to be denied even the bare necessities of life.

Mandela himself does not need his face to be emblazoned on a one ounce gold coin to gain international recognition and respect. He is already one of the best known people alive today and widely respected in many quarters. The question is whether those responsible for the coinage in South Africa will have the imagination to recognise the marketing opportunity of selling gold at a premium by stamping the head of the most internationally famous of all South Africans upon each blank and calling it a Mandelarand.

Mandela might be persuaded to lend his profile for this purpose provided that any premium obtained over the gold price was directed towards a specific project. I have in mind the rebuilding of the shanty town known as Crossroads, that affront to human dignity which visitors to Cape Town pass by on their way from the airport to the genteel surroundings of the Mount Nelson Hotel.

Enlightened self interest has never lost its appeal to investors, some of whom even as you read this, are rediscovering the attractions of gold having spurned it for the best part of 13 years.

Not only might investors profit from buying gold in the form of Mandelarands, but some of the least privileged people in South Africa would gain a lasting and tangible benefit from their perspicacity. Thus would be created a memorial to Mandela's leadership which would bring lasting improvement to the lives of thousands of his followers.

Is it likely that this proposal will ever come to the attention of those in South Africa who could make it a reality? Regretfully the answer must be no, for South African exchange control prevents influential South Africans from becoming unitholders and therefore being recipients of this Newsletter. Ironically the ANC has expressed the sensible intention of abolishing both exchange control and the dual currency, but that won't happen overnight.

It is therefore highly unlikely that you will ever have the opportunity of owning a Mandelarand even if such a coin was minted. Moreover, the rules prevent an authorised unit trust such as Mercury Gold and General Fund from holding gold on your behalf, even though the ownership of the far more risky and volatile gold shares is entirely acceptable!

All this talk about Mandela reminds me that some years ago the labour government in Australia decided to honour Mr. Mandela by changing the name of Rhodes Avenue in Canberra, to Mandela Avenue. Some wag was overheard asking the Premier, Bob Hawke, who had received his degree at Oxford, whether he would prefer in future to be known as a Mandela scholar. (**217. 13/5/93**)

With the date for the new elections announced, Julian speculates as to whether this will finally ignite investors' interest in SA gold shares.

On a more cheerful note, it has been announced that the first multi-racial elections will be held in South Africa on 27th April 1994. The announcement should lead to calls for an ending of sanctions. Those Funds who have been prevented by sanctions from investing in South Africa will have to decide whether to believe those of us who have been telling them that an ounce of gold in the ground in South Africa can be purchased at a fraction of the cost of an ounce of gold in the ground in other parts of the world. If ever they become so convinced, their buying will boost the value of our Fund which is more than 50 per cent invested in South Africa already.

We now read that Argentina is attracting the international mining community in droves. There is nothing wrong with Argentina. And looking for gold is a perfectly harmless pursuit, but why the international mining community takes not a blind bit of notice of the knockdown value placed on existing mines in South Africa, but rush like sheep to South American pastures, which may or may not be greener, I have not so far managed to fathom. Investors in gold shares have cottoned on to where the value lies even if the international mining companies have not. The FT Gold Mines Index of South African shares, in which over 50 per cent of the Fund is invested, has risen 258 per cent since the beginning of this year. As unitholders of the Fund all we can say is, Don't cry for us Argentina – we're laughing. (**223. 5/7/93**)

As South Africa's first non-racial elections loom, Julian ponders whether the essential foreign capital needed for the new era will be forthcoming.

The best advice that a potential investor in South Africa can receive is to avoid the temptation to go there too often for fear of coming back more enthusiastic about the country than is prudent.

Having just returned from South Africa as a guest of brokers Frankel Pollak, whose 17th annual investment conference has just finished, I should know. I was not alone. There were more than 80 of us foreign delegates this year, many from America. As we travelled round the country in our air-conditioned bus, our hosts totted up the number of investment dollars managed by the passengers' employers. It came to around a trillion dollars! I hope the bus driver got a good tip for delivering us safely! No doubt our hosts were calculating the potential commission if only a tiny portion of that money were ever to find its way into the South African market.

While we do not know the final total of funds recently raised for investment in South Africa, we suspect that it is likely to be in the region of a billion dollars. Some of this will not be deployed until the uncertainty of the election is resolved. In anticipation that this "wall of money" will go in anyway, my visit convinced me that we should increase our exposure from 42 per cent to 46 per cent of the Fund without waiting for the election result.

Of course the delegates were not just there for their health. They wanted to find out whether a country which had been out of bounds to so many of them for many years had now become a fit repository for their client's savings. I am not suggesting for one moment that the fact that South Africa is the world's best kept tourist secret would in any way affect their investment decisions, only that if they did decide to do so, next year would see them return with their wives and children in tow. And who could blame them. If the political changes which are taking place go reasonably smoothly, it is hard to think of a country more blessed with every conceivable tourist attraction. First world comforts at developing market prices. What better reviver for exhausted Fund Managers?

Tourism is a great employer of unskilled labour and improving job opportunities is an important component of what the new government has got to provide in order to meet the reasonable aspirations of the people.

One of the most memorable moments of our visit was an address by a leading figure in the ANC who had something of a reputation as a firebrand. She told us that she was constantly being urged to lower the expectations of her followers. How, she asked, could she possibly be expected to lower the expectations of people whose aspirations were largely limited to the provision of running water, electric light, a roof over their heads and sufficient food to eat? She hardly needed to point out (but that did not stop her) that the lack of any one of these facilities would be totally unacceptable to any in her audience. Few of us disagreed with that, judging by the applause, yet there is much controversy as to how these aspirations might best be met, especially in a country where capitalism seems to so many people to have failed them.

My best guess is that the new government will want to be seen to be doing something. Let us hope that what they do will not unwittingly have the effect of turning off the tap of foreign investment which seems ready to flow if the transition goes smoothly. A big if, admittedly. **(246. 2/3/94)**

Julian challenges the SA Mining Houses again, this time to analyse their low ratings in an international context.

In an attempt to increase shareholder value I asked the Mining Houses if they could think why South African gold shares were so lowly rated compared to their foreign counterparts. Here are some clues.

1. The only time investors are told what proven and possible reserves they are buying in a South African mine is when a prospectus is published. The competition gives this information at every possible opportunity so investors can work out for themselves how much they are paying for every reserve ounce.

2. Very few South African mines have any "blue sky", partly because they are confined to mining a specific lease area. There is, in fact, nothing to stop a

mining company taking a stake in another mining company. Driefontein, for instance, owns 20 per cent of Gold Fields of South Africa.

3. The mining laws in South Africa discourage foreign mining companies from investing in South Africa because the local mining companies can hold onto mineral rights indefinitely, thus tying up the most prospective ground. This also explains why the local Mining Houses are dying to invest abroad. When this was drawn to the ANC's attention, they proposed changes in the law, but the locals cried foul and the proposals have been watered down.

4. The South African mining companies express their costs in rands per kilogram which means little to an international investor who thinks in terms of dollars per ounce. Reserves are expressed in tonnes whereas foreign gold companies talk of thousands of ounces. Gold is the ultimate international currency but little effort is made by the producers worldwide to standardise their reporting procedures. Why make investment in gold shares simple when you can make it complicated?

5. The most highly rated international gold companies try to present themselves as "growth companies". They endeavour to show how their reserves increase each year. They need to. Few have lives of even half those of the South African mines.

6. South African mining companies are less adept at "mining the market" than their foreign counterparts. They are seldom seen at presentations by North American mining companies trying to learn how the competition presents itself to the investing public.

7. Senior mine management tend to hold options over the shares in their controlling Mining House rather than in the shares of the individual mines which they run.

If you can think of any other reasons I will gladly pass them on. (**246. 2/3/94**)

Dissent breaks out in the ranks of black South Africans as Zulus riot in Natal ahead of the 27th April election.

I hardly need to point out to you that these are testing times for investors in unit trusts holding significant investments in South Africa. What is both surprising and gratifying is that despite the horrendous news emanating from that country, there have been only modest redemptions of the units.

Perhaps your recent experience of what can happen when you buy a completely friendless market was enough to keep you aboard through the current bout of turbulence. Instead of fastening your safety belt or affixing your parachute, perhaps the best thing you can do is simply turn off your television sets until after the elections on 27th April 1994.

Some of us have seen it all before. Of course, this time it is different. At the time of the Sharpeville massacre or the Soweto uprising, everyone was convinced that political change could not come about without bloodshed and there was not much doubt in most people's minds whose blood was going to be shed. Buthelezi was considered a bit of a hero in the eyes of most white South Africans. Now he is cast as the villain of the piece.

Tragic as the current situation has become, there are some grounds for optimism. The troubles in Natal seem to be having the effect of uniting all those who have an interest in making a success of the New South Africa, even if they do not always see eye to eye politically. Unlike in other countries in Africa, South Africa has a sizeable white tribe with nowhere else to call home. And now that the die is cast, they see it as being in their best interests to try and make a go of it. The rest of the world too, having contributed to the changes which have taken place through the imposition of sanctions, have a moral and financial responsibility to ensure that the changes they have wrought do not degenerate into the very chaos that the old regime was trying to prevent.

For our part, we should focus on what the place may look like in three or four months time when, hopefully, the dust has settled. By then, those who hesitated to invest in these uncertain times will find themselves competing with others to get their required weightings. (**250. 14/4/94**)

Julian continues to consider whether foreign capital will begin to flow into South Africa and also notes that gold's role as a harbinger of inflation may be affecting its price to the detriment of SA-bound foreign currency flows.

The other country which has been out of favour with the Americans until very recently is South Africa. There were times in the past when people suspected that the Americans were bearing down on the gold price in order to make life uncomfortable for what was seen as an unacceptably racist regime.

Now the tables have completely turned. The Russians are in dire straits but there are few votes in America for providing untold millions of dollars to bail them out. South Africa is now back on the "straight and narrow" and needs all the help it can get to ensure that Mr. Mandela's moderation and statesmanship is rewarded. It is unthinkable that lack of funds should prevent the new rulers of that country from meeting the reasonable expectations of the least privileged members of their society. If these are not met, the backlash could be too ghastly to contemplate.

If only Mr. Greenspan had not publicly declared his belief that gold is a reliable barometer of inflation, there would appear to be nothing standing in the way of gold rising in sympathy with commodity prices. This would have the effect of curing two birds with no pain, if you will excuse the solecism. Whatever Mr. Greenspan does, you may conclude from the following chart that gold is about to rise in any case.

It could be argued that a rising gold price would provide much needed help to both Russia and South Africa without the American public noticing.

Unfortunately, Mr. Greenspan is in danger of being hoisted with his own petard because if gold goes up people will then think, like him, that inflation is just around the corner. Although you and I might think it desirable for the gold price to rise, he may not see it that way. However, just in case it does slip the leash, we thought you should at least be aware of the consequences, namely that South Africa and Russia will be helped.

On another subject, you may have noticed that the Fund has been behaving less well than we led you to believe it would following the successful conclusion of the South African election. It is as if people are feeling a bit liverish after all the celebrations!

Pre-election euphoria seems to be giving way to second thoughts on the part of foreign investors who have shortsightedly, in our opinion, been reducing their South African exposure until they can see the way ahead more clearly. The lacklustre gold price has not helped either, with base metals stealing all the limelight. **(255. 20/5/94)**

Julian returns to the subject of the gold mining industry's profitability, and speculates that South Africa's return to world respectability could boost gold share ratings.

Commonsense would suggest – would it not – that in the long run, a share index should reflect, over time, the profitability of the companies which comprise that index?

In other words, an index not only tells you about comparative value year-on-year, it also tells you something about the market's expectation of future profitability.

Take the South African Gold Mines Index for instance. We have worked out that historically since 1985 the JSE Gold Mines Index has sold at an average of 16.7 times the industry profit margin per ounce. This quarter we calculate that the industry will make an average distributable profit of R167/oz. The index is currently at 2200 so the index is currently selling at only 13.17 times the current profit margin.

Put another way, if the index was now selling at its historic relationship to the profit margin, it would now be 2421 or 10 per cent higher than it is. Obviously the market thinks that the prospect for the industry is less bright than it was in former times – but is it?

The industry's profitability is affected by a number of factors, not least of which is the rand gold price. That, in turn, has a great deal to do with the R/$ exchange rate. Gold, after all, is sold for dollars. If the rand is weak against the dollar, companies which sell their produce for US dollars but whose costs are incurred in rands, do very nicely thank you. The recent weakness of the rand against the US dollar and the consequently enhanced profitability of the industry bears witness to this truth.

There is reason to hope that this already satisfactory situation may be dramatically enhanced in the fairly near future.

South Africa is swiftly returning to the community of nations and rejoining the financial alliances from which she was previously excluded under the previous regime. The IMF, for instance, seems willing to play its part in the financial reconstruction of South Africa after years of deterioration caused by sanctions. The trouble is the IMF does not approve of countries which have dual currencies. For this reason, among others, it is government policy to do away with the dual currency as soon as possible. It would probably have happened already if South Africa's foreign exchange reserves were sufficiently robust to withstand large scale selling of the currency by locals wishing to disinvest. So far, almost everyone there has said they favour merging the financial and commercial rands, but so far they have not dared do it.

My personal view is that the fears of the authorities are probably unfounded and that in reality international cooperation will enable the financial rand to be abolished sooner rather than later.

This will probably be brought about by the commercial rand falling from the current R3.60/US$1 to about R4.20/US$1, a devaluation of 16 per cent. At the same time, the financial rand could well rise some 13 per cent from R4.73 to R4.20. All other things being equal, foreign holders of South African gold shares would benefit by some 13 per cent, due to the improvement in the financial rand. (**258. 21/6/94**)

The pursuit of the issue of undervaluation is continued against the background of Gengold's switch to a more transparent stance in providing mine reserve information.

Enlightened self interest has prompted us to expend much energy, and even more ink, over recent months drawing the captains of the South African mining industry's attention to the fact that their gold shares are undervalued compared to those in other parts of the world. More importantly, we have been suggesting that it is within their power to do something about it. In fact, we made no secret of the things we thought they should do if they really wanted to increase the asset value of "The New South Africa Limited", to say nothing of our own. We set them out in Newsletter 246 of 2nd March 1994.

Since little notice is taken in South Africa of what shareholders – particularly foreign shareholders – have to say (we are thought not to understand South African conditions), imagine our surprise when this quarter Gengold suddenly broke with tradition and published their calculation of the number of ounces which remain to be mined at each of their mines. This information happens to top our list of the things we have been urging the Mining Houses to do!

There were few surprises in their calculations, but if the other Mining Houses follow Gengold's example, it may help to put a stop to the wilder flights of fancy of those who from time to time find it to their advantage to try and show that South African gold shares are already fully valued.

More interesting was the immediate reaction of the South African brokers. Almost before the briefings were completed, we received comments pointing out that an ounce of gold in South Africa was being valued by the market at a fraction of what it would be valued at, if the Great Prospector in the sky had decided to deposit the gold in almost any other country.

Here is what Martin & Co. one of South Africa's top rated brokers, had to say about Gengold's revelations.

	BEATRIX	BUFFELS	GROOTVLEI	KINROSS	LESLIE	ST HELENA	UNISEL	WINKELHAAK	AMERICAN BARRICK	NEWMONT GOLD	HOMESTAKE
MARKET CAP (U$M)	472	109	27	298	25	96	43	140	6,670	4,039	2,799
REC OZ (000)	9,806	1,513	1,164	6,218	604	1,489	3,289	5,336	29,300	21,500	17,400
MARKET CAP/OZ	48	72	23	48	41	64	13	26	228	188	161

"The table shows Gengold's first attempt at addressing the issue of stating life of mine recoverable gold. It should be recognised that at higher gold prices these numbers can increase significantly. It is interesting to note that Beatrix, the group's flagship producer, has a capitalization per ounce lower than both Buffels and St. Helena. By comparison American Barrick is capitalised at $228/oz. The question that needs to be answered is whether the restrictions facing South Africans justify the relatively low valuation?

1. SA mines are ring-fenced and growth is limited to contiguous areas whereas the North Americans can invest anywhere, using existing tax bases to offset development costs elsewhere.

2. Offshore mining companies may view the low value placed on the SA ounce of production as an opportunity to increase reserve bases. Some new projects in South America are valued at $30/oz; in addition there will be

further development costs. Unisel could be acquired for a low $13/oz as a going concern with blue sky potential.

3. Political risk is still an issue. Elsewhere in Africa this does not appear to affect valuations; Ashanti gold in Ghana is capitalised at $100/oz, with a military dictatorship in place and restrictive currency systems to boot.

4. Production costs are important bearing in mind the depth of SA gold producers. Beatrix produces at $204/oz, comparable to Barrick's $191 /oz yet it has a capitalization one fifth that of Barrick.

As SA mining companies start to disclose reserve data, we believe the market will begin to focus on the low valuations and some rerating is possible."

The genie is now well and truly out of the bottle and the great debate may have started as to why South African gold shares are so undervalued. (**262. 28/7/94**)

The post-election flow of investment into South Africa remains modest, and Julian warns that it takes time to mobilise resources, especially with expert advice so thin on the ground after decades of Apartheid.

Investors and gnus have something in common. When they get something into their heads – like the need to all go in the same direction – nothing seems to stop them until, for no apparent reason, they suddenly all choose to go in the other direction.

This investor behaviour results in the well-known phenomenon that a stock market goes up until it stops going up and then it goes down until it stops going down and then it goes up again. But not necessarily in that order.

It may be the geographic location but it seems to me that South African investors are more prone to gnu-like behaviour than most. Perhaps we should blame the scribblers. It seems that having little else to write about now that the violence has ceased, the press is confined to reflecting disappointment that the waves of money which were expected to flow into South Africa are only arriving in a trickle.

The fact of the matter is that it takes time to mobilise resources. A good deal of portfolio money has clearly gone in already, otherwise the South African market would not have been one of the best performing markets in the world this year, as it was last year. The investment climate looks almost too healthy for its own good, yet TRANSFIT, the Group Financial Services Treasury newsletter starts off a recent bulletin as follows:–

"... Such tranquillity has not prevailed for many years and it should eventually have a positive impact on the economy, the investment climate and in the financial markets."

It then goes on to say that the trade surplus was 18 per cent up on last year. Inflation has fallen to 7.1 per cent year-on-year. The March production index increased by 6.3 per cent, following the 6.5 per cent rise in February. There is still thought to be a possibility that the current weakness of the rand will eventually be reflected in rising import prices. As it is, the organ seems almost disappointed that the prices of imported goods only rose 2.7 per cent in March compared with 3.1 per cent in February!

Of course if the gnus are responding negatively it is much easier for the scribblers to go on writing the market down. But like any good bull market, it climbs a wall of fear whatever they write. We don't take a lot of notice of all this gloom, preferring to use setbacks as buying opportunities. Luckily this contrariness has not so far done us any harm: the Fund is hitting all time highs almost daily, despite the fact that gold shares in other parts of the world are anything but chirpy. The size of the Fund has now passed the £370 million mark.

What seems to be being overlooked by those who are impatient for foreign investment in South Africa, are the difficulties being faced by the brokers and bankers who wish to participate, in finding people with the necessary skills and experience to advise on a market which has been virtually closed to outsiders for so many years. Such people are rarer than hens' teeth but once recruited they will only earn their keep if they get on the telephone and get their clients to buy South African shares. (**267. 1/9/94**)

With the Fund heavily committed to South Africa, Julian visits the country again and is amazed by the lack of bitterness on the part of the new black leadership, but worried by the scale of the work still to be done to raise the standard of living of the masses.

Nearly half our Fund is invested in South Africa – a higher percentage than most of our competitors and maybe even some of our unitholders feel entirely comfortable with.

The fact that we have such a large commitment to South Africa may reflect a certain pig-headedness on behalf of your Fund Manager whose distrust of conventional wisdom is only tempered by his experience that the market is very seldom wrong.

The justification of being a contrarian is that when the market changes its mind, as it appears to have done in the case of South Africa, it can be very rewarding. If you doubt me ask anyone who had held this Fund for the last couple of years. Having benefited from the change in investor perceptions, it is all the more important that we guard against falling in love with the stocks that have treated us so well.

Obviously a contrarian strategy has its dangers, but people who invest in mining shares are no strangers to that phenomenon. They mitigate the risk by limiting their exposure. We have often said that 2.5 per cent of this Fund in portfolios is about the right holding for conservative investors. As your Fund Managers, we can play our part in continually monitoring the risk by grasping opportunities to visit the countries in which we are invested.

For this reason, I accepted an invitation to speak in Johannesburg last week at the Frankel Pollak Vinderine annual conference which, this year, attracted a record number of overseas delegates. This conference offers existing and potential investors a chance to meet the "great and good" and take the temperature of investor attitudes towards South Africa. I was accompanied by Geoff Campbell, who has recently joined us to help run this Fund. He is staying on in South Africa for a further week to visit the companies in which we have invested and will be reporting to you on his return. If you would like a copy of my paper, please ask.

There is no doubt about the political miracle which everyone recognises as having taken place in the country. Some bemoan the fact that the economy is still not growing at the 4 per cent necessary to make inroads into the high levels of unemployment. Circumstantial evidence, however, suggests that the official figures do not give an accurate reflection of what is happening in the economy.

During a visit to SAPPI, the leading pulp and paper manufacturer, it became clear that local demand for newsprint and packaging is running at levels which suggest that the real economy is expanding at a far faster rate than that indicated by the official figures. We got the same story from a leading viniculturist who indicated that the greatly enhanced demand for his wine from the local hotel and restaurant industries, to say nothing of burgeoning export demand, was making it difficult for him to keep up with demand. I wish the same could be said for those of you who try to produce wine competitively in France!

By far the most impressive event of the week, and one which somehow epitomised the change of attitudes sweeping the country, was a visit to Robben Island to see the prison in which President Mandela was incarcerated for 27 years. We were shown the cells and the now famous lime pit in which they had to work, by three of the people who were incarcerated with him. Their description of life as political prisoners, told with great eloquence and an astonishing lack of bitterness, was extremely moving.

It might be thought that such a large portion of a lifetime spent in prison would give rise to feelings of revenge, but instead it simply seems to have resulted in a determination to ensure that political prisoners will never again suffer a similar fate in the new South Africa.

Obviously some of those who were imprisoned are now in positions of great power and influence. Others who do not have the necessary education to find gainful employment are not so lucky. There is no social security in South Africa.

To them the wasted years have been followed by nothing but continued hardship for them and their families. The formation of a Trust Fund to help them and their families was announced during our visit. We should all be grateful for their forbearance. (**285. 21/2/95**)

5. South African Mining House Fees

One of Julian's major crusades was against the system established by the South African Mining Houses whereby they charged substantial fees to group gold mines for technical and administrative services. In the initial stages of his campaign – which Julian had started while still on the buy side at James Capel – his at times forensic questioning on the issue annoyed and puzzled the houses and won him few friends among South African brokers, who relied upon the goodwill of the Mining Houses to support their business. In due course the points that he was raising became better understood, particularly the point he made time and time again about the way that the Mining Houses were protected from falling dividends from their mines as they had the fees to fall back on, which gold mine shareholders did not have. When he and a group of European and South African investors took hold of Rand Mines fees were abolished and the rest of the industry quickly followed suit.

The opening shots in a battle over SA Mining House fees that was to climax years later with Julian's backing of the reorganisation of the old Rand Mines group.

There has been a lot of talk recently about how the South African gold mining industry, once the lowest cost producer of gold in the world, has become the most expensive. What is not revealed, and should be, is the amount of money the individual gold mines have to pay the Mining Houses for the services they provide. How else can we shareholders decide whether we are getting good value for money? In many cases the Mining Houses are by no means large shareholders in the mines they administer, but they are believed to be amply rewarded, if not by the mines' dividends, which are few and far between these days, but by their fee income.

If you were to ask a mine manager who has been required to perform miracles in order to keep his mine profitable, whether he felt that people in Head Office were being asked to make equal sacrifices, I expect he would come up with the same sort of answer that you hear in the City these days whenever the subject of overheads is raised. My hunch, although I cannot prove it, is that there is a hidden element in South African gold mining costs which could be made even less visible without doing any harm to overall mine efficiencies. Perhaps someone will reassure me that my suspicions are without foundation. (122 .3/1/91)

Julian shows how Mining House fee income, once a fraction of dividends received, is now on a par with dividends received.

I am grateful to a Johannesburg broker, who prefers to remain anonymous, for his estimate of the fee income received by the Mining Houses for administering the gold mines under their control. In the old days the management fees represented a fraction of the dividend income derived from the individual mines they administered. Now, as you will see from the table below, my broking friends have calculated that future management fees will just about equal future dividends – until the gold price goes up, that is. For the time being it looks as if fees are a more reliable source of income for the Houses than dividends.

To me it seems logical for the Houses to do all in their power to keep the marginal mines alive through this period of low gold prices. Their reward will come when non-South African gold mining companies, which do not enjoy the benefits of the Mining House system, fall by the wayside. The Houses who do allow their mines to go to the wall will find themselves with neither dividends nor fee income, not just for a year or two, but forever. It is for this reason that I think that marginal mines may not be quite such dangerous investments as most people think they are.

Here is the table which shows the expected fee income versus the dividends which my anonymous friends think will accrue to the Mining Houses in future. If Mr Ramaphosa wants a share of the dividends he will be disappointed as far as most of the marginals are concerned. There probably won't be any dividends until the gold price recovers. If he wants a share of future fees, it will be in his interest to help keep the marginal mines in being just as much as it is in the interest of the controlling Mining Houses to do so. Not all will survive and we are bound to be caught holding one or two which bite the dust, but the rewards of holding the survivors should be very great even if we have to wait a while to reap them. (129. 14/3/91)

		1986 – 1990 (Rm)		1991 – 1995 Est (Rm)	
ANGLO AMERICAN	Dividends	1131	64%	767	42%
	Fees	637	36%	1045	58%
	Total	1768	100%	1812	100%
JCI	Dividends	123	50%	84	29%
	Fees	122	50%	209	71%
	Total	245	100%	293	100%
GENCOR	Dividends	450	69%	401	63%
	Fees	196	31%	236	37%
	Total	646	100%	637	100%
GOLDFIELDS	Dividends	1106	78%	724	64%
	Fees	309	22%	409	36%
	Total	1415	100%	1133	100%
All Companies	Dividends	2810	69%	1976	51%
	Fees	1264	31%	1899	49%
	Total	4074	100%	3875	100%

Julian explains that the fees/dividend issue leads to directors of individual marginal mines encouraging these mines to stay open, allowing the controlling houses to continue to benefit from fees paid.

You should know that these are the horrible decisions that are having to be made by the directors of many of the mines we hold in our portfolio. In my experience human beings do not make tough decisions until they have to. By that time it can be too late. That is why I have been warning you that some of our marginal mines may not survive until better times come. I say some, but hopefully not all! The survivors will make us a fortune.

One disadvantage the South African gold mining industry suffers is that, unlike their foreign competitors, the directors and managers of South African mines are not also shareholders in their enterprises. Their personal financial interests generally lie with the Mining Houses which employ them. Since the marginal mines don't pay dividends when times are bad, their contribution to the Mining Houses comes in the form of the management fee as I explained last week. Thus the mine management have a greater vested interest in keeping the mine going than in making it profitable.

I would like to see the directors of the mines keeping their directors fees rather than handing them on to the Houses who appoint them. Directors fees are not enough to make any difference to the fortunes of a Mining House but would provide an incentive for senior management to take tough decisions earlier if they had more to lose personally if their mines became unprofitable. Furthermore I would like to see directors and senior mine employees having share options in the mines they manage and not just in the Mining Houses they work for. (**130.** 21/3/91)

Julian calls for more transparency over the effect of the Mining House fee structure on the actions of directors, in their dual capacity as directors of both Mining Houses and the underlying gold mines.

You may recall that in a recent Newsletter I gave the legal definition of ore: "Ore means metalliferous material that can be mined and processed at a profit."

In South Africa, at some mines things have come to such a pretty pass that whole sections have had to be closed down with the tragic loss of thousands of jobs. In such cases there is no argument about it. What was ore last year no longer is! Even now, things are not quite what they seem.

As you probably know, the system that has evolved in South Africa is somewhat different from that pertaining in other parts of the world. In South Africa each mine is part of a stable of mines run by the various Mining Houses.

Frequently the Mining Houses own fewer shares in the mines they manage than would normally represent control. That does not really matter too much since Mining Houses have valuable contracts with their mines to provide technical, financial and secretarial services.

When times are good the mines earn enough profits to take care of the fees and to pay dividends to their shareholders. But when times are bad there is an enormous temptation for the controlling Houses to mine the remaining reserves at breakeven, in order to prolong the period over which fees will be payable. Thus, if gold remains depressed for any length of time, it is possible to envisage the poor old shareholder ending up with nothing – no dividends, no ore reserves and a worthless share certificate. Never mind, the Mining Houses get their fees.

Personally I have yet to be convinced that the system is altogether fair to shareholders. I think a case could be made for requiring directors of the individual gold companies, who are for the most part also directors of the controlling Mining Houses, to be more forthcoming on the subject of fees they charge in their capacity as directors of the Mining Houses and the fees they pay as directors of the individual mines. It would also be interesting if they highlighted the effect the fees have on their ore reserve position. It should not be too much to ask that shareholders be entitled to a fair share of the revenues derived from the remaining ore reserves. (**174. 12/5/92**)

Julian raises the issue of Mining House discounts to assets and wonders whether the fee structure may explain part of the discount.

I asked the Chairman of one of the Mining Houses represented at the Smith New Court conference if the directors ever gave any thought as to why their company sold at such a large discount to its assets and how much money would be released if the discount were abolished. He replied that the discount was the equivalent of R3 a share or a total of more than R4 billion (or US$1 billion). The need to recapture some of those missing millions had given birth to the recent debate about "unbundling". He himself was at a loss to know why the shares of the Mining Houses sold at a discount, since some of his pet theories as to why they did so had recently been disproved in practice.

In order to be helpful I put forward the suggestion that the discount might represent the present value of the cost of running the company for the next 20 years, discounted at 6.5 per cent. You may say that the trouble with this theory is that the controlling company's overheads are meant to be more than covered by the management fees charged to the companies administered by the Group. But the way I look at it is that the management fees are just as much part of a Mining House's income as are dividends received from its underlying investments. What is worrying is that a 25 per cent discount to the assets implies that the average investor thinks that only 75 per cent of his investment in the average Mining House will be put to productive use.

It could be argued that the market is calling into question the whole system under which many of South Africa's leading companies operate, but any suggestion by the ANC or others that the system might be improved upon, is met with a solid wall of vested interests arguing that any interference would lead to a dramatic loss of confidence on the part of foreign investors and should therefore not be attempted in the interests of the country as a whole. A suitable case for the South African equivalent of a Royal Commission headed by an independent Chairman such as Lord Hanson, if you ask me. (**196. 17/11/92**)

Julian returns to the subject of executive loyalties and wonders whether directors should be more nakedly exposed, in a financial sense, to the fortunes of the underlying assets which make up the leading South African Mining Houses.

The trouble with the South African Mining House system is that the directors of the mining companies are motivated by the Mining House they work for rather than by the mines which their Mining House owns. Many of them are directors of both.

If only the directors and senior executives of the South African gold mines held shares and options in the mines themselves rather than in the Mining Houses which control them, they and we would have a community of interest. Elsewhere in the world, directors of gold mines have to think whether their actions will affect their own pockets, but the conflicts of interest which beset South African directors of companies seem awesome to one when compared with their peers in other countries.

They tell me that if I think shareholders of the individual mines are disadvantaged by the system, I should buy the Houses and get the fees that way. The trouble with that argument is that the Mining Houses sell at a discount to the value of the underlying investments, let alone the present value of their future earnings from fees. The market seems to be telling us something about the financial efficiency of the system. Otherwise the value represented by the Houses' discount to net asset value would not have gone to "money heaven".

It is said that the pool of technical expertise available within the Mining Houses is always at the disposal of the individual mines. What they don't add is whether the individual mines need it or not! Elsewhere in the world, if mines want advice they pay for it when they need it. The pool of expertise is, I believe, largely there for the benefit of the shareholders of the mining finance houses but is paid for by the shareholders of the individual mines. That does not help us since we are shareholders of the individual mines. You can see why I am considered a nuisance for daring to raise the matter for debate.

If the South Africans really want to enhance shareholder value, they will allow the individual mines much more freedom to do their own thing in future. Correctly motivated, the directors of individual mines could do wonders for their shareholders.

Once it becomes generally respectable to invest in South Africa, the first foreign mining company which decides to apply international norms to the South African mining scene will not only make a fortune for its own shareholders, but it will change the thinking in South Africa itself. New mines in South Africa are likely to be joint ventures between local and foreign mining companies. If you ask me, foreign mining companies will be hard to convince that they should be paying fees to the local Mining Houses. If the locals want foreign partners to share the risk, they may well have to accept their culture too. We unitholders would welcome that. (**222. 24/6/93**)

Julian explains the rationale behind his push for control of Randgold & Exploration (Rand Mines), and his strategy to break the SA fees structure through control of what was South Africa's oldest and smallest Mining House.

You may have seen in the papers that we joined with other shareholders to exercise our rights to remind the Board of one of the companies in which we are invested that companies ultimately belong to their shareholders and that directors who do not listen to what their shareholders have to say, run the risk of being replaced by those whose hearing is better.

About 18 months ago we bought about 10 per cent of Randgold & Exploration, a small South African Mining Finance House which controls four marginal mines, ERPM, Harmony, Durban Deep and Blyvoors. At that time, the market must have been taking a gloomy view about Randgold's future since we were able to buy our stake for R1.5 per share which effectively represented a discount to the cash in the company's balance sheet. We therefore acquired for less than nothing the mineral rights, which if exploited successfully could be extremely valuable. We also acquired the holdings in the underlying mines and the management fees which were at that time, and still are, the company's only source of income.

The shares of Randgold have since risen to R9 but they still sell at a substantial discount to their asset value, possibly as much as 50 per cent. It is this discount that we wish to see unlocked. But all our suggestions to the previous Board as to how this might be achieved, fell on deaf ears. Not only that, every brokers' circular and every press commentator told us we should be selling our shares. In seeing value in them, we appeared to be the only ones in step. The series of misfortunes which have befallen the company, made us fear that unless something was done, there was a serious risk that the company's detractors would be proved right and that it would eventually be driven into the ground.

Fortunately we came across a group of South African entrepreneurs who shared our views as to how shareholder value might be enhanced. We were persuaded to give them our proxy to call an Extraordinary General Meeting and change the composition of the Board to one more in sympathy with our views. This has now been done.

There are a number of ways in which we perceive that shareholder value can be enhanced. First of all, no value is given by the market to the company's sole source of income, the management fees, which last financial year provided Randgold with income of some R50 million. In fact, the market attributes a negative value to them – with some justification. The old directors of Randgold are also directors of each of the underlying mines, so the underlying mines already enjoy the benefit of their skills. It is our view that if the mines did not have to pay this fee, they would have more money available to reward shareholders who have gone without dividends despite the record rand gold price. One of the major shareholders is of course Randgold. We too are major shareholders in Harmony.

We contend that Randgold shares would actually go up if they sold the management contracts back to the mines in exchange for shares! We think the shares of the underlying mines would go up too because each mine would become master of its own destiny. If the mines were well run and returned to profitability, their share prices would respond. If not, there would be nothing to stop them being taken over by someone who thought he could do a better job.

The present system encourages an attitude of mind that if anything goes wrong at a mine, big daddy is always there to bail them out. The local mine management derives too little personal benefit if things go well and takes too little responsibility if things go badly. Under the present arrangements, it is difficult to reward excellence and it is therefore difficult to attract ambitious people to work at marginal mines. Without sufficient incentive for the senior management at the mines, the shareholders also suffer. Under the new management all this is likely to change. (**266. 25/8/94**)

JCI's large asset discount demonstrates to Julian that its fee income gets no market credit.

An eagle-eyed broker skimming through the JCI Annual Report just published, noticed that last year the company derived R61 million after tax and Head Office expenses from fees payable by their mines for services rendered by Head Office. You would have thought that the market would place a positive value on such a certain source of income, however, JCI shares sell at a discount to their assets so the market is ascribing no value to these services.

It would be interesting to know whether the mines who received these services believed they were getting value for money but we are unlikely ever to find out since the senior management of JCI is also on the Boards of the underlying companies who presumably benefit from their management skills at their own board meetings.

Perhaps they would be well advised to repackage these so-called management contracts into revenue royalties and then sell them to Franco Nevada, whose shareholders place an almost unbelievably high value on such instruments. (**270. 6/10/94**)

Julian picks up an unlikely ally in his battle against Mining House fees in the shape of South Africa's former Foreign Minister Pik Botha.

As a contrarian, I find it particularly difficult to please the commentators over the short run. This fund is overweight South Africa. The reason for this is two-fold.

First it seems to me that there is more room for improving the profitability of the South African gold mining industry than any other. I believe that this perception is becoming more and more widely recognised, but it will not happen overnight.

The other day we nearly fell off our chairs in disbelief when we read that no less a figure than Mr Pik Botha, formally Minister of Foreign Affairs during the Apartheid regime and now Minister of Mines in the Government of National Unity, was quoted as saying that South Africa's management contract systems were "quaint and anachronistic" and needed to be reviewed. "It seems to me that management needs to change, to rid itself of possibly archaic practices, rigid structures and blinkered thinking ... The tendency is to blame labour [for steadily escalating unit costs] and to cut costs by retrenchment ..." And he does not even receive the Newsletter! (**310. 23/8/95**)

Julian continues his battle to force the Mining Houses to reconsider the fees structure, noting that Gencor has followed Randgold's example – but JCI and the others stand resolutely pointing the other way.

Last week we suffered a deep disappointment. For some time now we have been trying to convince the Mining Houses in South Africa that the system that has evolved over the years seems to be becoming less and less advantageous to their own shareholders and more disadvantageous to the shareholders of the individual mines. If the system really was of benefit to the shareholders of the Mining Houses, their share prices would presumably reflect that benefit. Instead of selling at a sizeable discount to their assets as they do at present, they would be selling at a premium reflecting the perceived added value to be derived from fees, mineral rights held in perpetuity and the skills which are assembled at the various Head Offices but paid for by the mines. If the Houses themselves wish to employ large quantities of people to further their own business aims, that is their affair, but we find it hard to accept that the shareholders of the underlying mines should meet the cost of employing these wizards.

As you know, we did have some success in changing the management philosophy at Randgold, even though we had to change the Management itself in order to achieve this. The discount to assets has been eliminated now by Randgold. Its share price goes from strength to strength. Gencor has done many, but not all, of the things which were pioneered by Randgold. They too, have virtually eliminated their discount and outperformed the market in the process. Both companies have drastically reduced numbers employed at Head Office and both have given added responsibility to management at the mines. Randgold has exchanged its management fees for additional shares in its underlying mines so that Randgold and the minority shareholders, such as ourselves, now have a community of interest never before seen in South Africa. In the next two weeks, when the quarterly reports are published, we shall see whether the mines which have been set free to mind their own affairs have performed better or worse than those who have had the benefit of the services provided by Head Office.

The main justification for continuing with a system which has long been discarded by mining groups outside South Africa, is said to be that skills are in short supply and that a central team of technical professionals can offer economies of scale and the transfer of core technologies from one mine to another and from one country to another. You would think that those companies which do not organise themselves in this way would fall further and further behind those who do not enjoy the advantages of having a large Head Office staff. RTZ, for instance, the largest mining company in the world, "struggles" along with a Head Office staff of 230 people. Closer to home Gencor has recently reduced its Head Office gold division head count from 140 people to 40 and Randgold has reduced its from 128 to 15. JCI employs around 400 people in its Head Office.

We have built up a large holding in JCI, in anticipation that the stellar share price performance of Gencor and Randgold would not have escaped their notice. We hoped that by now they would be showing signs of following in their footsteps. Instead, their annual report contains long passages devoted to the well-worn arguments for continuing with past practices. Would it be too cruel to suggest that they sound a bit like a well-worn gramophone record on the HMV label?

Before someone points an accusing finger at us we brazenly admit to wanting to have our cake and eat it. We complained that Randgold would not listen to us as its major shareholder, we in the same breath complain when JCI has to listen to its largest shareholder, Anglo American. Anglo American has set its face against making the reforms we have been calling for, as has Gold Fields of South Africa. Needless to say that these two companies sell at colossal discounts to their assets. Their "missing billions" are too numerous to count. But neither company has a reputation for caring much about its share price. JCI Limited revealed in its annual report that its discount to assets at 30th June amounted to a staggering R1.5 billion, which rightly belongs to the shareholders, but which has gone to money heaven. Before I go to heaven myself, I could ask for no greater prize than to have helped recover JCI's missing billions for you, the unitholders, to spend while you are still earth-bound. All the signs are that we will have to wait until the new black shareholders take control of JCI Limited from Anglo American. They will certainly be interested in the enhancement of shareholder value even if the present owners are motivated by less worldly principles. (**317. 16/10/95**)

The cracks in the fees system in South Africa continue to widen, but the industry's giants still refuse to budge.

It is now becoming clear to everyone, to a greater or lesser degree, that the current structure of the industry is creating an impediment to the harmonious, efficient and economic management of the mines. There was some adverse comment from members of our group about what was perceived to be bloated and bureaucratic Head Office structures paid for, it was thought unfairly, by one set of shareholders namely those of the individual mines, for the benefit of the shareholders of the Mining Houses.

In response to these criticisms, some Mining Houses are making strenuous efforts to display greater transparency with regard to who is paying for what. Others, like Randgold, have eliminated any conflict of interests by exchanging their management fees for additional shares in the mines they previously administered. This has enabled Harmony, for instance, to pay a dividend for the first time in three years. Randgold's interest as a shareholder in Harmony now coincides exactly with ours. If Harmony needs specialist help or advice it can employ outside consultants.

Gencor and Anglovaal, following Randgold's example, show encouraging signs that they may soon scrap the practice of charging management fees to the mines they administer. It is probably no coincidence that the market has rewarded these three companies by almost completely eliminating the discount at which their shares sell to their asset value. In so doing, they have succeeded in returning what we call "the missing billions" to their rightful owners, the shareholders. The management of these companies have selflessly given up, or are seriously considering giving up, a stream of earnings which helps maintain their lifestyle. The market, on the other hand, places no value on these earnings, suggesting perhaps, that it believes that only a small fraction of these fees end up enhancing shareholder value.

The payment of management fees has been likened to a rich man employing his own full time personal physician. The South African gold mines are anything but rich at the moment and are busy cutting dividends to their shareholders left, right and centre. Notwithstanding this, they are obliged to continue paying fees to their "personal physicians", the Mining Houses, whose much vaunted pool of specialist skills do not seem to be much good at preventative medicine since many of the mines are now clinging onto life by a thread! Would it be too cruel to suggest that the mines might be in better health today if they had had to fend for themselves since birth? All the Mining Houses we saw gave patient consideration to these points. We can only speculate as to the reaction of three of the largest, Anglo American, DeBeers and Gold Fields of South Africa who were unfortunately unable to make anyone available to speak to us. (**322. 25/11/95**)

Perhaps Julian's finest hour as he flies down to Johannesburg to do battle with the rapacious Mining Houses over management fees and draws blood.

Some wag once said that if God had not wanted shareholders to be sheared, he would not have made them to behave like sheep. To ram (whoops!) home the point, shareholders will be referred to as shearholders throughout this newsletter.

As you know, we have been pressing for some time for the abolition of the management contracts which bind the South African gold mines to their controlling Mining Houses and which are in grave danger of bringing the whole industry into disrepute.

There is quite a lot of evidence to suggest that the message has at last got through to the senior echelons of the South African mining industry that these contracts are doing them more harm than good in the eyes of shearholders and moves are now afoot to dispense with them – but at a price. We take very little credit for this change of heart, ascribing it more to the realisation that foreign capital will soon be required if the next generation of deep level mines is to be financed. The penny is beginning to drop in South Africa that shearholders, particularly those who rely on No 33 King William Street, will not be investing fresh capital in the country if they are to be gouged so mercilessly by the terms of the management contracts.

The stark reality is starting to sink in, that if steps are not taken to ensure that South African corporate governance is brought into line with international best practice, the cost of capital for new mining projects might be adversely affected, thus threatening their viability.

This week, Extraordinary General Meetings of shearholders took place in Johannesburg to facilitate the mergers of certain gold mining companies in the Gencor and Anglovaal groups. In both cases the schemes of arrangement included the abolition of the dreaded Management Contracts. Unfortunately for us shearholders the quid pro quo for the cancellation of the management contracts was R127m in the case of the Gencor mines and R81 million for the Anglovaal mines. Since the shearholders of the gold mines concerned were not asked to approve the contracts when they were originally put in place and since, in the case of the Gencor contracts, shearholders were not allowed even to see the contracts, the cancellation for which they were being asked to pay R127 million, we thought that the time had come for a posse of us to justify the management fee you pay us by flying to Johannesburg, whistle in hand, to see if we could stop you being sheared in public. We don't pretend to be saints, but we know that if you are sheared too frequently without us at least trying to protect you, you have a perfect right to take your business elsewhere.

Fortunately we held enough shares in some of the merging companies to be able to affect the outcome of the meetings. Other shearholders, the investment community in general and those who signed fairness opinions (they were only opinions!) seemed to find nothing wrong with the proposals, so immune have they become to the sight of investors walking around Johannesburg stripped naked!

You may have read in the papers that Gencor eventually agreed to modify their original proposals by agreeing to the appointment of three independent, non-executive directors to the Board of Evander Mines who will review the cancellation terms in order to give shearholders reassurance that they have not just been fleeced yet again. We are very pleased that Gencor responded to our concerns in this way, and as a result we were able to give the Evander Gold Mines merger our whole-hearted support.

Shearholders of the gold mines in the JCI, Anglo American and Gold Fields groups will just have to wait their turn in the shearing shed. Those in the Randgold, Gencor and Anglovaal groups who have now taken their haircut will meanwhile enjoy the following benefits arising from the cancellation of the management contracts:–

- The fees which were previously paid to the shearholders of the Mining Houses will instead accrue to the shearholders of the individual mines and will become part of their distributable income.
- The mine managers will no longer feel bad about paying the Mining Houses for services they felt they did not need or get.
- If another mining company feels it could manage the mines more profitably than the incumbent management, there is no longer anything to stop them bidding for the company in the normal way. The management contracts are no longer a poison pill. Foreign mining companies will at last be able to try their luck in South Africa. This could do nothing but good for the ratings of South African gold shares.
- It will be in the interest of the Mining Houses to maximise the share price of their underlying mines (rather than their management fees) in order to discourage predators. The interest of the Mining Houses and the interests of the shearholders of the individual mines have converged. This is actually a major step forward for Lambkind.
- Employees, incentivised for the first time with options to buy shares in the company for which they work, rather than in the controlling Mining House, will no longer need to wonder where their loyalties and their career prospects really lie.
- South African Fund Managers may for the first time be persuaded that there is merit in buying individual gold mines as well as the Mining Houses which own them. This in itself could enhance the value of South African

gold shares which have now become relatively more attractive investments due to the cancellation of the management contracts.

- Foreign shearholders will no longer have to suffer the injustice of paying ever higher management fees (part of which are based on revenue) every time the Rand devalues, while at the same time seeing their own dividends, if there are any, reduced by the amount of the devaluation.

We managed to persuade Gencor, if not Anglovaal, to appoint genuinely independent, non-executive directors to the Board of at least one of their gold companies. Rick Mennell, the Deputy Chairman of Anglovaal, gave a personal undertaking to consider doing so in public. We succeeded in getting a genuinely independent, arm's-length review of the price paid for the cancellation of the Gencor management contract, though we did not have quite enough firepower to insist on a similar undertaking from Anglovaal.

We believe that independent directors can do nothing but good for the mines, especially if some of them are from overseas. Having taken one small step in the direction of achieving better ratings for South African gold shares, we can only hope that others with similar interests to our own will now raise their heads above the parapet and do their bit to get the average South African ounce of gold in the ground rated at better than the current US$39/oz. Even if we could only achieve an average price per South African ounce in the ground, of only half that placed on an ounce in the ground in Ghana, we would enjoy an uplift of 29 per cent in the value of our South African holdings. With 47 per cent of the portfolio invested in South Africa, no effort is too great if it results in an enhancement of shareholder value of that magnitude. (**363. 7/11/96**)

6. Base Metal Shares – The Fund's General Holdings

It is interesting that in the early days of the James Capel Gold and General Fund the portfolio was largely invested in base metal shares, with only a scattering of gold shares. The reason for this was that at the time of the Fund's launch Julian took the view that gold shares were materially overvalued, and base metal shares were in contrast very cheap. Bearing in mind that his reputation as a broker had been built on his position as London's leading expert on gold and gold shares, Julian's support for base metal shares may have appeared a little perverse, and on occasion Julian did acknowledge this. However, as a good broker, value and cheapness were paramount to Julian.

Julian, the Fund just eleven weeks in existence, extols the virtues – and cheapness – of base metal shares.

The recent strength of base metal prices is shaping up beautifully to make those who have been recommending the sale of these shares look ridiculous. All the signs are that when the second quarter's earnings are published in the early weeks of July, we will be looking at annualised earnings of less than five in many cases. Investors are just beginning to twig to this probability and are buying in anticipation that a lot of words are going to have to be eaten by the mining analysts.

I rearranged our portfolio to take account of this when I saw buying interest starting to build up. We are now very heavily weighted indeed in this sector of the market, having added to our existing positions in the market leaders to the maximum extent allowed by the rules. In order to achieve this I jettisoned the portfolio's underperformers and took profits in some of the shares which have served us well. (**11. 14/6/88**)

Julian reduces his gold exposure while talking up base metal prospects.

In the next six days we will be getting the quarterly results from the North American base metal producers which form the nucleus of the Fund. Their publication should cause even those who have failed to notice their attractions up to now to sit up and take notice. The trouble is that at this time of the year there is no shortage of attractive assets on display on the beaches, but it is often too hot to do much about it, other than to take notice!

What I am trying to say is that, in the next few days, you will be able to see whether or not my somewhat unconventional approach to running a gold Fund is on the right track. I could, in those circumstances, hardly have sold the very companies which I believe will shortly demonstrate the logic of my approach, just because they had run up rather faster than was good for them in the short term. Let them have their reaction and that will give you your chance to add to your holdings.

All I did, therefore, was to marginally reduce our gold exposure, in case the rather droopy looking gold price is telling us that the three-year bull market is coming to an end. One of the tricks of the trade is to sell when "good" news does not put prices up. You would have thought that the shooting down of the Iranian jet liner would have put $10 on the gold price. At our morning meeting on Monday it was not even mentioned as a factor which would affect it – rightly so, as it had no effect whatsoever on the price. (**12. 5/7/88**)

Julian, who was always an admirer of De Beers, again lauds the qualities of the diamond giant.

While I was away, De Beers came out with doubled profits for the first half of 1988 and this firm estimates that they are now selling on 3.7 times 1988 earnings. As you know De Beers is one of the world's great businesses, controlling as it does some 80 per cent of the world's production of gem diamonds. It does this by maintaining a stockpile which it adds to when the demand for diamonds is weak, and sells from when the demand exceeds supply. It handles the sales of diamonds of such diverse countries as Russia, Australia and Tanzania, none of which are well-known supporters of South Africa. They market their production through De Beers because it suits them to. No one else could do it better. So much so that only a comparatively small proportion of De Beers' profits comes from the production and sale of diamonds from South Africa. De Beers is a fully international business, the bulk of which is conducted from its offices in No 2 Charterhouse Street, London, where it keeps its stockpile of diamonds and where the 150 or so leading diamond merchants assemble ten times a year to receive their allocation of the world's diamond production.

The demand for diamonds this year has been so strong that it has enabled the recipients of these parcels to sell them on to lesser mortals at a substantial premium, without even having to go to the trouble of opening the parcels. The producers who sell their diamonds through De Beers don't like to see their production being sold too cheaply, therefore De Beers increased prices by 13 per cent during the first half of 1988 and this in turn has led to a doubling of profits in the first half of this year, compared with the first half of last year. In spite of this, the parcels are still selling at a premium, which leads people to the conclusion that a further price rise is on the cards for later this year. This is leading analysts to increase their forecasts of earnings, and the consensus now seems to be that De Beers is selling on about 3.7 times the likely earnings for this year. I have seen it suggested that if De Beers were to move their Head Office from Kimberley to Gaborone in Botswana, the shares would probably double, since the Americans have no quarrel with Botswana. If they moved to London their shares would probably treble! People fear that the Americans will be forced to divest themselves of their holdings in De Beers due to sanctions legislation. Investors are tumid animals who tend to take an exceedingly short-term view and are reluctant to buy shares, however cheap, if they think the Americans are going to have to sell them. I take the view that all those worries are already reflected in the price and that is why, last week, some of your new money was spent on increasing our stake in De Beers to one full unit, or 7.5 per cent of the fund. (**18. 23/8/88**)

De Beers sparkles but falls, and Julian bemoans the lack of enthusiasm for equities in general.

One of the most reliable tricks of our trade is to watch what people do and not take too much notice of what they say should be done. It is sometimes hard to understand why the market does not respond positively to what is widely perceived to be good news. The most recent example of this, is the outstanding half yearly result announced by De Beers. Most brokers seem to be predicting that the company will earn around $2.75 per share this year, which puts the shares on 3.7 times earnings! All the brokers rate them a buy, yet they still go down. When good news results in cheap shares falling further, it tells you more about market sentiment than it does about the quality of the shares in question.

So how does this all affect us? Readers of this missive will be aware that despite its name, I do not want to buy gold shares for this fund unless they offer the prospect of getting more money out of them than we put in, in the first place. Gold shares are equities. Equities are jittery at the moment, worldwide. Equities are behaving more like they do in a bear market than in a bull market. I have therefore sought to protect our capital by buying high quality mining companies on low multiples, and this has worked well for us, as the following table shows. The figures are based on 1st April 1988, when the fund was started.

	PRICE 1ST APRIL	PRICE 5TH SEPT. 1988	CHANGE
Offered Price of units	50p	55.3p	+10.6
Australian Gold Index	1751	1730.4	-1.1
Canadian Gold Index	6738	6026	-10.6
S. African Gold Index	237.3	186.9	-21.2

(20. 6/9/88)

In his pursuit of value Julian became closely embroiled in the drawn-out battle for Consolidated Gold Fields, which started in 1988 with the bid from Minorco. Julian believed huge value could be unlocked by merging the Anglo American and Gold Fields groups.

Just as Minorco is valued by the market at a fraction of its true worth, so too, is De Beers. De Beers has three prongs to its business.

1. A stockpile of diamonds situated in London, worth $1.8 billion.
2. An investment portfolio, the income from which is used to iron out the fluctuating earnings of the diamond market. This portfolio is worth $2.95 billion.
3. The diamond business itself which this year should earn over $1 billion after tax.

The value of 1 and 2 together amounts to $4.7S billion and this compares with a total market capitalization of De Beers of $4.085 billion. In other words, the market is paying you nearly three quarters of a billion dollars to take the diamond business away! A negative value is being placed on a business that makes between $500 million and $l billion a year! You don't have to be a genius to see that something has to be done about that.

Even the Oppenheimer family are not so rich as to be able to continue to ignore such a gross undervaluation of their assets.

Apart from mining diamonds, De Beers buys and sells some 80 per cent of the world's diamonds for virtually all the producers including, it is said, the Russians. Much of this trade is conducted from London where a group of companies concerned with the buying, selling and marketing of diamonds, conduct their business. These activities, I am told, are likely to earn some $70 million this year, but if you know a better figure please tell me. Since the market appears to give no value to these activities anyhow, perhaps Minorco will be able to buy them for a reasonable price. The price I have in mind is $300 million or R1.153 billion financial rand. What a happy coincidence that would be! It would just about swallow up the overhang of financial rands and explain why the financial rand is behaving as if there was no danger.

Now you are starting to see the master plan unfold. It will be far more complicated than the one I have just described. In order to unlock the true value of the Anglo American group, the missing $1.5 billion in Minorco would first have to be found. To do that, Minorco will have to buy (or sell) Consolidated Gold Fields and put Charter and Johnson Matthey together eliminating the discount to assets of Charter. Then the De Beers' empire will have to be reshuffled, selling perhaps the London operating companies to Minorco. This would improve Minorco's earnings capability and its market rating.

Although De Beers is going to own less of Minorco, the plan must be to make its reduced holding more valuable.

Anglo American would also benefit from all this. It holds most of its De Beers' shares though Anamint which is more of a Diamond company than De Beers itself. Anamint will be a key player as the plan unfolds.

What, I can hear those of you who have got this far saying, has this got to do with us? Much more than you would think, is the answer. In my opinion, the enactment of the master plan is likely to create more wealth in the mining markets of the world than any other single factor. I have therefore invested heavily in it in recent weeks. Now, more than 30 per cent of the entire portfolio is committed to companies which are directly affected by this game plan. A huge amount of the balance is invested in companies which may be indirectly affected.

No private individual could possibly achieve this spread without seriously distorting his portfolio, but holders of our units have the whole play covered in one investment.

Let's hope, for all our sakes, that I have read the tea leaves correctly. (**30. 29/11/88**)

The tradition of promoting a Christmas Box of mining shares was first started when Julian headed James Capel's Mining Desk in the 1970s.

As far back as 1973 I noticed that the shares of the Mining Finance Houses like Anglo American & RTZ had a habit of performing particularly well over the Christmas period. The reason for this was a practice (which is now rather frowned upon) known as "window dressing".

This observation led to the creation of the James Capel Christmas Box which consists of a hamper containing about 8–10 Mining Finance House shares which, if purchased around my birthday on 9th December and sold on 31st January, enables its owner to finance his Christmas excesses at the expense of those who are unaware of the phenomenon.

Every year Capels publish the Christmas Box in their mining Newsletter and every year about three clients buy it. The others note its behaviour but cannot be bothered to clutter their portfolios up with ten mining shares for six weeks, despite the fact that the average capital gain achieved by the Christmas Box over the years has been 10 per cent or 85 per cent annualised. (**32. 13/12/88**)

Julian believed that Minorco's huge discount to its underlying assets would eventually be recognised by the market and lead to a significant value-enhancing leap forward in its share price.

If unitholders of the James Capel Gold and General Fund harbour uncharitable feelings towards their Fund Manager at this season of goodwill, they could hardly be blamed for that. Last week was not a good one for us!

I have been betting heavily, perhaps too heavily for comfort, on the ability of the new management of Minorco to set about finding the "missing millions" in a gritty and purposeful manner. The harsh treatment last week of Charter, Johnson Matthey, De Beers and Anglo American shares suggests that I have been expecting too much, too soon. The trouble, in these jaundiced markets, is that people form unrealistic expectations of the speed at which things can be accomplished. Steps in the right direction are interpreted as vacillation – as attempts to rearrange the deck chairs, rather than clear the decks themselves.

It is important that unitholders understand my perception of what is going on so that they can take appropriate action if they think I am on the wrong track. I say "perception", because unlike their foreign counterparts, UK Fund Managers like me have not yet had the opportunity of hearing at first hand from the directors of Minorco what they plan to do and how they plan to do it. I am simply basing my investment decisions for the fund on what I would do if I were them. Over 30 per cent of your money is invested in companies which would benefit directly or indirectly if Minorco succeeds in fulfilling the task to which it has set its hand. If they are perceived to be failing, you and I will be punished through our pockets.

So let me reiterate. Minorco, you will recall, is the company through which Anglo American holds its non-South African investments. All these investments like Consolidated Gold Fields and Charter have Boards of Directors of their own so there was thought to be little point in Minorco's directors trying to manage these assets twice over. Minorco came to look and behave more and more like an investment trust. Investment trusts tend to sell on huge discounts to their assets. In this case the discount became so gross that something had to be done about it. Minorco's assets are worth about $20 a share and the share price is $11.50. If the discount to assets can be eliminated, or at least reduced, the shareholders of Minorco will have up to $1.5 billion more than they now have.

The reason you get these huge discounts on companies like Minorco and Anglo American is that the profits made by the operating companies get "clipped" as they pass through the various holding companies on their way through to the top company. I have explained this in previous letters. What I perceive to be the task of the new look Minorco is to dear away as many of these intermediate companies as possible so that the profits of the operating companies can flow straight through to Minorco. These intermediaries should be wholly owned or sold. Minorco is setting about this task. It has made a bid for Consolidated Gold Fields. If it fails it will probably put its holding up for sale. I don't think it will fail, provided shareholders are allowed to be consulted. (**33. 20/12/88**)

Against the background of the cheapest base metal share market that Julian can remember he reveals his New Year resolutions for 1989.

I have only been in the mining game for 34 years, but I certainly have never seen leading mining shares offering such incredible value as they do today, even at peaks of previous cycles. That is why the Fund is stuffed full of them. As a broker friend put it, "Why travel steerage when you have a first class ticket?"

So any brokers reading this should know my New Year's Resolutions which I hope will help create order out of chaos in the mining markets, or if not there, at least in my own mind! They will note that I am resolved to go back to basics; back to the well-tried methods of valuing mining shares that I was taught when I started in the game.

1. I resolve not to differentiate between different types of metals when deciding which shares offer the best value. I bet RTZ didn't when they bought BP Minerals – why should I?
2. I resolve not to be diverted from pursuing a policy of "focussed excellence" when building our portfolio. The rules allow me to have 7.5 per cent of the Fund in seen shares. In other words seven shares may make up 52.5 per cent of the fund. At all times I will endeavour to ensure that my 7 largest holdings are the best seven mining investments in the world.
3. I resolve not to deal with brokers who rate gold shares on the number of thousands of dollars paid per ounce of annual capacity (unless they can explain to me what that method of valuation means).
4. I resolve to reward brokers who present their research in a way that ranks mining shares in order of "focused excellence".
5. I am resolved to require to know the present value of the future earnings of any mining share I buy before I buy it.

As with most New Year's Resolutions I expect to fail to keep them all, but I will certainly be trying. (**35. 7/1/89**)

Julian outlines the Fund's operating parameters and explains how he divides the portfolio in terms of quality.

You may be interested to know the constraints within which I am obliged to operate, in order to safeguard your investment by providing you with an adequate spread of shares:

1. I may not have more than 5 per cent of the fund in any one share; except
2. I may have up to 7.5 per cent in six shares; but
3. I may not have more than 55 per cent of the portfolio in less than 10 shares; and
4. I must have more than 20 shares in the portfolio!

In pursuit of my policy of "focused excellence", and acting within the constraints listed above I have decided to divide my portfolio into four divisions. The six "Royals" in the first division are allocated 6.5 per cent of the Fund each. The second division consists of four "Ladies in Waiting" which are allocated four per cent of the Fund each. The third division consists of about ten "Courtiers", having varying allocations, with the senior ones commanding 3.4 per cent of the fund each. The fourth division which will be strictly limited in size will fulfil the role of "Courtesans". They will provide a diversion from the serious business of the Court, and will enable us to have a good time when no one is looking!

You will see, at the grand parade being planned for next week, that the "Royals" consist of Phelps Dodge, Amax, De Beers, Freeport Copper, Minorco and Cyprus Mines. The "Ladies in Waiting" are Alcoa, Charter, Anglo American and Consolidated Goldfields. If you don't know by now what most of the ladies are waiting for, you have not been paying attention to these letters!

The senior "Courtiers" are Alcan, Reynolds, Asarco, Anamint, Englehard and English China Clays, but don't worry so much about them. The "Royals" and "Ladies in Waiting" is where 55 per cent of your money is invested. As you know, much will depend on the outcome of Minorco's bid for Consolidated Gold Fields. I contend that if Minorco succeeds, it will gain much credibility and the ripple effect will do us no end of good. If it fails, my contention is that our shares are already so cheap that it will do us little permanent damage. If you don't agree, sell your units now while the going is good. Battle is about to commence: those with no stomach for the fight, let them depart. For the remainder – see you in the breach. (**36. 17/1/89**)

And here is the portfolio divided as described above, with a very small exposure to gold at this stage in early 1989.

JAMES CAPEL GOLD FUND – PROFILE   25 Jan 1989

Rank / Name	Cost	% of Total	Cue. % Total	Sug. % Weight	Cue. % Total
				Suggested	
Royals					
Freeport CU	1,092,187	6.5%	6.5%	6.5%	6.5%
De Beers	1,053,348	6.3%	12.9%	6.5%	13.0%
Phelps Dodge	1,052,245	6.3%	19.2%	6.5%	19.5%
Amax	1,047,887	6.3%	25.4%	6.5%	26.0%
Minorco	1,047,291	6.3%	31.7%	6.5%	32.5%
Cyprus	1,036,173	6.2%	37.9%	6.5%	39.0%
Ladies in Waiting					
Alcoa	656,311	3.9%	41.9%	4.0%	43.0%
CGF	654,311	3.9%	45.8%	4.0%	47.0%
AAC	646,072	3.9%	49.7%	4.0%	51.0%
Charter	642,219	3.8%	53.5%	4.0%	55.0%
Courtiers					
Anamiat	568,483	3.4%	56.9%	3.5%	58.5%
Reynolds	552,024	3.3%	60.2%	3.5%	62.0%
Alcan	552,278	3.3%	63.5%	3.5%	65.5%
Asarco	548,487	3.3%	66.8%	3.5%	69.0%
Bougainville	523,483	3.1%	69.9%	3.0%	72.0%
Falco	498,202	3.0%	72.9%	3.0%	75.0%
ECC	487,983	2.9%	75.9%	3.0%	78.0%
Whim Creek	416,358	2.5%	78.4%	2.5%	80.5%
JMAT	370,001	2.2%	80.6%	2.3%	82.8%
Englehard	294,985	1.8%	82.3%	1.8%	84.6%
Sub-total	13,739,328	82.3%			
Courtesans	1,202,901	7.2%	82.3%		
Cash	342,500	2.1%			
Unreal. Profit	1,401,417	8.4%			
Total	**16,686,146**	**100.0%**			

Running a fund reminds Julian of his (misspent?) youth.

Running a fund reminds me of my bachelor days – a new temptation every week. I could never resist temptation then but advancing years makes it easier now. I am no longer to be seen chasing anything that moves. From my broking days I know there are some Fund Managers, much favoured by the brokers, who simply cannot resist pursuing the movers. They are obviously nimbler than me. Whenever I try it I am invariably too late. For me it is easier to buy into weakness. (**48. 26/4/89**)

Julian discusses shareholder returns and the importance of dividends when investing in wasting assets like mining shares.

Have you noticed how short a time it takes for directors of companies to convince themselves that they can make better use of your money than you can? I suppose it is only natural. By the time they have clawed their way up to the top of the corporate tree, it must be hard to believe they are not a great deal closer than the rest of us to the Great Investor in the sky who knows it all.

Directors of mining companies are now enjoying the sort of prosperity they could only fantasize about two or three years ago. Now they are making the sort of profits that stockbrokers felt were no less than their due before "big bang" blew them into oblivion.

It is interesting to contrast the behaviour of the directors of gold and base metal companies. When the gold miners were enjoying prosperous times a couple of years ago, they flooded the market with new paper to finance their exploration and expansion plans. Investors were only too keen to buy their paper, thus virtually guaranteeing that sufficient new gold mines would be started to ensure that the gold price would fall to levels which would render the paper they had bought worth less.

Now it is the base metal miners who are prospering. They are flush with cash, but do you think they are taking steps to finance increased production by selling more of their shares to the public? Not a bit of it! They did that in the late 1970's and reaped the whirlwind in the mid 1980s. Far from selling more shares, they are using their cash mountains to buy in some of their existing shares. Rather than increasing productive capacity, they are spending their new found wealth on reducing costs lest base metal prices should ever revert to the crisis levels of a couple of years ago. They have, to give them their due, also been paying rather higher dividends.

By a combination of these actions they try to convince us they are doing all in their power to increase shareholder value. I don't really believe them, do you? I think they would add more to shareholder value if they paid out to their shareholders a much larger slug of their windfall profits. After all we did not complain when we got nothing at all when metal prices were low. We realised that there was nothing the directors could do about metal prices – except try to survive. Having caught sight of the cornucopia, we now want our fair share of the overflow.

So I take a contrary view as to how best to improve shareholder value. I tell the musing company directors I meet that you, the unitholders, would be happier to buy units in the Gold & General Fund if only they offered a reasonable yield. Phelps Dodge can be used as an example of what many North American mining companies could afford to do if they wanted to. The brokers tell me that P.D. will earn between $12–15 per share this year, out of which they are expected to pay a miserly $2.40. This provides a yield of just 4 per cent at the current price of $58. Why shouldn't they at least double the dividend? Then our fund would offer a decent yield, as any fund investing in wasting assets ought to do.

If I could tell you that this fund offered you an annual yield of 5–6 per cent in addition to the near 40 per cent capital gain we managed to achieve in year one, I think you would be sorely tempted to add to your own holdings and tell a few of your friends about the fund too. That could more than double the size of this fund to over £50 million. Where would all the new money go? Back into shares like Phelps Dodge, of course! If only the mining industry could see they have a vested interest in keeping you happy we would all be richer.

Instead of the directors using our money to keep their shares up, the shares would rise on their own because there would be more buyers than sellers in the market place – the best reason I know for shares to go up.

So do we think the directors of mining companies will ever allow the cornucopia to overflow in our direction? You know the answer. If pigs had wings it would be neither sane nor sanitary to go out to lunch!

Meanwhile, back on the ranch, are the directors of gold mining companies buying back their own shares? Of course not. They too recognise their shares are far too expensive, and are they using their expensive paper to take over cheap base metal shares? Not on your life! They could not do that without the risk of damaging their multiples.

I am an unashamed reactionary. I would like to go back to the well-tried nostrums which have stood the test of time. Mining shares are wasting assets and mining companies should pay a decent dividend so we would all know where we stood. Now, everyone is in a muddle and here I am trying to unravel it on your behalf. (53. 25/5/89)

The fund underperforms both gold and gold shares, much to Julian's chagrin.

You have noticed! We are going through one of those depressing periods when the fund is underperforming both gold and gold shares. This gives my peers their chance to say "I told you so", so at least some people are deriving pleasure from our misfortunes! With the advantage of hindsight I should have taken remedial action by taking profits early in September. Then the number of ounces of gold which could have been exchanged for 1,000 units of the fund reached a record peak of just under 3.5 ounces. The charts overleaf show that the rise in the units had become somewhat overextended. If you remember, it was in early September that the shareholders of ConsGold received their cheques from Lord Hanson. I was obviously not the only one buying mining shares in anticipation that some of his money would find its way into the mining market. In the event not much did, which was disappointing. **(65. 29/9/89)**

Julian turns optimistic for mining shares as the first signs of a bottom to the downturn are spotted.

While on the subject of short-termism, I wonder if you have noticed how preoccupied people have become with the timing and magnitude of the "landing" which the world economy is going to make. The closer we get to touchdown, the sooner we can get on with the refuelling which will facilitate the next take-off. If you ask me, the market is in some danger of "falling upstairs". By groping about in the abyss you can sometimes trip on the first step. Markets are supposed to be forward looking. When, I wonder, will they start focusing on the next upturn? Is it really necessary to touch bottom first?

Once people are satisfied that we are past the trough of metal prices for this cycle, they will start discounting the recovery, just as they are doing with gold. In fact there are two metals which are perceived to be at, or close to, their lows of this cycle. One is aluminium, the other is gold. The downside risk in both metals is perceived to be minimal, yet aluminium shares in North America sell on seven times earnings, whereas gold shares are selling at nearer 30 times. No prizes for guessing which ones we hold most of.

All this talk of soft and hard landings has caused mining people to think long and hard about long-term metal prices. If you ask a dozen mining men what metal prices they are factoring into their calculations, their consensus of opinion will shock you deeply. I have been consistently at the low end of the range, but the gap between me and my peers is narrowing. The only thing I know for certain is that when everybody thinks the same way we will all be wrong, but will we be wrong on the high side or the low side? I have a suspicion that we are going to be wrong on the low side. The reason I say this is that I believe that within a year the authorities will be going for growth again and additional production will be needed. Falling interest rates could well lead to a renewal of inflationary pressures. None of this would be bad for metal prices, so once people have concluded that we are through the trough, they may well be prepared to put mining shares on multiples closer to those of the market as a whole. It is not difficult to paint a very bullish scenario for the mining markets along these lines if you want to. (**66. 4/10/89**)

Julian postulates that mining shares are at least as cheap as the general market.

As a contrarian, something tells me not to be a gnu and follow-my-leader! If you think about it, one of the reasons that people are having second thoughts about the general level of markets is fear of excessive corporate borrowing, especially in the States. The mining industry, which used to be heavily in debt, has now reduced its borrowings to very manageable proportions. Although metal prices are falling, prospective multiples, even on lower projected metal prices, compare favourably with those of the market as a whole. As you know, the multiples people pay for trough mining earnings is normally higher than the multiple of the market as a whole. Gold shares on current multiples of 30 are a good example of this as were sky-high multiples of base metal shares during the mid 1980's. All the forecasts of future trough earnings I have seen indicate that mining shares are still selling on prospective multiples that are less than, or similar to, those of the industrial markets. If that is the case, why should I ditch them? (**69. 26/10/89**)

In nostalgic mood Julian returns to the subject of the Christmas Box of mining shares and how the concept came about, and confidently predicts another bumper performance as the festive season looms.

During Christmas week, when markets go dead as the senior practitioners slip away to the sun for their mid-winter break, hoping their departure will escape the notice of those who are required to remain at their posts; the rearguard spends much time eating and drinking and contemplating how lovely it would be if the next 12 months were better than the last. In other words the future tends to be viewed at this season of the year through an alcoholic haze of optimism which gets reflected in share prices albeit on narrow volume. In the old days, the now discontinued practice of year-end window dressing also made its contribution to the seasonal firmness of muting share prices. The mining industry is nothing if not incestuous! A little judicious year-end buying did no harm to published asset values in the bad old days.

I know this because all too often it was I who was left behind to man the fort having been quite unable to convince my colleagues that even one day of my annual holiday entitlement remained unused.

Having nothing better to do, I remember in 1973 setting about calculating the percentage gains that had been made in the past five years by investing in a small portfolio of Mining Finance Houses over the Christmas and New Year periods. To my astonishment I found out that the percentage gain was easily enough to finance the Christmas excesses of the most devoted Bacchanalian. A little further research revealed that the most favourable time to invest was at the start of the three week Christmas stock exchange account and sell at the end of the following account. This was further refined so that purchases are now made on my birthday, 9th December, and profits taken on 31st January.

Of course not everyone wanted to clutter up their portfolios with all ten shares which comprised what we christened the James Capel Christmas Box. Although the Christmas Box idea became well known in mining circles as a result of us bringing it to their attention year after year, few people actually participated, preferring to buy one share which hopefully would be representative of the whole. Sometimes they were lucky in their choice, sometimes unlucky, but the Christmas Box itself managed an impressively consistent performance. It has risen an average of just over 10 per cent each year for the last 20 years during the Christmas Box period.

I particularly remember the Christmas Box of 1979. I was in Australia at the time and the papers were full of the long-term attractions of investing in the mining industry during the decade of the 1980's. If you can believe it, the Christmas Box appreciated 39 per cent between 9th December 1979 and 31st January 1980!

Now, here we are, ten years later at the beginning of a new decade. Mining shares are much cheaper than they were then, selling as they do on between 6–8 times earnings. The gold price has only very recently turned from a bear market into a bull market. Everything looks set for another sterling performance for this year's Christmas Box. (73. 6/12/89)

Julian highlights the issue of risk and then ponders the attractions of the closed Bougainville mine in PNG, the shares of which for decades have fully mirrored the nursery rhyme antics of the grand old Duke of York.

Our portfolio is inevitably exposed to this type of political risk. That is one reason why you should demand a good yield on a Fund like this. Political risk is almost unavoidable with a diversified portfolio. I may not be able to avoid the risk, but being aware of it is to some extent to be forewarned. If we are going to accept the risks, we may as well do so in shares which have fallen a long way like Bougainville rather than in ones like Renison, which is trading within a whisker of its high.

Between 1985 and 1988 when everyone thought there was no greater risk of investing in Bougainville than there was in Porgera, you could exchange between one and two Bougainville shares for one Renison share. The unthinkable has happened to Bougainville and you can now exchange no less than seven Bougainville shares for one share in Renison. I am only a simple Fund Manager, but it seems to me that the value of the metal still left in the ground at Bougainville is proportionately no greater or less than the value of the metal still left in the ground at Porgera. If you believe, as I do, that gold is likely to appreciate in real terms over time, all that has happened is that the Bougainville gold which should have been produced today at a relatively low gold price will stay in the ground and be produced tomorrow at a somewhat higher gold price. As far as copper is concerned I have to admit that my long-term forecast for the copper price is somewhat lower (28 per cent!) than the current price, so it is bad news for Bougainville that it cannot take advantage of current favourable prices for copper.

But who knows, if Bougainville was producing, the copper price might be lower. Overall it would be surprising if the profit margins to be earned when the mine eventually reopens are vastly different from those which would be earned now if the mine was operating normally. The thing that is markedly different is the price of the shares.

Of course the market may well put a lower rating on Bougainville's profits in future due to their recent unfortunate experience with the political risk. That's their privilege, but in my opinion the same lower rating should similarly be applied to Bougainville's more fortunate neighbours. The fact that they have not so far been affected by political risk does not mean the risk does not exist.

Since I contend that the political risk has been discounted more in the shares of Bougainville than it has in the shares of Renison I have been reducing our Renison holding and adding to our holding in Bougainville.

You may think I have finally taken leave of my senses, but the whole purpose of this Newsletter is to let you know what I am doing with your money so that you can form your own opinion about my sanity. If you take the view that I am not sane enough to look after your money, you can always sell your units, which are within a whisker of their all time high. Against all conventional wisdom I just happen to think that the risk/reward ratio is in favour of the stock which has already halved. (**78. 16/1/90**)

The issue of mines as wasting assets is reviewed again.

You know my views. Mines are mines whether they produce gold, nickel or copper. A mine is a wasting asset and its value depends on how much more money you expect to get back over its life than you invested in it in the first place. There is little doubt that we will get our money back in the base metal mines we own but most gold mines haven't a snowflake's chance in hell of giving investors their money back over the life of the mine, unless the gold price goes to levels which most people would not dare to bet on. Of course if gold does go up to those levels, the chart suggests that base metals will follow suit so we won't miss out.

So what I am saying is this. Perhaps the cheapest "gold" share is a Phelps Dodge, RTZ or Amax. I hope so, because we have large holdings in all of them. Not only are base metal prices low at the moment, but the returns offered by base metal shares are better than those offered by gold shares. The time to buy mining shares is when the market is low and when the metal is low. Gold itself may be low, but gold mining shares are anything but low. (**83. 21/2/90**)

Mining shares just get cheaper and cheaper, much to Julian's frustration.

As we have found out all too painfully over the last few weeks, the pursuit of long-term value does not prevent one losing money in the short term. What I believe it will do, however, is enable us to outperform over the long term.

In an attempt to ameliorate the pain, I thought you might like to have the vital statistics of those companies which both Ord Minnett and Capels rate as "super buys" on their slippery slopes. May I remind you, a "super buy" is a share with potential to rise at least 60 per cent from its current level before it becomes a "must sell" on the slippery slope.

For the uninitiated I should explain that the figures under IRR (Internal Rate of Return) tell you the real return the brokers expect from each mining company over the next 20 years at the current share price. These can be compared with the current rate of return of 4.3 per cent obtainable by investing your money in a UK Index Linked Bond of similar maturity.

The PE ratio column shows the number of years it will take for each company to earn its current share price. If it takes eight or nine years just to get your money back in earnings, the remaining 11 or 12 year's earnings provide the potential return on your investment over 20 years. You can see why I don't like buying mining shares on PEs that are higher than their remaining mine life! I know there are anomalies in the tables, but both brokers stand by their figures.

The companies listed below represent 31 per cent of our portfolio. In addition we have large holdings in certain companies which have not yet been analysed for slippery slope purposes such as RTZ, (8.14 per cent of the fund) and DeBeers (3.3 per cent) which will probably qualify as "super buys" when they are analysed in this way.

Price $	ORD MINNETT	IRR %	EPS $ – 1991 – PE	
24.50	Amax	10.32	2.45	10.0
A$ 2.15	N. Broken Hill	9.8	0.26c	8.3
A$ 1.54	Ashton	9.0	0.20c	7.7
A$ 1.25	Bougainville	8.8	n/a	n/a
62.375	Alcoa	7.7	7.60	8.2
20.00	Alcan	6.9	2.38	8.4
57.50	Phelps Dodge	6.6	7.10	8.1
52.25	Reynolds	6.2	5.25	9.9
24.75	Asarco	6.1	2.6	9.4
AS$ 4.52	Western Mining	5.9	0.49c	9.2
	Average	**7.7**		**8.8**

CAPELS	IRR %	EPS -1991-	PE
Amax	14.3	3.22	7.6
N. Broken Hill	14.2	0.30c	7.2
Reynolds	13.6	7.17	7.3
Asarco	13.0	3.52	7.1
Western Mining	12.3	0.62c	7.3
Alcoa	11.9	8.00	7.9
Alcan	11.6	2.60	7.7
Phelps Dodge	10.5	8.90	9.2
Bougainville	9.7	n/a	n/a
Ashton	8.8	0.20	7.7
Average	**11.99**	**7.67**	

In addition to the "super buys" mentioned above, there are a number of companies in the portfolio which are rated as "must buys" by the brokers, namely shares which offer a return more than 50 per cent higher than the return offered by an Index Linked Bond. Included in this category are shares like Freeport McMoran, Franco Nevada, Teck, Cyprus Minerals, Comalco and Freeport Copper. These account for a total of 17 per cent of the fund.

Lastly in the "safe" category we have the South African Bonds which help to keep our yield of 4.3 per cent in place. They account for about 5 per cent of the whole.

Thus you can see that at least 65 per cent of the fund is invested to give a real return of 50 per cent more than that offered by an Index Linked Bond.

What's left is mainly gold shares. These have been giving me a headache since they will not give the required returns unless the gold price itself goes up in real terms as it looked as if it was starting to do around the year-end.

It is particularly galling to have had to suffer our recent losses which, as you know, I did my best to avoid should the gold price falter. It was this fear that caused me to try to buy "paper gold" last December. The metal has in fact fallen far less than the shares and is far more marketable so we would have been comparatively well off if the rules had permitted us to invest in the real thing. (See Issue No 74)

Secondly, by restricting our exposure to gold shares to about one third of the Fund and concentrating on the better value base metal miners, I thought we would be protected if things went wrong for gold. In fact the prices of base metal shares have fallen more than 20 per cent this year whereas most metals are now higher than they were on average in the last quarter of last year. As you can see there is no justice in this world, just better and better value. (**91. 2/5/90**)

The human/social problems of closing mines.

Some people think that mine closures will soon cause supply and demand to be brought into line. I think it may take rather longer. It is not just the mining companies' reluctance to close down mines when they become unprofitable, it is the knock-on effect on whole communities which attracts the attention of government and makes the decision making process so tortuous. The evil day is delayed or postponed in the hope that divine intervention will cause a stay of execution. (**98. 20/6/90**)

Wars tend to be bullish for metal prices and, with Kuwait being a major oil producer, there is also the prospect of inflation to help gold.

The invasion of Kuwait was interpreted bullishly by the commodity markets. Wars use up considerable quantities of largely irrecoverable metals and some people remembered that metal prices were strong during the Korean and Vietnam wars.

You will have noticed that the shares of the leading base metal producers suffered badly in the stock market collapse which followed the invasion. It was interesting to compare their performance with the performance of the metals themselves. Metal prices were unchanged to firmer. In contrast, metal shares were down between 3 and 6 per cent in a day. What have investors in commodities heard that investors in commodity shares have not?

Gold held its value as it often does on these occasions, but it did not increase as much as some people thought it might. Gold shares held steady but the marginals we hold need a strongly rising gold price to really show their paces. They could still get it. Last week I drew your attention to how cheap gold had become relative to oil. If the rise in the oil price is inflationary then gold should benefit from that. If it is deflationary, real interest rates should fall and high real interest rates are poison to the gold price. (**105. 8/8/90**)

Julian returns to the subject of mining companies selling at a discount to their underlying assets, and again highlights Minorco, Anglo's overseas mining vehicle.

To my way of thinking there is logic in mining companies selling at a discount to their assets. After all, most of them are fairly fully invested all the time and when markets are depressed they would probably find it hard to sell their assets for their full market value should they need to do so.

Should they decide to sell one asset and buy another, the chances are that the company they bought would, in the short term, provide much the same return as the company they sold. Shareholders would not notice much difference in the short term.

The point I am making is that buying the shares of a mature, fully invested Mining Finance House is unlikely to provide an investor with as good a return as he could have obtained for himself by buying the underlying assets of that Mining House; unless, of course, the Mining House were to sell at a substantial discount to its underlying assets – which is normally the case.

The interesting exception to this rule occurs when a substantial proportion of a mining company's assets are in cash. If Minorco, for instance, thought it could obtain say a 10 per cent real return by buying BP Mineral's interest in Olympic Dam for US$460 millon (as it says it wants to) an investor in Minorco itself would get a better return than 10 per cent since he is able to buy US$460 million of the same cash for US$276 million because Minorco sells at a 40 per cent discount to its assets. So, whereas Minorco would receive a return of 10 per cent on the money it invests in the project, an investor buying the same project through Minorco would receive a return of 16.6 per cent. Using exactly the same money. Obvious, really, when you put it that way.

Since commentators generally seem to approve of Minorco's attempt to buy into a world-class mineral deposit with a 200-year life in a stable country, Australia, I thought we should do so too by buying Minorco shares at a 40 per cent discount.

I have therefore invested about 5 per cent of the Fund in that company. It is reassuring to note that the shares are now gaining increasing favour with the broking fraternity who, one after the other, are putting out buy recommendations on the stock, just as they did recently and successfully with Placer Dome. Let's hope they are as right with their recommendation of Minorco as they were with Placer Dome! (**195. 11/11/92**)

7. Gold Shares and Elephant Traps

In the eyes of many of his City peers Julian Baring was simply the "gold guru" who, as a broker, topped the Extel Analysts survey in the gold sector for many years. As an investor, he was a believer in getting the trend right and then positioning himself in the most appropriate way to benefit from the sector's rise. This led him to spend long periods underinvested in gold shares, and when the market started to run he would buy the marginal South African gold mines rather than the lower cost leaders in order to gain maximum exposure to the inherent leverage in marginal mines as gold rose. His interest in gold shares was primarily in the South African sector, which was still the dominant market when the Fund was launched. Having said that, Julian was always on the lookout for value in gold shares wherever he could find it.

Julian underlines the importance of return from gold shares, quotes Warburg to support his view, and also points out the way that over his career the valuations on gold and mining shares have yawed around unpredictably.

In mid August, Warburg Securities published an interesting circular on the subject of US Gold Mining Shares. Since I entirely agree with its findings, I would like to share them with you. I am sure they won't mind! After all some of us at Capels have been saying much the same thing ourselves but not so pithily.

Speaking about the valuation of North American gold shares they say:

"The main relative valuation tools remain price/earnings and price/cashflow ratios, capitalization per annual ounce, and, occasionally, ore reserve ounces per share. All give widely disparate values and none are really satisfactory so we have re-investigated a simple form of the net present value method. Keeping it very simple we have merely discounted at 10 per cent our estimates of net earnings in present day terms that would be derived from presently declared measured and indicated ore reserves."

In other words they have gone back to basics. They have come to the earth-shattering conclusion that if you put your money into a hole in the ground, you should do so in the expectation that you will get more money out of the hole over the life of the mine than you put in in the first place – plus interest. They want a return of 10 per cent per annum, so they have discounted their estimated net earnings at 10 per cent per annum.

Personally I think 10 per cent is a bit high – 5 per cent would be enough. After all gold is meant to at least keep pace with inflation, so to ask for 10 per cent on top of that seems a little greedy. However, if they think that is reasonable, who am I to argue? Perhaps it explains why some of them are so rich!

What is important to me is that a firm of Warburg's standing has had the courage to come out in public and print the words I have underlined. It reminds me of the boy in Hans Andersen's fairy tale who drew the attention of the crowd to the fact that the Emperor had no clothes! You will remember, everyone knew the Emperor had no clothes, but were too polite to say so.

The broker who has a go at changing the market's current perception that the only mine worth owning is a gold mine, is going to make a fortune for his firm if he succeeds. I know, because I am partly responsible for the market gaining that perception in the first place. When I first started it was conventional wisdom that the owner of a mine which produced that "barbarous relic", gold, was a mug. What you had to do, to make your portfolio perform, was to buy the Mining Houses. Hands up all those who know what multiple RTZ, De Beers, Anglo American and Selection Trust sold on in the early 1970's. You wouldn't believe me if I told you, so different were they to today's.

Some of you may remember what people used to say, which was that every time they bought a gold share, they found to their horror that it was a Mining House that had sold it to them and vice versa. Needless to say, since the Mining House knew more about gold shares than the average punter, it was the Mining Houses who invariably made the share dealing profits.

In due course, the punters recognised that buying gold shares was a mug's game and that the smart thing to do was to buy the Mining Houses direct and let them make the share dealing profits.

Changing that perception was a real uphill struggle, since Mining House shares had become star performers and gold shares were wasting assets which required yields of between 10 and 15 per cent to take care of the amortisation. Now, gold shares yield almost nothing and Mining Houses are virtually given away. C'est la vie.

But you didn't buy the Fund to read about my curriculum vitae. You will just have to trust me not to miss the turn round in the gold market when it comes. I'll certainly be trying not to. **(19. 26/8/88)**

Julian reiterates his view that gold shares are expensive equities at the moment, complains that mines of longer-term interest to him have sold gold forward, somewhat de-linking from the metal, and notes that the Fund cannot buy gold metal.

I have pointed out many times before that gold shares are equities, so I find myself between a rock and a hard place. Not only are gold shares equities, but they are expensive equities. Authorised unit trusts such as this one are not allowed to buy the metal. Some ingenuity has to be employed to make sure that we are not left behind if the gold price does in fact break upwards, without taking too much risk if it does not.

I have been altering the percentage holdings in the portfolio to give greater emphasis to gold related investments and slightly less emphasis on the more general investments. I will be more specific when I have completed this programme. Don't worry, what I am doing is not a change of course, it is more like an adjustment to the sails.

The difficulty I face is that many of the gold mining companies I would like to buy for a breakout of the gold price, have already sold forward a significant proportion of their future gold production for the next three years. Therefore they will not get the full benefit of the higher gold price even if it occurs.

In other words gold shares don't look cheap enough relative to gold. Unfortunately, the powers that be won't allow us to buy the metal even though it is much less volatile than the shares. If any of my readers can come up with a gold look alike which would not fall out of bed if equity markets collapse, I hope they will tell me. Otherwise perhaps you could embark on a little gentle lobbying of the Powers that Be. (**31. 6/12/88**)

Gold shares continue to rally but Julian is sceptical of the value on offer.

I have to admit that this continuing rally in the international gold share markets is unnerving but try as I may I still cannot find as good value in the gold share market as I can in other areas of the mining markets. Therefore I think I must say to you again, as I have in the past, that if you believe that we are on the brink of a breakout in gold and gold shares which I am not anticipating you would probably be better off in a fund more heavily weighted in gold shares than this one is. I have to tell you this from time to time although it hurts me to do so. Those who have stayed this far have done better than those who have left, however I accept that one day it may be right to be more heavily weighted in gold shares than I am, and it is going to be difficult for me to rearrange our portfolio in good time. I repeat, I still don't think it is right to move heavily into gold shares, otherwise I would already be starting to do so. You, as individuals, have more flexibility than I do if you want to move quickly. Not only is it difficult for me to alter course quickly, I also happen to think it would be wrong to do so. I am not going to change tack until I am sure.

Consider for a moment the reasons why the siren voices are encouraging us to buy gold shares now. They draw attention to the rising levels of worldwide inflation which are causing the authorities so much concern at the moment. Do you think you can have falling commodity prices at tunes of rising inflation? I rather doubt it. If copper is going to go up alongside gold as people seek to buy real assets as a hedge against inflation, why should gold shares on multiples of 20 be preferable to base metal shares on multiples of 4–6?

The other side of the same coin seems to me to be the fear in the minds of investors that the measures taken by the authorities to combat inflation through high interest rates may cause a recession. Obviously that would be no good for base metals but I can't see why gold would be a beneficiary. Normally high interest rates are bad for gold since it increases the cost of holding it. Last time gold did well at a time of high inflation in the late 1970's, Bonds offered investors a negative rate of return; a far cry from the present situation where high real rates of return are available on Bonds as interest rates rise. Bond holders were caught by negative interest rates too recently to have already forgotten the lessons learned so painfully at that time. (45. 30/3/89)

Julian worries about missing the real turn in the gold market but cannot bring himself to jump early.

What I must not do is miss the real turn in the gold market when it comes. When it does come I must have enough cash ready to grasp the opportunities. I do not want to find myself scrambling to get out of existing holdings at bad prices in order to get into gold shares at strongly rising prices. In order to do the right thing I will have to force myself to sell too early, a difficult enough thing to do when multiples are high, let alone when they are at record lows. Getting the balance right is what you are paying a management fee for. For the moment you should know that running this Fund is like driving in fog. I am not doing anything adventurous until it lifts. If all this makes you feel you should not be adding to your holdings just yet, I would only remark that by trying to double guess the market you will probably miss it. One of us guessing at a time is quite enough and without your participation I won't have the wherewithal to buy the bargains when they present themselves. (48. 26/4/89)

Julian alludes to the public service side of the Fund, whereby he buys stock when everyone is selling and sells stock when everyone is buying. He also revisits the issue of getting your money and more back over the life of a gold mine.

Some people think that gold is money. Is it? If it is, then a gold mine is a money mine. If you invest in a money mine you should surely expect to get more money out of the mine than you put into it in the first place. Believe it or not, most people who invest in gold mines don't seem to mind that they have little hope of getting more money back than they put in. Perhaps they think they will get lucky and sell their shares to someone else on the greater fool theory. At anything like current gold prices, there isn't an earthly hope of getting your money back in earnings over the life of the average gold mine (except certain South African mines) yet when the gold price rose a few dollars last week on the news from China, the telephone never stopped ringing. "Get in," they said, "it's your last chance to buy gold shares." I felt like Lady Godiva without her hair. As you know, we have less gold shares in our portfolio than Lady Godiva had goldilocks!

There is an old saying: "When the ducks quack, feed them." We did, and now we have even fewer gold shares than we had before!

I was reminded of the Bateman cartoons. The man who ... A budding cartoonist in the office put pen to paper to show you how I felt when everyone was buying and we were selling, it's a lonely feeling I can assure you!

Now that the gold price has fallen and the shares are cheaper than when we sold them, I feel better. Even now I am summoning up the courage to buy them back when the ducks decide to sell what they have so recently bought. They won't until after 30th June if you ask me.

This Fund seems to perform a public service in that it sells gold shares when the crowd wants to buy them and buys them from the crowd when the crowd wants to sell them – provided we can do so at a profit. So far this has worked well but there will come a time when we will buy them and hold them. Then you will see we are a gold Fund after all! **(55. 13/6/89)**

Julian returns to the issue of buying marginals, rather than low-cost producers, when the gold price starts to run.

You all know where I think the best value lies in the mining markets, but no one seems to care about value when exposure to the "barbarous relic" is what is required. Gold rules people's hearts, not their heads. Once a new bull market gets going in gold shares, you can expect to enjoy a few months during which the game of "pass the parcel" can be played with impunity. At times like this, gold shares are for trading in, not investing.

Because it looked at the end of last week as if the party was about to start, I did not wait for the lights to go up before significantly increasing our gold exposure. Forty five per cent of the fund is now gold-orientated as opposed to about 20 per cent last time I wrote to you. I shall increase this exposure further as opportunities present themselves, but not at any price, because it seems to me that the falls in base metal shares are already being overdone. What is needed is a well-rehearsed balancing act. You must be wondering whether Blondin Baring is the right man to carry you across the great divide!

Since the fund is too large to move entirely into gold, I have decided to go for the rather more highly leveraged shares on the basis that if gold moves to the $420 level, for instance, we want to reap the maximum advantage for the minimum exposure. Needless to say this policy goes against the advice of most of the broking fraternity who keep urging me to buy only the lowest cost producers. This is exactly the right advice when the gold price is falling, but we don't like to be holding gold shares at all when the gold price is falling!

What we are doing, rightly or wrongly, is taking the view that the gold price has broken out of its two-year bear trend. When it is widely perceived to have done so, people will want to buy the shares which will benefit most from an upward trend in the gold price, not the ones which will benefit least.

Obviously the shares which will benefit most are those which were feeling the pinch the most before a rising gold price came to their rescue. This policy will enable us to continue to hold a significant exposure to the leading mining companies which provide the good, safe long-term value that we seek. (**70. 31/10/89**)

The Fund begins to change its balance towards favouring gold shares over more general mining counters, and Julian reminds us of the perspicacity of his astrologer friend.

As George Seebohm used to say "the market is very seldom wrong!", yet everything I read and write has been saying that gold shares are crazily overvalued. Everyone, that is, except the astrologer I told you about in Newsletter 58 who said that a great bull market for gold, and by implication the shares, was going to start in August 1989 and last a year. I pooh-poohed him then, but I wouldn't pooh-pooh him now. You need a good miracle to make people believe. I call a 43 per cent rise in the FT Gold Mines Index since August the nearest thing you will get to a good miracle in 1989.

If what I am saying makes any sense to you, the implication is that I am currently being over-cautious with our money. From now on I shall invest all the new money which is pouring into the Fund into a mixture of gold shares and paper gold until two thirds of the Fund is in gold and gold related assets and one third is in general mining shares. This is a major change of policy and you should be the first to know about it.

At present we are about 50/50 Gold and General but the gold shares I have bought are generally the most marginal ones, namely those which will respond best to an improving gold price. In that way you get maximum bang for your buck but have less of your wealth exposed to the risks. Buying paper gold will greatly reduce our risk and will counterbalance the volatility of the type of share I am buying. (**72. 30/11/89**)

As the Fund finally begins to build up its gold exposure, Julian runs into EU (then European Community) problems with his desire to hold on to paper gold.

I have greatly appreciated your uncomplaining support over what has been a rather frustrating three months. We are now well on the way towards getting the portfolio looking how I want it to, namely, one third in mining shares, one third in paper gold, one third in bonds and gold equities. I am constrained to some extent by my determination to keep the Fund's yield as close as possible to 5 per cent. That in itself may be no bad thing. It discourages me from buying speculative, non yielding prospecting and developing companies. Obviously the more paper gold I buy, the more difficult it will be to compensate for the lack of yield on the gold portion of the portfolio. The lesser volatility of gold compared with gold shares and its superior marketability should certainly reassure you that your sleep will not be interrupted by some calamity which results in my being unable to sell if I want to. Gold is a very liquid investment, you can always sell it in quantity. The same is not always true of gold shares.

I hope you are sitting down. Since writing the previous paragraph the trustees, who had previously approved our purchase of paper gold, discovered that although there is nothing in the UK rules to prevent us from holding paper gold, the UCITS regulations which govern all authorised unit trusts in the European Community specifically preclude us from acquiring either precious metals or certificates representing them. We have therefore been obliged to sell the least volatile portion of our portfolio, namely the holdings of paper gold which I had been acquiring. Life was not meant to be easy, but to preclude people from holding the less speculative investment does not seem either sensible or reasonable. We must try and get the rules changed. Do you know anyone that could help? (**74. 14/12/89**)

Julian worries both about his post-Christmas liver and a weakening gold price.

The gold price is reacting rather like my liver to the excesses of the Christmas festivities. No matter, the brokers reassure me, gold won't fall below its 200 day moving average of $380/oz. The trouble is that if it does, they have no contingency plan – we are on our own! The closer the gold price gets to $380, the more nervous everyone will become and the more reluctant to buy gold shares for fear of what will happen to them if the $380 line is breached. I know we humanoids should not behave like this, but we do! (**76. 4/1/90**)

Julian starts to worry that the market is beginning to reassess, negatively, the value of gold producers, as gold stumbles and gold production begins to rise – anticipating the ten years of pain that stretched into the new millennium.

My principal worry at this time is not that the gold price is behaving badly per se, but that we may be witnessing the start of a reassessment by the market of the values placed on the shares of the producers. Anyone who has worked in the mining business for more than a few years remembers only too well the collapse in base metal shares in the mid 1980's, following the inflationary excesses of the late 1970's. The present generation of mining company executives will certainly not forget. The survivors lived through five years of sheer misery as metal prices resolutely refused to rise to levels which provided them with a profit. On the contrary, they had to wage a seemingly unending battle for survival by reducing costs to levels which many would have sworn were unachievable at the beginning of the decade. They were forced into this because prices of base metals fell, for five whole years, to levels in real terms not seen since the great depression of the 1930's.

There was no point in exploration geologists finding new base metal deposits when most mining companies could not make a profit from those they were already mining. The bankers would not finance them even if they did. Between 90–95 cents in every exploration dollar was therefore spent looking for gold. Although gold had fallen from the dizzy peaks of 1980, it still achieved average prices throughout the 1980's which provided the producers with a respectable return.

If the mining industry spent the lion's share of every exploration dollar for the best part of a decade, looking for one metal, it should surprise nobody that they found such a lot of it as to depress the price! This seems to be exactly what has happened with gold, but still the price has not fallen far enough to stop the expansion in production, although there are signs of it slowing down significantly. (**96. 6/6/90**)

Julian points out that his favouring of base metal shares over gold shares has led to G&G outperforming peer funds with a heavy weighting towards gold.

For the best part of ten years, the mining industry has been mining more base metals than it has been finding. If world growth continues for another two or three years at anything like the rate we have seen in the recent past, the dearth of new production will really make itself felt in the mid 1990's. It looks as if there is a real possibility of a base metal boom in the making. Will you be a beneficiary of this or will near term discomfort have shaken you out of your units?

As you know, I had already factored in the point our mining friends were making. That is why the Fund is so light in gold shares (25 per cent) and so heavily weighted towards the base metals. Notwithstanding this, my colleague Rob Weinberg's devastating speech to the Boston Gold Show which was reported in last Saturday's *Financial Times*, and to a lesser extent my own cautious remarks about gold shares in last week's letter, unsettled a number of you and resulted in some redemptions.

I cannot stop the markets doing whatever they have to do, any more than King Canute could stop the tide coming in. What I can do is to take precautions and this I have been doing, not altogether unsuccessfully, I hope you will agree. Since the Fund started in April 1988 it has risen some 35 per cent compared with a fall of about 5 per cent in the average gold sector fund, according to the Micropal statistics.

I have explained in recent letters how the Fund has avoided being swept away by the fall in gold shares and I have described how the Fund's investments have been structured to take advantage of the opportunities in the base metals that we have identified. There is not a lot I can do about short-term market fluctuations caused by short-term movements in metal prices without running too great a risk of being excessively liquid when the recovery starts. (**97. 13/6/90**)

With Minorco beaten by Lord Hanson for Consolidate Gold Fields, Julian thought that Hanson's stake in Newmont would be difficult to sell because of its high valuation.

Well how wrong I was! No lesser figure than Jimmy Goldsmith has acquired the stake in exchange for his forestry interests. Would you believe it? Lord Hanson has suddenly decided he would rather be involved with chopping things down than digging things up. He has bought Goldsmith's forests for $1.3 billion and that gives Goldsmith exactly the amount required to buy Newmont. "Not called Goldsmith for nothing", I can hear you say.

Has Sir James bought value? After all, if you think about it, Newmont has said that it controls 20 million ounces of gold in the ground. Capels have assumed that they will find more and have credited them with 24 millin ounces. That implies that Goldsmith has paid $116 for every ounce in the ground. Newmont tells us it costs $214 to dig each ounce up and their overheads are at least $50 per ounce, so just to break even, a gold price of $416 (in 1990 dollars) will be needed over the life of the mine. A mining company wanting to take over Newmont would require a real return of not less than 6.5 per cent, which is what we try to achieve. This return would require a gold price in 1990 dollars of $509/oz over the remaining life, compared with today's price of $367. Sir James is obviously content with a much lower rate of return than that, regarding Newmont as a preferable alternative to gold bullion which, unless it rises, gives no return at all.

This simple arithmetic makes me think that there may be more to this deal than meets the eye. You cannot help but admire people who are prepared to make such huge bets using their own money. Sir James does not have the appearance of a masochist to me so he must be taking a very bearish view of everything else to take that sort of gamble on gold. He may well be right but if he had wanted to back his judgement, he would have found it impossible to do so in the normal way in that size. Hence the attraction of acquiring the Newmont stake. Being rather smaller, we have greater flexibility as to timing. I share Sir James' view that gold will have its day again, but I see its role as helping to solve a financial crisis not to prevent one. Gold shares are equities. What worries me is what might happen to equities in the meantime.

I mention all this because it helps to explain why I have been so reluctant to follow the fashion for buying gold shares on sky-high multiples, preferring to stay with the base metal producers and marginal gold shares. The galling thing is that this conservative approach has not protected us more, though there are signs that our policy may at last be starting to pay off. The leading gold shares are now suffering a serious disease known as "multiple contraction" and are now falling faster than the marginals we own. These are beginning to be seen for what they are, an option on the gold price. The whole point of options is that you don't have to commit much money to them while you are waiting for what you expect to happen. I view many of the marginal gold mines as a cheap 20-year option on the gold price. Newmont Mining may be an option on the gold price but it certainly cannot be described as a cheap one. (**113. 18/10/90**)

While again scratching his head over sky-high gold shares valuations, Julian forecasts that with gold production running behind demand the gold mines able to survive will eventually reap their rewards as gold recovers.

With gold at current levels there are an uncomfortable number of companies which do not make $30/oz profit. Most make more than that if you just take the cash costs of producing an ounce of gold. But shareholders are often surprised at the paucity of the net profits attributable to them, even from those companies which boast of having cash costs of around $200/oz. If companies reported net profits per ounce instead of earnings per share, all would be revealed. But they will not do that, for who wants to be seen producing a precious and rare metal at a profit of less than the cost of replacing it.

As you know I have difficulty in understanding why an industry in such a pickle commands share market ratings so much higher than that of the market as a whole. That is why this gold fund only has about 20 per cent of its resources exposed to that industry. The market is at last beginning to twig that all may not be well and the prices of the most popular gold shares have started to fall quite severely in recent weeks, as Lord Hanson and others know only too well!

It occurs to me that a miner has to sell his gold in order to pay the wages, whereas the buyer of the metal itself has the advantage of being able to wait for his profit. The buyer of the gold itself knows that the industry is replacing less gold than it is mining, so he deduces that those companies which cannot replace their reserves or who pay too much to do so will be forced out of business. Those companies which have plenty of reserves in the ground will still be around to enjoy the extra profits that higher gold prices will eventually bring even if they have a very lean time while they are waiting. After all, there comes a time when businesses are valued in their assets rather than on their earnings stream as any farmer will tell you. (**114. 25/10/90**)

Julian finds an ally in Canadian broker First Marathon who cannot see value in market favourite Hemlo even after a 50 per cent fall in less than a year.

It has been some time since I tried to spell out my investment policy and how I see the outlook. My recent letters have been stressing the lack of value available in the golds despite the severe falls seen this year. For example, the Toronto Gold and Silver Index is down 36 per cent from its February 1990 high, but some senior stocks have done worse than that.

As you can see, we have done badly ourselves – but not that badly!

Surely, I can hear you say, after such huge falls you should be buying. Not according to First Marathon Securities who put it this way in their latest missive.

> "Let us look for example, at Hemlo Gold. In its most recent quarter, Hemlo reported earnings of $0.13 per share, with revenues averaging US$400/ ounce. There were no unusual items. If we assume a similar relationship between revenues and costs for the remainder of the 20 year mine life, this means that Hemlo Gold shareholders can expect total undiscounted earnings of approximately $10 per share ($0.50 x 20). For those who think that this is somewhat simplistic, we should point out that since Hemlo's Golden Giant mine opened in 1986, the company has, to date, reported an average less than $0.50 per share in earnings despite consistently mining above ore reserve grade. Hemlo currently pays out $0.20 per share in annual dividends so that the current dividend yield is just over 2%.

On this basis, Hemlo, even after a 50% drop in price over the last ten months, does not appear to be a bargain and continues to have absolutely no appeal to those who value companies using rigorous fundamental methods. A similar comment can be made about many of the other senior golds."

If anything, I think First Marathon are being rather generous! According to work carried out for me by Smith New Court, Hemlo needs a gold price of $533 for the rest of its life in order for a buyer at today's price to get his money back, let alone a return on his money.

So, despite the fact that gold shares have had such a large fall, I am not inclined to commit our precious cash to them just yet.

What I do think, however, is that sooner or later the market will get it into its head that the growing lack of profitability of the gold mining industry will soon lead to cutbacks and closures, just as it did with the base metals industry in the 1980's. At some point, and it is not yet, investors will take the view that insufficient gold is being produced to satisfy the growing needs of the jewellery industry. The same fears exactly, that affected the market in 1970 when gold was $35/oz and the jewellery industry was consuming every ounce produced.

At that point investors will return to the gold market just as they did in the early 1970's and their entry will probably coincide with a reduction in the real rates of return currently offered by bonds which make it so unattractive for investors to hold the metal at present.

I am addressing this situation by holding the nearest things I can find to options on the gold price, committing the minimum amount of money for the maximum amount of gearing. I hold those companies which will rise the most when the gold price turns, namely the marginals – a high risk policy, since some of our mines may not live to tell the tale. That is why I keep a relatively small exposure to each and only 10 per cent of the Fund altogether in this type of share. (**118. 21/11/90**)

One of Julian's biggest coups was the Fund's stake in Western Areas, the buying of which he likens to taking out a cheap option on the gold price.

As you know the Fund has built up its liquidity in recent months and now has about 30 per cent in cash and bonds of one sort or another – hence the yield.

Despite the fact that gold shares, worldwide, have been falling – in some cases quite dramatically – the Fund in recent weeks has remained comparatively unmoved around the 51p level. Part of the reason for this is that the 20 per cent of the Fund which is invested in gold shares is invested in marginal mines which have already taken a beating and are unlikely to fall much further. Mining shares are usually valued on the basis of what they can earn. But when the gold price falls to levels at which they cannot earn anything, they become valued as an option on the gold price.

To give you an example; Western Areas, a marginal South African gold mine with costs of $380/oz is only likely to make any profit at current gold prices because it is selling its production forward. In other words, you can no longer value it on its earnings potential since there are virtually no earnings. Because of this the shares have fallen to levels where each ounce of gold in its reserves is valued by the market at only $7. If, by a miracle, the gold price was to go up to $500/oz, the profits of Western Areas would rise from between $5–$10/oz to $105–$110/oz. Where else could you buy a 15-year option on the gold price rising to $500/oz at a cost of only $7/oz?

Generally speaking I take the view that the gold price itself has little downside from current levels because there are an increasing number of mines, like Western Areas, which are having to phase out uneconomic production in order to stay in business. Cutbacks and closures will start having an effect on the gold supply in 1991 or 1992 and this may well encourage investors to think of gold as a one way bet.

Although a good case can be made for suggesting that the gold price may not have much further to fall, it is quite another matter to suggest that it is likely to rise far enough in the near future to justify the current price of the average gold share. To my mind, it is much more likely that gold shares will fall to reflect the current gold price than it is for the gold price to rise to justify current share prices. **(119. 29/11/90)**

The impending war to reclaim Kuwait from Iraq fails to move the gold price and gold shares.

The fact that we appear, at the time of writing, to be on the brink of war would normally be expected to stimulate interest in gold and gold shares. When it appeared that war might be averted the base metal component of our portfolio rose in sympathy with Wall Street and our golds declined. The reverse occurred when it appeared that war was becoming more likely. If someone had told you six months ago that war was going to break out in the Middle East, and at the same time there was going to be a banking crisis in the United States, you could surely be forgiven for thinking that gold, the so-called asset of last resort, would be heading skywards. In the event very little has happened.

It is all your fault! If you, the public, buy gold funds, the funds have to buy gold shares. Since the funds are probably already underinvested, a little buying interest on your part could well create a bit of a scramble. It has not happened so far but it could. This Fund, as an extreme example, is only invested as to about 30 per cent in gold shares because I can find so little value in them at current gold prices. That would all change with gold at US$500/oz but the metal shows little signs of wanting to head in that direction at the moment. (**123. 10/1/91**)

Julian continues to take a relatively upbeat attitude towards the South African gold mining industry, believing that the poor experience elsewhere in Africa will save it from nationalisation and that a recovery in the gold price, and therefore the Fund's marginal mines, may not be far away.

The fact that people in South Africa are so depressed about the gold mining industry may be no bad thing. In its current state it hardly seems propitious for the ANC to embark on a policy of nationalisation. Neither is there much point in increasing taxation on an industry, one third of which is making a loss. When push comes to shove therefore, a more representative government may well turn out to be more rather than less sympathetic to the plight of the gold mining industry, particularly to the marginal mines, since a great mass of potentially redundant miners are about to become voters.

It will be all too easy for an aspiring member of parliament to point out that the present government's policy of protecting the value of the rand will lead to mass unemployment in the gold mining industry. It will not have escaped the leaders of the NUM and others that you can pay a miner whatever he wants if you allow the rand to fall far enough, though what he will be able to buy with his enhanced pay packet is another matter. The present government pursued exactly that policy, until recently, for slightly different reasons and no unemployment resulted until the policy was reversed. My own guess is that a future government will not be able to stomach the political consequences of a strong rand for long and that the surviving marginal mines will be the greatest beneficiaries of any weakening in their resolve to protect the currency. If you doubt me, visit Zimbabwe.

There is much discussion about the power wielded by the National Union of Mineworkers and fears are expressed that the mining industry could all too easily go the way of the Zambian copper mines. I had the opportunity of meeting Mr Cyril Ramaphosa, the Secretary General of the NUM, during my visit and he left me in no doubt that he was well briefed on all sides of the argument. He certainly came across as a person you could do business with. What is often overlooked is that he too has a constituency. The fact that his answer to a question, particularly a trick question, may not always satisfy the questioner is certainly no reflection on his ability to understand the consequences of his actions.

You may not be surprised to hear that much of my time was spent discussing with people in the gold industry whether my rather unconventional policy of buying the marginal mines, rather than the leaders which everyone recommends except Williams de Broe, is justified by the facts. I was particularly keen to gain reassurance that the mines we are holding are not going to be the stretcher cases; in other words that their parent Mining Houses will find it worthwhile to ensure their survival through this tricky period in order to continue to derive management fees when better times come.

I am satisfied that most, if not all the mines we hold, will be helped by their "parents" to survive a low gold price for a couple of years or so if there is a harvest in the end worth reaping. I think that any adverse effects on the gold mining industry brought about by a change of government in South Africa will be felt less by the marginal mines than by the leaders. I think that the bearish sentiment about the gold price is reaching fever pitch. I think that the South African gold mining industry is in a better position to survive a period of low gold prices than the gold mining industries of other countries, partly because it has more fat to shed than do its competitors and partly because South Africa has more to lose through the demise of its gold mining industry than have other countries. I think that the eventual lifting of sanctions will add some foreign investment to an already buoyant local demand for South African equities. This demand for equities should overflow into the depressed gold sector as soon as there is any renewed hope for the gold price.

You have to buy shares when nobody wants them. This week I bought a quarter of a million Venterspost for £55,000. A year ago those same shares would have cost me £275,000. I know because I paid that much for them a year ago! Last week I bought a quarter of a million Libanon for £62,500. A year ago they would have cost £330,000. As far as I know both companies still have roughly the same amount of gold in their ground as they had a year ago. It's just valued differently, that's all.

One day you and I are going to wake up to find that gold in the ground is valuable after all. While the price is low the industry should be mining as little of it as possible. Why mine something valuable and sell it at a loss? So long as the gold price is below the long-term cost of digging it out, gold is more valuable if left in the ground. I perceive that gold is beginning to look cheap if you think of it as a currency and is obviously cheap if you think of it as a commodity. If that were not so, the jewellery industry would not have been able to absorb all new annual production plus some 800 tonnes of forward sales as well. (**127. 27/2/91**)

Julian's optimism that his buying of marginal mines will be vindicated in due course by a strengthening gold price remains undimmed.

I personally believe that the necessary steps can and will be taken to ensure the survival of most but not all of the marginal mines and I am backing this hunch with our money in the belief that too much is at stake for many of them to be allowed to fail. Being cautious by nature I have also increased our exposure to some of the low-cost mines on the grounds that if I am proved wrong about the marginals and they go out of business then the consequent rise in the gold price will benefit the higher-cost mines which, unlike their foreign competitors, have resisted the temptation to sell their production forward.

If you think about it, gold bottomed on 25th February 1991 at $357.5/oz which was then the equivalent of R970/oz. Today the gold price is only $4 higher but the equivalent rand price is now R985/oz. Things are not always what they seem. All that has to happen is for gold to go up $10/oz and the rand to fall a further 10 per cent against the dollar and hey presto, you have a gold price in rand terms which used to be the equivalent of $425/oz back in February!

Better still, the great majority of investors have not noticed what is going on. When did you last see an article extolling the virtues of gold shares in a Sunday newspaper for instance? The only articles I have seen have been those which point out that in the last six months, unit trusts which specialise in gold shares have been among the worst performing funds in the entire universe, and so they have! If many people seriously thought that they might be the best performing funds in the next six months, they certainly would not be languishing at their present levels. My guess is that gold-based unit trusts will be among the best performers in the next six months. Would anyone care to bet against that? (**130. 21/3/91**)

Gold remains becalmed, but Julian reveals that the Fund has been buying gold shares in recent weeks.

Just so with gold. Neither you nor I have the faintest idea what the gold price is going to be this afternoon let alone in one or two years time! All I know is that when it goes up everyone will expect it to go higher and if it goes down they will say I told you so. Gold shares look an awful investment just now as doom and gloom envelop the producers, but believe me if the gold price starts heading for $400/oz, gold shares will not stay at present levels or anywhere near them, however expensive they may appear to be on fundamentals.

That is why I have been building up our gold holdings in recent weeks. The luxury of being able to buy when the market is falling is not given to those who have the task of running straight gold funds. They, like me, get redemptions when the gold market is low but all they have to sell is their gold shares. We on the other hand, can sell other things to meet redemptions and that helps to increase the percentage of the Fund invested in gold shares. By selling more than we need simply to meet redemptions, we can also buy the gold shares others are selling. This policy has resulted in our direct gold percentage increasing to 40 per cent. It is not as much as I would like, but it is more than double what it was three weeks ago. (**132. 11/4/91**)

KB Securities' note on different valuations of Cluff Resources, when considering the parent company and its Zimbabwean subsidiary, catches Julian's eye, leading him to point out that exchange controls may lead to local markets putting a high value on stocks due to the limited choices facing local investors.

Monitor published by Kleinwort Benson Securities. It said, and I quote:–

"Despite increased profits, higher gold production and weaker sterling, Cluff Resources fell heavily during the quarter, underperforming even the South African index in dollar terms. With production growth feeding through, Cluff looks undervalued at present."

Cluff Resources is an interesting stock since it was one of the first mining companies to invest in Zimbabwe after independence apart, of course, from those which were already operating there. Cluff's Zimbabwean subsidiary is now quoted on the Zimbabwean Stock Exchange and is very highly rated. Kleinwort's mining experts tell me that every ounce of gold in the ground owned by Cluff Resources is valued by the market at US$32 but the same ounce of gold owned by Cluff's Zimbabwean subsidiary is valued at US$75. Can you believe that?

In fact you often get these anomalies, but what strikes me as intriguing is that an ounce of Zimbabwean gold in the ground appears to be valued by the market more than 50 per cent higher than an ounce of South African gold. If my arithmetic is right the average South African ounce is valued at about $20.

We know that an ounce of South African gold has always been less highly valued than an ounce of Australian or North American gold because conventional wisdom says that the political risk is so much less in those countries. That may be so, but I have always found that the value of a share is also influenced by the amount of money available to buy it.

If that were not so, gold shares generally would be rated like other mining shares. After all, gold mining is about turning rocks into profit just as much as is base metal mining. Base metal mines are not highly rated because there are plenty of shares available for the comparatively small number of people, such as us, who are mad enough to want to buy them.

The point I am leading to is that in a closed economy like Zimbabwe where the pension funds and insurance companies are fenced in, they can only buy what is available to them.

So it is in South Africa. The institutions are locked in and have to invest their cashflows. That is why over the years they have been "buying back the farm", not because they are any more certain of their own future than we are but because they have to do something with their money. In due course foreigners will realise that the available supply of South African gold shares has shrunk as more and more of them are absorbed by the locals, never to appear again – at least not at these prices.

Those of you who are long in the tooth will remember how we Brits used to buy plantation shares on yields of 12 per cent and sell them to the Malaysians on yields of 8 per cent. It was the fashionable thing to do for many years. Then one day the locals, who had become prosperous, decided to hold onto the shares they had bought on an 8 per cent yield through thick and thin, so the game changed and those foreigners who had invented the rules suddenly found to their cost that the rules had been changed by the locals who looked upon plantation shares more as growth stocks than yield sweeteners.

I do not want to excite you but I believe that exactly the same thing will happen in South Africa. But a combination of sanctions, a low gold price and worries about political risk are likely to ensure that foreign investors are underweight in the one sector of the gold market that is likely to do best.

Not only will the South African gold shares go up most when the gold market recovers – it always does because local investors love gold shares – but the likely lifting of sanctions in the next few months will at last enable a section of the investment community (like the Japanese) who have been precluded from buying them, to participate. Furthermore, low gold prices could well lead to a weaker rand and that in turn will help boost the profits of the mining industry. As I explained last week, logic would suggest that a more representative government in South Africa will be unable to resist the social pressures created by the current exchange rate policy. It is my guess that after a valiant effort to stem inflation by keeping the rand at an unsustainably high level, the currency will go the way of all flesh and devaluation hedges will once again become all the rage for the South African institutions. (133. 19/4/91)

Julian looks at the comparative attractions of Newmont and Randfontein as they relate to market value, expressed in terms of production ounces.

People will in fact pay less for an ounce of gold in the ground once they realise that it costs nearly as much to produce it as it can be sold for. Therefore the name of the game, if you are trying to persuade a Fund Manager to buy shares in your gold mining company, is to gloss over two vital ingredients which make up the value of a mining share. First you must try not to mention the word "overheads" at all and then you should scrupulously avoid drawing the Fund Manager's attention to the cost of buying the ounce in the first place.

Let me give you an example. There is a widely held share in North America called Newmont Gold which is considered to be a blue chip investment. It costs Newmont Gold only $210 to extract an ounce of gold but the overheads bump that cost up to $273/oz. Since they can sell their gold for $357/oz, it does not take a genius to work out that they currently make a profit of $84 per ounce.

The snag comes when you find out that in order to participate in that profit you have to pay $182 for the privilege of owning the ounce in the first place. You would need a gold price of $455 to come out all square. I need hardly remind you that gold currently sells for $357/oz.

If you really think the gold price is going to $455/oz, you might prefer to own Randfontein. Their total costs are $354/oz, $81 higher than those of Newmont Gold. The great difference is in what you have to pay for the privilege of owning an ounce of Randfontein's gold – a mere $11/oz compared with $182 for Newmont Gold's ounce.

If the gold price goes to $455, in order to break even you could pay up to $90 for an ounce of Randfontein gold. That would value a Randfontein share at $10.50 compared with today's price of $3. That is why we have got over a million pounds invested in Randfontein and not a penny piece invested in Newmont Gold.

If Jimmy Goldsmith, who has invested more of his own money in Newmont Gold than the whole value of this Fund, is right in saying that gold will have its day, it will be interesting to see, when gold has its day, who has made the best investment, you or he. (**135. 15/5/91**)

Julian continues on the same theme.

Let me give you an example. James Capel and Co. Limited have calculated that taking gold at $400/oz, the average South African gold mine will earn $113/oz on every ounce it owns for which you pay $46/oz. The average Australian gold mine will make $90/oz for which you pay $123/oz and the average North American mine will make $77/oz for which you pay $145/oz. The trouble is, investors do not think of it that way. They do not relate what they pay for a share with what they pay for an ounce, although they cannot own the ounce unless they buy the share! The gold price is beyond the control of the mining companies and there is not a lot they can do to increase their profit margins except sell gold forward, which in turn tends to depress the price. So, when times are bad, the diminishing profit that the company can make on each ounce of gold should be reflected in its share price since it is the share price which determines how much is paid for each ounce.

That is why I try to buy gold shares which already value every ounce of gold in the ground at a low figure. If each existing ounce is valued at a low figure – and by that I mean below $50/oz – any additional ounces found can make a big impact on the share price. Similarly, any improvement in the gold price has a far greater impact on the price of those shares which place a low value on each ounce in the first place.

The moral of the tale seems to be that if general disillusionment with the behaviour of the gold price is going to lead the market to pay less for each ounce in the ground, the less we pay for the ounce in the first place, the less, in theory, we should stand to lose. This is exactly the opposite of what has been happening in real life! The shares which have fallen the most seem to be those like Venterspost, Western Areas, Libanon and Doornfontein, all of which are more than 40 per cent below their recent peaks. None of these shares value an ounce of gold in the ground above $10! Perhaps someone has heard that these companies are not going to survive, in which case each ounce in the ground would be worthless. I have bought this type of share with my eyes wide open, being prepared to accept that one or two such marginal mines may not survive. What does seem to me unlikely is that all of them will go bust. For one thing there are too many potential voters working in those mines for the government to allow too many of them to close down. My guess is that they would rather let the exchange rate take the strain. If some gold mines do go the way of all flesh, that in itself should have a beneficial effect on the gold price. In that case the survivors in our portfolio will do very well. (147. 28/8/91)

Looking at gold shares as long-term options on the gold price – with a little prompting from Carr K&A.

Or finally you might decide to back your judgement by investing in gold shares by joining the Starling School of Gold Investment. David Starling of Carr Kitcat & Aitken, who has been dealing in the gold share market for more years than he or I care to remember, started me thinking, when he suggested that gold shares could perhaps be considered as long-term options on the gold price; options which finally expire when the last ounce has been mined.

When you buy a gold share, you buy the after tax profit which the mining company makes on each remaining ounce of gold it owns. If it costs the company $320 to mine each ounce and if the shares value each ounce in the ground at $20, then at the present gold price of $347/oz it will make a profit of $7 per ounce. However, if the gold price returns to $392/oz, the profit margin, all other things being equal, will go up from $7/oz to $52/oz!

It is for this potential increase in profitability that we unitholders are patiently suffering our present discomfort because, as you are by now only too fully aware, gearing works both ways. Not everyone thinks of gold shares as long-term options on the gold price, so the shares sometimes don't behave as if they were long-term options. I happen to be attracted by David Starling's theory, so perhaps it is not surprising that the shares I like do not always coincide with the preferred flavour of the market. So far this has not harmed us since a growing number of gold analysts have become disillusioned with their own methods of evaluation and are now casting around for new ones. As you know, when everyone likes the same song they get bored of hearing it and this keeps the record industry gainfully employed. It's the same with investment theory – fashions change.

Since you like to know exactly what I am doing with your money I will tell you that we have developed a "pop chart" which combines two important criteria, the potential percentage gain that each share should achieve if the gold price returned to its "fair value" price of $392/oz coupled with the requirement that shares only qualify for inclusion in our portfolio if the cost of producing each ounce, plus the cost of buying each ounce, is less than $350/oz.

To be perfectly frank with you, our portfolio is not perfect in this ratio. One or two shares have crept in which do not meet our criteria, due to the entreaties of the "silver-tongued brigade" whose persuasive powers can sometimes weaken the resolve of even the most hardhearted Fund Manager. However you will be pleased to hear that the great majority of our holdings meet my criteria, which by no means exclude quality stocks. That may be why I am not as dismayed as some people are by recent events in the gold market. For the record our gold holdings value each ounce in the ground at $50; whereas the average profit margin on each ounce we own, based on $392/oz gold, is $70. (**148. 4/9/91**)

Julian ponders his tough stance on gold share valuation techniques.

The other problem facing investors in gold shares is that the well-established techniques used to value them are gradually being discarded as previous methods become more and more discredited. At times of change it is hard to know which new method will become fashionable. When I first started this Fund, brokers used to tell me that if they used my methods of valuation they would not be able to recommend any gold shares. They would all be too expensive. Bearing in mind their subsequent behaviour, that seems to have been no bad thing. In other words, the methods I use are starting to look more realistic. Whether they become conventional is anybody's guess, but if they do most American and Australian gold shares still do not look good value. That worries me because if the shares that most funds hold continue to look expensive, then if they get cheaper still, they may well drag down with them the shares that do represent good value. That seems to me to be a risk worth taking when compared with the risk of not being fully invested at the bottom of the market. (**151. 25/9/91**)

Julian worries about the high levels of debt required to finance gold mine development, and also that so much gold gets sold forward as part of the process.

Last week I visited a number of gold mines in Nevada, courtesy of Bunting Warburg who provided their clients with the opportunity of seeing for themselves some of the gold mining operations of mainly Canadian companies operating in the USA. Much as I admire the technical skills of the Americans and the wild beauty of the desert State of Nevada, that admiration pales into insignificance when compared with the admiration I have for the bravery of those who are prepared to pay current market prices for most North American gold shares!

For the record the mines we visited were owned by Viceroy Resources, Lac Minerals, Echo Bay, Franco and Euro Nevada, American Barrick, Newmont Gold and Pegasus Gold.

As a result of my trip, my admiration for the Americans' technical expertise and their work ethic has, if anything, increased. I remain to be convinced that the natural qualities of the state of Nevada are enhanced by the plethora of one-armed bandits but self control was never my strongest suit. If I had won a jackpot perhaps my perceptions would have been different!

It seems a shame that so much gold, which the miners assure me is a valuable product, is having to be produced at a loss in order to pay the mining companies' interest bills. I do not expect the shareholders of the banks who have lent money to the gold miners to see it that way. The trip has persuaded me that mining operations should not be financed by debt, even cheap debt. The chances are that the cheap debt will not turn out to be nearly as cheap as many people now think it is.

I remain concerned at the willingness of the mining industry to continue selling gold that has not yet been produced even at these low levels. To do so at a time when most of them tell you that they believe gold to be below its long-term value, is not only shocking, it is lemming-like. (**153. 16/10/91**)

A return to the subject of comparative market valuations per ounce of producing gold mines.

Those of you who enjoy absurdities will like the one which was pointed out to me this week by John Lydall of First Marathon, a Canadian broker of like mind. He mentioned that Lac Minerals had earned about 9 cents a share in the last six months and was priced at C$9. Royal Oak had earned approximately the same, but was priced at C$0.9. Both are gold producers, but if you want to buy Royal Oak's ounces in the ground you have to pay $20 each for them; whereas if you prefer Lac's ounces, each will cost you $150. Since I could not tell the difference between an ounce of gold produced by Lac and one produced by Royal Oak, I bought the cheapest. I hope you don't mind!

The point I am making is that the less you pay for an ounce in the ground, the more profit you are likely to make on that ounce when the gold price goes up.

I have a rule which I try to stick to. I do not always succeed – human frailty – but at least I try. I do a simple sum. I add what I pay for each ounce to what it costs the company to mine that ounce. Then I add the company's overheads per ounce. If those three items added together come to less than the current gold price I buy the share.

How can the gold mining companies which own ounces of gold in the ground that are valued by the public at ludicrously high prices, turn the public's gullibility into hard cash for their shareholders? Most companies' stated aim is to "Enhance shareholder value". They should be straining every mental sinew to find a way of converting the over valuation of their reserves into the folding stuff.

The most obvious thing that an over valued mining company can do is to use its paper to acquire an undervalued company's shares. That would suit us very well because we hold the undervalued companies! In other words, the ones that appeal most to us on their own merits, are the very ones which should also appeal most to predators.

I always ask the directors of these over valued companies how much they are prepared to spend looking for an ounce of gold to replace their reserves. They always tell me that the ounces they have already found cost them between $20–$30/oz. I then ask them if it is getting easier or more difficult to fund new ounces and they say "More difficult, stupid, otherwise gold would be a base metal!" I should explain that more difficult is another way of saying more expensive.

"Would you be prepared to pay $35, $45, $55," I ask them, "stop me when I have gone too far."

So far I have not found a single mining company which is prepared to pay more than $60 for an ounce of gold in the ground (except Minorco, but they are special). Why? Because they know as well as I do that if they paid more than $60 it is unlikely that they will be able to make a return on the money they spent on getting the gold out of the ground.

If the mining industry is not prepared to pay more than $60 for an ounce in the ground, why should investors be prepared to pay up to $200? Could it be that they have more money than experience. Never mind, it's all a game really; a game which few play and of which even fewer bother to learn the rules. Clever people find the world of gold too restricting, so the field is left to stupid people like me. Since I am incapable of understanding what most brokers tell me about gold shares I prefer my home-grown methods of valuing them. As the season of the mistletoe approaches, KISS seems to be as good an acronym as any for those who purport to advise others on the gold market. Keep It Simple Stupid so that old-timers in the gold market like me can understand what you are talking about. If the simple methods we use do not work, why on earth should this Fund have the reputation of being the one to beat? (**156. 15/11/91**)

With reference to Newmont Gold, Julian considers the issue of how gold mines calculate reserves.

Newmont Gold, a leading company with comfortably high grades, shows in its 1991 annual report, exactly how their proven and probable ore reserves are calculated. So important are these figures that I am going to risk boring you by quoting them in full.

"Newmont Gold Company's estimate of its proven and probable ore reserves is set forth in the table below. The proven and probable reserves were determined by the use of mapping, drilling, sampling, assaying and evaluation methods generally applied in the mining industry. NGC's calculations with respect to the estimates as of December 31, 1991 and 1990, are based on a gold price of US$400 per ounce. NGC believes that if its reserve estimates were to be based on gold prices as low as US$300 per ounce with current operating costs, reserves would decrease by approximately 16 per cent for 1991. Conversely, if its reserve estimates were to be based on a gold price of US$500 per ounce with current operating costs, reserves would increase by approximately 16 per cent for 1991."

The point that has to be made is that Newmont Gold is indeed fortunate not to have too much marginal ore. Many other companies must wish that their ore reserves were only depleted by 16 per cent at a gold price of US$300/oz.

I wish that it was as easy to establish the true position with all gold companies as it is for Newmont Gold. At 31st December 1991 NGC had reserves of 20.116 million ounces which they say would have to be reduced to 16.9 million ounces at a gold price of US$300/oz. The market capitalization of Newmont Gold is about

US$4.4 billion so if the worst came to the worst, you would be paying US$260 for each ounce m the ground. It costs about US$200 to extract each ounce so you would be paying US$260 for a profit of US$100. Not too inviting, but a great deal better than some.

How do I avoid the elephant traps? I work out what gold price is required in order for us (not the mining company) to break even. In the case of Newmont Gold, I calculate that an investor paying US$42.50 per share would need a gold price of US$416 in today's money to get back, over the life of the proven and probable reserves, what he put in today.

Much as I admire what Newmont Gold has achieved, the shares are just too fashionable for my taste. I prefer those of Freeport Copper and Gold where I reckon they need a gold price of US$246 to break even. Better still, each ounce of their proven and probable reserves only costs us US$54. That's why Freeport is our largest holding. Nothing wrong with Newmont, mark you, except the price people are prepared to pay for it.

This is the season for elephant hunting. Many gold companies are recalculating their reserves. Gold analysts are always encouraging me to pay ever more for blue sky. But experience tells me that you can lose far more money, and quicker, as a result of ore reserves having to be reduced due to low metal prices, than you can make from ore reserves being enhanced by exploration – unless you are a very lucky investor. (**173. 6/5/92**)

Julian muses on the different attitudes among Mining Houses to their marginal mines, and the importance of income to an underperforming SA gold sector.

For my part, I try to protect our interests by ensuring that our larger investments are in shares in which the Mining Houses themselves have substantial shareholdings. Such an investment is OFSIL, our largest South African investment, representing 5.7 per cent of the Fund. OFSIL is a holding company of Freegold, the largest gold mining company in the world, producing some 110 tonnes of gold a year. As such, it is an important potential contributor to Anglo American's gold earnings and despite its marginality, its reserves are mined at a grade which provides the group with substantial dividend, as well as fee, income.

The South African specialist at Smith New Court predicts that a shareholder in OFSIL, buying the shares cum the final dividend recently declared, will have received 16 per cent of his purchase price back in dividends in the next 13 months. Such optimism caused me to increase our shareholding knowing, as I do, how much you like income.

Furthermore, for some reason best known to itself, the market values the shares of OFSIL at a sizeable discount to the value of Freegold. That being the case, it would be nice if the directors of OFSIL distributed the underlying shares of Freegold to us, the shareholders. After all we own them already.

Unfortunately, our other marginal mines in South Africa are not so important to their parent Mining Houses as OFSIL is to Anglo American. They have been having a dreadful time recently and are largely responsible for the disappointing performance of our units. It is certainly too late to sell them now. The gold price has fallen further than many of us expected a year ago, so mines which were marginal at that time are now in "intensive care" and those that were "middle of the road" are now marginal. We have a larger exposure to South African gold shares than any of our competitors. The chart shows the underperformance of the South African gold shares so far this year. I still maintain that when the gold price turns the South African gold shares will perform the best. They always have! (**174. 12/5/92**)

Julian argues that investing in gold shares may be the cheapest way of getting exposure to base metals.

Bearing in mind that gold shares, due to their scarcity value, are far more volatile than base metal shares, the contrarian investor might share my view that the cheapest way of taking an interest in base metals is by buying a gold share! That may sound a strange thing to say, but look at it this way:

In 1986, when the gold price was trading at about US$450/oz, gold shares were discounting a gold price at least US$150/oz higher. Two things seemed obvious to me at the time. Firstly that gold was far better value than gold shares and secondly that if the shares were right to be predicting a gold price of US$600/oz, the chances that the copper price would remain below 60 US cents/lb were virtually nil. It would likely rise in sympathy with gold to at least 75 US cents/lb. Low margin copper mines which were struggling with 60 US cents/lb copper would be making a packet with copper at 75 US cents/lb. Thus I argued that the cheapest "gold shares" were in fact two copper shares, Magma Copper and Inspiration Resources. This advice surprised people at the time but when both shares doubled, they quickly acclimatised themselves.

Today, exactly the opposite is the case. It may not have escaped your notice that three leading base metal companies, RTZ, Phelps Dodge and Alcoa, are achieving all-time highs, though the metals they produce remain very depressed in real terms. Since the shares of these companies are now higher than they were when metals peaked in 1989, the market must be expecting most metal prices to double by the peak of the next cycle in two or three years time. I don't disagree with that prognostication.

As the market is very seldom wrong, the question you should be asking yourselves is this. If base metals have the capacity to double to the peak of the next cycle in the next two or three years, is gold likely to remain at US$337/oz? If the answer to this question is yes, you should sell your units. If you take the opposite view, you should be buying more. After all, the FT Gold Mines Index has already fallen 70 per cent from its high in just over two years, so if you do decide to be brave, you are certainly not getting in at the top! (175. 21/5/92)

Julian's lifetime lesson on dealing in marginal gold mines.

When I was a broker, it took the best part of 20 years and four bear markets to teach me not to recommend my clients to sell their marginal mines at the bottom of the market. To save time, I would just like to let the brokers know that this particular "poacher turned gamekeeper", is not about to take their advice to sell my marginal mines now, however much they try to persuade me.

Those of you who remain unitholders will surely approve of that. (179. 19/6/92)

The puzzle of why there is such a value differential between doppelgangers Ofsil and Freegold.

The largest gold mine in the world is comprised of a number of smaller mines in the Orange Free State which were merged some years ago to form Freegold. This mammoth mine, which produces over 100 tonnes of gold a year, can be bought through three different companies, Freegold, Ofsil or Welkom. The reason for the retention of three companies, when one would do, is to enable investors to own up to 15 per cent of the mine by holding up to 5 per cent of each of the three holding companies. You see, some mutual funds are not allowed to hold more than 5 per cent of any one company because it is thought that small investors should be protected from having too many of their eggs in one basket.

The way round that technically is for a mine to be owned by a number of holding companies. The danger is that if something were to go wrong with the mine itself all the holding companies would suffer and the investor might find, to his surprise, that his exposure was not confined to 5 per cent at all. It reminds me of these Names at Lloyds, who found that they were exposed to more risk than they thought they were taking on.

Ironically, what has happened in the case of the Freegold mine is that it is valued quite differently by each of the three holding companies. For instance, we hold Ofsil, which sells at a discount of 16 per cent to the value placed on the same mine through Freegold. Put another way, to bring Ofsil into line with Freegold, the price of Ofsil would have to rise 19 per cent!

If Ofsil were to rise by that amount, this Fund alone would benefit to the tune of £375,000 or just over 112p per unit. But that is too selfish a way of looking at it! The shareholders of Ofsil as a whole (and they include Amgold and, indirectly, Anglo itself), would benefit to the tune of US$154 million. We are constantly told by the directors of mining companies that their aim is to "enhance shareholder value", so it would be interesting to know why Ofsil's management does not choose to enhance the value of Ofsil by simply distributing its holdings of Freegold shares to those of its shareholders who would like to receive them. Those, who for any reason are quite content to continue to hold Ofsil shares at a 16 per cent discount, could elect not to receive the Freegold shares to which they would be entitled.

There is a precedent for all of this. Recently Elsburg distributed its holding of Western Areas shares to Elsburg shareholders, eliminating, in their words, "a costly structure that served no useful purpose". The move was estimated to save shareholders R350,000 per annum, at a one-off cost of R800,000. The Freegold mine is far larger, so it would be reasonable to assume that the saving would be commensurately greater.

When I was a young man, I used to carry the bags of one of the senior partners of my firm, when he travelled abroad. I remember being shocked by the fact that he never bought his entitlement of duty free goods because he couldn't be bothered to go to the inconvenience of carrying them home. Some people are just so rich that they don't need the hassle! If this Fund were hitting new highs every day, I dare say I wouldn't worry about an extra penny or so on the price of our units, but gold mine investments have been so appalling recently that it hurts to see nothing being done to eliminate a shortfall of US$154 million in the value being placed on our largest single investment. Perhaps, if you were to write to the company, that would do the trick. They certainly do not take any notice of me! (**183. 6/8/92**)

Problems for the gold mining industry as only high grading and forward selling keeps corporate heads above water.

Thus the industry is in dire straits. The South Africans who resisted forward selling, when others were putting downward pressure on the gold price by doing so, are now bearing the brunt of the current pressures. But the rest of the industry cannot be complacent since the bulk of their forward sales will be used up within the next 18 months and in current conditions it is not so attractive to put more forward sales in place.

Without forward sales, much of the North American and Australian gold mining industry would already be making losses. Some already are, even with forward sales. It seems that if the sight of gold mines actually closing is the only thing which will make investors believe that the gold price has hit rock bottom, they may not have long to wait. The gold mining industry is now engaged in a fight against time. The question is, will the high cost South African mines run out of high grade ore before their competitors run out of high-priced forwards.

Once closures start, investors, like vultures, will descend on the gold price. The price will start rising and a virtuous circle will ensue. High grading will cease, thus reducing still further the amount of gold available for sale. That is just what happened in the 1970's.

The same was true of the base metal markets in the mid 1980's. Years of over-capacity and inefficiency led to depressed metal prices, which ultimately forced some producers under. Like the Phoenix from the ashes, most of the base metal mining industry rose again, emerging leaner and fitter and, so long as metal prices remained firm, highly profitable. Perhaps a few deaths in the family (but hopefully not close relations of ours) will prove a blessing in disguise to the gold industry as a whole. No one, however, is prepared to lay down his life voluntarily for the greater good.

I can tell you that running a fund in the current circumstances is not my idea of fun, any more than it is fun for those of us who hold it. All I can say is that the laws of supply and demand are immutable and look as if they are shortly going to be tested yet again. When that happens, those of us who are still there to tell the tale should reap a rich harvest. Meanwhile, after you with the laughing gas! **(186. 3/9/92)**

With SA gold shares under intense pressure Julian baulks at regulations from taking out ASA calls.

Although it is just as hard to see how sentiment could ever recover in the South African market, we should bear in mind that if this level of violence continues, many of the conditions would exist which could give rise to a military coup or at least the re-imposition of a state of emergency. Politicians of all races must realise that if they do not cool it, far from leading South Africans to the promised land, they will find themselves en-route to another Yugoslavia.

So, just as the Nikkei did exactly the opposite to what people thought it would, so it seems possible that the oversold indicator will once again prove its value and tell us when it is time to buy South African gold shares, against our better judgement.

The question was how the Fund should try to take advantage of an oversold situation. We already have more than enough exposure to the political risk and I am reluctant to increase it still further. In fact, we would be more than happy if the indicator is proved right yet again.

We had it in mind to buy November US$40 ASA calls for US$0.5 selling sufficient of our South African holdings to finance the purchase. Unfortunately the SIB Regulations, 1991, prevented this course of action since it could be construed as "speculation", notwithstanding the fact that it has certain defensive qualities.

A 21 per cent recovery in the shares of ASA could be expected to result in a fourfold rise in the ASA November US$40 calls. Such a prospect appeals to me and if the buy/sell indicator declines to minus 10, I will be sorely tempted to "speculate" for myself even if I am not allowed to do so for you. (**187. 10/9/92**)

Julian again brings up the subject of the South African gold mining industry's inefficient working practices as the market batters the shares.

I mention these two companies (Golden Shamrock and Zapopan) because their 40 per cent plus share price appreciation in the last month has helped to lessen the adverse impact of the appalling performance of our South African shares.

Even in South Africa, there is perhaps a small glimmer of hope with Mr Mandela's public recognition last week of the fact that unless the politics can be sorted out fairly soon, the economy will be so weakened that no government, of whatever hue, will be able to create the wealth needed to provide even the bare necessities of life for the majority of the population.

A couple of weeks ago the London Society of Mining Analysts was addressed by Clem Sunter, the Chairman of Anglo American's Gold Division. He made the point that most of the easy things the gold mining industry could do to stay alive had already been done. Some tough decisions would soon have to be taken.

This was brought home to us recently when the Managing Director of Harmony, one of our "marginal" mines, said that even if the miners were prepared to change their working practices and work a seven-day week, the mine had only two more years life left. The following day he changed "two years" to "many years", but the damage to the share price had been done. Costs last quarter were $US385/oz so there is an urgent need to reduce them by at least US$45/oz.

If abandoning the lower grade areas of the mine and working a seven-day week is enough to restore profitability, you have to ask yourself why the entire gold mining industry in South Africa is not adopting working practices widely adopted elsewhere in the twentieth century.

In a desperate situation like that faced by Harmony, rather than run the risk of losing their jobs and their homes and risking the town of Virginia becoming a ghost town, surely the workforce would prefer to take a 10 per cent cut in salary and then reduce costs by about US$20/oz. Furthermore, the directors should be asking themselves whether, in the circumstances, their company should be subscribing to the World Gold Council and the Chamber of Mines at a cost of say US$5/oz. Then there are the fees payable to the controlling Mining House. In other words, when people say there is nothing more that can be done to save the mines, short of a devaluation of the rand, you should take it with a pinch of salt. Peggy White for Chairman I say.

Peggy White has made a fortune for the shareholders of the Canadian mining company, Royal Oak, including us, by buying marginal mines and taking unpleasant desicions in order to make them profitable. She would have a field day in South Africa where there is plenty that can still be done to reduce costs. Unforauntely, in my experience, the really difficult decisions are seldom taken until it is clear to all that there is absolutely no alternative. By the time, the patient is often so weakened that survival is not certain.

The dire straits in which the gold mining industry in South Africa finds itself calls into question the whole rationale of the mining system. There is much talk of the desirability of "unbundling" the Mining Houses' underlying assests. You can't help wondering whether it makes sense for a raft of highly paid senior Mining House executives to be involved in the administration of the samller gold mining companies, some of which are capitalised at less than US$25 million. There is much to be said for handing the mine managers a bundle of share options and leaving them to fend for themselves just as they do in Canada and Australia. Like any other "small business" marginal gold mines simply cannot afford the luxury of Mining House overheads. If the Mining Houses want the fees which the gold mines pay them they should "put up" or "shut up".

Of course, I don't pretend to have a monopoly of good ideas as to how to save costs in the gold mining industry, but if by chucking a few controversial rocks into the settling pond, I start a thought process in anybody's mind which leads to even the smallest cost saving, no harm will have been done.   (188. 18/9/92)

Julian bemoans the poor performance of gold shares when compared to the performance of the gold price itself, a phenomenon well understood in today's market.

The conventional wisdom that gold has become just another commodity deserves further consideration in the light of the currency upheavals which have taken place since 1st September, a period which includes Great Britain's withdrawal from the ERM.

To set the scene, here is the price of an ounce of gold in the currencies of the producing countries since 1st September 1992 plus the price in sterling, the currency of the majority of our unitholders.

GOLD PRICE IN	1st SEPTEMBER	24th NOVEMBER	per cent CHANGE
US$	342	335	-2.0
£	172	222	+29.0
A$	477	488	+2.3
C$	410	440	+7.3
SA Rand	934	1011	+8.2

Source: James Capel & Co. Ltd

In contrast to the behaviour of gold in local currencies, the performance of the shares has been quite extraordinary. Here are the indices to prove it.

INDEX	1st SEPTEMBER	24th NOVEMBER	per cent CHANGE
FT Gold Mines Index £	79	64	-19.0
Australian Gold Index A$	1108	952	-14.1
Canadian Gold Index C$	5341	5057	-5.3
JSE Gold Index Rand	954	765	-19.8

Source: James Capel & Co. Ltd

It is hard to believe, yet true, that since 1st September 1992 a sterling investor would be 29 per cent better off today if he had been entirely invested in gold; whereas he would be 19 per cent worse off if he had chosen to be entirely invested in the FT Gold Mines Index. Since the beginning of this Annus Horribilis the FT Gold Mines Index has lost no less than 55 per cent of its value!

Why have the shares not reflected the recently improving profit margins of the gold industry in their local currencies? The answer is that the miners, with certain notable exceptions, have already sold their immediate production forward and covered the currency at the same time. It no longer matters what the gold price does in local currency, the gold miners have chosen to insulate themselves from the very thing that makes gold shares go up or down, namely the volatility of the gold price!

Of course, by selling forward the miners have helped to depress the gold price by forcing the market to absorb more "spot" gold than it would otherwise have had to. Now that they have achieved penury for all of us, we find ourselves in no position to benefit when the gold price does rise in local currencies, as it is doing at present. We have suffered the agony, but unless we are very choosy about which gold shares we hold there is a good chance that we shareholders are going to be denied any ecstasy. The growing realisation of what is happening to us is being reflected, as you can see, in the performance of the gold share indices. (25/11/92)

The Fund's exposure to South African gold shares pays off as gold revives.

As you know, markets have a way of going up until they stop going up then going down until they stop going down and then going up again. The gold share market personifies this behavioural pattern, as the Americans would put it, but it won't go up until the last bull has sold and it won't go down again until the last bear has covered.

What excites me is that, since metal prices started to turn up in mid November, we have started to outperform all the other gold funds whose South African exposure is lower, but whose exposure to Papua New Guinea is higher than ours. Needless to say, this is a most welcome change from being constantly at the bottom of the short-term performance league tables.

Although it would be nice if this change of fortune removed us from the bottom of the class this year, it has probably come too late to alter our position. Next year, however, could be a very different story. So confident am I, personally, that things will be different next year that I have bed and breakfasted my own units to establish a loss for tax purposes. (199. 8/12/92)

Julian re-emphasises that gold mines are wasting assets and so must at least return a shareholder's investment, and that dividends are consequently vital to the process.

In contrast to the modem fashion, we have always taken the view that a mine is a wasting asset and that a sensible investor in mining shares should look to get his money back over the life of a mine, plus an adequate return on his money.

Current practice has it that the business of a mining company is to replace its ore reserves over time by exploration or acquisition. Thus, it is thought reasonable to value a mining company as if it were an industrial company which uses its depreciation allowances to replace its worn-out plant.

Although it is certain that an industrial company can buy new machines to replace its old, experience tells us that it is much more difficult for a mining company to continue to grow and at the same time at least replace its depleted ore reserves with others of similar or greater value. The faster a mining company depletes its ore reserves, the more pressing becomes the task of replacing them.

As investors in mining shares, we are interested in the amount we are called upon to pay for each ounce in the ground and the profit to be derived from mining that ounce. We are more interested in profits per ounce than earnings per share.

Our South African holdings are generally single mine companies with depleting resources. Therefore, dividends are all-important. Normally available cash, after capital expenditure and taxes, is paid out in full. Dividends go up or down in line with profits, which in turn are determined by the gold price, operating costs and production levels. (**201. 7/1/93**)

Julian highlights a problem, still with us today, whereby a leading Australian junior (in this case Golden Shamrock) operating successfully overseas gets no credit or interest from Aussie investors.

Last Tuesday, before the early morning mist had cleared from the Iduapriem Mine site in the mountains of the Western District, the famous talking drums of Ghana were summoning the local populace to attend the official opening of the mine by their President, Flt. Lt. Jerry J. Rawlings.

If you did not hear the drums, you probably first got wind that the mine had been opened when you read Wednesday's Financial Times. This information probably came to you via a more efficient, but less romantic means of communication, known as satellite technology.

Those who heard the drums, and there were many, were not disappointed. The mine is a showpiece, built and operated by a small group of Australian mining professionals. Little did the locals comprehend or care that their mine was the product of a textbook example of international financial co-operation.

Most of them, living in such a remote area, had probably never seen their President in the flesh and anyhow their minds were concentrating on the culinary delights of the sumptuous feast which the mining company had laid on for them.

Those of us whose connections with the mine privileged us to attend its opening, had plenty of time to reflect on the achievements of all concerned. Ghanaians, like most Africans, don't feel that their effort to attend has been adequately rewarded unless speeches last for a proper length of time and are repeated in full, in the lingua franca, to ensure that great men's words are well understood by all.

In fact the mining concession was originally acquired by a Ghanaian, passed on to an Indian and thence to an Australian. Finance was provided by a courageous and entrepreneurial American on the recommendation of an experienced South African explorationist. Additional loan capital was raised by a consortium of German, Swiss and Dutch banks under the auspices of the International Finance Corporation (IFC). The IFC retains a 20 per cent interest in the mining company,

Ghanaian Australian Goldfields Limited, alongside the Ghanaian Government with its 10 per cent shareholding and board representation. The Mercury Gold and General Fund started buying Golden Shamrock, which controls Ghanaian Australian Goldfields Limited, in June 1991 at about 7p. We now own 8 million shares valued in the market at 24p or, about 4 per cent of the share capital.

Not only is the mine under Australian management, the plant was erected by Minproc, an Australian company specialising in the construction of such plants. The plant was built within time and on budget and has suffered no serious teething problems. Huge credit must be given to the Australians' contribution to the first of a new generation of gold mines in Ghana and to the farsightedness and courage of the American financier.

The shares of Golden Shamrock are owned principally by the Concord Group in America who provided the original equity capital and by AOG and ourselves. Conspicuous by its absence has been any Australian equity participation. Not a single Australian institution, apart from AOG, has a meaningful holding. Perhaps someone should arrange to send the talking drums to Collins Street, Melbourne and Pitt Street, Sydney and then we will find out whether the Australian institutions can hear them from there. (**208. 25/2/93**)

The strong performance of SA gold shares puts off gold disbelievers as they worry about chasing an already hot market.

One of the delights of the investment game is watching people who have been wrong-footed by the market trying to justify their position instead of admitting their mistakes and going with the flow. Their cries of caution make no difference whatsoever to the eventual outcome but they do enable bulls of the market to buy more shares at cheaper prices than would otherwise be the case. Our pleasure is therefore savoured with gratitude as we watch investors climb a wall of fear.

How do I know? Because I was badly wrong-footed myself 17 years ago when, in 1976, I turned bearish of gold shares after the market had already fallen 84 per cent. Fortunately my mentor was quick to point out to me the error of my ways, thus enabling me to change tack before too much damage had been done. Otherwise I would have missed the subsequent rise of 690 per cent in the market which took place in the next four years. So let's look at some of the things that the disbelievers are saying.

First they say that they could not bring themselves to buy a Fund or a market which has already more than doubled this year. That is like saying that because a horse came first in the Derby it could not possibly be expected to win L'Arc de Triomphe. Surely what matters is how the Fund is invested and whether the underlying investments have the potential to catch up with their peers. Since our

Fund was started in April 1988, South African gold shares have halved. To get back to where they started they would have to double. 50 per cent of the Fund is invested in South African gold shares. (**218. 20/5/93**)

Once more Julian returns to the subject of owning gold rather than gold shares (something that his Fund cannot do) in the light of the tendency for gold shares to materially outperform gold in the early stages of a gold bull market.

Finally there is the conspiracy theory that Mr. Soros and Sir James Goldsmith got together to ramp the market. No one bothers to explain how Mr. Soros could have put US$400 million into the gold market unless he had found a natural seller. Peter Munk of American Barrick said he had been approached but was not prepared to sell. Sir James Goldsmith when he first bought his stake in Newmont made no secret of the fact that he would lighten his holding at an appropriate moment. Bearing in mind that Newmont shares are probably no cheaper than any other North American gold mining company, why should anyone be surprised if Goldsmith grasped the opportunity of exchanging half his holding for the real thing – gold. It makes perfect sense to me since previous bull markets have seen the gold price rise by at least 70 per cent from their lows, such are the swings of the golden pendulum.

After all, gold shares are equities and Goldsmith has often expressed his distrust of equities now that world markets are making new highs. Gold on the other hand is no one else's liability. It does not promise to pay you anything. You either own it or you don't. In the 1987 crash, equities, including gold equities, lost more than 30 per cent of their value in two days, but gold went up in value. It makes perfect sense for the prudent investor to have some of the real thing to balance his portfolio of shares.

Alas, the authorities don't see it that way. They don't allow authorised unit trusts like this to own bars of gold on which the mining costs have already been paid by someone else. Gold is considered too speculative, so we like Mr. Soros have to make do with far more speculative and highly geared bits of paper called gold shares. At the beginning of a new bull market, gold shares will way out perform the metal. The skill will be in managing the portfolio when the shares eventually become over-valued compared with the metal. At least you will have the Newsletter to keep you informed about how we are coping with this problem. In the meantime don't listen to the Jeremiahs – all they will succeed in doing is to rob you of your just deserts. (**218. 20/5/93**)

Julian begs his unitholders to hold on as the gold share market corrects.

In the recent rise, the shares got a bit ahead of the game and the correction we have seen in the last couple of weeks is not only healthy, having blown away a good deal of the froth, it also gives a splendid opportunity for those who feared they might have missed the boat, to climb aboard.

So don't listen to those who now tell you to take your profits and run. Hold onto your units. If you don't, you won't be able to sell them to the very same people who are telling you to sell now. Once the market's future behaviour has convinced them that they too should own some gold shares, you could then be helpful and let them have yours!

Not many miners see this letter, but those who do might like to calculate what would be the cost to the shareholders of covering their forward sales if my predictions are proved right. At the same time they might also like to calculate how much the shareholders will gain if the gold price falls far enough to enable them to cover their forward sales at an acceptable profit. My calculations show that the potential loss is four times the potential profit.

If the acceptable profit is greater than the possible loss, then they should continue to behave as if we are still in a bear market and do nothing. If they find their possible loss is many times greater than any realistic forecast of the profit they might make by doing nothing, they should cover their forwards immediately. I am told they may not find it quite as easy to do so as they thought it was. I am told the bullion banks are unenthusiastic about covering forwards early. Never mind that, just remind them that they don't own the mining companies, we do. **(221. 17/6/93)**

A new FT Gold Mines Index representing all gold share markets – not just, as formerly, the South African market – could ironically underline the importance of the SA sector in a world context.

If you want my prediction, it is this: the new FT Gold Mines Index will draw the attention of a wider audience to the fact that the South African gold shares represent 27 per cent of the index but produce 45 per cent of the total profits of the companies which comprise that index.

Over time, this anomaly is likely to be rectified by those Fund Managers who find themselves overweight in North America and underweight in South Africa. The argument that the South African gold shares have to stand at a discount due to the political risk does not explain why the South African industrial market sells on a higher multiple than the FT-SE 100 Index. Nor does it explain why the South African gold shares have been the best sector in the entire market so far this year.

Does the political risk of investing in South Africa look so much less than it did six months ago, or about the same? Political risk has not stopped the FT Gold Mines Index from rising over 200 per cent since the beginning of this year.

No; the real reason why South African gold shares stand at such a big discount to their peers is that they offer little or no "blue sky". All the mineral rights in South Africa are held by the Mining Houses, but no value is attributed to the Mining Houses by the market for these mineral rights. Perhaps the market believes that a new government will politely ask the mining companies to produce or get off the prospect, to paraphrase a popular expression, so that others can have a go.

If I were a director of the Mining Houses, I would arrange for the mineral rights to be shared with the mines in my group whose fees, after all, paid the technical staff who were employed to find and develop those mines in the first place.

That would enhance the value of the mines since they would immediately acquire the "blue sky" which is so highly valued elsewhere. As the major shareholder of the individual mines, the Mining Houses would see their asset base enhanced. It would also upset a wider spread of foreign investors if the government decided to free up South Africa's mineral wealth in a way which was considered unfair or unreasonable.

To end on a rather different subject, the market now appears to have got over its jitters occasioned by the rumoured sale by Mr. Soros of his gold and the feared disposal of some of France's gold reserves. The South African gold shares having fallen by some 25 per cent from their highs in July are now starting to recover. Some of you have sensibly been using the setback to buy more units. This has resulted in new money coming in almost every day throughout the correction. At last the penny seems to have dropped that corrections in bull markets provide buying opportunities. (**227. 19/8/93**)

Julian once more expresses admiration for Peggy Witte whose career as a mining mogul fell foul of the late 90s gold bear market.

The best example of the way gold Fund Managers respond to this type of management is the Canadian company, Royal Oak, run by a determined and charismatic lady called Peggy Witte. Royal Oak has enjoyed the most spectacular share price performance as the market responds to the management's heroic efforts at making a virtue out of the necessity of forcing down costs. No one expects her to win all her battles, but she has won enough to make many investors prepared to give her the benefit of the doubt when the going gets tough, particularly as she takes great trouble to meet her foreign shareholders at least twice a year to ensure they are fully "au fait" with what she is doing with their money. (**242. 17/1/94**)

Following a visit to Australia Julian muses on the enormous amounts of dirt that have to be mined before gold can be exposed and sold, and draws a comparison with shareholder returns from gold shares.

Having had the opportunity to visit the operations of St. Barbara, Plutonic Resources, Newcrest, Resolute Resources, Delta Gold and Poseidon Gold, I am now a world authority on large holes in the ground which seem to me to add character to an otherwise featureless topography, whatever the environmentalists say.

It occurred to me, as I gazed into the umpteenth open pit, how much we investors have in common with the miners. What gets between the miners and their gold are millions of tonnes of overburden which have to be removed before they can get at the final few thousand tonnes of pay dirt. If they are lucky, they derive some cashflow as they go down but in many cases, the big pay-off does not come until there is no more waste to remove and only ore has to be carted up from the floor of the pit.

Of course I will be accused of over-simplification, but it seems to me that the overburden that investors have to get through before they can get their gold is even thicker. Our overburden is the share price. In other words, we cannot derive any benefit unless we buy the shares and that means paying our entrance fee up-front too. We may be lucky and get a small dividend as the mining company digs deeper, but the chances are that the mining company will have plenty of other things to spend its money on without having to worry too much whether we are receiving enough to amortise our investment. After all, if a mining company is too generous to its shareholders, it may not have sufficient funds to replenish its reserves – a fate with certain similarities to death!

All this understandably makes mining companies very careful with their feasibility studies. Unlike investors, who can in theory "pass the parcel", a mining company is virtually stuck with its investment. The miner knows that he is not going to get his final pay-off until the end of the mine's life so the pay-off has to be discounted back to the day he first committed the money.

Many investors do not seem to see it that way; they prefer to look upon gold shares as collectables which give pleasure but no income. When half the market thinks of gold shares as collectables, it makes it hard for those of us who think of them as investments to get a decent return. In other words, the market is prepared to pay more for an ounce of gold in the ground than the profit the mining company can make by mining that ounce.

Such extraordinary behaviour can only be explained in one of two ways. Either the market has a touching belief that gold mining companies will always be able to find more gold than they mine or, that the gold price will rise sufficiently to make the sums add up.

We are only prepared to buy gold shares which promise to give us more back than we put in. Gold mines which sell their gold forward do not appeal to us since they put a cap on the gold price. It is one thing to accept a zero discount rate and take the chance that a rising gold price will provide an adequate return, it is quite another to buy a piece of paper that has more resemblance to a bond. Bonds demand a rate of return.

It is argued that since people who buy gold require no income, there is no need for gold shares to provide any. Last year I had the good fortune to win a sovereign from Ord Minnett for picking the five gold shares to appreciate the most in 1993. The fact that I have not yet received the sovereign should not worry me since gold is meant to hold its value over a long period, so it does not matter when they give it to me. Ord Minnett are a reputable firm and they can easily afford a sovereign so I have absolutely nothing to worry about, but the sovereign is in their pocket, not mine. I am beginning to want a rate of interest to compensate me for the time value of money. The question is when will gold share investors start thinking the same way. **(247. 17/3/94)**

Julian continues to be puzzled by the high price that the market can put on gold discoveries, particularly when compared with the value applied to mined gold.

Almost all mining company executives are familiar with the fact that the market sets great store on new discoveries. Those who do not know this are usually employees rather than shareholders in their companies. We always ask our visitors how much it costs them to find an ounce of gold. The reply is invariably "less than US$15/oz". Of course, a good deal of un-poetic 'liesence' (sic) is brought to bear on this subject, since if it really only costs US$15/oz to find gold, it would soon cease to be a precious metal! The truth, of course, is that we only see miners who find gold. The others are much too busy searching for it and lack the time to mine the market!

Our next question is far easier. "How much does the market pay for the ounces that you have found?" Market capitalization per ounce of reserves is a familiar yardstick. Indeed, the *Financial Times* showed on its Companies and Markets front page on the day after the Ashanti float what the market was paying for an ounce of gold in reserves in all the major producing countries. They showed that Ashanti's ounces were being valued at US$92/oz compared with an average of US$140/oz in Australia and US$160/oz in the Americas.

It occurs to us that gold mining is a pretty good business to be in if you can find it for less than US$15/oz and then have it valued by the market at US$140/oz or more. It seems obvious to us that unless an Australian miner can earn more than US$140/oz for mining his ounce, he would be better off leaving it in the ground and spending any cash he may have on trying to add to his reserves. If he does not have enough cash the market will be only too happy to provide it by taking a placement of his shares.

You have no doubt already guessed our next question. "What," we ask "is the profit that you make by mining an ounce of gold at your property?"

The answer to this question by those who perceive they may be approaching an elephant trap, is normally accompanied by a good deal of throat clearing and shuffling of papers. The profit is almost invariably less than the market is already paying for the ounce in its un-mined state. Every ounce removed from the ground at a typical profit of say US$60, is one less ounce remaining in the ground on which the market places a value of US$140. Yet miners like digging deep holes in the ground and continue to mine their reserves at a cost in excess of US$200/oz rather than spend US$15/oz on finding more. "Why would you want to do that?" we enquire with the pained expression of a shareholder who catches his Board selling his company's assets for less than what the market will pay for them. **(253. 9/5/94)**

The Fund is a large holder of giant Western Areas and Julian speculates that as the globalisation of the gold share sector develops South African mines such as WA will be increasingly valued in line with their global peers.

There is another reason why the publication of ore reserves is so important, it demonstrates on an ongoing basis to the mine workers and the government alike, how the life of a mine is affected by costs. If costs increase, or the gold price decreases, some of the ounces will no longer be economic to mine and the reserves will fall by more than the amount mined during the year. Conversely, a rise in the gold price or a reduction in costs, will increase the mineable reserve as extra ounces become payable. Those of you who follow mining shares closely will remember how, only two short years ago, people were predicting that the South African gold mining industry, which currently gives direct employment to 360,000 and indirect employment to an estimated further 195,000 people, would be less than half its present size within a few years because most of the high cost mines would have become un-payable.

Of the new revelations, by far the most interesting to date is the published reserves of Western Areas which surprised the market by announcing reserves of 22 million ounces. Western Areas is in the process of merging with South Deep to form a single entity with reserves of just over 60 million ounces. That puts it in the super league of world gold mines with comparable reserves to American Barrick/Lac Minerals, Driefontein and Placer. The largest Australian mine, according to JB Were & Son is the super pit at Kalgoorlie (GMK) which currently boasts over 20 million ounces. The capitalization of Western Areas and South Deep combined is US$1.2 billion, roughly the same as the combined capitalization of Homestake Australia and GMK who own the super pit which contains about a third as much gold. The South Africans have much to do before they can claim that their mines are valued in line with world-class gold shares elsewhere. They are at last addressing the problem, that is why we remain heavily overweight in that market. There is no doubt that their efforts are being rewarded as is evidenced by the fact that the South African gold shares continue to be the star performers this year, as they were last. (**270. 6/10/94**)

Mexican devaluation impacts upon the Fund's Latin American gold stocks in an unexpected way.

The turmoil in the emerging markets sector following the devaluation of the Mexican peso has resulted in a flight to duality. Investors in the Latin American countries got a rude shock when they woke up to the news that the value of their investments in Mexico had fallen virtually overnight by 40 per cent. Emerging markets had been doing so well! If Mexico could give them such an unpleasant surprise, who could blame them from wondering what other shocks were in store? Many unitholders in the emerging market funds did not even wait to see what would happen – they took to the hills!

The hills they took to were the usual sanctuaries. The Swiss franc, the German peutschmark, the US dollar and a little bit into gold. Gold, unlike Mexican Peso Bonds for example, has the advantage of being no one else's liability.

As Fund Managers, we know only too well what happens when investors take fright. This newsletter endeavours to keep you abreast of what we are doing with your money, but from time to time it may also serve as something of a shock absorber. No doubt a psychologist could explain why human beings feel better about losing money if they think they know why they are losing money! I mention this because the Mercury Gold and General Fund has not come out unscathed from the South American debacle. We do, after all, have nearly 4 per cent of the Fund invested there.

Our largest South American holding is that "wonder stock" Buenaventura, the Peruvian gold miner which owns the Yanacocha deposit in partnership with Newmont Gold. Last year, Buenaventura rose 150 per cent from Soles 4.90 to Soles 12.26, but the recent combination of a lacklustre gold price and the Mexican crisis caused the share to fall 34 per cent from its high at one moment.

"What," we can hear you ask, "has a devaluation of the Mexican peso got to do with the price of a Peruvian gold mine?" The answer, of course, is not a lot. However, the price of a share can sometimes have less to do with its fundamental value than with the number of people who want to buy or sell it. In the case of Buenaventura, Emerging Market Fund Managers facing massive redemptions, have little choice but to sell whatever they can sell. Once Buenaventura had fallen 34 per cent, a number of us did want to buy them, especially when we saw that the flight to quality was helping the gold price to recover. Within 48 hours the shares had recovered to Soles 9.90, 24 per cent from their low.

We have to admit that we are somewhat mystified by the way gold has been performing recently. We keep being told that there is insatiable demand from the traditional buyers whenever the price falls below US$375/oz, but its failure to reflect in any meaningful way the extraordinary strength of other commodities is rather surprising. It feels as if there has been a persistent seller preventing the metal from getting its head above water. One theory is that Arab interests concerned with the liquidation of BCCI may have been disposing of significant quantities of gold to meet their obligations. Happily that unfortunate saga is now said to be drawing to an end. We will probably never know what caused gold to behave so sluggishly, but when it starts to go up again, we won't care what the reason was. Looking back however, we will wonder what on earth stopped us from taking advantage of such a wonderful buying opportunity. (**280. 16/1/95**)

Julian points out his "lobster pot" thesis, explaining that large gold share funds must start to alter their course well ahead of any trend change.

Trying to stand in the way of such a sea change in sentiment and argue that actually gold has not behaved too badly compared with Bonds and equities is a bit like lying down on the track in front of an express train and expecting it to stop. It is far more tempting simply to go down into the bunker with everyone else and wait until conditions improve, or simply sell out of the market.

Selling out of the gold sector is certainly what investors in the world's gold funds have been doing. We know from experience that the gold market is very much a one-way street. The great difficulty from our point of view, is trying to anticipate when the flow is going to be reversed. With a Fund this size, it is no good waiting for the first signs of a reverse in sentiment. By that time it is too late. We have to anticipate the change well in advance. You can liken it to the captain of a tanker whose radar has broken down, having to alter course in order to avoid the rocks long before the warning flash of the lighthouse comes into view. We did alter course before the warning lights were visible but not enough to escape unscathed from the wreckage. The very same predicament is being faced by Fund Managers in the emerging market funds, some of which also hold gold shares. No wonder the behaviour of gold shares under such circumstances, bears little relationship to the metal which guides their fortunes; a metal which

A gift to Julian Baring from the South African desk of Deutsche Morgan Grenfell on the occasion of his retirement in 1996.

From this you can tell that the price of gold is as unpredictable as a one arm bandit. All you can do it buy it when it is down, sell it when it is high and the shares likewise.

Geoffrey Campbell (third from left) visiting Buryatzoloto, Siberia in 1995.

Fieldwork at The Savoy – Julian with his wife (Isla) prepare to pay for their set menu. Paddy Linakar who ran the gold fund at M & G felt left out as the sovereign could only cover the cost for 2.5 people at the time.

"You may have noticed the recent uptick in the Indian economy which coincided with my wife Isla's arrival there on holiday three weeks ago. Her enthusiasm for shopping is becoming internationally renowned for kick starting the economies of the emerging markets she visits."

Julian in retirement in 2000. He became known as "Le potier Anglais" in his village in Provence.

Graham Birch,
director, *1993–2010*

David Baker,
portfolio manager,
1992–2001

Trevor Steel,
portfolio manager,
1992–2001

Richard Davis,
managing director,
portfolio manager,
June 1994

Evy Hambro,
chief investment officer,
natural resources –
managing director,
July 1994

Catherine Raw,
managing director,
portfolio manager,
July 2001

Graham Birch and Justin Baring
Fundraising for the Julian Baring
scholarship, *2009*

The BlackRock Natural Resources Team.

knows nothing of the agonies and uncertainties suffered by those of us who invest in it.

With nearly 50 per cent of the fund invested in South Africa, we have been particularly badly affected by the fact that South Africa has been much harder hit than the other gold markets, partly no doubt because South Africa has also been affected by what has been going on in the emerging market funds. What has been most scary for both us and the emerging market funds, is that the South African gold shares have fallen a long way on relatively little volume. In this "seller only" environment, even the shares of quite well-known major gold mining companies have turned out to be "lobster pots" – easy to get into and much more difficult to get out of. (**282. 26/1/95**)

Trouble in the South African mines led by wage negotiations leads investors to favour North American gold stocks, much to Julian's frustration but also understanding.

There is no question that the South African gold shares have been the worst performers since last year's high. We had already anticipated that they had reached unsustainable levels when we wrote the Newsletter on 4th November 1994 which carried the headline "Trees Don't Grow To The Sky". At that time, as a defensive measure, we invested in base metal shares and in addition we switched a portion of the portfolio from individual South African gold mines into the South African Mining Houses. This turned out to be a relatively successful strategy although it was not enough to prevent the Fund price retreating some 20 per cent. As gold shares have fallen back towards attractive buying levels (see table) and redemption's have had to be met, we have reversed this strategy and reduced our non-gold investments from 30 per cent to 13 per cent of the portfolio. We are thus fast becoming a pure gold fund again.

Of course, the South African gold shares are not languishing for no good reason. In fact, it is quite hard to find any South African mining share to get excited about. Apart from Western Areas (our largest holding) and Beatrix (which we don't hold) where is the sizzle? Apart from Randgold where is the blue sky?

Wage negotiations are about to start with the African miners asking for wage rises of between 19–70 per cent. There is little chance of such a claim being met and this raises the possibility of a strike. Unpayable shafts may have to be closed down permanently. The mine owners seem demoralised, not knowing what to do. White miners fear to maintain discipline underground. Safety seems to be becoming an increasing worry. In 1994 one life was lost for every 50,000 ounces of gold produced valuing each life at US$18 million of foreign exchange earnings or a mere US$2.8 million of net profit. And this year the figures are likely to be even more gruesome. No wonder foreign investors are dumping their South African gold mines in favour of the greener pastures of North America. They are taking the view that if everything goes wrong in South Africa, the gold price has only one way to go and that will more than justify paying a premium for American reserve ounces.

Those of us who have been round the South African race track more than once in a life time recognise the feeling we are now experiencing. At the time of Sharpeville and the Soweto riots we felt just the same way. Before President Mandela was elected there was huge uncertainty and much bloodshed but those who sold out at much the same valuations as prevail today rued the decision within a year.

As we stand, many South African gold shares are selling on yields of about 8 per cent based on currently depressed earnings. Not a bad yield while waiting for better times. SG Warburg Securities tell us that at present with profitability so low the mining industry is effectively only working for the shareholders for one day a month. If the workers chose to go on strike that day Warburgs say (tongue-in-cheek) that it will eliminate shareholder returns! The other side of the same coin proves the old saying that the threat of imminent death concentrates the mind wonderfully.

Will the South African miner go down the same path as the Zambian copper miners or the UK coal miners, dockers and car workers who chose to do less than a full days work for an affordable wage thus bringing their industries to their knees in the process? Does the market believe that black South Africans, after all they have been through, will learn nothing from other people's experience? Or will our belief that realism will prevail turn out to be yet another triumph of hope over experience? (**296. 18/5/95**)

Julian calls for fundamental reform in the South African gold mine industry.

So, much remains to be done to bring the South African gold industry back from the brink. It is clearly nonsensical for a capital intensive industry to only work for 250 out of 365 days of the year, as at present. This anomaly is at last being addressed and should be rectified by the end of this year. It is old fashioned, to say the least, to have one man one job. Current thinking is to have smaller but more highly paid teams underground who can do each other's jobs. These teams should in due course be able to achieve one blast per day, whereas at present a blast is achieved every three days. Where these improvements have already been introduced, the increase in productivity has been most encouraging.

The excessive bureaucracy which has been allowed to grow up around the industry over the years makes decision making painfully slow. The Chamber of Mines which negotiates wage rates with the unions for the whole industry is part of the bureaucracy. The system which has evolved results in wage settlements which take little account of ability to pay. It has a similar effect to that of reducing the speed of a convoy to the speed of the slowest ship. The richer mines have little incentive to bear down rigorously on costs. All they have to do is better than the poorest mines.

There is an urgent need to devolve power down to the mines from Head Office and to incentivise the senior management at the mines themselves. At present if you ask most mine managers who they work for, they become confused. They should be in no doubt. They should be given options in the mining company they work for to ensure that they have a community of interest with the shareholders. Where these common sense reforms have been introduced the results have been spectacular.

Obviously these reforms cannot be introduced overnight, but when they are, the rewards for the long-suffering shareholders should be great. We think those who earn their livings from this once great industry have been given such a shock by what has happened to them recently, that this time nothing can stop the much needed reforms from being introduced. If they aren't we're dead! (**322. 25/11/95**)

Julian calls for the South African gold houses to look at the issue of board composition.

In our view, the study currently being undertaken by the government into the governance of the mining industry should give consideration to what is the most desirable composition of the boards of the individual gold mining companies. It should bear in mind that the interests of the Mining Houses do not necessarily coincide with those of the shareholders of the individual mines. The system cries out for the appointment of genuinely independent non-executive directors, but the question is whether a system that has endured for over 100 years is capable of changing of its own accord and whether sufficient outside pressure can be brought to bear to bring South African practice into line with international practice. Our rantings as major shareholders of some of the individual gold mines have had about as much effect on the Randlords as the sting of a tsetse fly on an elephant. (**329. 19/1/96**)

Julian calls for more incentivisation of South African gold mines management.

With over 40 per cent of our portfolio invested in South Africa we have a vested interest in any strategy which might lead to an increase in the valuation placed by the market on South African gold shares. We have often suggested that shareholder value could be enhanced by emulating the more successful policies adopted by gold mining companies elsewhere. Incentivising the management of the individual mines with options on shares of their own companies, rather than options in the controlling Mining Houses shares over which they have much less influence, could have a most beneficial effect on shareholder value. They seem most reluctant to do this, with certain notable exceptions. Individual gold mining companies have no opportunity to prospect outside their own lease areas. They are therefore denied the high value placed on the "blue sky" enjoyed by their foreign competitors. (**334. 26/2/96**)

The Fund continues to favour an overweight position in South African gold shares. Julian explains why, and also how it has been able to effect fundamental change in the industry through its control of Randgold.

One of the questions we are most often asked at presentations for the Mercury Gold and General Fund is "How can you sleep soundly at night when you have such a massive over weighting to South Africa in the Fund?" South African gold shares represent about 21 per cent of the James Capel Global Gold Index, whereas some 42 per cent of our Fund's portfolio is invested in that country.

The principal explanation is that unhedged South African gold shares provide the best gearing to a rising gold price. What we pay for a South African ounce in the ground is now considerably less than what we, as shareholders, get for it once it has been mined. Nesbitt Burns, the Canadian broker, tell us that a gold price of US$500/oz would be needed for that to be the case in respect of the large North American gold mines. The plummeting rand has recently transformed the profitability of those South African mines which have resisted the temptation to sell forward.

But there is another reason why we are so attracted to the South African gold shares. It is because there are so many things that can still be done to enhance shareholder value. Only the will has been lacking to make the necessary changes to a mature industry that has become too set in its ways.

It was just over two years ago that we, together with like-minded investors, seized an opportunity to bring about some of the changes which we thought, if tried, would have the effect of enhancing shareholder value. We were able to vote to install new management at Randgold, the smallest of the Mining Houses. The new management agreed with us that the huge discount to the assets at which Randgold shares (R7.00) were then standing could best be reduced by tackling certain fundamental issues. Furthermore, they were prepared to put their own money where their mouths were before embarking on the necessary changes (which are listed below).

- Reversing forward sales contracts since these have the effect of depressing the gold price and reducing the imperative of keeping down costs.

- Monetising the mine management fees by exchanging them for shares in the underlying mines. The management contracts can so easily cause a conflict of interest between the shareholders of the individual mines and the shareholders of the controlling Mining House. Management contracts can prevent badly run companies from being taken over by allowing control to be exercised without a significant shareholding.

- Attempting to get value placed, where no value previously existed, on the "blue sky" normally associated with exploration acreage. It is only exploration acreage that has the potential to turn a mining company from a wasting asset into a growth stock. It has been the custom in South Africa for this acreage to be held by the Mining Houses, but due to the discounts at which they sell to their assets, a nil or even negative value is apparently placed on them by the market. More value would be unlocked if they were owned by the individual mines.

- Ensuring that the senior management of each gold mine is incentivised with share options in the company he works for, rather than in the controlling Mining House. The existing system stops him thinking like a shareholder of his mine and divides his loyalties.

- Breaking down the entrenched bureaucratic hierarchy which exists within the mining industry thus separating the face worker from the chief executive by what must seem like impenetrable layers of management.

- Giving top priority to mining profitable ounces rather than maximising tonnage hoisted through improved grade control and the more efficient use of geological skills on the mines.

- Paying more attention to shareholder relations by arranging roadshows and improved presentation of the quarterly results. South African institutions have long since become disillusioned with the gold mining industry and are hugely underweight in the sector. International investors are a more fertile field to foster investor relations.

That was the checklist we wrote down on the back of an envelope just over two years ago before the new management took over. Now, two years later, every item on the checklist has been addressed. The shares have risen from R7 to R23, far outpacing the other South African Mining Houses. For us this outstanding record has been marred by two events. First, to our shame we failed to keep the faith and sold our holding before the shares got to R14, having multiplied our original investment sevenfold. Randgold too forgot themselves and sold a limited amount of gold forward just before the price went rocketing up on the devaluation of the rand.

Notwithstanding these two blunders and despite Randgold's original game plan being greeted with much hilarity and mirth, not to say scepticism when it was announced, it is now being copied with variations by some of the other Houses. The floodgates have been breached. We are about to get our reward. (342. 20/5/96)

Julian bemoans the South African gold industry management's tendency to meddle in financial engineering rather than mining engineering.

Those of you with long memories will remember that a few people in senior positions in the South African mining industry lost their jobs ("pour encourager les autres") on account of the horrible losses they incurred by unsuccessful currency dealing. After that it became unfashionable to put one's job at risk in this way and it was many years before forward selling and currency hedging became acceptable once again.

What discourages people from investing in South African gold shares is that companies cannot be relied upon to resist the temptation to become currency speculators. If only the companies could be persuaded to earn their management fees by expending more of their skills on mining engineering, directed at producing the maximum amount of metal at the minimum cost and less on financial engineering, we would find it a great deal easier to analyse the companies and make sensible predictions of their earnings potential.

We have feared for some time that a nasty accident would occur sooner or later as a result of unwise currency speculation or forward selling. It is therefore of little comfort that our fears have been borne out.

Until someone has to take the consequences of his actions, this undesirable activity is likely to continue to the detriment of overall market sentiment. In the meantime shareholders will not only have to bear the pain of the losses incurred they will also have to suffer from a lower value being placed on the market as a whole than would otherwise be the case. If South African companies cannot make hay when the sun shines, God help us when the rainy season starts. (352. 16/8/96)

Fund favourite Western Areas' forward sales initiative trashes its share price despite a strong rally in gold.

Last November's forward sale trashed the price of Western Areas, from which it has taken a whole year to recover. It did not prevent the gold price from rising to US$417 shortly thereafter, sparking a 30 per cent rally in the gold share market. These forward sales do affect the supply/demand for gold and the price, whatever the experts say, and sometimes they are the cause of investors giving up the unequal struggle. With equities world-wide hitting new highs, investors get tempted to sell their gold shares in order to join the bandwagon.

We always say that investors buy and sell gold shares in order to relieve pain. The pain of holding gold shares when they are falling and everything else is rising becomes too great, so people sell. The shares then become oversold and the bears of gold get squeezed and the gold price rallies. The pain of having sold at the bottom and seeing the long-awaited rally enriching those who have held on through thick and thin, becomes too great to bear so they buy back. There is nothing we can do to change human nature! The best antidote for investors is to imitate an ostrich. (**360. 8/10/96**)

Julian continues his crusade to have South African gold shares valued in line with their global peers, and ponders on whether foreign groups will invest in the SA industry in due course.

And then of course there is the unfinished business to be attended to. I have in mind the unfinished business of helping to get South African gold shares the ratings they deserve. This year has not been easy for those of us who believe that the South African mining industry has it within its power to get its gold shares rated more like their international peers. They have been slow in bringing about the changes needed to put them onto a level playing field. It seemed so obvious to us what needed to be done this time last year, but it has taken far longer than we expected for the changes to be instituted. Good progress has been made during the year, even though it may be hard to detect it from a distance.

For much of this year it seemed as if all momentum for change had been lost. This is evidenced by the fact that although the Rand price of gold has been soaring, South African gold shares have been plunging. However, the fact that it is difficult to see the movement of the minute hand of a clock, does not mean that time stands still. Changes are taking place. One day soon, you will wake up to find that the industry has changed radically. That is when you will start seeing the re-rating for which we have been waiting so impatiently.

Already we are starting to see the South African broking fraternity focusing on the growth potential of the new style gold companies which are emerging as a result of the Evander and Avgold mergers. (See last week's Newsletter). It should not be long now before we see brokers making comparisons between the values offered by these new companies, unencumbered as they now are by stultifying management contracts, and those offered by their international competitors.

If, magically, one or both of these new super mines could be plucked out of the ground in South Africa and deposited in North America, they would be valued at a multiple of what they are now valued at. Of course magicians are in short supply these days and there is little chance of anyone picking up South African ounces and putting them where investors would like them to be. But it is possible to convert a Russian, South American or Indonesian ounce into a North American ounce, provided that ounce is owned by an American Company. We have seen this trick performed on numerous occasions. The technique is called "mining the market" and it requires much less effort than mining the deposit. We have frequently said that it is a scandal that not a single foreign mining company has seen fit to invest in South Africa since a democratically-elected government was elected in that country.

One day some brave North American mining company will take the plunge and planeloads of North American mining analysts will then be flown out to see what they have bought. What they will see will bear little resemblance to the awful things they have read about in the papers. Circulars will be written extolling the far sightedness of the American company and how cheaply they have added ounces to their reserves. The cost of the average South African ounce in the ground is currently US$39. The market pays more than US$200 for the average North American ounce. You don't have to dilute your share capital much to acquire lots of South African ounces if you run a North American gold company. In North America, gold shares are revered as a type of super currency. In South Africa they are hardly rated at all. Mix the two together and you get super currency with super value.

What is crystal clear from this distance is that South African gold shares will not be re-rated so long as South African corporate governance is out of line with international best practice. International investors find it hard to accept the pyramid structures which are so much a part of the South African corporate system. They feel vulnerable to exploitation in the absence of genuinely independent non-executive directors sitting on the Boards of the gold mines to protect the interests of minority shareholders. And they have noticed that the directors of the gold companies hold no shares or options in the individual mines but have shares and options in the Mining Houses. People think that this must result in horrendous conflicts of interest. (**364. 14/11/96**)

8. The Essence of Valuation –
What you Pay and What you Get

Julian had very firm opinions about the subject of valuing mining shares, particularly gold shares. He held to the view that when being considered for inclusion in the G&G Fund any mine needed to have the potential to return at least what he was paying the market for the shares. It was therefore the case that he was very keen for brokers to have long-term metal price forecasts as part of the process.

Julian explains his approach to brokers over valuation.

The other thing I ask them (the brokers) to tell me is the present value of the future earnings of the companies they recommend, discounted at 5 per cent. I tell them I accept full responsibility for the long-term metal prices I ask them to use in their calculations. These are as follows; Gold $320/oz, Copper 90c/lb, Aluminium 80 c/lb, Zinc 50c/lb, Lead 35c/lb, Nickel $3.00/lb. If they know better, particularly in the short term, I encourage them to use their own metal price forecasts but only for the next 12 months or so.

This approach entails the adoption of a whole new valuation method for mining shares. I bet it was the method used by RTZ to value the mining companies they acquired from B.P. We all applauded the deal done by RTZ and this was reflected in their subsequent share price performance. If I use the same method, perhaps our fund will behave as well as RTZ has! There is some reluctance to provide these figures, but those brokers who oblige are getting most of our business. (39. 31/01/89)

As far as gold shares are concerned, he (Rob Weinberg of UBS) looks upon them as collectables. That's original I had not thought of them that way, but that is what they are. The price of gold shares has nothing to do with their earnings capacity, merely with the number of people who want to buy them at a given time. That being so, it's hard to see why so much research is done into their earnings capability. I'm joking of course, but with gold shares it seems to me you need the advice of a mass psychologist more than that of a mining analyst. (**50. 9/5/89**)

Sufficient now to remind you that mining shares which offer a better return than UK Government Index Linked Bonds are categorised as "may buys". Those which offer a return 50 per cent greater than that are termed "must buys'. Conversely those which offer a return of up to 50 per cent lower than an Index Linked Bond are termed "may sells' and those which offer even less than that are categorised as "must sells". Got it? As the shares go up and down each day, they change their position on the "slippery slope" and we buy them or sell them accordingly.

Since dreaming up the idea of the "slippery slope" another category of stock has been invented, known as the "super buy". "Super buys" are rare as Bongos. They are shares which offer a potential profit in excess of 60 per cent from the current market price to the "must sell" level. (**57. 5//7/89**)

The habit of brokers to direct Fund Managers finds little support from Julian.

You may recognize it as the "slippery slope" method which has been perfected by Ord Minnett with no little encouragement and much financial inducement from you and me. Others, less mercenary than Ord Minnett, prefer to continue with their practice of "handing down the tablets" – and why shouldn't they? Fund Managers are not expected to think for themselves! The great attraction of our method is that it throws up long-term values which are, by their very nature, unaffected by short-term considerations. When the short-termites get into a lather and ditch their shares at depressed levels, it often brings them within our buying range.

That is just what happened last week with Phelps Dodge. Having paid a special dividend of $10, the shares fell by $13, putting them into our "super buy" category. I am happy to tell you that the "slippery slope" rules forced me to buy 6,000 additional shares below $65 and they have since recovered to $71. With a bit of luck they will soon recover the whole dividend, just as the shares of Inca did when they paid their own special dividend some months ago. Phelps Dodge remains one of the cheapest mining shares in the world, offering investors an exceptionally generous return on their money. (**66. 4/10/89**)

Julian once more spotlights Phelps Dodge one of his favourite value shares.

People are understandably depressed by the decline in base metal prices, but don't forget the profit margins are still more than satisfactory. Breakeven costs at Phelps Dodge are in the 60–65 cents range, compared with the present copper price of 108 cents. That is not what I call living on the breadline!

At the present price of Phelps Dodge ($58) and assuming a long-term copper price of only 75c/lb, Phelps Dodge is currently offering investors a real return of 6.9 per cent. That may not seem much to you, but it is nearly twice what you can get on a 20-year Index-Linked Bond. (**71. 23/11/89**)

Julian baulks at the high ratings of North American gold.

As I write, the gold price and gold shares are having a breather after their hectic rise of the last few weeks. Brokers had become alarmed at the prices people were paying for gold shares. Here are Shearson's estimates, for example, of the prospective PE ratios of North American gold shares, based on two gold prices next year, $400 and $500/oz.

You can see why up to now I have been reluctant to own many of these shares. Since it will take 21 years for the average N. American mine to recoup its present share price in earnings, given $500 gold, I would rather own the metal. After all, gold is $409 now and if it is going to go to $500, that in itself is a potential gain of 22 per cent. However, with investments, things are not always what they seem. (**72. 30/11/89**)

The value attractions of base metal shares catches Julian's eye.

Scotia McLeod have produced the following charts for me. The charts show the real price of metals since 1967, expressed in 1990 dollars. They also show the actual price of the metals. Inflation makes it hard to know at any moment whether the metals are cheap or expensive. I have indicated (with a +) the long-term prices in 1990 dollars that I am using for calculating the value of our mining investments. All this sounds a bit complicated, however it is worth trying to follow what I am trying to do, because if I am wrong it's going to cost you!

Perhaps the most controversial forecast is that for copper. I perceive that the cost of producing copper is falling in real terms and therefore I am loath to use past prices to forecast the future. If, as you can see, I were to use the historic long term price of copper in order to forecast future copper prices, the copper industry could make well over 100 per cent profit on every tonne produced. It would not be long before copper mines became as fashionable as gold mines! I doubt if that will happen but as far as I know there is no God-given-reason why they it should be any less profitable.

Even using these down to earth metal prices, base metal shares offer rates of return which stack up favourably against most industrial equities. It therefore seems to me to make perfectly good sense to include a smattering of this fund in balanced portfolios. (**92. 10/5/90**)

1990 PE Ratios

Company	$400	$500
AmaxGold	39	23
American Barrick	50	38
Echo Bay	36	18
Freeport Gold	36	20
FMC Gold	21	12
Homestake	42	16
Placer Dome	27	18
Average	35.5	20.7

Favourite Phelps Dodge again!

Taking current copper prices, Phelps Dodge is earning at the rate of $18.50 a year which at $60 puts them on a PE of 3.2 times earnings. Put another way, in the time it has taken you to read this note, Phelps Dodge has earned about $3,600. Not a bad reward for 3 minutes work! (**107. 20/8/90**)

Julian's request to brokers after business.

On a different (but not altogether different) subject, I thought you would like to know that whenever the brokers ring up urging me to buy a gold share I now ask them to answer a few simple questions to make sure I am buying good value. I thought you might like to see the questions.

So far none of the brokers I speak to have been able to answer the last question in the affirmative, despite the fact that their normal circulars are full of buy recommendations. Of course, they too are in the business of feeding ducks so you can hardly expect them to behave like tobacco companies and issue health warnings with their products.

Caveat Emptor, I say.

FINANCIAL ARITHMETIC

	Question		Answer	
1	How many Proven / Probable ounces are stated by company		0	oz
2	How many ounces do you think you are buying Careful now!		0	oz
3	Deduct ounces earmarked to repay gold loans (oz) (they belong to the bank)		0	oz
4	Net ounces in ground (=No 1+No 2+No 3)(oz)		0	oz
5	No shares fully diluted		0	M
6	Share price US$		$0.00	
7	Market Capitalization (US$)		$0	M
8	Market Cap as % of value of gold in the ground	0%		
	Basis $400/oz	0%		
	Basis $500/oz	0%		
	Basis $600/oz	0%		
	Basis $700/oz	0%		
	Basis $800/oz	0%		
	On basis No 24		0%	
	Current gold price	$386		

FINANCIAL ARITHMETIC

9	Market cap per ounce of resource (=No 7/No 4) (US$/oz)		0	/oz
10	What are the cash costs per ounce (US$/oz)		0	/oz
11	In order to calculate overheads.....			
	a) Latest net profits in local currency (millions)	0		M
	in US$ millions	0		M
	b) Ounces produced in that period (oz)	0		/oz
	c) What was the profit per ounce US$	0		/oz
	d) What was the net profit per ounce (a/b)	$0		/oz
	e) SO THE NET COST PER OUNCE WAS (c–d)	$0		/oz
	f) The overheads per ounce (incl tax) were (e–No 10)	$0		/oz
	(Excluding tax…)			
	g) What was the effective tax rate? (percent)	0%		0%
	h) Tax per ounce paid (d/l–g)–d)	$0		/oz
	i) Therefore untaxed overheads (f–h)		$0	/oz
12	What is the company's effective tax rate likely to be?		$0	/oz
13	Deduct/Add profit or loss/oz if all forward sales closed out today	25%		/oz
14	Deduct/Add Net Cash/Debt in balance sheet (excluding gold loans) $/oz		0	/oz
15	Deduct/Add other factors per ounce			/oz
16	Gold price needed to breakeven (No9/(1–No 12) + Sun 10 – 15	$0	$0	/oz

VALUATION ANALYSIS

17	What is the mine life (number of years at assumed production rate)		0	Years
18	Do you look for a real return on your money when making an investment?		0	
19	If YES what real return do you seek?		$0.0%	
20	What total undiscounted profits are needed to achieve this return? US$ million (No7/return factor)	$0		M
21	How much does this equate grossed up for tax? US$ million (No 20/(1–No 12)	$0		M
22	What is current profit margin No 11d		$0	/oz

23	What profit margin is required per oz to give desired return? (No 21/No 4	$0	/oz
24	So what gold price per oz is required to give that profit margin? (No 10+No 23+ No 11+ No 13+ No14+No15)	$0	/oz
25	What ore required undiscounted profits (No 20/share)	$0.00	
26	Using table below apply percentage discount to check calculation	$0.00	
27	Is the answer to number 22 a reasonable assumption of the gold price in today's money that is likely to prevail over mine life.		
28	Share price needed to justify current gold price (No 8/No 10/No 11i/No 13/No 14/No 15) x (1/ No 12) x No 4 x return factor/No 5	$0.0	
29	Gold price needed to justify current share price No 24	$0	
30	In the light of answer to No 26 are the shares good fundamental value?		

YEARS MINE LIFE

		1	2	3	4	5	6	7	8	9	10	11	12	13	14	15	16	17	18	19	20
DISCOUNT	2.0%	0.98	0.97	0.96	0.95	0.94	0.93	0.92	0.92	0.91	0.9	0.89	0.88	0.87	0.86	0.86	0.85	0.84	0.83	0.83	0.82
RATE	6.5%	0.94	0.91	0.88	0.86	0.83	0.81	0.78	0.76	0.74	0.72	0.7	0.68	0.66	0.64	0.63	0.61	0.59	0.58	0.56	0.55
	10.0%	0.91	0.87	0.83	0.79	0.76	0.73	0.7	0.67	0.64	0.61	0.59	0.57	0.55	0.53	0.51	0.49	0.47	0.46	0.44	0.43

(108. 30/8/90)

The required return on the Fund's investments.

What I have been doing, as you know, is basing the return required on our investments on metal prices which I believe can be sustained in the long run. In nearly all cases such prices are well below current prices. If at those metal prices the shares offer a real return which is 50 per cent better than we could get by investing our money in a 20-year Index Linked Bond, I buy them. The higher the return they offer, the more I try to buy.

As you have seen, we can be caught between a rock and a hard place by adopting this investment policy. Let's take copper as an example. The copper price is currently $1.28/lb and falling, bringing copper shares down with it. The copper price on which we base our long-term earnings projections is 79c/lb. If the copper price is going to fall to our long-term price, it is inevitable that copper shares will fall too, even though they already provide the returns we seek, based on 79c/lb copper. (110. 26/9/90)

More thoughts on the issue of rates of return and metal prices.

When considering what metal prices should be used in order to calculate mining company earnings in the future, it is as well to keep an eye on historical prices, expressed of course, in today's money.

Capels have come up with an interesting table which gives the prices of various metals since 1934, the year the gold price was raised from $20.67/oz to $35/oz.

206

It shows (A) what price each metal should now be if it had kept pace with US inflation since 1934; it also shows (B) the price in 1990 dollars that each metal has averaged since 1934. Also given (C) are the metal prices we are projecting in order to calculate future earnings for the companies in our portfolio. These can be compared with today's prices.

METAL PRICES SINCE 1934

		A	B	C		
	ACTUAL PRICE 1934	1934 PRICE IN 1990 dollars	AVERAGE 1990 DOLLARS	PRICE NOW	PROJECTED PRICE	
COPPER	USc/lb	$8.5	$78.4	$122.3	$122.0	$80.0
ALUMINIUM	USc/lb	$23.3	$216.6	$105.2	$84.0	$75.0
ZINC	USc/lb	$4.2	$38.7	$57.4	$62.0	$53.0
LEAD	USc/lb	$3.9	$35.9	$52.1	$36.0	$26.0
NICKEL	USc/lb	$35.0	$325.4	$334.9	$419.0	$315.0
GOLD	USc/oz	$34.7	$322.6	$273.7	$393.0	$400.0
PLATINUM	USc/oz	$36.5	$339.0	$411.7	$488.0	
SILVER	USc/oz	$48.0	$445.9	$542.7	$468.0	$550.0

When forecasting future price levels we have to bear in mind that improved technology can reduce costs considerably. Copper is a case in point. In 1980 Phelps Dodge was producing copper at 80c/lb whereas with solvent extraction they are now producing it at 50c/lb. This helps to explain why most of our projected base metal prices look so mean compared with historic prices.

A couple of weeks ago I was making the point that it is a great deal easier for us Fund Managers to decide what return we want to achieve on the funds entrusted to us than it is to forecast metal price. I mentioned that it would be helpful to know the gold price required to cause the average gold share to provide a real return of 6.5 per cent over the remaining life. All I then have to do is decide whether that price looks attainable.

W.I. Carr were the first brokers to respond to this request and they provided the information for their universe of gold shares. Their findings are attached (I have underlined the stocks we sold). You can see that they calculate that a gold price of $558/oz (1990 dollars) would be needed from now on to allow the average gold share to offer a real return of 6.5 per cent. That is 43 per cent higher than today's gold price. (**112. 11/10/90**)

Gold Price $385

	PRICE US$	SHARES M	MKT CAP	PROVEN & PROBABLE RESERVES	MKT CAP /OZ RES	ANNUAL PROD OZ	LIFE YEARS	6.5% DISC FACTOR	TOTAL COSTS /OZ	PRETAX PROFIT /OZ	PROFITS DISC -6.5%
BMG	6.88	72.3	492	4.3	116	330	13	0.661	2.31	154	102
HEM	11.5	87.5	1006	5.76	175	428	13	0.653	212	173	113
AU	13.38	60	803	3.94	204	360	11	0.700	212	173	121
ICR	4.63	166.2	770	5.82	132	715	8	0.758	285	100	76
FGL	9.38	65.5	614	1.89	325	320	6	0.809	158	227	184
NGC	39.38	104.9	4131	20.7	200	1700	12	0.677	273	112	76
ECO	11.5	99.1	1140	12.64	90	803	16	0.615	332	53	33
PGU	11.13	24.7	275	3.09	89	337	9	0.736	343	42	31
HM	18.75	79.5	1491	14.72	101	1150	13	0.665	316	39	26
ABX	19.88	133.5	2654	19.9	133	573	35	0.393	321	64	25
LAC	7.63	121.2	925	6.33	146	773	8	0.757	370	15	1
BIG	3.5	57.6	202	4.35	46	600	7	0.778	387	-2	-2

North American Gold Producers
Profit Margins and Market Cap per ounce

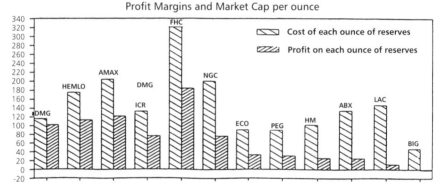

Julian raises his hurdle rate for mining shares returns.

As you know I try not to buy a real return of less than 6.5 per cent. I still think that a hurdle rate of 6.5 per cent is reasonable. After all, until three months ago, according to the "slippery slope", only about 10 per cent of the mining shares we follow offered as good a return as that and even now, after the massive falls we have seen, only about one third of them offer that return. The trouble is those that do, have fallen with the rest of the market and now offer much more than 6.5 per cent. Most of our large holdings now appear to offer a prospective real return of between 7.5–10 per cent! I wish, with the advantage of hindsight, I had not been so eager to buy them as soon as they hit the 6.5 per cent target.

Are you sitting down? I have just read the last paragraph to Capel's strategist, Alastair Ross-Goobey, who tells me that the real return on equities in the UK since 1918 has in fact been 7.5 per cent and in America 7.8 per cent. (Takes a bear market to discover something like that – typical!) From now on our hurdle rate has got to be 8 per cent, since mining shares are riskier than equities. **(115. 31/10/90)**

Julian continues to ponder long term rates of return on gold shares and the required gold price.

The table gave me an idea. If we know the total cost to a mine of producing each ounce, we can of course establish the pre-tax profit which each ounce produces at any given gold price. We can then make the admittedly crude assumption that the mine will make broadly the same profit from each ounce mined in future. We can calculate what we are paying for each remaining ounce (market cap per ounce of reserves) so it is easy to see whether we are buying value. Overleaf is how the picture looks if gold averages $385/oz (1990 dollars) from now on.

You don't have to be Einstein to see that, at the current gold price, you are paying more for each ounce than the profit each ounce will produce. In most cases, much more. Obviously a much higher gold price is required to provide value. Here is the same table assuming gold averages $556 (1990 dollars) in future instead of today's $385. I leave it to you to decide whether this is likely.

You can now see that much better value is provided. Capel's work shows that for the average mine to give a 6.5 per cent real return a gold price of $556 is required. That is why the second table has been calculated using that figure.

I personally find it hard to believe that gold, which has averaged $290 (1990 dollars) for the last 56 years, will average $556 from now on. In fact, the owner of an ounce of gold has almost exactly maintained his purchasing power over the last 50 years, for which he should be duly grateful. Why the market should apparently expect him to be endowed in the future with nearly twice the purchasing power that he now enjoys escapes me, but that is what gold shares seem to be implying. **(116. 8/11/90)**

North American Gold Stocks
Profit Analysis & Market Cap per Oz of Reserves for the third quarter 1990

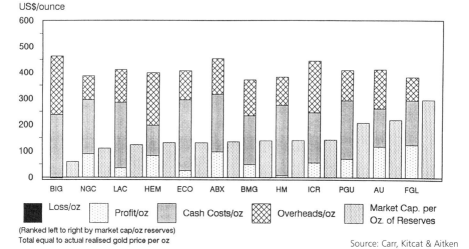

(Ranked left to right by market cap/oz reserves)
Total equal to actual realised gold price per oz

Source: Carr, Kitcat & Aitken

Julian once more looks at gold mine valuations and wonders whether the reserve base of many mines can actually be mined at a profit at a time of low gold prices.

Following on from last week's Newsletter, Carr Kitcat & Aitken have kindly produced a bar chart which shows a breakdown of the revenues of selected North American gold shares.

The left-hand column is divided into three segments. The bottom segment (the dotted portion) shows the profit per ounce earned last quarter by each company. Above that (in grey), is the cash cost of extracting the gold from the ground. The hatched segment is derived by deducting the profit per ounce and the cash costs per ounce from the total revenue per ounce. I call these overheads. They include depreciation, exploration expenditure, interest and Head Office expenses.

The right-hand column attempts to show how much a new shareholder is paying for each proven and probable ounce in the reserves of each company.

I can already hear the cries of "foul" coming from the mining industry because no account is taken of possible and inferred reserves over and above those that are designated "proven and probable". That's fair enough, but how many companies are finding more reserves than they are mining? If anything I suspect we may be in for a few nasty surprises at the year-end, since ore reserve calculations at the last year end were probably based on a higher gold price and lower costs than we now have. Maybe we will see a speeding up of the recent trend for proven and probable reserves to be reduced. I have been looking at one particular company this week which would not have made any profit at all if it had not sold all its production forward at very high prices a couple of years ago. As far as I know, the definition of ore reserves is "ore which can be mined at a profit". Surely not a profit which depends solely on forward sales?

So if I am being unfair to some companies by only valuing their proven and probable reserves I am sorry about that.

There is a compensating factor however. For the purpose of this exercise I have assumed that the investor requires no return on his money. It has admittedly been acceptable in gold mining circles to ask for no return but this is becoming less so by the day. In very simple terms, if you want a return on your money that return has to come out of the available profits. Where else can it come from except from the portion of the revenue that you get? In every case the available profits are already smaller than the amount you have to pay for them. The market, therefore, is already discounting further discoveries or a higher gold price, or both.

The arithmetic of achieving an adequate return from the current level of net profits is so horrendous that I do not want to spoil your Christmas by spelling it out to you, but it does help to explain why only 20 per cent of the Fund is committed to gold shares. **(117. 15/11/90)**

Julian struggles to find value in the global gold mining sector.

In their summary of Gold Fields Mineral Services authoritative review "Gold 1992", Warburg Securities drew attention to the fact that in 1991, the Western world's gold mining industry produced 1782 tonnes of gold or 57.3 million ounces at a pre-tax cost of US$308/oz.

With gold now selling for US$338/oz, the industry is making US$30/oz before tax, or say US$25/oz after tax. My guess, and it's only a guess, is that at the current gold price the proven and probable reserves of the gold mining industry are sufficient to last about 12 years. All things being equal, the total net profit that the industry will make over the next 12 years is therefore US$17 billion.

So how much is the market paying for this future profit? The answer is US$37 billion, which is the market capitalization of all the world's gold shares. Obviously the shares should not be worth more than the future profits they generate. Unlike industrial shares, mines are wasting assets. However much they assure you to the contrary, you cannot be certain that miners will be able to replace the ounces they mine each year, with new discoveries. Much money has been lost by taking them at their word. To pay US$37 billion for US$17 billion of future profits does not seem very sensible to me. It means the market is paying US$58/oz for a profit of US$25/oz.

Clearly investors in the shares are expecting the gold price to rise sufficiently to give them a profit of US$58/oz otherwise they will get back less than they put in. Furthermore, investors usually want a return on their investment. In order to get their money back, plus 6.5 per cent per annum, a profit margin of US$90/oz would be needed.

In other words, with costs of US$308/oz plus a requirement for a US$90/oz profit margin, the gold price has to appreciate to just under US$400 in today's money in order to provide an investor with a 6.5 per cent return. Either the gold shares are still much too expensive and will have to fall some 60 per cent in order to give a sensible return or the gold price has to rise to US$400/oz.

One thing 25 years in this game has taught me is that the market is very seldom wrong. It is good at getting the balance right between risk and reward. The other thing I have learnt is that commentators are far smarter at explaining a move in the market than predicting it. So personally I believe that it is more likely that the gold price will rise to US$400/oz than it is for shares to fall a further 60 per cent from here. As you hardly need reminding, South African gold shares have already fallen 72 per cent in the last 2.5 years, the Australians have fallen 48 per cent and the Canadians 42 per cent. Gold itself has fallen 20 per cent. (**178. 11/6/92**)

Julian looks at the proposed Newmont/American Barrick merger.

Let's imagine, therefore, that gold was the only money in the world. If you wanted to buy shares in a gold mine you would have to pay for them with gold. You would not be pleased with your broker if he bought you a gold share whose earnings were less during its mine life than you paid for it in the first place.

I really do believe that gold is a form of money. I don't always succeed, but at least I try not to buy gold shares which will never earn enough profits to repay the capital (your capital!) I put into them.

That is why we do not own either of the shares which were in the news last week. Two of the market's favourites, American Barrick and Newmont Mining, are proposing to merge. The market approved. Both shares went up. Here is Smith New Court's estimate of how the two companies' earnings in 1992 will combine into a single entity. What they don't tell us is how much each company and thus the combined group, will make on every ounce nor do they divulge how much each ounce costs you.

Using Smith New Court's figures I have calculated the vital statistics we really need to know, namely earnings per ounce and market capitalization per ounce. Here they are:—

		NEM	ABX	Pro-forma Combined*
Price	($)	36.125	20.25	20
No shares	(mn)	67.7	117.7	259
Market cap	($ bn)	2.4	2.4	5.2
1991 P/E		19	40	24
1992 P/E		19	25	21
Current reserves	(mn oz)	20	19.5	39.5
1990 production	(mn oz)	1.8	0.6	2.4
1991 production	(mn oz)	1.6	0.65	2.25
1992 production	(mn oz)	1.4	0.6	2.5

* including 100% NGG

It seems the market is prepared to pay $131 for each ounce of gold on which the expected profit is $99. Thanks, but no thanks!

When I tell the brokers who urge me to buy this sort of value that you would not be pleased with me if I did so, they usually tell me that I don't understand the gold market. They are quite right. I don't! (**137. 05/06/91**)

		Newmont Mining	American Barrick	Combined (incl 100% of Newmont Gold
1982	Earnings Per Oz (EPO) (What SNC think they will earn every oz)	$91	$86.7	$98.6
	Market Cap Per Oz (MCO) (What you hope to pay for every oz)	£122	$122	$131

Julian looks at cashflow vs cash paid on the Fund's largest gold holdings.

The following table shows my estimate of what you would have to pay for an ounce of gold in the ground (market capitalization per ounce of reserves) at the six largest gold investments we own in each country and how much cashflow each ounce will generate, assuming a gold price of $350/oz on average, over the life of the mine.

213

	What you pay (US$/oz)	What you get (Cashflow US$/oz)
AUSTRALIA		
Arimco	$50	$81.0
ACM Gold	$103	$114.0
Forestania	$73	$90.0
Bougainville	$7	$52.0
Golden Shamrock	$34	$52.0
Ore Search	$43	$50.0
Average	$52	$73.0
SOUTH AFRICA		
Ofsil	$16	$16
Randfontein	$12	$19
Southvaal	$15	$34
Hartebeestfontein	$22	$39
Western Deep	$28	$42
Average	$19.2	$30
NORTH AMERICA		
Freeport Copper	$55	$112
Glamis Gold	$76	$97
Franco Nevada	$138	$177
TVX	$75	$62
Viceroy	$84	$108
Royal Oak	$37	$33
Average	$77.5	$98.2

James Capel & Co. tell me that the average Australian ounce costs $127 and should return $70. The average North American ounce costs $119 and should return $101 and each South African ounce costs $33 and should return $88.

What we have paid for our ounces is a great deal less than the cost of the average ounce in each country, so our portfolio should be defensive if we are going to have to put up with depressed gold prices for any length of time. (**168. 19/3/92**)

The issue of how much you pay for gold shares against what you can expect to get in returns continues to exercise Julian.

In their summary of Gold Fields Mineral Services authoritative review "Gold 1992", Warburg Securities drew attention to the fact that in 1991, the Western world's gold mining industry produced 1782 tonnes of gold or 57.3 million ounces at a pre-tax cost of US$308/oz.

With gold now selling for US$338/oz, the industry is making US$30/oz before tax, or say US$25/oz after tax.

My guess, and it's only a guess, is that at the current gold price the proven and probable reserves of the gold mining industry are sufficient to last about 12 years. All things being equal, the total net profit that the industry will make over the next 12 years is therefore US$17 billion.

So how much is the market paying for this future profit? The answer is US$37 billion, which is the market capitalization of all the world's gold shares. Obviously the shares should not be worth more than the future profits they generate. Unlike industrial shares, mines are wasting assets. However much they assure you to the contrary, you cannot be certain that miners will be able to replace the ounces they mine each year, with new discoveries.

Much money has been lost by taking them at their word. To pay US$37 billion for US$17 billion of future profits does not seem very sensible to me. It means the market is paying US$58/oz for a profit of US$25/oz.

Clearly investors in the shares are expecting the gold price to rise sufficiently to give them a profit of US$58/oz, otherwise they will get back less than they put in. Furthermore, investors usually want a return on their investment.

In order to get their money back, plus 6.5 per cent per annum, a profit margin of US$90/oz would be needed.

In other words, with costs of US$308/oz plus a requirement for a US$90/oz profit margin, the gold price has to appreciate to just under US$400 in today's money in order to provide an investor with a 6.5 per cent return. Either the gold shares are still much too expensive and will have to fall some 60 per cent in order to give a sensible return or the gold price has to rise to US$400/oz. **(178. 12/6/92)**

Julian continues to worry about the issue of gold mine returns.

We have been doing our sums on the South African gold mines' profit margins. You may find it just as hard to believe the figures as the market does, but that will not deter me from giving them to you.

215

We have looked at 22 South African mines which account for some 90 per cent of that country's gold production.

These mines are capitalised at US$7.7 billion and taking the average of four brokers' estimates, have reserves of some 327 million ounces. In other words, all those ounces are priced by the market at US$23 each. The industry is currently making a profit of about US$27 on each ounce it produces, so effectively you are paying US$23 for each ounce and you will receive US$27 for each ounce, assuming today's gold price. Now look what happens if the gold price continues on up to US$400/oz. You would still be paying US$23/oz but the profit per ounce would be US$47. Instead of receiving US$4/oz more than you paid, you would receive about US$24/oz more after tax. That, in the trade, is called gearing! (**182. 30/6/92**)

For an investor to get his money back on a 20-year asset, a dividend yield of 5 per cent is required. Over the last 20 years or so the market has valued the shares of Vaal Reefs, a leading South African producer, on an average annual yield of 7.1 per cent to a South African investor. In other words, a South African investor has been prepared to accept a real return of 2.1 per cent per annum over and above the yield required to get his money back.

Of course someone who bought Vaal Reefs 20 years ago would have got his money back in dividends many times over (the shares were 32 rand in 1973, the subsequent dividends have amounted to 199 rand and the share price is now 138 rand). We have worked out that whenever the dividend has been increased sufficiently to give a return of more than 7.1 per cent the shares have tended to perform particularly well as the previous chart shows. (**201. 7/1/93**)

The Fund searches for cheap ounces in Ghana and Fiji.

Our search to buy cheap gold in the ground has taken us far and wide. In Ghana we bought cheap gold at the Iduapriem Mine owned by the Australian mining company, Golden Shamrock, when we paid US$20 for each ounce, now valued by the market at US$39/oz. In South Africa, gold in the ground can currently be bought for around US$24 per ounce, but the profit derived from mining each ounce is likely to exceed the cost of buying it by a far wider margin than is available elsewhere in the world. That is why 43 per cent of our Fund is invested in South Africa. In North America and Australia we follow the same principles. In North America we have been selling shares where the ounces have become "expensive" in order to buy cheaper ounces in Australia and now even further afield, in Fiji.

Fiji's only gold mine is owned by Emperor Gold Mines, a company which in better times had a market capitalization of A$208 million, more than five times the current market capitalization. Each ounce is now valued at US$29. In the last fortnight we had the opportunity of purchasing 7.7 per cent of the entire company, which produces 145,000 ounces of gold per year. As very often happens, the market bad become preoccupied with the problems which had beset the company and had lost sight of the future potential of the mine. After all, there are not many gold companies where such good fundamental value can seemingly be bought. As mentioned above, at the current share price, the market is only valuing Emperor's 685,000 ounces of gold in the ground at US$29/oz. The broker, Pru-Bache, calculates that with gold at US$350/oz, Emperor has the ability to earn US$67 on each ounce it produces; more than twice the cost of buying that ounce in the first place. (**207. 18/2/93**)

The issue of what you get back from a gold share rumbles on.

Gold is money, whether it be in a bank vault, in the ground, or in the palm of your hand. It stands to reason, therefore, that a gold mine is a money mine. If gold was the only money, investors in gold mines would take more care than most do at present, to satisfy themselves that they were likely to get more gold back from their investment than they put in. We do go to great lengths to calculate what we are paying for each ounce in the ground and how much profit each ounce is likely to generate, on average, over the life of the mine. To put it in financial jargon for the benefit of any broker who may read this and want our business, we compare the market capitalization of a gold company with the net cash flow which will be generated over the mine life. If the net cash flow is smaller than the market capitalization, it will be difficult to persuade us to buy it. (**316. 5/10/95**)

Sky high PEs and miniscule dividend yields dog the gold share sector

At one of our morning meetings last week I was drawing the Team's attention to the fact that, in contrast to the past, mining brokers nowadays seldom, if ever, mention yields or price earnings ratios (PERs) when discussing gold shares.

I reasoned that the lacklustre gold price had resulted in a dearth of Es to go with the Ps and as for dividends, yields were so small as to be hardly worth mentioning. The reaction to this outburst was totally unexpected. "Its all your fault", I was told, "If you stopped insisting that the brokers told you how much you were paying for each ounce in the ground and then stopped asking them how much you were likely to get for each ounce once it had been mined, (what you pay, what you get) the fashion for buying stocks with exploration potential would never have achieved its current popularity."

My colleagues may be prone to exaggeration but they have a point. Gold shares enjoy ratings that most other shares can only dream about. The Chairman of a leading base metal company once quipped that when he died he would like to be re-incarnated as the CEO of a gold company with his current company's earnings. The multiples paid for most gold companies' earnings are so high that no broker, hoping to get anything other than a sell order, would dare mention the PER and although mines are wasting assets, yields on gold shares don't seem to matter any more. Everything now depends on "growth". Growth of production, growth of reserves, exploration success, earnings growth and sheer size are what the market wants these days. (**356. 11/9/96**)

9. Assessing Value – Barrick, Western Areas and Bre-X

Julian found it very difficult to find value in the shares of Canadian incorporated American Barrick now simply Barrick Gold, but knew that ownership of Barrick's shares would have boosted portfolio performance in the 90s. He believed that superior value was offered by South Africa's Western Areas and he built up a major holding which boosted the Fund, particularly during the mid nineties run in SA gold shares. He was less enamoured by the value prospects of exploration stocks where he was very conservative. The Fund, however, did dabble very successfully in Bre-X but it was not the sort of trade that Julian was comfortable with.

American Barrick

Amazed by Barrick's ability to raise equity with the shares selling on a PE of 60, Julian suggests that the company buys gold bullion with its new funds, dump it in an open pit and mine it a second time, enhancing the imputed value as related to its PE.

When a company thinks its shares are too cheap it often asks its shareholders' permission to buy its own stock in the market. When a company thinks its shares are too expensive, it arranges a placement of stock to satisfy the "ducks" when they are quacking.

If you would like an example of the duck feeding scenario, may I suggest you make a case study of American Barrick whose Chairman, Peter Munk, is the master at giving the public what they want. What the public wants is the shares of American Barrick and he knows they are prepared to pay through the beak for them. American Barrick is capitalised at over US$3 billion, significantly more than the world's largest nickel company, Inco. Never mind the fact that Barrick makes only one tenth the profit that Inco makes or that the nickel price is going up far faster than the gold price; it's Barrick shares that the ducks require.

Mr Munk has therefore once again courageously succumbed to the temptation of giving the public more of what they think is good for them. I say courageous because he knows perfectly well that when he did that in the past, investors had a nasty habit of subsequently biting the hand that fed them.

Last week he issued 5 million new shares of Barrick at $22.625 on 60 times historic earnings to raise $113 million for the treasury. No doubt some of this money was taken off the street in order to participate in the placement. Have no fear, it will be back there soon earning about 13 per cent per annum for Barrick shareholders. This interest alone will have the effect of increasing Barrick's earnings by 33 per cent compared with last year, at a cost of less than a 5 per cent dilution in the share capital. The additional gold production this year will be a bonus!

Why bother to get your hands dirty mining gold when you can grow your company's earnings just as well by feeding ducks?

Of course, what he could now do is to use the money he has just raised to go out and buy 295,000 ounces of gold at $384/oz. These ounces could then be thrown into the open pit and mined all over again. The market, in its wisdom, is valuing the company at about US$5,000 per ounce of annual production. By increasing "production" by 295,000 ounces, Mr Munk could theoretically increase American Barrick's value by $1.47 billion at a cost of $113 million per annum without having to suffer the cost of mining.

The placement of shares is, of course, perfectly legal. The placement of gold coins round open pits is anything but legal though I cannot for the life of me see why! Can you?

Anyhow, American Barrick is to be congratulated on what it has done and if history is anything to go by it won't be long before the other gold companies "follow my leader".

Lord Hanson springs to mind as someone who is long of duck fodder at the moment and he, even now, must be rubbing his bands at the thought of what the ducks might pay for his feed – unless, of course, they have already been satisfied by Mr Munk's collation.

What all this goes to show is that gold mining shares have a magical quality about them which makes people who invest in them seem a bit dotty. "Takes one to spot one, I can bear you say. Mr Munk's personal holdings of American Barrick are held through Horsham Corporation, in which we too have a modest holding. Do you think Horsham subscribed to more American Barrick: shares on 60 times earnings? Of course not; that would have been taking duck feed out of one pocket and putting it in another. Fortunately for Horsham the shares of Barrick rose more than 5 per cent after the placement so they were better off than before without having to spend a penny, if you will excuse the expression. (**108. 30/8/90**)

Julian sings the praises of South Deep as a value investment.

I said in my last Newsletter that I would try and come up with a cheap way of paying the school fees. The largest unexploited deposit of gold in the world is owned by a South African company called South Deep. They own some 22.5 million ounces of gold, about the same as American Barrick. James Capel & Co.'s mining research department ("Capels") tell me that if you want to buy South Deep's ounces, you pay $4 each for them. If you prefer those of American Barrick you have to pay $146 for each of them. They estimate that it will cost $294 (1991 dollars) to extract each ounce at South Deep and that the costs at American Barrick will be $215. They have calculated that to get the money you put in, back over the life of the mine after tax, a gold price of $298 (1991 dollars) will be needed at South Deep and $398 at American Barrick.

The reason for this huge discrepancy is that most of American Barrick's ounces are financed and in production, whereas those of South Deep are at this stage a twinkle in the mine manager's eye.

By the time you have to pay the school fees, however, things may be rather different. By that time South Deep will be in production and American Barrick will be a mature situation. According to Capels' calculations, if South Deep in a few years time were to be valued as American Barrick is today, the shares of South Deep would have to rise from $2.00 to $30. Of course, an ounce of North American gold will always be more highly valued than a South African ounce as Mr Munk, the Chairman of American Barrick, never ceases to remind us. So even if you don't do your school fees sums on the assumption that an investment in South Deep should appreciate by 1,378 per cent by the time you have to start paying the school fees, it certainly should make a significant contribution.

Do we hold South Deep shares in the Fund? What do you think? **(144. 6/8/91)**

Julian notes that building reserve ounces in the ground can do wonders for valuations when the miner concerned is American Barrick.

The analysis of how much is paid for an un-mined ounce of gold and how much profit will be generated on that ounce is the fundamental basis of our research. Such basic arithmetic is too simplistic for the market, particularly in North America where, as a result of rising gold share markets, increasing values have recently been placed on ounces in the ground. As far as the smarter players are concerned, the trick is to buy cheap ounces which then get re-rated by the stockmarket under their ownership. A sure-fire way of increasing the value of the directors' share options! Over the centuries people have been unsuccessfully looking for a way of turning base metals into gold. Now at last, some have successfully discovered how to turn gold into nearly three times its value in paper money.

Growth in earnings per share is the name of the game. The most famous player is American Barrick which has perfected the art of convincing the market of its ability to grow by expanding production and at the same time protect itself against the vagaries of the gold price by judicious forward selling.

In order to achieve this you have to demonstrate that you have plenty of reserves to provide the tonnage for your ambitious expansion plans. Many miners still say it is not worth drilling for reserves which will not be mined for many years, but they tend to be spectators, rather than players, in this game.

Pegasus seems to have perfected their game to such an extent that they have even managed to bank their profits. Their quest for this, the ultimate prize, started only six months ago in Australia when they bought 35 per cent of Zapopan.

According to Bunting Warburg, in April this year, Pegasus had just over 4 million ounces of gold in reserves for which the market was prepared to pay US$86/oz.

Following Barrick's example, Pegasus then increased its reserves by 22 per cent, to 4.9 million ounces, mainly by acquiring 720,000 ounces of gold in the ground at a cost of US$26/oz through the purchase of 35 per cent of Zapopan. Zapopan is an Australian gold mining company which owns one of the largest undeveloped gold projects on the map, the financing of which can largely be met from the cashflow from Zapopan's existing operations, plus gold loans, with little recourse to shareholders.

As the market started to recognise these newly acquired ounces, Pegasus shares rose from US$12.25 to US$17.00, thus valuing both existing ounces and the newly acquired ounces owned by Zapopan at US$98/oz. Not only was the market persuaded that it was sensible to pay US$98/oz for what the company had recently paid US$26/oz; it also revalued the existing reserves by US$12/oz, a 14 per cent increase.

"Super Alchemy" was achieved last week when Pegasus turned most of its newly acquired ounces into cash without even having to go to the trouble of mining them. The company sold 3.25 million of its shares to the public at US$17 a share, thus banking US$55.25 million, sufficient to monetise approximately 75 per cent of the ounces which had so recently been acquired for US$19 million. (190. 1/10/92)

The road to investor approval followed by North American gold mines.

Without doubt, investors in American gold shares are playing the "growth" game. Scotia McLeod have recently summarised the rules of the game, stating that the "key to good performance is growth in earnings and cashflow through: a) production increases, b) cost cutting, and c) reserve increases." With the ground rules well understood in American mining circles it has been a relatively simple task for the North American gold producers to give the market what it wants, in one form or another. American Barrick having invented the rules, has bought the technique down to a fine art.

Hot on the heels of American Barrick has been Placer Dome and most recently Lac Minerals. It took a new management at Placer Dome to really understand the current rules which basically enable mining companies to "mine the market" and their reserves at the same time. The difference this knowledge makes to the share price has been staggering. Against a declining gold price, Placer Dome has risen 26 per cent in the past six months as the company concentrated on upgrading its resources and achieved a reduction in the cost of producing each ounce. The actual profit the companies make on each ounce, compared with what investors are asked to pay for each ounce, is not presently considered important according to current interpretation of the rules. (**210. 18/3/93**)

Barrick outlines its hedging numbers.

Admittedly some hedged gold producers have performed well too. American Barrick for instance has gone to great lengths to explain to shareholders that due to its superior reserve base and strong balance sheet the company has the ability to roll forward its forward positions if at any time the spot gold price exceeds their forward price, thus enabling the company to maximise profits. American Banick has 27.2 million ounces of gold in its reserves out of which a little over a quarter has been sold forward at an average price of US$423/oz, US$58 above the current spot price.

If you spread the advantage they have gained over their total reserves it will give them an extra $16/oz over and above what they would have got if they had not hedged. Good news unless the price of gold goes over US$407/oz. (**229. 3/9/93**)

Graham Birch looks at the issue of cost in developing gold mines in Russia against aluminium projects.

The original questioner persisted. He asked "Why is it then that gold mining companies are prepared to go in and buy up projects and aluminium companies are not?" Bird said that it was because the biggest gold mines were relatively small businesses compared with even a small aluminium project. The amount of money involved in developing a typical gold mine is only 5–20 per cent of that required for an aluminium smelter. The costs involved in Russian gold mining are, he argued, thus relatively low compared to the billion or so dollars that would have to be expended on a Russian aluminium project. In other words, a small company with entrepreneurial flair can rapidly develop Russian gold deposits but an aluminium project is a "non-starter" for any but the largest companies.

This caused a certain amount of consternation around the table. Not many of the people present had realised that there was such a discrepancy. This may be because the market capitalizations of gold mining companies frequently bear little relationship to the absolute size of the underlying business. To highlight the point it is perhaps worth comparing the USA's leading gold producer with the USA's leading aluminium producer (based on figures for the year ended December 1992. Source: Ord Minnett).

Company	AMERICAN BARRICK	ALCOA	BARRICK AS % OF ALCOA
Revenue (US$m)	540	9491	6%
Net Income (US$m)	175	196	89%
Cashflow (US$m)	252	879	29%
Dividend Yield (%)	0.3%	2.3%	13%
Market Capitalization (US$m)	7954	6115	130%
Book Value (US$m)	993	3604	28%
Placer Dome	27	18	
Average	35.5	20.7	

Although Barrick has done some very clever things with gold options and futures and thus will generate a little more net income than Alcoa this year, it is nonetheless quite clear from this table that Alcoa is a bigger business than American Barrick in all major respects bar one – market capitalization. Why do investors place this premium on the shares? It certainly isn't because of management skills (both companies are highly regarded in this department) and it surely can't be because the up-side earnings power of American Barrick is any greater.

Alcoa in its current annual report states that as a measure of our improved operating performance, we believe that if we had today the price levels that existed for our product line in 1988–89, our earnings would be about US$300 million more than the US$900 million we achieved at that time. Such a time will come again. Ord Minnett has calculated for us that for American Barrick to earn this amount of money (US$1,200 million) from its relatively modest revenue base, the gold price would have to rise to US$1220/oz! I will leave you to make up your own mind as to which of these two companies has the greatest chance of earning a billion dollars at the peak of the next cycle. (**239. 6/12/93**)

Julian once more considers the value of Barrick shares and Peter Munk's midas touch in raising funds for his other interests using Barrick paper as a guarantee.

By now you may have guessed that the company concerned was American Barrick and the executive was Peter Munk. His success with the company has made it the top pick of the broking community, almost without exception. The result is that American Barrick is now the most highly valued gold share in the world. No one has a larger vested interest in turning Barrick's super-share rating to advantage than its largest individual shareholder. Any of us lesser mortals who fails to study what he is doing is likely to miss a trick or two. If gold was the only currency, this is how an investor might look at an investment in American Barrick, assuming today's gold price of U$381.1/oz.

	US$ bn	Equivalent Tonnes of Gold
Gross value of ore reserves	12.4	1011
Less cash costs	5.7	465
Less overheads and tax	2.0	165
Less capital expenditure	0.3	25
Profit for shareholder	4.4	356
Barrick's market capitalization	**7.4**	**608**

Thus, it can be seen that potential investors in American Barrick are being asked by the market to swap 608 tonnes of gold today for 356 tonnes over the next 18 years (the current reserve life). This is by no means unusual for North American gold companies.

There are various explanations for what might otherwise be seen as irrational behaviour by investors. First, they may well believe that ounces of gold will be more valuable in future. As mentioned earlier that could not be the case if gold were the only currency. Our estimates suggest that in Barrick's case it would require a gold price of U$524/oz for an investor to get his money back over the life of the current reserves.

Alternatively, investors may believe that the company will find sufficient additional ounces to make up for the apparent shortfall. Some companies have better records than others on this score. Barrick, with its excellent record, needs to find an extra 13 million ounces or about 40 per cent more gold in order for an investor to get back as many ounces as he invested. That is a tall order by anyone's standards, but they have done it before.

Thirdly, investors may take the view that the quality of the management is such that they will work the same miracles in the future as they have in the past. Just as it is possible to confuse genius with a bull market, so it should not be forgotten that world-class deposits of gold do not grow on trees. If they did, gold would not be a precious metal.

What the founding shareholders of Barrick have done is to diversify their holdings, exchanging their shares in Barrick for shares in The Horsham Corporation. Horsham in turn has invested in Clarke Oil & Refining, the fifteenth largest oil company in the USA and in property on the outskirts of Berlin.

The market started by having doubts as to whether Mr. Munk's Midas touch would extend to oil and property, but as time goes by, they seem to be giving him the benefit of the doubt. The really clever thing that Horsham has done is to use its Barrick shares as a means of raising cheap loan finance. With the backing of Barrick paper they have been able to raise a US$600 million, 25-year debenture at an interest rate of 3.25 per cent which represents a 300 basis point discount to the price the US government has to pay for a similarly dated treasury bond! In the very same week De Beers Centenery, which controls the non-South African diamond interests of De Beers, raised £150 million in 8.25 per cent guaranteed unsecured loan stock due 2009. The yield to redemption on a UK government gilt maturing in 2009 is 6.84 per cent. Like Horsham, De Beers said that it didn't need the money but was always interested in new good funding opportunities.

Bearing in mind that diamonds have held their value far better than gold over the years, it says a lot about the quality of the financial wizardry that Mr. Munk can bring to bear on the companies he manages. Perhaps that is the best reason why his shares are so highly rated that we cannot afford them! (**245. 11/2/94**)

Barrick bids for Lac and the issue of the cheapness of South African gold raises its head again.

The genie is now well and truly out of the bottle and the great debate may have started as to why South African gold shares are so undervalued. Two excellent examples of the difference in valuation placed on South African and non-South African shares presented themselves this week.

American Barrick made an offer of 0.43 of its own shares for each Lac Minerals share, valuing Lac Minerals at US$1.54 billion. Lac Minerals is a Canadian Company with interests in Chile, Peru and Canada. American Barrick produced

1.6 million ounces of gold last year and Lac Minerals produced 1.0 million ounces. The combined market capitalization of the two companies, if the bid is accepted, will be in the region of US$8 billion for 2.6 million ounces of annual production.

Anglo American's annual report for 1994 has recently been published. It shows that the mines it controls produced 9 million ounces of gold (3.37 million ounces attributable) and that the whole company generated a profit of around US$487 million. The following table summarises the situation.

	MARKET CAP (US$M)	NET INCOME (US$M)*	1993 PRODUCTION (MOZ)	MARKET CAP PER ANNUAL OZ
AMERICAN BARRICK	8,000	200	2.60	3,077
Plus LAC MINERALS	12,400	487	3.37	3,649

Year end December 1993 for American Barrick plus Lac Minerals. Year end March 1994 for Anglo American.

Of course only 27 per cent of Anglo American's assets are in gold and it is not therefore just a gold mining company. Directly and indirectly it controls 33 per cent of the world's largest diamond company, De Beers, and its foreign interests are held by Minorco (US$5.2 billion) in which the Corporation owns 45.6 per cent and that is to say nothing of its South African industrial interests held through its 49.9 per cent interest in AMIC which is valued by the market at US$2.7 billion. Anglo American is a colossal business by world standards, but although South African industrial businesses sell on higher ratings than many industrial businesses outside South Africa, South African mining shares are valued at a fraction of those elsewhere in the world.

At Western Areas' present price of US$14.20, we calculate the 9 million ounces of gold in the ground are valued at US$61/oz with South Deep's valued at US$13/oz. The merged company would own 38.4 million ounces of gold valued at US$27/oz.

This compares with the US$171 which the market would be paying for each ounce in the ground owned by American Barrick and Lac Minerals combined if the bid is successful. American Barrick's highly rated paper values each of its ounces in the ground at US$228. Lac's ounces are valued at US$83/oz. The combined value is US$170/oz on which, we calculate, they will generate a cash flow of US$132/oz with gold at US$408/oz.

If American Barrick wanted to buy the combined reserves of Western Areas and South Deep, they could double their reserves for a mere 16 per cent dilution in their share capital! But like many other investors, American Barrick resists the temptation to own South African ounces however cheap they may appear. We don't mind, our investment in Western Areas was acquired for 61p per share and the dividend this year is likely to exceed 70p! The shares meanwhile have risen to £9.29, a rise of 1,423 per cent in a little over 18 months and they still yield 6.6 per cent.

Indeed, it is true to say that holders of this Fund enjoy a larger exposure to Western Areas than do the shareholders of JCI, the controlling Mining House. (262. 28/6/94)

Geoff Campbell travels to Nevada.

The Goldstrike mine, operated by Barrick, has been using autoclave technology for several years to process its sulphide ores. Measured by gold output it is the largest mine in North America and is one of the most technologically advanced. At the end of our tour around the mill (full of gleaming pipes and computers) we were shown the results of one day's work. Laid out on the table were five, 1,000 ounce gold bars the size of house bricks with a total value of US$1.9 million. To mine such a massive amount of gold requires a huge amount of equipment. Goldstrike runs a fleet of 73 mining trucks each capable of carrying the weight of a Jumbo Jet.

Controlling such a large and expensive fleet of trucks is too complex a task for one man and, in line with most of the large North American mines, the job has been given over to a computer. The computer decides where the trucks go to pick up a load and where the load should be taken. This task is complicated by the fact that part of the Goldstrike mine is owned by Barrick and part by Newmont Mining. Since ore from different parts of the mine has different owners, each has to be treated separately. Barrick has gone a stage further with its technology and all the mine trucks are fitted with satellite receivers so that the computer knows where all the trucks are to within 10 metres. Barrick reckons that having such precise information gives it the edge in controlling and utilising this valuable fleet. (314. 21/9/95)

Barrick continues to back gold price hedging but hints that the issue is always under review.

Barrick's Chief Financial Officer Randall Oliphant said "Barrick continues to be committed to gold hedging, but we aren't stuck in the mud ... this was not done on the basis of a prediction of the gold price but rather in response to the changing realities of the gold market itself". What he means by this is that the rising interest rate on gold has pushed down the contango on gold futures to such an extent that forward selling has become relatively less attractive. It has become progressively harder for Barrick to generate additional revenue through forward contracts. Barrick's hedging strategy generated a revenue boost of US$77/oz in 1992, US$49/oz in 1993, and US$18/oz in 1994. Who will say that it will provide any boost in 1996?

Barrick is arguably the most progressive gold mining company in the world. It has a remarkably consistent track record of growing earnings and production. It was one of the leading proponents of gold hedging and this has been an important plank in its strategy. So successful has Barrick become that it is hardly surprising that more and more companies gradually followed suit and jumped on the forward selling bandwagon. Now that Barrick has fired the retrorockets, it is not unreasonable to expect other companies to start covering. The bullion dealers are now running scared because in trying to cover, mining companies are likely to find that the gold market is rather tight. Getting the gold back that they have sold short could be difficult because the metal has already been dissipated far and wide and is now adorning millions of women (and men) all over the world, particularly in the Far East. Barrick's 3 million ounce buyback (carried out at prices between US$385 and US$395/oz) has pushed the gold price up US$27/oz. What is going to happen when numerous other companies trek down the same path? (**331. 2/2/96**)

Julian and Peter Munk have lunch and Julian notes that Barrick has begun to unwind some of its forward sales.

We had the pleasure of lunching last week with Peter Munk, Chairman of Barrick Gold Corporation. When the perpetrator of the cult of forward selling and the most vociferous opponent of the practice meet on neutral territory, you can guarantee a lively discussion. Last week's lunch resulted in just that. But the smartest businessmen are those whose ideas are not set in stone. We agreed there were times when it was sensible to sell forward and that there were times when the practice became just too dangerous. All the good that a sensible and well-thought out forward selling policy had achieved for Barrick over the years, and one which had been widely copied within the gold mining industry, could be undone almost overnight by a strongly rising gold price, through an unwillingness to reverse a policy which had hitherto been very successful.

We discussed the danger that forward selling was becoming counter-productive and with that in mind Barrick had unwound one third of its forwards. Having made that important decision it would be surprising if their new policy was immediately reversed. It seems far more likely that a further unwinding of the outstanding futures positions will take place as opportunities presented themselves.

As a gold mining company grows larger, it becomes increasingly difficult both to replace the ounces mined each year and at the same time grow the reserves sufficiently to increase production in the future. Inevitably the balance eventually tips in favour of allowing a rising gold price to provide the increase in earnings that the market demands, but you can't have your cake and eat it. If you have sold your gold forward at a fixed price, you can't expect to enjoy the full gearing to a rising gold price.

It has been a painful business for us not being invested in one of the great success stories in the gold market since we started the Fund in 1988. This resulted in our Fund underperforming Barrick, particularly in the early years of the Fund's existence, although we have outperformed the company's share price in more recent years as the following chart of the relative performance shows. Now that they have shown flexibility by covering one third of their forwards, it is becoming increasingly difficult for us not to do the decent thing and invest your money in this quality investment. When we do we'll let you know.

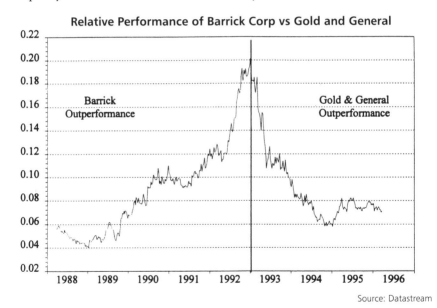

Relative Performance of Barrick Corp vs Gold and General

Source: Datastream

(337. 22/3/96)

Western Areas

The Fund is a large holder of giant Western Areas and Julian speculates that as the globalisation of the gold share sector develops South African mines such as WA will be increasingly valued in line with their global peers.

There is another reason why the publication of ore reserves is so important, it demonstrates on an ongoing basis to the mine workers and the government alike, how the life of a mine is affected by costs. If costs increase, or the gold price decreases, some of the ounces will no longer be economic to mine and the reserves will fall by more than the amount mined during the year. Conversely, a rise in the gold price or a reduction in costs, will increase the mineable reserve as extra ounces become payable. Those of you who follow mining shares closely will remember how, only two short years ago, people were predicting that the South African gold mining industry, which currently gives direct employment to 360,000 and indirect employment to an estimated further 195,000 people, would be less than half its present size within a few years because most of the high cost mines would have become un-payable.

Of the new revelations, by far the most interesting to date is the published reserves of Western Areas which surprised the market by announcing reserves of 22 million ounces. Western Areas is in the process of merging with South Deep to form a single entity with reserves of just over 60 million ounces. That puts it in the super league of world gold mines with comparable reserves to American Barrick/Lac Minerals, Driefontein and Placer. The largest Australian mine, according to JB Were & Son is the super pit at Kalgoorlie (GMK) which currently boasts over 20 million ounces. The capitalization of Western Areas and South Deep combined is US$1.2 billion, roughly the same as the combined capitalization of Homestake Australia and GMK who own the super pit which contains about a third as much gold. The South Africans have much to do before they can claim that their mines are valued in line with world-class gold shares elsewhere. They are at last addressing the problem, that is why we remain heavily overweight in that market. There is no doubt that their efforts are being rewarded as is evidenced by the fact that the South African gold shares continue to be the star performers this year, as they were last. (**270. 6/10/94**)

Julian gives Western Areas another value plug.

As you know, one of the reasons that this Fund has performed relatively well in the last two years is because we have a predilection for marzipan. In other words we try to sweeten the portfolio with what we call "marzipan stocks" in the same way that a Christmas cake manufacturer applies a layer of marzipan to his Christmas cakes in order to give them added flavour.

One of our most successful investments has been Western Areas, a South African gold share which was very much out of favour when we bought it two years ago for a mere 60p per share. They are now selling at £11.23 per share. An excellent example of what a little dollop of "marzipan" can do! Western Areas is now our largest single holding.

231

Western Areas' next-door neighbour is South Deep, a new mine on its southern border. A couple of years ago South Deep was the bargain of the century. We hoovered up as many as we could up at 145p, a price which valued the whole company at a mere £57 million. With ore reserves of 30 million ounces, at that time gold in the ground was being valued at US$3/oz, the best out-of-the-money call on gold you have probably ever seen. South Deep are now £10.45. High quality marzipan if ever there was any!

Last week it was announced that Western Areas and South Deep are to merge. The merger will result in substantial savings in the cost of developing South Deep since the cost can be set against Western Areas' profits to reduce the overall tax burden. The combined company will have reserves of 54 million ounces equivalent to US$17/oz. That compares with the average South African cost per ounce of US$39.

In order to put the enlarged Western Areas into perspective it is necessary to compare it with its peers. There are not all that many gold companies in the world which can boast reserves and resources of more than 30 million ounces. Here are some of the few examples. We have included their market capitalizations and what you pay for each ounce in the ground.

COMPANY	GOLD RES. & RESOURCES (Moz)	WHAT YOU PAY (U$/OZ)	MARKET CAP. (U$M)
American Barrick	40	192	7,660
Placer Dome	28	173	4,855
Newmont Gold	50	67	3,330
Driefontein	45	68	3,057
Kloof	40	51	2,026
Freegold	47	37	1,743
Vaal Reefs	52	33	1,715
Western Areas/South Deep	54	25	1,342
Star Mining	26*	5	136

Based on Star's 35 per cent interest in 75 million ounce resource at Sukhoi Log   *Source: SG Warburg, MAM*

The table clearly shows how attractive the merged Western Areas/South Deep company looks by South African as well as by international standards. So despite the fantastic run that both these companies have enjoyed in the last two years the merged company remains one of the most attractive large gold shares on offer anywhere in the world.

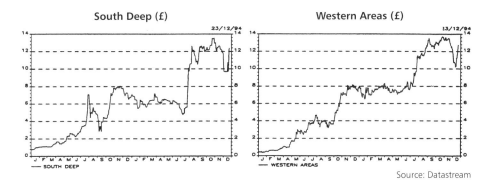

South Deep (£)   Western Areas (£)

Source: Datastream

Two years ago, when many investors had given up on gold as an investment and when South Africa remained a pariah in the investment community, shares in Western Areas and South Deep were a bargain. The charts below show how they have performed as investors has increasingly focused on the outstanding value on offer.

(278. 22/12/94)

Geoff Campbell describes a visit to Western Areas.

During my stay in South Africa I visited Western Areas, the largest single holding in the Fund and one of the best examples of a company that is undertaking the re-engineering process. Western Areas recently merged with its neighbour, South Deep, to form a company that has one of the largest deposits of gold in the world. The statistics of the proposed development are staggering. The resource figure is quoted at 60 million ounces and the company is embarking on a R2.7bn (US$750 million) capital expenditure programme. Western Areas has been going since 1961 and the new development will extend the mine life by at least another 47 years. The world's deepest production shaft is being sunk to a depth of 2,750 million to develop and access the lower levels of the ore body. The depth of this shaft will be twice the height of Ben Nevis! At the deeper level, the ore body is very thick and can be mined using mechanised equipment, thereby bringing down the cost of extraction. Along with improved technology, one of the things that has enabled Western Areas to embark on such an ambitious programme has been an improvement in work practices. The company believes that it can achieve still further improvements in cost and flexibility. A project of this scale takes time as well as a great deal of money. Full production from the enlarged mine is not expected until 2003. For many years the mine will consume large amounts of capital to fund the development. This money will come from three sources, the shareholders in the form of a rights issue, retained earnings and from Western Areas' tax shelter.

If a company uses retained earnings, which is one of the most efficient means of funding, there will necessarily be little or no dividends while the project is cash negative. Of course the shareholders get their return in the form of super dividends once the development is completed and the project turns hugely cash positive.

That suits us because the UK tax man takes half our dividends but none of our capital gains. We would have been happy to forgo any dividends in Western Areas for the next few years in return for helping to finance one of the most significant gold mines to be developed this decade. This is, after all, quite a normal state of affairs in North America and Australia where gold mining companies regularly make use of retained earnings and gold loans to develop new projects and to finance exploration.

In the end Western Areas decided on a compromise. It will pay a reduced dividend which, since the company is cash negative, will have to be funded partly with our money from the proposed rights issue; robbing Peter to pay Peter so to speak. Shuffling cash around is a nil gain exercise at the best of times. However in this case there is an added sting.

Assuming Western Areas' proposed rights issue is R500 million, we will be investing an additional R22.5 million (£3.9 million) in the company. During the next five years we will get this back in the form of gross dividends, assuming a modest dividend payout, but we will be taxed on these dividends, so in fact we will only get back about half what we put in. Others do not see it that way. Some Western Areas' shareholders are miffed that the dividend has been reduced at all! They can't have their cake and eat it! Maybe it's not just the workers on the mine that need to be more flexible.

The job of providing development capital for new projects has traditionally been the role of the mining finance houses. They use dividends from existing mines to finance new projects. Since dividend income is free of tax in South Africa, it pays a mining finance house to get its return partly in the form of dividends and partly in the form of fees. We don't get the benefit of the fees and we are taxed on the dividends which, in the case of Western Areas, are paid for out of the proceeds of the rights issue. The established mines have got used to paying full dividends and the shareholders got used to receiving them. A bit like the driller who drills and the helper who helps, neither does the job of the other.

The new South Africa will have international investors who are used to companies taking full advantage of the capital sources at their disposal namely, equity, debt and retained earnings. In an internationally competitive market it pays to make the best use of all your assets and not discourage the foreign investors which everyone in South claims are essential if the country's development plans are to be fulfilled. (**286. 2/3/95**)

Julian shines the spotlight on the merged Western Areas/South Deep operation.

The Fund's largest holding, Western Areas, has been performing well in recent weeks. Earlier this year the company, which now makes up over 9.5 per cent of the portfolio, acquired all the assets of South Deep Exploration for 36.3 million shares. The combined operation has an estimated reserve of 60 million ounces making it one of the largest gold mines in the world. In June, the company issued 13 million new ordinary shares in a rights issue to raise R509 million which will be used to fund the development of surface and underground infrastructure at the South Deep ore body. We followed our interest in the rights issue, subscribing for half a million shares at the issue price of R40. Since then shares have performed well and are trading at R55, a 37 per cent increase in sterling terms. This has contributed to the 12 per cent increase in the price of your units since the end of June compared with a 7.4 per cent rise in the FT Gold Mines Index.

In our view Western Areas has the best growth prospects of any gold company in the South African sector and will therefore remain a core holding in your Fund.

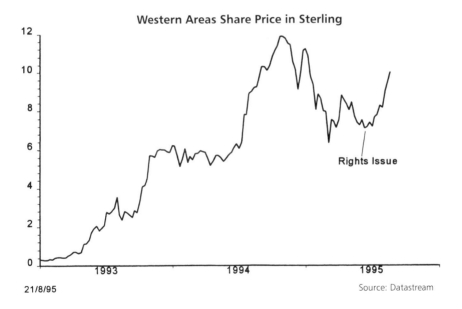

Western Areas Share Price in Sterling

21/8/95

Source: Datastream

(309. 21/08/95)

Describing the giant South Deeps project.

Advanced technology is being applied at Western Areas, the Fund's largest single holding. Western Areas is currently developing one of the largest undeveloped gold deposits in the world, the South Deeps orebody. Everything about this new project is world class and world beating. The new mine will have the single deepest vertical shaft in the world, with a target depth of over 2.75 km and the largest single headframe in the world. But the development of this new project has not been without its challenges. And in a storyline that would entertain even the most critical Hollywood director, the mine development team pushed their resources to the limit to progress the sinking of the main haulage shaft at South Deeps. The challenge was to staunch a huge inflow of water when shaft sinking hit a fissure. Water is contained in huge underground reservoirs, trapped within the rock sequence. As the shaft started to fill with water the action had to be swift and precise. In a series of nail biting manoeuvres the solution was to plug the base of the shaft, and thus the fissure with cement, pumped under high pressure from the surface. In the closing sequences, underwater divers, kitted out in full scuba gear, were on hand at the base of the shaft some 450 metres below the surface. Tom Cruise, eat your heart out!

As the engineers finished telling this particular story, we were convinced that these challenges were well within the capabilities of the excellent engineering team at Western Areas. By October the crew will continue shaft sinking ever deeper, if a little behind schedule.

In the South Deeps development, Western Areas has one of the brightest futures of any gold company in South Africa, if not the world. The company's gold reserves dwarf most of its competitors. But all those 64 million ounces of gold are only valued by the market at US$23/oz. What is apparent is that the market fails to give any value to the ounces that will be produced by Western Areas beyond 20 years. It also fails to appreciate that the South Reef is an extremely robust orebody – capable of withstanding a gold price as low as US$250/oz. On current forecast production levels, the mine has a life of over 40 years. If the market can be convinced that Western Areas will bring this gold production forward in time more ounces of gold will be mined in the 20 year "window", thus boosting the value of the company. The company has a number of options available to it to increase its gold production beyond its forecast. The most obvious is to construct another even deeper shaft to the south of the South Deeps mine. Technology is now available to sink a single vertical shaft to a depth of 3.5 km. Unfortunately the lead time for a new shaft will preclude any benefits in the near term but the potential value is there. (**358. 29/9/96**)

Bre-X

The Newsletters continuously describe how unless Julian believed that the gold price or shares were over-valued the purpose of the Gold and General was to offer investors the best gearing possible to a rising gold price. The fund always owned those companies that were the cheapest (as measured by their reserves in the ground) rather than provide investors with exposure to the high-risk exploration stocks. As he would say it the Fund made a point of avoiding "lobster pots" (companies which are easy to get in to but difficult to get out of). This discipline paid off around the time of the exploration boom that came after the discovery of Bre-X and Diamond Fields.

Drawing on his experience of the "Aussie" nickel boom of the 1960s, Julian explains his aversion to exploration plays.

That said, the slippage of the gold price back into its 1995 trading range is a great disappointment to all of us. Gold shares are, of course, geared investments and we have naturally taken precautions to reduce your discomfort as we pass through this area of turbulence. In particular, we have made sure that the Fund's cash balances are topped up (circa 5 per cent) and that the exposure to "junior exploration plays" is negligible. As we stressed in previous newsletters, we have felt for some time that the exploration stocks are a little frothy. Bre-X Minerals, for example, is currently the third most highly valued gold share in the world, having a market capitalization of US$3.4 billion before a single ounce of gold has been poured and before any money has been raised to fmance a mine! In such a hot-house atmosphere it is no wonder that Canadian registered gold shares command a premium in the international market! Indeed some Australian gold companies are busy seeking listings on the Toronto Stock Exchange, hoping to bask in some reflected glory. Relative to Diamond Fields and Bre-X, junior exploration stocks look very cheap to the unwary – but not as cheap as they will look soon if they don't find something. In the current climate "yet to be discovered" ounces are valued very highly.

Those of us who are getting long in the tooth have seen it all before during the Western Mining and Poseidon nickel booms in Australia in the late 1960's and early 1970's. The same phenomenon occurred in the gold booms of 1970–74 and 1976–80 and to a lesser extent in the gold share boom which followed the Soros and Goldsmith foray into gold in 1993. By keeping our exposure to the exploration stocks to a minimum, we are knowingly sacrificing short-term performance with the aim of avoiding the inevitable pain when the bubble bursts. Knowing how few discoveries eventually turn into profitable mines, we boringly prefer to give you your thrills by spicing our portfolio with already producing mines which would do particularly well if the gold price were ever allowed to rise. Other funds are better than us at picking the hot exploration plays and those who do so successfully thoroughly deserve to earn their school fees. (**245. 11/2/94**)

Graham Birch recounts how frothy the market had become.

Hot Money, Cold Feet

The phenomenal exploration success driving the share prices of both Diamond Fields and Bre-X has generated a huge amount of wealth for mining equity speculators. Just look at the combined value of the two companies:

1 January 1994	C$98 million
1 January 1995	C$246 million
1 January 1996	C$3,527 million
18 April 1996	C$6,765 million

Those that are lucky enough to hold shares in these companies are now doubtless starting to look around for areas to reinvest the quick and spectacular profits. Those who do not hold shares and who watched in anguish on the sidelines are desperate to make sure that they don't miss out next time. Either way it is hardly surprising that one of the most common questions asked of stockbrokers is "tell us the name of the next Bre-X or next Diamond Fields?"

This of course is easier said than done. However, brokers are always a wellspring of optimism and so there is no shortage of suggestions. Furthermore, investors have become so trigger-happy in their search for the next pot of gold that they would appear to be throwing caution to the wind. This ultimately looks like a recipe for future problems as it has led to the development of a speculative bubble rather reminiscent of 1985–1987 and to a lesser extent 1993. Indeed there is now reason to believe that the market is placing a higher price on exploration assets than it is placing on developed mines! The market is prepared to do this because the prospective capital gains that can be delivered by "blue sky" are currently way in excess of the relatively pedestrian earnings yields available on the mines themselves. As in most walks of life, dreams are so much more exciting than reality.

Timbuktu Gold is an interesting example of this phenomenon. A few days ago this junior Alberta listed stock stunned the market with spectacular intersections from its Mali gold property. The stock leapt upwards to C$30/share – capitalising the company at over C$600 million – not bad for a company which has only received drill results from two holes.

A subsequent broker's report suggested that while highly speculative the company might eventually discover a 50 million ounce orebody. Sadly for the "instant millionaires" who hold Timbuktu, the stock is now suspended while the Alberta authorities probe various irregularities.

Despite the fact that the stock has now been suspended, Timbuktu proves beyond any doubt that a new category of ore reserves now exists which we have christened; "Soon To Be Discovered" ounces or STBD for short. Because the recent exploration successes have been enjoyed primarily by Vancouver, Toronto and Alberta listed companies it is Canadian investors, above all others, that have lost their capacity to feel vertigo. Perhaps not surprisingly therefore, it is the Canadians who are prepared to pay the most for STBD gold. This has not gone unnoticed by the market and the latest game being played by corporate brokers is to take humdrum Australian exploration companies, re-list them in Canada and watch an immediate upwards revaluation take place – often of substantial proportions. Being able to add value simply by re-listing in another country is something which shouldn't really happen in today's world of high-speed communications and instant money flows. For those who are prepared to listen, an alarm bell is faintly ringing in Canada.

Now at this point we would like to reassure you that your Fund's exposure to these high-priced, highly-speculative situations is very low. We never held Timbuktu and we have completed the sale of our Bre-X at a very good profit. In fact, if we add up all the positions in the Fund where the company has neither production nor a bankable feasibility study it amounts to only a fraction over 3 per cent of assets. (**340. 23/4/96**)

The Bre -X story was so "exciting" that David Baker was sent to check out what all the fuss was about.

Sydney Australia is one of the world's beautiful cities, and a great place to live. So now that I have been down under for 18 months, I decided it was time to buy a roof over my head. I recalled my father's advice from younger days, "Son," he said "there are only three rules to buying real estate, location, location, location." Well I couldn't quite afford the waterfront, but I do live in a very nice part of town and hopefully my father's advice will pay off in the longer term.

Location is all important, and not surprisingly, the mining game is all about having the right address. Some locations are the equivalent of Mayfair on the famous Monopoly board and others, the Old Kent Road. But as in any real estate frenzy, when prices defy gravity you should never resist taking your profits.

The "hot spots" of the world are dominated by a few regions, some better than others, but as with that one magic ingredient, the potential for the mighty "elephant". If you scan through the Mercury Gold and General Fund's portfolio you will get an idea of where we believe the "hot spots" of the mining world are right now. Regions that come to mind would include West Africa, Peru and South East Asia. But the Mayfair of the "mining Monopoly board" is now Indonesia, or more specifically an address in East Kalimantan. Mining companies from around the globe are falling over themselves in their efforts to secure the best possible ground in the region and investors, particularly those from North America, are bidding up the share prices of companies with properties along this golden corridor.

But what has sparked this excitement? The catalyst of what appears to be a sudden rush of blood to the head of investors, has been one of this decade's most remarkable gold discoveries. An "elephant" to dwarf all other "elephants" which, even this time last year, was nothing but a sparkle in a geologist's eye. The deposit is Busang, and the owner of this prime piece of real estate is a company called Bre-X. The share price of Bre-X has appreciated from little over C$2.50/share to the equivalent today of C$194/share. Now that is serious wealth creation and probably one of the main reasons that entrepreneurs, investors, hairdressers, dentists and taxi drivers in Canada are abuzz with the "gold rush fever".

As for the Mercury Gold and General Fund, it is a case of been there, done that. We first invested in Bre-X at around C$50/share, which after the stock had risen from C$2.50 per share was a major leap of faith. What gave us that "leap of faith" was actually putting our footprints on the deposit, and last November, we did just that.

Our journey took us from Sydney to Jakarta and then by helicopter into the jungles of Kalimantan. The deposit has been formed by previous volcanic actions and the geologists describe how this monster was formed at the crossroads of a major fault system. Volcanic action from the depths of the earth enriched the deposit with gold and each time the volcano attempted to break through the surface, more gold was deposited in this huge system. This is the one that all geologists dream about. But just how big is this elephant. The alterations have been mapped over a 7 km strike, and market scuttlebuck suggests that we should be confident with a total resource in the region of over 40 million ounces of gold, but even this could be conservative.

Such a bonanza gold find by a "junior" mining company (although this junior is now capitalised at around US$3 billion) poses a serious dilemma for the major North American gold mining companies. These companies are mining gold at an alarming rate. For example, Barrick has to replace the 3 million ounces of gold that it mines every year just to keep the larder stocked. What would they give for a dowry of "40 million ounces plus" in their resource inventory? The market speculates that Barrick or maybe Newmont will not be able to resist putting their hand into the cookie jar and mounting a bid for Bre-X and its "elephant". Whilst the market speculates, we can take profits, and that is just what we have done. In fact, the company has put the "for sale" sign on the deposit, keen as it is to secure US$1 billion for 25 per cent of this monster.

The spotlight is well and truly on Indonesia and although location, location, location can be the key to spectacular returns, reinvesting your profits into the next "hot spot' is the key to growing the money tree. Investors in North America appear to have turned the world upside down. The mining companies have drill rigs scattered over the developing world from Peru to Indonesia to Ghana. And as the hint of spectacular returns entices even the more wary investor into this inflating bubble, the risks are getting larger and larger. A North American broker recently told me the story of his visit to the dentist. He was given a filling and the latest hot stock in Peru; at the barbers having his hair cut he heard another two tips, one in Argentina and one in Venezuela, and on the way home in the taxi after a long day in the office his tally of hot gold stocks was up to six and his geographic spread had moved into Tanzania and Ethiopia.

The fact is that the market has to be able to attract new entrants with mouth-watering stories of "King Solomon's Mines" and thus maintain its inflated level.

But, although Bre-X has been widely recommended, not one of the "new experts" in gold exploration has mentioned South Africa. Yet South Africa has some of the largest gold deposits in the world, comparable even with the mighty Busang.

Take Western Areas for example. Assuming that Bre-X has 40 million ounces of gold in the ground, Western Areas has at least 50 per cent more, but whereas Bre-X will not be mining its gold for at least three, if not four, years and still has to finance its mine at Busang, Western Areas is well under way to producing 1.4 million ounces per annum, and the project is fully funded so shareholders will not be asked to contribute any more to the project's development.

	BRE-X	WESTERN AREAS
Market Capitalization	US$3.1 billion	US$1.4 billion
Resources	40-60 million ounces	6.5 million ounces
Market Cap per ounce	US$78–52/oz	US$21.5/oz
Capex to production	Substantial, yet to be funded	Construction under way, fully funded

It is a topsy turvey world; not only does Western Areas have a similar resource inventory but the market is only willing to assign US$21.5/oz for each of Western Areas' un-mined ounces, only 40 per cent of what it is willing to pay for ounces in

Indonesia. Even though Western Areas has sold 7.5 million of its ounces forward, that seems to be too great a discrepancy between two deposits of similar size! (**344. 6/6/96**)

David Baker highlights the difficulties in being contrarian at the time of the Bre-X excitement.

Prior to our visit to South Africa it was easy to believe that the South African gold industry was struggling to survive; gold production continues to fall and costs appear to rise relentlessly. As such, South African gold shares are frowned upon by the international investor. Why bother playing this dull and unexciting market when such riches as the fabulous Busang deposit in Indonesia can ignite the imagination of eager analysts? South Africa continues to hide its light under a bushel while the rest of the world's gold companies compete furiously for investment dollars. (**358. 26/9/96**)

Trevor Steel was also sent to Brazil to investigate if there may be significant deposits in the recently opened up territory. He also points out the Fund's successful short term trade in Bre-X.

As we have often said in this Newsletter we are not in the business of gambling your money on the chance of exploration successes. We will, on occasion, back companies at the exploration stage when we think that a small company really has the potential to become a very big company because of the significance of a discovery. Of course, the classic example of this type of company is Bre-X, which discovered the massive Busang deposit in Indonesia last year. We bought Bre-X at C$50/share, after a member of the team had visited the property, and sold four months later at C$150/share. At Black Swan's Cata Preta property, insufficient drilling has been carried out to establish the potential of the deposit but needless to say we are watching very closely. (**361. 21/10/96**)

The Bre-X scandal breaks and Graham Birch and Geoff Campbell recount a near miss.

"Insignificant amounts of gold"

Thus was described the mighty Busang deposit in Indonesia that until recently was reckoned to be the largest gold discovery in recent times. Only a few weeks ago John Felderhof, Senior Vice-President of Bre-X, stated in public that the deposit could contain as many as 200 million ounces. All this has been thrown into doubt and confusion following the comments by Freeport McMoran Copper and Gold, currently carrying out a due diligence programme on the property with a view to a joint venture. The company announced after drilling its own holes to verify the Bre-X exploration that its own tests so far revealed "insignificant amounts of gold".

This was not an early April Fool's Day joke and at the time of writing there has been no adequate explanation for the massive discrepancy for what Bre-X thought was there and what Freeport's work would suggest. Bear in mind that many respected mining companies have taken a close look at the property with a view to a joint venture with Bre-X.

Both Barrick and Placer Dome showed keen interest in the property and it was only the fact that Freeport effectively shut them out of a deal that they are not now in Freeport's position.

Initial studies of the property did not over-turn anything untoward in the ore reserves calculation, but then no one else has drilled any of their own holes until now. Furthermore the well-known firm of Kilbom were involved in preparing the resource calculations. Over the past three years, PT Kilbom Rekayasa carried out resource studies and modelling based on geological data, sample and assay information provided to it by Bre-X. A press release from Kilbom states that the conclusions and recommendations provided in the various studies are believed to be prudent and reasonable and are founded on calculations and observations that were performed to accepted industry standards. However the calculations are dependent on the validity of samples and assaying of those samples. Kilbom goes on to say that it did not drill, did not take the samples, nor did it assay those results.

Investor's confidence is shaken

At this point in our newsletter, we would like to reassure investors that we do not own any Bre-X shares. We are thus in the fortunate position of being able to watch the unfolding saga from a relatively safe distance. Whatever the reasons for the assay discrepancy, one thing is clear; investor confidence in exploration shares has been severely shaken. Bre-X shares are suspended and exploration stocks across the board have taken a hammering. Investors are probably thinking if such a thing can happen to Bre-X then it can happen to anyone and will simply want to be out of the sector at any cost throwing the baby out with the bath water in some cases.

Other investors will be in the unpleasant position of having to meet margin calls. For the purpose of margin calculations the valuation of Bre-X has been set at zero until the stock commences trading. Anyone who bought the shares on margin or has borrowed against a holding in Bre-X has to come up with the full amount owing without delay. This means there will be a lot of forced selling of assets by shareholders of Bre-X. It is a fair assumption that people who own Bre-X will tend to own other high risk exploration shares and following recent experience they will sell those other exploration shares in order to meet margin calls.

Limiting the exploration risk.

The preceeding table shows what happens when investors want to get out at any cost; share prices plunge. Fortunately our readers will not be familiar with the names in the table because the Fund has never owned any of these shares. The Gold and General Fund has always been constructed in such a way as to give its unitholders the maximum exposure to a rising gold price by owning fundamentally undervalued gold producing companies. Exploration shares are not particularly sensitive to movements in the gold price and, as is now patently obvious, they are very risky. Furthermore it is very difficult to apply any sort of fundamental analysis to exploration companies. They either find gold or they do not; it's a win or lose situation, a bit like a lottery ticket. Or in the case of Bre-X, they find gold and then they do not. We simply do not want to overload our unitholders with these types of non-quantifiable risks and our exposure to pure exploration stocks is minimal. At the present time the Fund has a mere 1.1 per cent of its assets invested in pure exploration stocks and a further 4.3 per cent in companies that are in the process of developing mines. In other words 94.6 per cent of the Fund's assets are invested in companies with producing assets.

If exploration stocks are so risky, why have any at all in the Fund? The first reason is that they do sometimes give excellent returns and we believe that our rigorous investment process and detailed analysis will help us to avoid some of the "elephant traps". The second reason for owning exploration shares in a mining portfolio is that exploration provides the pipeline of future projects to the mining industry. If we are to be fully abreast of what's going on in the mining industry, we have to keep an eye on exploration. And it's very difficult to keep an eye on exploration if you do not invest in it. (377. 1/4/97)

10. The Route to Success – Selling High and Buying Low

When you are investing with a contrarian mindset Julian always questioned whether the miners were in a bull or bear market. Over the course of his career he had "war wounds" to prove that he had experienced several protracted periods of bear markets and he used those experiences to orientate himself at any given point in the cycle. The rises and falls from the lows and highs were a key tool to aid him on this path.

In 1970, before one of the great bull markets of all time, no one wanted to buy gold shares which were then viewed as high-yielding, wasting assets, with falling grades and rising costs. Base metal shares today are just about as unpopular as gold shares were in 1970. Gradually, gradually people are beginning to wonder whether, by ignoring them, they are in danger of missing another opportunity of a lifetime. (**10. 7/6/88**)

An early comment on timing in relation to share buying.

Many people in the investment world don't seem able to decide whether they come to work to collect share certificates or to collect money. If they work to collect share certificates, you would think that they would buy them on weak days, because they can get more of them that way. If they work to collect pound notes, you would think they would sell shares on strong days, because you can get more pound notes for shares when they have just gone up! If you think that is what happens in practice, you have got another think coming, but from what I have seen in the last week, the unitholders of the Gold and General Fund know exactly what they are collecting. Of course, when money comes in on weak days, it gives me a chance to buy more of the shares I like at favourable prices, so it helps us all. (**14. 19/7/88**)

Investing with the pack and its consequences.

Have you noticed that as soon as people get into a market place they behave instinctively, like shoals of fish, flocks of sheep or collections of gnus? They are happiest when following each other. Once they have decided which way they want to go, it is hard to divert them.

That is why at the risk of being over-simplistic, it is easy to see (especially with the advantage of hindsight) that markets go up until they stop going up and then down until they stop going down! So, to be a successful investor you have to be a trendie, going with the flow until the tide turns. The hard bit is knowing when to stop. When a market is high, there are many more reasons to buy it than sell it, otherwise it wouldn't be so high. Conversely, when a market is low there are many more reasons why it should fall further, than rise. That is why we all find it so hard to change tack. At tops and bottoms of markets, the reversal of the existing trend looks like a temporary aberration. All the reasons you were so bullish or bearish are engrained in your mind and it's hard to jettison them just because a trend line on a chart has been breached. (**16. 1/8/88**)

The danger of strong rallies in bear markets.

Once, or sometimes twice, in the course of a bear market you get a jumbo rally of 40 to 50 per cent. I don't think this particular one is going to turn into a jumbo, (they are usually preceedcd by a state of near panic and that was not the situation before this one started). I have therefore ignored it in the expectation it will blow itself out before long. The market does not seem to believe it either, otherwise gold shares would have been responding more positively by now. (**23. 27/09/88**)

In my opinion, the right price for a share is when it reaches a level where you don't know whether to buy it or sell it. (**37. 25/1/89**)

The market is very seldom wrong.

When I first started in this game in 1967, there was a delightful old Partner of the firm called George Seebohm who had an uncanny knack of reading markets correctly. Like most of us of the old school of stockbroking, he would be the first to admit that detailed analysis did not come as second nature to him, yet he was one of the canniest investors I ever met.

Whenever I had a rush of blood to the head about a particular stock or market, he would invite me to lunch with him at the City Club and he would say, "Julian, don't overlook the fact that the market is very seldom wrong". I must tell you that over the years I have found that maxim worth remembering whenever I was tempted to make definitive statements about what should be where, regardless of what the market was indicating. (**72. 30/11/89**)

Don't forget, the best time to buy mining shares is when the market is low AND when the metal is low. That way you have two things going for you. Either the metal price will rally and the earnings will be better than the market expects OR the market will go up, dragging your mining shares with it. Better still, both will rise together, giving you enhanced earnings and multiple expansion. In other words, in a bull market investors are prepared to pay a higher multiple for a given level of earnings, just as they are doing with gold shares at the moment.

So, to answer the question, the excellent performance of our gold shares is being masked by the downward pull of our base metal shares, but the more the base metal shares fall, the nearer we get to the reversal. This Fund does not have all its eggs in one basket in case someone drops the basket. Put another way, this Fund is designed to provide the ballast, so to speak, of your gold exposure. You want increased excitement, you should not have much difficulty in finding it for yourself, but make sure someone tells you when to sell. It is easy to make money in the mining market in boom conditions, but the "tall poppy" syndrome usually ensures that you give most of it back when the bubble bursts.

The reason why the Fund is not being left behind by its peers is, as I have learnt over the last 20 years, that brokers always recommend the wrong stocks at the beginning of a new bull market. They always urge us to buy the low-cost leaders, whereas of course the high-cost marginals are the ones whose profits benefit most. It is the high-cost marginal mines which this fund has been buying and it shows up in our performance figures. When this type of stock starts to find favour with the brokers, which it tends to do when the gold price has moved up to a level at which the marginals are no longer marginal, then they can have our stock and we will buy the low-cost leaders because they are safer. But that moment has not come yet, though I am sure it will. (**81. 6/2/90**)

Hanging on to marginal gold mines.

My predicament, and I like to tell it to you straight, is this. Should I hold onto our marginal mines which look perilously close to the "plimsoll line" at the present gold price (in fact some of them are now loss makers); or should I abandon them in favour of the low-cost mines which will enable us to sleep better, but which do not have the same upside potential if the gold price starts to go up again? Others more timid than I are already dumping the marginals and buying the leaders. I think that most of you know that you are taking a higher than average risk in a Fund of this nature. This Fund is invested in those mines which do best when the gold price goes up i.e. the marginal mines. The corollary to that is that those self same mines are likely to do worst when the gold price is falling – hence my decision to restrict the portfolios exposure to this danger.

Despite the fact that gold and gold shares have fallen severely and are now closer to the bargain basement than they were in January, the institutions almost to a man, have now become very bearish, usually a reliable sign that we are close to a low. Come back private clients, all is forgiven! Private clients don't care about quarterly performance. The market surely shares our optimism about the direction of the gold price, since Kleinwort Weekly Mining circular tells us that North American gold shares are selling on an average of 31 times 1989 earnings! In order to bring the PE ratio down to a lower figure than the remaining life, you need a higher gold price in the future than we had in 1989 and that was $384/oz. I still think the gold price is destined to go higher and I still think the best time to buy mining shares is when the metal price is at a low ebb. The fact that institutional investors are finding a thousand reasons why they should not doing so only encourages me to believe that we are on the right track. If I have learned anything in the last 25 years it is that you can often do best by betting against the crowd. So don't be down hearted, better times are on the way. **(89. 4/4/90)**

Betting against the crowd.

As you know I prefer to bet against the crowd. I take the view that every extra day the supply disruptions last, the more difficult it will become for deplenished stocks to be built up. Every day that passes brings us closer to the next economic upturn. The improvement in commodity prices which would accompany an economic upturn is anything but discounted by metal shares at current prices. Don't forget the multiple on Wall Street is close to 14 times earnings, whereas the sort of stocks we hold are selling on between 7–10 times most people's estimates of this year's earnings. **(92. 10/5/90)**

Gold shares as options on the gold price.

Mining shares are usually valued on the basis of what they can earn. But when the gold price falls to levels at which they cannot earn anything, they become valued as an option on the gold price.

To give you an example; Western Areas, a marginal South African gold mine with costs of $380/oz is only likely to make any profit at current gold prices because it is selling its production forward. In other words, you can no longer value it on its earnings potential since there are vinually no earnings. Because of this the shares have fallen to levels where each ounce of gold in its reserves is valued by the market at only $7. If, by a miracle, the gold price was to go up to $500/oz, the profits of

Western Areas would rise from between $5–$10/oz to $105–$110/oz. Where else could you buy a 15-year option on the gold price rising to $500/oz at a cost of only $7/oz? (**119. 29/11/90**)

Judging the pain threshold in a falling market.

If in bull markets, brokers' circulars contain more buy recommendations than sell recommendations, would it not be reasonable to expect that in bear markets their circulars would contain more sell recommendations?

Judging from the circulars I receive, most of which contain buy recommendations, we are still very much in a bull market. Or is it that many of the analysts are too young to recognise a bear market when they see one? Those of us who have spent our working lives in the mining markets have experienced more than our fair share of bear markets.

One of my earliest recollections was of the bear market for copper in the 1950's brought about by a previous boom in copper prices which had led to the substitution of copper by aluminium in the overhead power line market. Anglo American had helped to finance the Kariba Dam which was to provide cheap power for the copper mines in Northern Rhodesia. You can imagine the look of disbelief on the directors' faces when they heard that the power lines taking electricity from Kariba to the copper belt were to be made of aluminium!

So that you can make up your own minds whether we are in a bear market or a bull market, I am publishing this week some long-term charts of selected indices, courtesy of Smith New Court, for your perusal. People in the securities industry will tell you that business has been bad since the crash of 1987 and judging by the volumes they certainly have a point. But that does not mean that share prices have been declining since the crash of "87, far from it. Having looked at the charts you may decide that the World Capital Index peaked in December of last year and has only fallen 18 per cent since then. A fall which is inconvenient but by no means disastrous. My previous experience tells me that markets do not bottom out until most investors have decided that such is the pain they have suffered that they will never, ever invest in equities again! That pain threshold is normally reached when markets have lost more than 60 per cent of their value. The following table shows the falls in the FT Gold Mines Index which I personally have ridden and survived since coming into the industry in 1967.

Bear Markets	FT Gold Index at Previous High	FT Gold Index at Low	Percentage Fall
1976	525	79	86
1982	559	181	68
1986	735	186	75
1989	497	155	69
1990	379	151	60 (to date)

This year the FT Gold Mines Index has lost 60 per cent. Those of you who remember the Western Mining and Poseidon nickel booms will have painful memories of the money that was won and lost in the late 1960's and early 1970's. And then there was the bear market in UK equities which terminated in 1974, having lost 73 per cent of its previous value in two years.

So if you conclude from these charts that we are in a bear market, you may also wonder whether it has been going on long enough or far enough to wash out the weak holders yet. What we must not do is fight the trend. More important than that, we must avoid the greatest elephant trap, namely the rally which often takes place once a market has fallen about 25 per cent from its high. At that stage, people often conclude that the market must be cheap and they throw their money at it hoping to recoup what they have lost since the peak. If they are not extremely nimble they find they have fallen into the elephant trap, become impaled on a spike and suffer a slow and lingering death.

If you want to know why this Fund is 30 per cent in cash and bonds it is because I think we are in elephant country.

This will be my last offering this year and for that at least you can be grateful. Next year will probably provide us with the buying opportunity of a lifetime and I am determined to have the wherewithal to take advantage of it. In the meantime I leave you with a chart which shows the performance of this Fund so far this year compared to that of our competitors. Surely those who stay the course can look forward to having a lovely time when the recovery eventually takes place. After all, never once since 1976 has the gold market risen less than 145 per cent from the bottom of one bear market to its subsequent peak. (**121. 13/12/90**)

In a falling market the Fund is once more biased towards non gold stocks.

In the meantime, into the breech steps Burns Fry, the Canadian broker whose conventional analysis of the North American gold industry can be transformed in the twinkling of an eye into any form you like. In a matter of days, rather than months, they have produced for me a piece of paper on which they have calculated that a gold price of $487/oz is needed for the average gold share in their universe to offer a 6 per cent real return. Although they could not immediately tell me how far the shares would have to fall to give a 6 per cent return on the current gold price of $367/oz, they did work out that given a gold price of $400/oz the Toronto Gold Mines Index would have to fall 38 per cent from today's limit to 2909. At that level it would be 63 per cent below last year's high of 8000.

If you think that is impossible, remember the FT Gold Mines Index has already fallen 65 per cent from last year's high. Our Fund has fallen 36 per cent. I am not proud of that but it could have been worse.

Now it seems to me that if there were a real danger of the gold share market in North America declining a further 38 per cent from here, you would wish me to exercise extreme caution in the investment of your money in this area. Rest assured, I am. At the last count less than one quarter of this Fund was exposed to gold shares generally and of that portion less than a quarter was invested in North American gold shares. **(126. 07/2/91)**

Julian worries about not having firepower as the market weakens.

What is difficult is to arrange our affairs in such a way as to provide cash for those wishing to exit the Fund and at the same time, find money to build up our holdings of gold shares at current depressed levels.

I want to rub in the point I am making. It is a fact that the lowest level the FT Gold Mines Index ever reached was 43.5 on 26th October 1971 when gold was still close to $35/oz. At that time the FT All Share Index was about 180. Therefore, at the worst possible moment for the FT Gold Mines Index, it represented 24 per cent of the Ft All Share Index. It now represents less than 12 per cent of that Index. Half its previous low point. I do not know, and nor I suspect do you, when the pendulum will start to swing the other way again. All I do know is that sooner or later it will start to swing back in our favour. You may be clever enough to get out and get back in time to catch the turn, but if so it will probably have more to do with luck than good judgement. **(128. 6/3/91)**

Julian's assistant makes a wise observation on the market.

My assistant, Denise Bennett, whose irrepressible sense of humour helps to keep her sane, relishes telling friends and clients that our new telephone number in delightful Docklands is 955 fifty fifty.

Her short career as a Fund Manager has persuaded her that the odds of us getting your investments right are not dissimilar to our telephone number. After all, for every buyer there is a seller and they can't both be right! I try to improve the odds by buying when shares have fallen a long way and sell when they have risen. Gold shares have fallen a long way and base metal shares have risen, so I am adding to our gold holdings and top slicing our base metal holdings.

Nearly 53 per cent of the Fund is now in gold shares. You may recall that the percentage was nearer 16 per cent a couple of months ago. (**134. 8/5/91**)

As bearish sentiment grows Julian senses the end of the gold bear trend.

So don't let's worry about investors who behave like gnus. Once the fundamentals start asserting themselves and the gold price starts going up, investors will want part of the action. They will reinforce the uptrend just as they are now reinforcing the downtrend. They will forget overnight all the reasons why they were so bearish in August 1991. At present they think that they have identified a continuation of the overall downtrend which has prevailed for the best part of 11 years. But they bad better watch out. They may find that the trend is bottoming out and that they cannot talk it down much further.

I do hope I am not being pig-headed, but the more obituaries I read for gold, the more I think we cannot be far from the bottom. Bear markets only reverse themselves when there is nobody left to sell. We cannot be far from that now, surely! (**146. 21/8/91**)

Marginal gold mines do best in a bull run but mines can be too marginal.

I have never hidden from you that this strategy has its risks. So far the rewards have compensated us for those risks but obviously, when the market is feeling liverish, we will do less well than our more respectable competitors who eschew "marginal mines". My point is that "marginal mines' are to be avoided when they can only break even at a comparatively high gold price like $425/oz. In other words when the gold price itself is vulnerable. As I see it, the gold price is about as low as it will go at $355/oz so I am content if my marginal mines are roughly breaking even at the current gold price. Having reduced their costs they will do extraordinarily well when the gold prices does go up a little. This is not necessarily so in the case of mines which have lower costs per ounce than our marginals but where the investor has to pay a high price to buy each ounce. What good is it to you to pay $125/oz for a mine with costs of $300/oz? You still need $425/oz to come out all square, but at that price the marginal mines we own will be making us a fortune. It is very important that unitholders fully understand this point. I do not want you to be holding units on false pretences! (**147. 28/8/91**)

Everyone has become totally bearish and dispirited. Those few of us who remain bullish are rendered powerless to act by the continuing stream of redemptions which force us to go on selling at very depressed levels when we know we should be buying. No wonder falls get overdone and rises too! You know me, I refuse to sell when the market is flat on its back and I am not going to give you any encouragement to do so either. (**152. 4/10/91**)

Julian warns against selling when the market is flat on its back.

What we are experiencing now is a recurrence of the usual syndrome associated with bottoms of markets which are characterised by total lack of interest accompanied by an uncontrollable urge to throw ones money away! If history is anything to go by this won't change, unfortunately, until the units have risen more than 50 per cent from their low (they are only up about 35 per cent so far). Then people will wake up to what is happening and start buying units again. That in turn means that I shall be buying back the shares I am now having to sell to meet redemptions, at prices 20 per cent or so higher than they are today. (**154. 23/10/91**)

The gold bears begin to depress Julian.

I don't know about you, but I find the ever-shriller tones of those who hold no gold shares, entreating us to sell ours, is starting to depress me. They keep telling me the gold price is going nowhere except down and now the bear trend of gold shares is so clearly established (the FT Gold Mines Index has lost nearly 60 per cent of its value in real terms since January 1990 and 87 per cent of its value in real terms since its peak in 1980) they find the courage to recommend that we should now call it a day.

If successful investing is about buying an improving trend of profits, perhaps you will forgive me for continuing to invest your money in a sector which is managing to keep its head above water in exceedingly adverse circumstances.

When the trend of the gold price reverses, the distributable profit, which currently represents a mere 4 per cent of revenue, will enjoy a spectacular renaissance! If I switch out now, I know I will never be clever enough to get back in again at the right moment, but as I have said before, the only way to be sure of underperforming a market is not to be fully invested at the bottom. I am not going to risk that. (**169. 26/3/92**)

Julian analyses past investment bubbles and looks at historic gold share bubbles as well.

Last week a client sent me a copy of an interesting article in a Morgan Stanley publication which gave some examples of burst investment bubbles. The article was designed to draw attention to what is going on in Japan, but the table overleaf which accompanied the article, omitted to mention the burst bubbles the gold market experienced in the last 20 years or so.

There have, in fact, been five separate booms and busts since I became involved in the gold market in 1970, all of which have contributed to the thickness of my skin.

It will be seen that people who bought gold shares at the peak of the market in 1975 would have said goodbye to 83 per cent of their money if they had sold at the bottom in 1976 but those who bought at the 1976 bottom, multiplied their money sixfold in the subsequent four years!

Those who bought at the top of the 1980 bull market and held on to the present day have so far lost 88 per cent of their money in real terms! These horrifying examples of disappearing wealth show that gold shares deserve a place in Morgan Stanley's "chamber of horrors" of burst bubbles. With gold itself down over 60 per cent from its 1980 peak, both gold and gold shares may be symptomatic of what is happening to the value of real assets in a deflationary environment.

	FT Gold Mines Index US$				Percentage Rise	Per Cent Fall
1970–1975	Low	110	High	980	790 per cent	
1975 –1976	High	980	Low	170		83 per cent
1976–1980	Low	170	High	1343	629 per cent	
1980–1982	High	1343	Low	340		75 per cent
1982–1984	Low	340	High	1050	208 per cent	
1984–1986	High	1050	Low	300		71 per cent
1986–1987	Low	300	High	790	163 per cent	
1987–1989	High	790	Low	290		63 per cent
1989–1990	Low	290	High	600	106 per cent	
1990–1992	High	600	Low	205		66 per cent
1970–1980	Low	110	High	1343	1120 per cent	
1980–1992	High	343	Low	205		85 per cent

Source: James Capel & Co. Ltd and Datastream

What worries people is that the problems of Japan could have a knock-on effect on the other markets of the world, some of which are uncomfortably close to their all-time highs. So far Japanese stocks have fallen 56 per cent from the December 1989 high. The FT Gold Mines Index (expressed in US dollars), having already fallen 85 per cent, may be relatively defensive.

Booms and Busts	per cent Rise Bull Phase	Length of Bull Phase (months)	per cent Decline Peak to Trough	Length of Bull Phase (months)		
Tulips Netherlands (1634–1637)	+5900	36	-93	10		
Mississippi Shares France (1719–1721)	+6200	13	-99	13		
South Sea Shares England (1719–1720)	+1000	18	-84	6		
American Stocks US (1923–1932)	+345	71	-87	33	?	?
Mexican Stocks Mexico (1918–1981)	+785	30	-73	18		
Silver US (1979–1982)	+710	12	-88	24		
Gulf Stocks Kuwait (1978–1986)	+7000*	36	-98	30		
Hong Kong Stocks Hong Kong (1970–1974)	+1200	28	-92	20		
Taiwan Stocks Taiwan (1986–1990)	+1168	40	-80	12		
Japanese Stocks						
Tokyo (1970–199?)	+35710	230				

* Appropriate   Source: Morgan Stanley Research

The measures which the authorities may be obliged to take to shore up the banking system and at the same time kick start the world economy, could have inflationary implications further down the road. It is therefore hard to believe that gold itself will remain depressed forever, though some would say the following chart of the FT Gold Mines Index in US dollars is looking decidedly droopy at the moment. Others would describe it as oversold and ready for a bounce.

What is interesting about this chart is that on many occasions the market has had a significant change of direction in June preceded by a selling or buying "spike".

Should the next bounce be sufficient to cause the index once again to bang its head against the main down-trend line, the market would have to rise 110 per cent from current levels. Although it is hard to believe that such a thing could happen again, I assure you that it was no less hard to believe it in 1982, 1986 and 1989.

What is so disappointing is that although gold itself has risen about 20 per cent in real terms since 1977, the shares of the South African producers have nearly

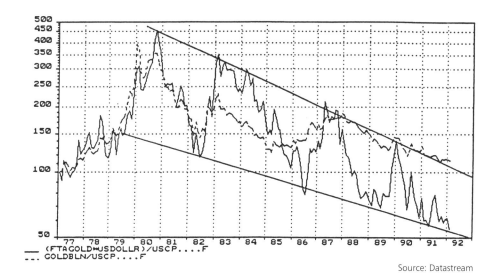

FTAGOLD⋈USDOLLR)/USCP....F
GOLDBLN/USCP....F

Source: Datastream

halved. And to think that Mr. Mandela wants to nationalise them! What has he heard, I wonder? (**171. 9/4/92**)

Julian wonders whether things can really get worse?

At the risk of rubbing salt into the wound, you may be interested to know that the FT Gold Mines Index reached its all-time low of 43.5 in October 1971 when the gold price was £17/oz (US$41.3). Today's Index of 94.6 is the equivalent, in 1971 money, to 14. So in real terms the Index is now about one third of what it was at its all-time low.

As far as the gold price is concerned, today's price of £184/oz is the equivalent of £27 in 1971 money. So, from their 1971 lows, you can see that gold has risen 59 per cent in real terms, while the shares have fallen by two thirds.

All this goes to show that the profit margins in the South African gold mining industry must be smaller now than they were in 1971 despite the fact that in 1971 the gold price had been fixed at US$35/oz since 1934! There are still profits, however, and when the gold price eventually rises those profits will increase dramatically as they did after 1971. Between 1971 and 1975 the FT Gold Mines Index rose by 980 per cent in dollar terms. Although it's hard to believe that history will repeat itself this time, the possibility of a major rally, if not a complete turnaround, is ever present and the lower the market goes the more impressive the rally is likely to be. (**180. 26/6/92**)

Finally, the first signs of a turnaround in the gold shares fortunes.

With the commercial rand starting to weaken, the gold price in rand terms has appreciated in the last week from R930/oz to Rl,000/oz, the additional profit going straight to the bottom line. So marginal have the South African gold shares become that a rise of this magnitude should enable dividends to be increased (Martin & Co. estimate by between 10 per cent and 40 per cent). With yields of 8–10 per cent already widely available, South African investors looking for a currency hedge are likely to do better in gold shares than in their favourite hedge stocks such as Charter Consolidated, Rembrandt, Minorco and Lonrho. After all an 8–10 per cent yield while you are waiting for a 20–30 per cent capital gain is not to be sniffed at. That is why we can't help thinking that greed may soon overcome fear. Let's hope so anyway. (**188. 18/9/92**)

Increasing the Fund's holding in Doornfontein the classic geared marginal.

One such mine in which we have a substantial shareholding is Doornfontein, a loss making South African producer with costs of US$385/oz and an annual production of about 200,000 ounce. The shares have fallen such a long way that the whole company is now only capitalised at US$10 million. It would have enough gold in the ground (5.2 million ounces) to last at least 20 years if costs could be reduced by 10 per cent, or if the gold price in rand terms were to rise by a similar amount – by no means an impossible dream. Each ounce in the ground can now be bought for US$2 at the present share price. I simply do not believe that it is impossible to find a way of keeping the mine from closing permanently. The prize is more than 5 million ounces of gold in the ground on which a profit can be made when times get better. Just 14 months ago, when the gold price was R1,057/oz, compared with today's rand gold price of R988/oz (-6.5 per cent), Doornfontein shares were nearly five times the present price. With touching faith in human ingenuity we bought another 350,000 shares last week at 15.3p. (**189. 24/9/92**)

Contrarian investing as Julian spots silver lining.

Even in Biblical times it was recognised that trends do not continue forever. Fortunes can change. The last shall be first. It is by no means unheard of for the worst-performing fund in one year to be among the best performers one year later. I have a friend in the Fund Management business who makes a habit once a year of selling the best-performing units in his portfolio and buying his Group's worst-performing unit trust. Judging by his lifestyle this system does not seem to do him any harm!

Here is the picture which has turned into a seemingly perpetual nightmare. No it is not of the north face of the Eiger, nor is it of Mont Blanc. It represents the performance of your units since January 1991. Having risen some 50 per cent in the first six months of 1991, they have fallen 32 per cent in the last 18 months or so. But the eagle-eyed or the eternal optimists among you will have detected what may possibly turn out to be a change of direction in our fortunes.

(199. 8/12/92)

When a market has fallen 83 per cent in the space of three years, a technical rally of 50 per cent from its low would still leave the market down a thumping 74.5 per cent from its high.

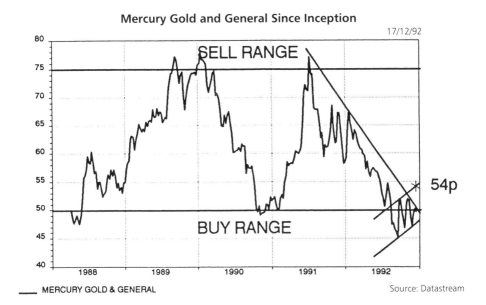

Mercury Gold and General Since Inception

17/12/92

SELL RANGE

* 54p

BUY RANGE

1988   1989   1990   1991   1992

―― MERCURY GOLD & GENERAL   Source: Datastream

(200. 18/12/92)

Gold shares begin to roar and the Fund soars.

In a moment to be savoured this week the price of our units surpassed 100p, having risen 92 per cent since the beginning of this year. The units have now doubled in just over five years not taking income into account. That is better than the FT-SE 100.

Is it time to sell your units? The answer is, not if you think the gold price is going to go up. In spite of their spectacular rises, South African gold shares are still not selling at their historical relationship to their latest distributable profit margins. In the last two and a half years the South African index has averaged 15.8 times the distributable profit margin. The March quarter's profit margin was Rl02/oz, so the index should now be 1611. It is currently 1393 having risen from 786 on 1st January 1993. Although the index is nearly back to its historical relationship with the profit margins, if you believe the gold price is going to go up to say US$400/oz, the industry profit margin would expand by R80/oz after tax to R182/oz, implying a potential level for the index of 2875, over twice today's index! Don't forget, 50 per cent of our Fund is invested in South African gold shares.

This week saw the publication of the South African gold mining quarterly reports for March. Distributable profit margins for the industry improved 18 per cent to RI 02 compared with the previous quarter. Some of the marginal mines produced spectacular profit increases.

Western Areas, of which the Fund owns 7.7 per cent of the share capital and which is now our largest single holding, increased its profits after tax from R3 million to R11 million, quarter on quarter. The shares responded to these splendid results by rising 17.2 per cent overnight.

Our second largest holding, Emperor Mines, rose 36 per cent during the week, reflecting an increase in reserves announced in the latest quarterly report.

Sumitomo Metal Mining warrants sprinted 49 per cent during the week proving that it is not just the South African shares which showed their paces this week. (**215. 28/4/93**)

Despite a soaring Fund Julian points out the disappointing long term record of gold shares and ponders the need to take profits during strong trends.

In case it has not already come to your attention, the Mercury Gold and General Fund has had a good run in recent months. In May it was 34.86 per cent up following its rise of 23.66 per cent in April, 22.47 per cent in March and 18.96 per cent in February. It has risen 134 per cent since the beginning of this year and is 111 per cent higher than it was a year ago – not bad for a Fund investing in a metal whose permanent demise was widely predicted during most of last year!

Notwithstanding this well-intentioned advice, gold shares have in fact proved themselves to be a pretty dismal long-term investment, as anyone who has held them through thick and thin over the years will tell you. They are nonetheless one of the most exciting means of accumulating wealth over shorter periods, as you have recently discovered.

Between 1970 and 1975 the FT Gold Mines Index rose no less than 790 per cent! Between 1976 and 1980 it rose by 690 per cent! Between 1982 and 1984 it rose 209 per cent, not to mention the rise of 163 per cent and 106 per cent in 1986 and 1989. As you can see from the following chart, the current boom has taken the index up 195 per cent from its low in September last year.

Gold shares will not go up if the overall direction of the gold price is down, so the first thing you have to decide is what the gold price is going to do.

I liken the performance of the gold market to the swing of a pendulum which swings, as pendulums do, until they cannot swing any further.

In 1980 when no one felt properly dressed unless they had a krugerrand about their person, the pendulum swung to its most extreme position when gold hit US$850/oz. The fall of 75 per cent or so, in real terms, to US$326/oz at the beginning of this year is now widely thought to have marked the limit of its swing in the opposite direction. The pendulum is now starting to swing back. So far the golden pendulum has retraced a mere 14 per cent of its path.

If you think of gold as a commodity, it is by no means unusual for commodity prices to double from the bottom to the top of a cycle, but it does not happen in six months. There have been five bull markets for gold since 1970 and with only one exception, 1990, none has witnessed the gold price rising less than 70 per cent trough to peak.

Bearing in mind the totally negative sentiment concerning gold in 1992, the transformation we have seen in 1993 is truly remarkable and augurs well for a repeat of past performances. (**220. 10/6/93**)

Julian takes up the issue of when to buy marginal mines with one eye on the highly profitable Doornfontein holding.

At the end of last year we were buying marginal mines. For example, we bought 1 million shares of Doornfontein at 10 US cents in November which are now priced at 128 US cents! Most people think marginal mines are far too risky to hold when the gold price is low so they sell them. Now that the gold price has gone up, marginal mines are less marginal so people feel safe in buying them for the gearing.

For my money – and it is – I prefer to reduce my exposure to "marginals" when the gold price is "high" and increase exposure to low-cost mines. The downside risk is less. Conventional wisdom has it that you should buy low-cost mines when the gold price is low in order to avoid owning a mine which goes bust. If you think the gold price is going down, don't invest in gold shares!

As far as the Gold and General Fund is concerned, I can reduce the risk by moving increasingly into quality mines and by increasing slightly our exposure to non-gold investments. This we have done.

Of course, some of you will say it is much too early to be making such defensive moves, but with mining investments it is better to move too early than too late. "Feed the ducks when they quack" is a good maxim for the mining market. The ducks are quacking loudly right now. (**224. 08/6/93**)

A word of caution from Julian summed up in the title of the newsletter "Trees don't grow to the sky".

Call me a spoil sport but it seems to me that international equities are looking rather unstable. Gold shares, which are equities after all, could well lose some of their buoyancy if shares in general are sailing into choppy waters. Since we are all grown-up people, I know you would expect me to tell you the good news and the bad with equal candour so you can make up your own minds whether I am taking appropriate action to safeguard your investment. (**273. 4/11/94**)

As Julian feared, gold shares run into difficult times in the second half of 1995.

World gold shares have had a dismal run recently. From the mid July high point of 2,064, the Ft Gold Mines Index, (which is a dollar index) has fallen by nearly 16 per cent to 1,738. In sterling terms the fall has been even worse. The Index is down by over 17 per cent (source Datastream) since mid September! Although we need no reminding that relative performance does not pay the school fees, it may be of some consolation to you that the Fund is only down 12.5 per cent from its recent high (mid price basis, source Datastream). There have been no sure-fire hiding places in the world gold share market and all of the country-specific gold indices have fallen. The worst culprit has been South Africa which is down by nearly 22 per cent in sterling terms from its recent high. This is bad news for your Fund, as South Africa comprises 40 per cent of the total assets. Offsetting this, to some extent, has been our "overweight" position in Australia (25 per cent of the Fund) which has performed relatively well. (**318. 31/10/95**)

11. Arbitrage – Contrarian Investing

A constant theme of Julian's was the rewards that can accrue to the brave investor – the contrarian – who can find value in mining shares when they are unloved and part company with them when everyone else has finally fallen in love with them. Here are a few more of his thoughts on the subject of contrarian investing.

Prospective PEs underline the attractiveness of base metal shares.

As a contrarian, something tells me not to be a gnu and follow-my-leader! If you think about it, one of the reasons that people are having second thoughts about the general level of markets is fear of excessive corporate borrowing, especially in the States. The mining industry, which used to be heavily in debt, has now reduced its borrowings to very manageable proportions. Although metal prices are falling, prospective multiples, even on lower projected metal prices, compare favourably with those of the market as a whole. As you know, the multiples people pay for trough mining earnings is normally higher than the multiple of the market as a whole.

Gold shares on current multiples of 30 are a good example of this as were sky-high multiples of base metal shares during the mid 1980's. All the forecasts of future trough earnings I have seen indicate that mining shares are still selling on prospective multiples that are less than, or similar to, those of the industrial markets. If that is the case, why should I ditch them? (**68. 19/10/89**)

Comparing the relative position of the Yen, the Nikkei and gold.

This week's chart shows how gold looks to the Japanese, both in terms of their stockmarket and as a currency compared with the yen. The top chart shows that in 1980 you could have bought 24 "Nikkeis' for an ounce of gold. Now the Nikkei Dow has risen and gold fallen so much that you can only buy 1.5 "Nikkeis' for an ounce of gold. As you can see that state of affairs seems to be being reversed. The chart seems to suggest that either the gold price is too low or the Nikkei is too high. I leave it to you to decide which. The lower chart tells much the same story. The inexorable rise of the Japanese currency against gold, which has been in progress since 1980, seems to be reversing. If the Japanese start seeking to protect themselves by buying gold, it is easy to see how the gold price could rise above $600/oz. (**84. 28/2/90**)

The global gold share market's value less than some major UK industrials.

I have often drawn your attention to the miniscule market capitalization of the world's gold companies. According to Carr Kitcat & Aitken, all the gold mines in the world are capitalised at about half the value of funds under management by one company, Mercury Asset Management! They just about equal the market capitalization of British Telecom or two brewing companies, Guinness and Grand Metropolitan, as Carr Kitcat & Aitken's chart shows. I hasten to assure you that the title of the chart is in no way intended to belittle any of the companies referred to, or their products, but merely to hint that if ever gold shares were to return to favour there might not be enough to go round.

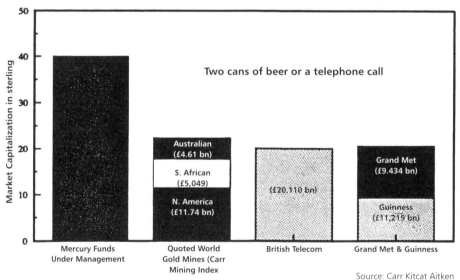

Market Capitalization of World Gold Shares (Bn Sterling)

Source: Carr Kitcat Aitken

If that does not impress you, Carr say that nearly half of all the gold shares are not available to buy, being held by other companies for control purposes. If you take that into account, they tell me that the free float of all the gold mining companies in the world comes to about 20 per cent more than the value of Hanson Trust! (**165. 26/2/92**)

Measuring the market value of gold shares as a per cent of global gold reserves.

A simple way of looking at it is to consider the value placed on all the world's gold shares and compare that with the value of the world's gold reserves. Ord Minnett provided me with the following figures which express the value of the shares as a percentage of the value of the metal in the ground at two gold prices, $350 and $414:

	$350 (now)			**$ 414 (28th August 1990)**		
	Total Cap $USm	Value of Res US$m	%	Total Cap $USm	Value of Res US$m	%
South Africa	8816	92855	9.5	12512	109834	11.4
Canada	6642	24220	27.1	11612	28650	40.5
Australia	5758	23205	24.8	8028	27448	29.2
USA	12791	36365	35.1	15440	43075	35.9
TOTAL VALUE	$34 bn	$177 bn	19.2	$47bn	$209bn	22.8

What this table shows is that when the gold price is depressed, as it is now, the shares are valued at 19.3 per cent of the value of the metal in the ground. When the gold price was 20 per cent higher, gold shares represented 23 per cent of the value of the metal in the ground. (**167.13/3/92**)

Gold and base metal shares mostly move in the same direction.

A glance at the chart shows that although the two companies produce completely different metals, their share price performance until recently has been very similar. This reinforces a fact to which I frequently draw your attention, namely that gold and base metals never move in opposite directions for long. Since we are always being told that gold is just another commodity, why should they?

What the chart shows is that the shares of Homestake are far more volatile than the shares of Alcan and that in the past you might just as well have bought Homestake if you fancied aluminium! And, of course, you can once again see the gap to which I referred at the beginning of this note when comparing the ratings of gold shares and base metal shares generally. (**185. 26/8/92**)

Julian once more draws attention to the continuing cheapness of South African gold shares against the rest.

The moral of the tale seems to us to be quite simple. The less you pay for an ounce of gold in the ground, the more likely you are to make a profit from mining it. Why then do investors pay an average of US$116 for an ounce of gold in the ground in North America when North American mining companies show it is possible to add to their reserves for roughly half that figure? Perhaps it is because only American Barrick and Pegasus have so far managed to achieve "Super Alchemy". We have always concentrated on buying cheap ounces in the ground which offer the prospect of providing a return greater than the cost of acquiring them. A fat lot of good it has done us, as you know, because most of such ounces are to be found in South Africa where it seems investors have become so disillusioned by what is going on that they couldn't care less if the ounces were given away, or taken away for that matter! (**190. 1/10/92**)

Cheap PGM shares.

Finally, a piece of useless information which rather appealed to me. Last week it was rumoured that the world's largest company, NTT, was about to tell the world that it had achieved cold fusion in the laboratory by means of a palladium catalyst.

Cold fusion mania caused the shares of NTT to appreciate by 10 per cent overnight, thus increasing its market value by US$6.7 billion. The entire platinum/palladium mining industry in South Africa is capitalised at a mere US$3 billion, less than half the increase in the overnight value of NTT! The price of palladium itself was unchanged. (**193. 23/10/92**)

Gold and its purchasing power over the long term.

When people say that gold is losing purchasing power, it is only partly true. Admittedly commodities generally are getting cheaper as technology improves but gold is holding its value relative to base metals.

We like to think that gold "money" is likely, over a long period, to be able to buy a constant amount of other commodities. After all, gold miners are subject to the same cost pressures as the miners of base metals, so it would be logical for the price of their product to move broadly in line with the price of base metals over a long period.

What has actually happened on average since 1975, is that the owner of an ounce of gold could have purchased a basket of 674/lbs of base metals. Believe it or not, the amount of base metals which can be bought with an ounce of gold today is almost exactly the same as the average of the last 18 years! We have chosen to start in 1975 because before that date gold was catching up with the other metals having been held down artificially at US$35/oz by Central Bank intervention for many years up to 1970. (**202.14/1/93**)

Newcrest reaches a buy point.

Of all the major Australian producers, Newcrest Australia would appear to have most to gain from a market re-rating on the lines of the North American producers. Newcrest is one of Australia's largest gold producers, with an estimated reserve base of just over 6 million ounces. Recently the company has fallen out of favour with Australian investors on the perception that the company has gone ex-growth. In fact the share price fell to levels at which it offered good fundamental value on what it had already found, let alone what it might find in future. At that point we could no longer resist them. Newcrest is now our fourth largest Australian holding. (**210. 18/3/93**)

Comparing Western Areas value with that of Canada's Viceroy.

Western Areas is one of the cheapest ways to buy gold in the ground. Smith New Court calculate that even following Western Areas 372 per cent rise from its low, it still only costs US$15 to buy each of the 5.1m ounces of gold in its reserves. This 400,000ounce producer is capitalised at only US$75 million! In comparison, the Canadian gold producer Viceroy, which produces a quarter of that amount of gold in California, is capitalised at US$200 million!

Whereas Western Areas has projected reserves of 5.1 million ounces, Viceroy has only around a fifth as much gold in reserves at its Castle Mountain mine in California, valued by the market at US$180/oz in the ground. Admittedly Viceroy's operating margin is significantly greater than that of Western Areas. This is a good thing when the gold price is going down but not so desirable when it is going up! Last quarter a 1.4 per cent rise in the gold price and a 3.8 per cent fall in the unit costs led to Western Areas' distributable profit margin increasing from R5 million to R11 million quarter-on-quarter! Despite these results, the over valuation of Viceroy relative to Western Areas is still very much in evidence. Just as South Africa is the cheapest major market in which to buy gold in the ground, North America is the most expensive.

Our strategy last year was to purchase large holdings in high-cost gold mines, in the knowledge that when the gold market turned it would be the marginal gold mines which would have the greatest upside potential. At current share prices we calculate that Viceroy requires a gold price of US$495 to break even, whereas investors in Western Areas should get their money back with gold at US$350/oz. If ever the gold price reaches the level already being discounted by shareholders of Viceroy, we calculate Western Areas will be generating profits of US$76/oz, five times what the market is currently paying for each ounce in the ground! (**216. 6/5/93**)

Julian continues to press the cheapness of South African golds.

The other thing which occurs to me is that South African mines are valued at a fraction of the value accorded to gold mines elsewhere in the world. Ord Minnett tell us that the market is paying US$50 for each reserve ounce in South Africa whereas it pays US$104 for an ounce in Papua New Guinea. In Papua New Guinea mines have actually been closed through political unrest and the government has been known to change the rules of ownership in the middle of the game. While uncertainty exists whether the same thing will occur in South Africa, an ounce of gold in the ground there will remain in the bargain basement.

In Australia, according to Ord Minnett, the market pays US$146 per reserve ounce and in North America the figure is a staggering US$162. Furthermore, investors and mining companies see nothing wrong in paying fancy prices for potential reserve ounces in South America where, as flavour of the month, the political risk is considered negligible.

The South Africans say the modest rating accorded to their mines is due to the perceived political risk. Yet their industrial market sells on a multiple not much different at 14.5 to that enjoyed by the UK market where the FT-SE 100 Index sells on 14.1 times earnings. (**222. 24/6/93**)

Changes to the FT Gold Mines Index to include non-South African producers are announced.

In the case of the North American mines you would be unlikely to get more money out than you put in, unless the long-term gold price is a great deal higher than it is at present. We have seen estimates that North American gold shares are already discounting a gold price of US$550/oz.

If most North American mines need a gold price of US$550/oz to justify their current share prices, I would rather own the gold itself, or better still those mines which could be expected to appreciate strongly if the gold price ever reached those dizzy heights.

If you want my prediction, it is this: the new FT Gold Mines Index will draw the attention of a wider audience to the fact that the South African gold shares represent 27 per cent of the index but produce 45 per cent of the total profits of the companies which comprise that index. (**227. 19/8/93**)

Julian and David Baker comment on the strong performance of base metal shares relative to a dull performance from base metals themselves. They also update the situation at Newcrest.

As you can see from the lower part of the chart, base metal shares have rarely been more expensive relative to base metal prices than they are today. At the bottom of the last cycle of base metal prices back in 1986, the base metal shares index and base metal prices were at parity. Now it is hardly surprising if base metal shares are starting to suffer from vertigo. In fact, the well-established bull trend line in base metal share prices seems to be breaking down and, as we have just discovered in the gold market, when over confidence evaporates and reality shines through, the market can come down to earth with a bump.

Base Metal Shares and Metal Prices

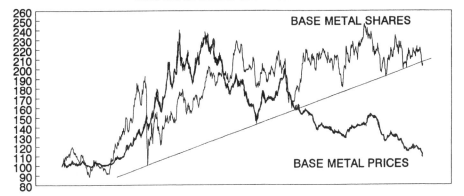

(232. 23/9/93)

Newcrest is our largest holding in Australia and still offers good fundamental value. The company has recently upgraded its exploration efforts at its Telfer Mine site, concentrating on extending the underground reserves. The main dome has been shown to have eight stacked high-grade reefs over a vertical thickness exceeding one kilometre. One of these, the MlO Reef, looks like one million ounces or more. Mineralisation exists at other domes around Telfer, and Newcrest controls 12 domal features. One prominent Australian broker believes that "the potential upside is enormous". This week the company indicated a resource in the order of

1 million ounces on the MlO Reef. The market is currently paying approximately A$150/oz for each ounce of gold and we estimate will generate profits of A$155 at US$408/oz. But further discoveries would transform the figures.

The relative cheapness of South African gold mines becomes ever more apparent. If someone could pick them up and place them in America, they would be valued at three or four times as much.

Since that can't be done, the best we can hope for is that some American mining companies will be brave enough to acquire some reserves in South Africa and see if the market values those mines as cheaply in American hands as it does in South African ones. (**235. 21/10/93**)

12. Sovereigns and the Savoy and other Pet Subjects

While Julian, both as a broker and then as a Fund Manager, was steeped in the mining industry and recognised widely as the leading authority in the sector, his interests ranged far wider than just mining. He was an accomplished potter, bought a château with a vineyard in Provence, and at one time was a racehorse owner. This section brings together some of the comments he made in the Newsletter about these activities, and about other subjects, including his famous Savoy dinner sovereign ratio, that he thought his readers might be interested in.

Savoy Dinners

One of the valuation ratios that Julian was famed for was the calculation of how many Savoy Hotel set dinners could be bought with one gold sovereign. The concept behind the ratio was that gold, although sometimes volatile over short periods, could be relied upon to keep its purchasing power value over the longer term, and Julian liked to measure this inflation proofing by reference to Savoy dinners.

Sovereigns and dinner at the Savoy.

I have in my possession a photostat copy of the set dinner menu at the Savoy in 1914, the last year you could go to the Bank of England and exchange a one pound note for a sovereign, or vice versa. The dinner cost 6/- (30p), so in 1914 you could entertain 3.3 people to dinner at the Savoy for a sovereign or a pound. In those days chicken from 7/- was more expensive than half a lobster at 2/6d!

A couple of weeks ago, The Sunday Times colour supplement did a feature on "The week before the war" (1939). They mentioned that a souper dansant at the Savoy cost 15/6d (78p). They also reported that a week before the declaration of war, the price of gold rose 6/- (30p) to 167/- or £835/oz. At that time a sovereign was £1.96, so just before the war 2.5 people could dine and dance at the Savoy for a sovereign, just like they can today.

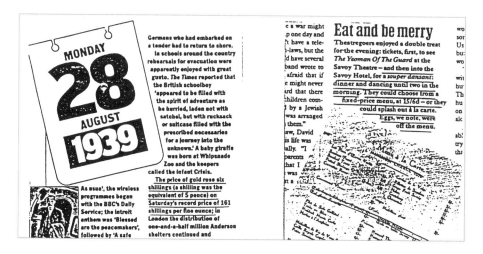

I remember being taken, on a special occasion, to dinner at the Savoy, in a party of four adults and eight teenagers, by my uncle in 1951. In those days the Savoy provided dinner, dancing and a cabaret! I remember marvelling, as a 15-year-old boy, that anyone could be so rich or so generous as to be able to remove £36, mostly in white livers, from his wallet to pay for the entire evening's entertainment for 12 people!

An ounce of gold in 1951 cost 248/- so a sovereign must have been worth about 60/3d- or £3. We must have quaffed the wine, since by the time we had finished, my uncle had spent the equivalent of a sovereign on each of us. (£54 in today's money). In 1951, gold had been fixed at $35/oz for 17 years so was obviously becoming cheap in real terms by then. Furthermore that particular dinner was to mark a special occasion and was probably priced accordingly.

Today, the dinner costs £21.67 exclusive of 15 per cent VAT and a sovereign can be bought for £54.14 so you can now take 2.5 people to dinner at the Savoy for a sovereign, just like you could before the war! For those who like this sort of useless information, here is a table which summarises the situation. VAT was introduced in 1973 so, in fairness to gold, I have excluded VAT throughout for the purpose of comparison.

As you can see overleaf, the average number of people who could have eaten for a sovereign in the years listed is 3.4. This proves to my entire satisfaction that either the Savoy is getting too pricey or gold is gradually going out of fashion. Probably a bit of both, since the Savoy seems to have been exercising some caution about raising its prices in line with inflation this year and gold is certainly less fashionable as an investment medium than it used to be. To make matters worse the mines are producing more and more of it.

Date	Cost of Set Menus (Ex VAT (m 1974)	Gold Price Price per oz (Ave)	Price of Sovereign *	Average per Sovereign
1914	.30p	£4.25	£1.00	3.3
1939	.78p	£8.35	£1.96	2.5
1974	£5.06	£67.83	£15.97	3.2
1975	£5.98	£72.34	£17.03	2.8
1976	£6.67	£69.34	£16.32	2.4
1977	£7.36	£84.56	£19.90	2.7
1978	£8.74	£100.65	£23.69	2.7
1979	£9.77	£143.54	£33.79	3.5
1980	£9.77	£263.74	£62.08	6.4
1981	£11.47	£227.29	£53.50	4.7
1982	£11.47	£215.67	£50.77	4.4
1983	£15.30	£279.12	£65.70	4.3
1984	£16.15	£269.68	£63.48	3.9
1985	£17.85	£246.00	£57.90	3.2
1986	£17.85	£251.00	£59.01	3.3
1987	£19.12	£272.00	£64.01	3.3
1988	£20.61	£245.00	£57.67	2.8
1989**	£21.67	£230.00	£54.14	2.5

In order for 3.4 people to be able, (once again), to dine at the Savoy for a sovereign, the gold price would have to rise to £313/oz or $485/oz at the current exchange rate, but gold shares are discounting at least that price already! In current circumstances I see little likelihood of the gold price rising to $485/oz, but undeterred, the majority of broker's circulars urge me to buy gold shares because at current prices they are said to be a lead indicator of what is going to happen to the gold price! What they don't tell me is how much I will lose if they are wrong. They never do – perhaps they never are! (**62. 4/9/89**)

Recalculating the Savoy dinner to sovereign ratio.

If you had been lunching at the Savoy last Friday you might have seen two of the largest individual shareholders of this Fund having their biannual lunch together.

Up until now, it has been the practice of the largest shareholder to buy lunch, which he was quite happy to do so long as the Fund was going up. Having to pick up the tab even when the Fund was going down was, he felt, a disincentive to the second largest unitholder! This practice has now ceased. If the Fund is lower than it was at the previous lunch, in future the second largest unitholder will pay. When it is higher, the present arrangement will continue. I thought you should know, it may affect the performance!

While at the Savoy we took the opportunity of checking on the price of the set dinner, now £35.60. That compares with 30p in 1914. In 1914 (the last time it was possible to exchange a pound for a sovereign) 3.3 people could enjoy the set dinner at the Savoy for a sovereign. Now only 1.48 people can dine at the Savoy for a sovereign. So either the Savoy is too expensive, which cannot be so since the restaurant was chock-a-block, or gold is far too cheap. If the old relationship were to be restored, and it lasted for many years, the gold price would have to rise to £499/oz or $813/oz, very nearly the price it reached at the peak of the market in 1980 when you could take 5.4 people to dinner for a sovereign.

You do not have to lunch at the Savoy to know that gold is too cheap at the moment. If it wasn't, the gold mining industry would not be living in such straightened circumstances and the jewellery industry would not have consumed 252 tonnes more gold than was produced in 1990. The trouble is that people always seem to think that whatever has been happening recently will go on forever, which it never does. When everyone becomes convinced that gold is going up there will be no shortage of explanations accompanied by a lot of beard-stroking and comments along the lines of "look where it's come down from, it is going to go much higher".

In anticipation of this, as you know, we have added significantly to our gold holdings. This Fund is now 75 per cent gold, 25 per cent general. That seems about right in the circumstances, since some of our general stocks are behaving very well at present. Freeport McMoran for instance, our largest single holding, went up 8.7 per cent last week and not many gold shares did better than that! (**139. 21/6/91**)

Julian updates the Savoy dinner/gold sovereign ratio.

On the other hand, if you think of gold as money, the price has now retreated to levels which give it pretty much the same purchasing power as it had in 1935. Gold is no longer expensive money as it was in 1980 when the owner of a sovereign (about a quarter of an ounce of gold) could entertain 5.4 people to dinner at the Savoy. Today, he can only entertain 1.7 people with the same "money". Since 1914, on average, it has been possible to entertain 2.33 people to dinner at the Savoy for a sovereign. To restore the purchasing power of gold in terms of Savoy dinners, the price of gold would have to rise to US$471/oz.

The price of dinner at the Savoy has more to do with people's standard of living than their cost of living. In fact, if gold had simply kept up with the cost of living, the price today would be about US$400/oz, a price widely accepted only two short years ago by the mining industry and investment community as being reasonably conservative for use in the valuation of gold mining investments. **(220. 10/6/93)**

Julian argues that dinner at the Savoy may well not be overpriced despite the hard economic times, but rather that gold is underpriced.

As I travel around the country urging people not to ignore gold in these uncertain times, I am amazed at the number of investors who seem to have got it into their heads that there may be some relationship between the price of gold and the cost of dining at the Savoy Hotel in London.

There are those who maintain that the price of gold should be more a reflection of people's <u>standard</u> of living, than of the <u>cost</u> of living. They contend that since people's standard of living is increasing faster than the 2 per cent increase in the annual gold supply, they do not find it at all surprising that the resulting shortfall is having to be met in one way or another by Central Bank sales, without which they maintain the gold price would be a lot higher.

It is undeniable that most of those lucky enough to be able to dine at the Savoy enjoy a higher standard of living than those whose preferred eatery is SHORTY'S HOT DOG STALL. You can bet your boots that both establishments charge as much as they think the market will bear, but even in these hard times you have to book early at the Savoy to avoid disappointment. That being so, it is hard to argue, much as one might like to, that dinner at the Savoy is over priced. Perhaps we are on safer ground in suggesting that gold may be cheap.

Chart 1 (following page) shows the price of the set dinner at the Savoy since 1914, the last year that a pound was freely exchangeable at the Bank of England for a sovereign. The chief cashier's "promise to pay the bearer the sum of one pound" has never meant the same since 1914; the authorities, no doubt fearing that the citizenry might, on the outbreak of hostilities, prefer to put its trust in something that could not be printed.

The Savoy has kindly let us have a copy of their menu for the "souper" of 1914. It cost 6/-, or 30p and differed little in fare from what is on offer today. The "foodies" among you might be interested to note that in those days chicken (7/-) was much more expensive than half a lobster (2/6)! One pound, (or one sovereign) would buy 3.3 dinners. Apart from the number of pound notes needed to buy the dinner, most other things at the Savoy are much the same as they were in 1914.

The venue is the same, the menu is much the same, and some cruel commentators have been heard to speculate that even some of the waiters are the same! I was lunching there recently with a satisfied unitholder who politely asked our waiter how long he had been working there. On being told that he was coming up to his 48th year there, he was provided with a tip of such magnitude as to restore completely the spring in his step! Apart from that, the price of the dinner has to cover the cost of the food, to say nothing of the cost of heating, electricity, laundry, etc. The exchange rate also plays a part, since many of the Savoy's patrons come from abroad.

You can see from chart 1 that the price of the dinner expressed in sterling, has risen 123 fold since 1914. In US dollars it has risen 38 fold and even in terms of gold, the most stable currency we know of, it has almost dou-bled. Put the other way round, as you can see from chart 2, gold would have to rise to US$791/oz for it to have maintained its purchasing power in terms of Savoy dinners!

The last time gold was expensive was in 1980. In that year a sovereign would have bought an average of 4.6 dinners or some 40 per cent more than the same sovereign could have bought 70 years earlier. The day gold peaked at US$850/oz in 1980, the owner of a sovereign could have entertained no less than 6.4 people to dinner, nearly twice the number that could have been entertained in 1914! But gold was expensive in 1980 a fact that in no way deterred most investors from owning it. Then 10–15 per cent of all Swiss portfolios were typically invested in gold. Now most Swiss portfolios contain no gold at all. How fashions change! Investors in gold have become rare birds. Only Messrs. Soros and Goldsmith have publicly owned up to owning the stuff in recent times.

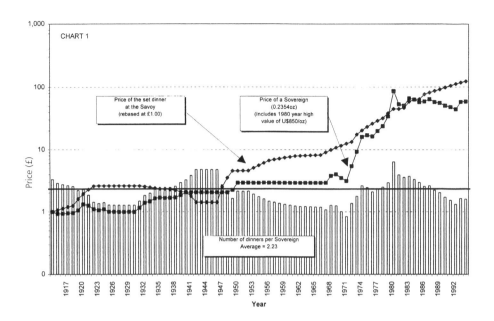

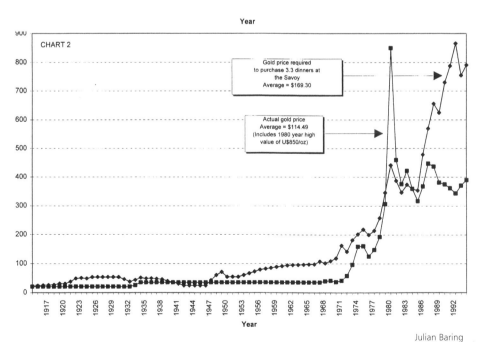

Julian Baring

277

Julian tracks the value of gold in relation to the US Dow Jones Index and finds that its relative value has fallen sharply over 15 years.

Last week we tried to prove to your entire satisfaction that gold has become very cheap relative to the cost of dining at the Savoy.

This week our chart shows just how cheap gold has become compared with American shares. As most of you know, gold has been underperforming American equities since 1980, but trends do not continue forever. It would not take much of a rise in the gold price or fall in the Dow for gold to break the bear trend which has been in place for the last 13 years. If we have anything to do with it, investors will be quick to take advantage of that eventuality.

If the gold price were to rise to the level which would enable the owner of a sovereign to buy the average number of Savoy dinners he had been able to buy since 1914 and if the Dow were to remain at its present level, the gold price would have to rise to US$530/oz. To give you a sense of perspective we have marked an asterisk to show how the chart would look if gold were to rise to US$530/oz.

CHART 1

GOLDBLN/DJINDUS

Source: Datastream

Our second chart is for the benefit of those who aspire to make their living trading Savoy dinners for gold and vice versa. As you can see, gold is "cheap as chips" compared to dinners, as it was before the gold price was raised to US$35/oz in 1934 and as it was before the Americans closed the "gold window" in 1970, when they allowed the dollar to float against gold in order to stop the drain on the American's gold reserves.

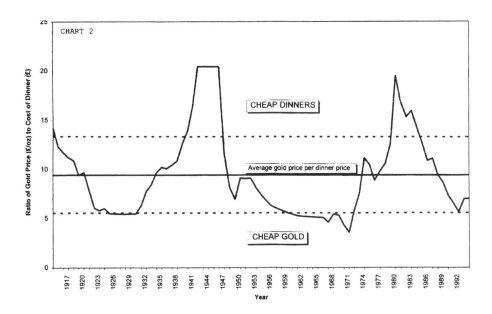

Bearing in mind the overwhelming evidence we have presented to you that gold is cheap and should be bought, it is all the more extraordinary that at a time when dollar weakness is making the cost of almost everything else rise in dollar terms, gold is getting cheaper. If anyone has any bright ideas as to why that should be happening, perhaps he would like to let us know. (**260. 8/7/94**)

The Horse

Although Julian worked himself and his team hard he was not "a dull boy" and knew how to relax. One of the more unusual things he did was to buy himself a racehorse which, as a financial transaction, was quite out of keeping with his investment philosophy as it related to value. Nonetheless Julian had some fun with the horse, though the final fate of the "investment" is not documented in the Newsletters – perhaps the "boys in blue" objected!

Having bought a horse as a short-term investment Julian decides to put it into training despite the cost of doing so. He names it "Golden General"!

A year ago, by a lucky mistake, I became the joint owner of a chestnut foal. To anticipate your next question, I won't reveal my partner's name but you will be relieved to hear she is one of us, a unitholder! The idea was to keep the foal in her field, feed it up and put it into the Newmarket yearling sales in November.

I happened to drop in to see the animal on the morning of the 2000 Guineas, but since the only thing I know about horses is that they are dangerous at both ends, it soon became apparent that I was totally unaware that if a horse called Nashwan won the Guineas, it would do us no harm since the animal we had bought was Nashwan's nephew.

The rest is history. The more classics Nashwan won, the less keen I became on the idea of selling our foal. My partner, on the other hand, took the more conservative view that putting a horse into training was normally a triumph of hope over experience. Notwithstanding, her husband and I have pressurised her into living dangerously and so the horse is to be sent to the veteran trainer Bill Wightman who has been practising his game even longer than I have. Everyone tells me that having a horse in training is like standing in front of the burning fiery furnace feeding in fivers, so I am only going to try it for a year.

If the horse shows any signs of flagging, the jockey will be instructed, in the words of Michael Edwardes, to "reinvigorate it". I am told that with horses this can best be achieved by whispering a word in their ear, but I won't mention the word for fear of upsetting the susceptibilities of my partner.

Of course, there are no prizes for guessing what this horse is going to be called, it has already been christened. "I name this foal GOLDEN GENERAL – may God bless him and all who ride him."

If he wins, I warn you here and now that I shall be pressing strongly for him to replace Al Oerter the dreaded discus thrower who adorns our advertisements for this Fund in the Sunday papers. If he loses, he will be shipped off like a remittance man to the colonies. Those of you who are into these things will want to know his ancestry. I am reliably informed that he has the same markings as his famous uncle but whether he can run as fast is what we are going to find out in the next 12 months or so.

Red God
Runaway Bride Monitor
Pink Tinge (USA)   Blushing Groom (FR)
Crepello   Takealetter (USA)
Sans le Sou   Busted   Blushing Scribe (USA) Golden General
Swing Easy (USA)   Swing the Cat   Broken Paws (1984) (b28th April 1988)
Catkin

You will be kept in touch with the progress of both of my Gold and Generals. The early omens are promising, as you will see. (**63. 12/9/89**)

Golden General's uncle does well in a big race in France, raising Julian's hopes.

Finally, you may have heard that "Uncle Nashwan" was beaten into third place in a big race in France last weekend. The omens are not all bad however. I hope you noticed that the winner was called Golden Pheasant! No relation of Golden General but obviously another member of the Glitterati! (**64. 22/9/89**)

Golden General begins training.

On a lighter note you may be interested to know that "Golden General" has now gone into training with Bill Wightman. I am told he spends his mornings lunging or being lunged which entails running round and round in circles. I know the feeling, don't you? At the moment, however, I think I know where we are going and I am planning to get there by the shortest possible route. (**72. 30/11/89**)

Julian visits Golden General in training and is pleased with progress.

Last weekend I called in to see how "Golden General" was getting on under the tutelage of his trainer, Bill Wightman. I can report favourably to you. Last week, for example, he was mounted for the first time (remember?) and his lad survived the experience!

In the course of our conversation it became clear that Golden General's long-term future depended to a greater extent on the performance of the Gold and General Fund than the latter's future depended on the winged hooves of the former.

You don't have to be as streetwise as Harry the Horse, Nicely Nicely Johnson or even Big Julie to see why any trainer worth his salt would want to hedge his bets by becoming a unitholder of the Gold & General Fund. We welcome him!

If he is as gentle with me as he is with my horse I can look forward to lots of carrots and not a lot of stick! I can't speak for the horse, but what greater indulgence could any Fund Manager seek from his supporters. (**77. 10/1/90**)

1990 is the year of the horse!

Finally I have a received message, which reads as follows: "Please remind your readers that 1990 is the year of the horse." Signed: Golden General. (**80. 30/1/90**)

Julian sees Golden General on the gallops.

P.S. Last Saturday I was allowed to watch Golden General on the gallops. He ran second! His trainer quaintly described his behaviour as "Christian". I pass this on to you in the knowledge that some of my most important unitholders are likely to declare that whatever virtues as he possesses they are by no means exclusive to that faith! I could not agree more. Meanwhile, I have to concede that "The General" is improving faster than the fund. I remain hopeful, however, that in the long run we will show him who has the most staying power. **(84. 28/2/90)**

A first outing for Golden General disappoints.

Finally, in case you haven't heard, Golden General took his time on his first outing in the 2.15 race at Salisbury last Thursday. So far behind the field was he that I thought there was a chance of his being placed in the 2.45! But it was not to be and rather like his owner's recent performance, the most charitable thing you can say about it is that surely he can only improve. **(92. 10/5/90)**

Julian outlines his thinking behind the Fund's dividend policy and ruminates on the returns he is getting from "Golden General".

As you will see in the manager's six monthly report, which should be winging its way to you shortly, I set great store by the dividend. First of all it encourages me to sustain the quality of the portfolio. Not many speculative exploration stocks offer a yield of 5 per cent! Secondly the need to pay a decent dividend reminds me that mines are wasting assets which should give their owners their money back in dividends over their remaining life of say 20 years. In other words, I need to aim to give you an average dividend of at least 5 per cent per annum for 20 years. With the discount, our reinvestment scheme will get you into the units at about 60p for reinvestment purposes. Even assuming no improvement in the dividend in the current year, you will be buying a yield of 4.2 per cent.

For myself, I have to admit that I need the dividend from the units to pay "Golden General's" trainer's fee. If he wins a big one I will be only too happy to reinvest his winnings in the Fund. The best he has managed so far is to come third in the 6.30 at Brighton, the prize money for which just about covered the cost of getting him there. I am not complaining; at least he was not tailed off like he was in his first two races. So pleased was I by his endeavours that I took it as an omen for the Fund itself and bought some more units for myself. They look cheap to me. **(102. 17/7/90)**

After an enjoyable but unsuccessful outing at Salisbury Julian cut his losses and parted company with Golden General.

The Fund

When the Fund launched 25 years ago it was priced at 50p, and its peak was seen at the end of 2010 when the income units traded at around 2000p. Julian believed that his experience as a mining specialist stockbroker could be transferred successfully into specialist Fund Management. He underlined his confidence in making a success of this mid-career switch by being a substantial owner of his Fund's units right from the start. Over the 25-year period house prices in Chelsea, where Julian lived, have risen by around eight times. The Fund at its peak (in 2010) was forty times up and is currently around twenty times up.

Julian lays down the Fund's basic investment philosophy.

The fund's investment philosophy is based on the perception that the market's love affair with gold shares and its hate relationship with base metal shares, is not well founded – what love/hate relationship is? Many people think that just because base metal prices have been rising strongly in recent months, they must be dangerously high. In the past when metals were high, it was always right to sell the producers, even though the multiples were very low. In the past as the chart shows, when the price of copper was high, it was high in real terms too, but it is not high in real terms, yet – so why sell copper shares?

In my eyes base metal shares are cheap but gold shares are fashionable. In this Fund we are going to try and buy cheap shares. It is my intention to update you on regular basis with the Fund's progress, with my "reasons in writing" for doing what I am doing. (**1. 5/4/88**)

Julian muses about the effect of spring and then summer on possible buying of the Fund, and reminisces about his membership of the Salisbury Club poker school in Rhodesia (Zimbabwe).

In the last two or three weeks (perhaps because spring is in the air) quite a few of you have been telling me that you have it in mind to add to your holdings in the Fund. All you are waiting for is a setback in the price. I must admit, exactly the same thought had occurred to me!

Unfortunately I don't see it as part of my job to run the portfolio in such a way as to purposely provide those of us who want to buy more with topping up opportunities. I may not be very good at it, but I am constantly doing my best to make the units go up rather than down! In fact I try to structure the portfolio so as to avoid doing too much damage to our wealth, even if one or two of our holdings hit an air pocket. In naval parlance it is called damage control. The thing about unit trusts is that they are not like individual equities which seldom grow to the sky. A unit trust's portfolio is constantly being pruned and replanted. In our case, the present portfolio bears little resemblance to the one I published in Issue No 6 about a year ago.

Of course I would welcome the extra firepower which any additional contributions of yours would provide. Without adequate cash, how am I to take advantage of the opportunities which so often occur in the mining markets during the long hot summer months? I daren't count on sufficient new money coming in to boost the Fund's liquidity, so without waiting for you to ante up I have recently increased our liquidity to 15 per cent with the summer doldrums very much in mind.

Running a Fund like this is reminiscent of my misspent youth. I used to be a member of the poker school at the Salisbury Club, Rhodesia. Probably to intimidate me the old-timers used to say that if I could keep my head above water in that school I could look after myself in any other. In order to avoid being fleeced I had to learn, not just how to make the best of the good hands, but much more importantly how to preserve precious resources when the cards were running against me. The best players seem to have the knack of staying afloat when the good cards are falling elsewhere. It's the same with investments. (**49. 2/5/89**)

A prospective buyer of the Fund explains to Julian how he relies on his astrologer for market timing advice.

Finally, I want to report on a dinner, given by a friend to introduce me to a prospective buyer of the Fund. When we got to the nitty gritty, I found he needed no persuasion. He had been consulting the astrologer who had so accurately predicted the gold boom of the 1970's. Speaking in an entirely matter-of-fact voice he informed me that the stars foretold that a new gold boom would start this August which would take the gold price to unprecedented heights. He was therefore only too happy to participate in any investment with a significant gold content.

When I asked him how long the boom was likely to last, he replied that his astrologer had recently joined the Great Astrologer in the sky and was therefore no longer available for consultation. So it looks as if we are on our own, unless any of you know of a substitute. If you recount this story in mixed company, you will find that the men tend to be rather sceptical. The ladies express no surprise whatsoever that the gold price can be foretold by the stars, but it's not their jobs that are at risk if astrology takes over. It's you who will be joining me out on Uranus! (**58. 13/7/89**)

The Fund passes the £60 million landmark.

I seem to recall that in the Autumn I told you that I hoped that this Fund would reach £60 million by the end of the year. I am pleased to tell you that this figure was passed last week and better still my Lords and Masters tell me that it is at last beginning to make a contribution to what is known in current parlance as the "bottom line". That's a relief, I enjoy contributing! (74. 14/12/89)

Julian urges those contemplating buying into the Fund to get on with it before they lose their nerve.

It is not my job to tell you how much the prudent man should invest, but I can tell you that when I was on my travels last week one Fund Manager said "I think you are right, I am going to invest 10 per cent of my speculative accounts in the Gold and General Fund, 7.5 per cent of my middle of the road Funds but nothing in my low risk Funds." I ventured to suggest that the conservative thing to do would be to reverse those percentages and on further reflection he agreed. The next morning his cheque was in the post.

It is one thing to agree what should be done, but it is quite another thing to actually put into practice what you have decided to do. That is the difficult bit and that is what determines whether you are a man or a mouse. There is always some reason why it would be better to put off the appropriate action "til another day. Perhaps the things you wanted to sell will be higher tomorrow, or the price of the Fund will be lower. I say, "Don't be a Whimp. If you have decided to do something, get on with it." Nine times out of ten, decisions get harder to implement, not easier, as time goes by and eventually they tend to go by default.

Last week, I was propounding these views to one unitholder who listened patiently with a resigned look on his face. When I had finished he said, "My portfolios are now 60 per cent in cash and 40 per cent in gold!" Obviously a man who puts his clients' money where his mouth is! No Whimp he! (**80. 30/1/90**)

The Fund plunges, much to Julian's discomfort.

If you are not feeling quite as sore as me about the recent performance of this fund, it is probably because you are not holding as many units! It may be of some comfort to compare the Fund's performance with other sectors of the market, though I have never been convinced that knowledge of the pain suffered by others makes your own any easier to bear. (**84. 28/2/90**)

Almost two years old, the Fund has both increased in size and outperformed the "Footsie".

It may be a bit much to expect this fund to go up when most of the markets of the world seem to be going down. It should however show reasonably good relative performance. Attached is a chart of the Fund's performance compared with the FT-SE 100 since inception. It looks like a 15 per cent outperformance in just under two years. It is not for me to tell you whether or not that is a satisfactory performance, but the chart may help you decide that for yourselves.

The other chart which I find interesting is the one which shows the flow of money into the Fund each month since we started. Don't forget, for the first 18 months or so the gold price was actually falling from $460 to $356 per ounce. That did not stop the Fund increasing from £3 million to £40 million. Since gold turned positive in October you can see that the size of the fund increased dramatically to about £70 million. The message seems to be that people perceived that gold had become too cheap last year but were waiting for the bear trend to be reversed before getting out their cheque books. (**86. 15/3/90**)

Julian bemoans the fact that reasons for buying the Fund are non-existent.

I have been racking my brains trying to think up reasons why anyone in his right mind would want to own a Gold Fund at a time like this. Try as I may, I have not been able to come up with a single reason – except that I can't come up with a single reason!

When you can't think of a single reason for buying something, the chances are that others playing the same investment game of "musical chairs" will be of like mind. The fact that there is any game going on at all is explained by the remaining players talking so much among themselves, in order to keep their spirits up, that none heard the music stop! Of course we have to bear in mind that those who have fallen out of the game have a vested interest in predicting disaster for the remaining participants. Someone, after all, has to be there to pick up the pieces and who better to do that than those watching from the sidelines.

What a contrast all this is to the euphoria which prevailed at the beginning of this year! Who at that time warned us of recovering stockmarkets, moderating inflation, increased Russian gold sales, liquidation of Middle Eastern gold stocks, declining oil prices and net disposals of Central Bank gold reserves, to mention but a few of the factors which have borne down on the gold price in the last few months?

Of course you can look on the bright side if you want to. None of these factors has pushed the gold price below the lows of last year or the lows (in real terms) of the previous two bear markets of 1982 and 1985. It was from those lows that so much money was made by the people who in those bleak times were talking so much among themselves, in order to keep their spirits up, that they didn't hear the music stop. (**95. 31/5/90**)

Julian bolsters the Fund's income return with the purchase of a South African parastatal Bond.

To compensate us for the fact that marginal mines pay no dividends at the current gold price, and the fact that they would probably have further to fall if the gold price falls further, I have invested in a South African quasi government Bond which is specially designed to appreciate in value if the gold price declines. This bond, called the Transnet 1991 Bear Bond, is currently yielding almost 25 per cent, which seems to be an adequate recompense for the lack of yield on our marginals.

The brokers like to tell me I should be selling our marginal mines and buying the leaders. I cannot however bring myself to hand someone else the upside potential. It may seem selfish but I think our interests would be better served by buying the marginals not selling them.

If the logic of all this escapes you, you probably should not be holding these units. The purpose of this Newsletter is to tell you what I am doing with your money and why, so you can decide for yourselves whether you think I am likely to impoverish or enrich you. (**103. 25/7/90**)

Julian explains one of the value parameters he uses in running the Fund.

When I was a broker I used to remind people running funds that mining shares never go up when the value of the metal they produce is going down. Judging by the recent performance of this Fund I have forgotten the facts of life – a clear sign of old age!

What I have been doing as you know, is basing the return required on our investments on metal prices which I believe can be sustained in the long run. In nearly all cases such prices are well below current prices. If at those metal prices the shares offer a real return which is 50 per cent better than we could get by investing our money in a 20 year Index Linked Bond, I buy them. The higher the return they offer, the more I try to buy.

As you have seen, we can be caught between a rock and a hard place by adopting this investment policy. Let's take copper as an example. The copper price is currently $1.28/lb and falling, bringing copper shares down with it. The copper price on which we base our long-term earnings projections is 79c/lb. If the copper price is going to fall to our long-term price, it is inevitable that copper shares will fall too, even though they already provide the returns we seek, based on 79c/lb copper. (**110. 26/9/90**)

Julian bemoans the collapse of gold shares since the previous Christmas but offers "Christmas Box" buyers a dealing discount for buyers of the Fund.

History shows that last year's worst performing sector often turns out to be one of the best performers of the following year. Even in Biblical terms the Good Book tells us "the first shall be last and the last shall be first". A year is certainly a long time in investment. When you think how extremely optimistic we all were about gold this time last year and how neutral we all are about it now, I think that makes the point. It is hard to believe today, that this time last year this Fund was attracting over £2 million a week!

Of course you won't want to clutter up your portfolio for the next six weeks with the ten or 12 mining shares which normally comprise the James Capel Christmas Box. But, you could buy a unit trust instead! The chances are that most, if not all the shares in the Christmas Box are in the Trust's portfolio anyhow. Nor need you be put off too much by the front end load which unit trusts charge when you buy them. In these hard times and because it's the season of good will, you can bet your boots that it won't be difficult to twist our dealers arms sufficiently to secure a satisfactory discount. In fact, I have done it for you. Provided you mention that it is your Christmas Box deal and that you are not taking commission as an intermediary, you will be able to secure for yourself a 4 per cent discount from the normal offer price. Eat your heart out Gerald Ratner! (**120. 7/12/90**)

Fund redemptions accelerate and Julian concludes that investors buy into the Fund when it has outperformed, i.e. they like to see units rising in price before plunging in.

You have to laugh! Last week I politely suggested that perhaps this was not the best moment to ditch units in the Gold and General Fund. I thought I put up rather a good case, but needless to say if anything redemptions accelerated! Serves me right for trying to influence your investment decisions, but at least I think I have learnt what motivates you to buy and sell the Fund; up until now it has been a bit of a mystery.

Here is a chart of the price of the units relative to the FTA All Share Index. Also shown in bar form are the net purchases and net sales of the units each month since we started. Investors in this Fund do not care much what is happening to the gold price. They buy when the units are outperforming the ETA All Share Index and sell when the units are underperforming the Index. If you share Jimmy Goldsmith's view that sooner or later gold will have its day, it would seem to me sensible to tuck some units away when they are low relative to the UK market, rather than high. But I'm sure you know best!

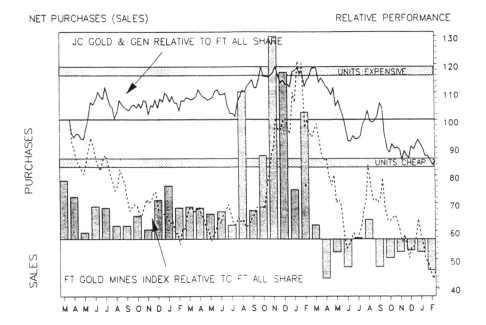

What happens in practice is, like a circus seal you feed me more fish when I perform well and keep me hungry when I perform badly. This method works well with seals and it certainly makes me try hard to please you. The more the UK market goes up, the more tempting it will become for investors to try their luck in the only market to be virtually left out of the recent rally in world stockmarkets. Strangely enough it is not easy to buy gold shares in quantity even now when very few people want to know. Heaven knows what it will be like when investors start to pay attention. We have got to get set before the crowd decides that our market is oversold. We will never buy value once they all start buying.

In the meantime the name of the game seems to be to try to double guess each other. I prefer to sell gold shares when they have risen a long way and buy them when they have fallen. You tend to give me money to invest in gold shares when they have risen a long way and remove your money when they have fallen.

No wonder the market is such a great leveller. Nobody likes tall poppies so we all do our best to top and tail them if you will excuse the mixed metaphor. You would think it would be different with the home-grown variety. I rather hoped that by keeping you in touch with what I am doing with your money you might be encouraged to help by resisting the temptation to sell units when you can get very little money for them. But why should you take any more notice of my advice than I take of the brokers who have been advising me to buy mining shares which seem to me to offer very little value? Despite redemptions, I continue to increase our exposure to the marginal mines which most brokers tell me I should be selling. Nearly 30 per cent of the Fund is now in gold producers compared with about 16 per cent a month ago. (**129. 14/3/91**)

Having under-owned gold shares in the Fund for a long time Julian begins to reverse the policy.

Last week I asked one of our erstwhile unitholders why they had been selling their Gold and General units. They replied that they perceived gold to be a "dead duck"! Until recently I did not have a quarrel with that view. Until recently we only had about 16 per cent of the Fund invested directly in gold mining companies. As you know, I am beginning to find value in gold shares now that they have fallen more than 60 per cent in the last year or so. This seems to be the time for me to add to our holdings, not to sell them! So while I am busy making the Fund more gold and less general, some of our unitholders have been voting with their feet since they have noticed that the gold price has been a bit weak and therefore feel the urge to sell anything with the name gold in it. My view, for what it is worth, is that it will not be long before they find that the duck isn't dead, only stunned, and that when it recovers it will get up and fly. I wish I could forecast when that will happen, but even if I could you would not believe me.

You may care to consider one further fact. At the top of the market just over a year ago, the large gold funds were about 5 per cent liquid. They are now about 12 per cent liquid. In order to get back to 5 per cent liquidity they would have to put $300 million of their cash into gold shares on top of anything extra you might feel inclined to give them to invest on your behalf.

Even at a time like this when the gold shares are being marked down in line with the gold price, very little stock is actually coming on offer which simply underlines the importance of being fully invested before a market turns rather than trying to chase stock after it has done so. I am doing my best to comply with this basic rule of investment but it is not easy. (**131. 27/3/91**)

Julian explains the unit price volatility of the Fund when sellers disappear and buyers appear.

You may have noticed about ten days ago the price of the units became more volatile than usual. The price of the units reached 70p at one stage as selling started to dry up and a few buyers emerged. When this happens the managers (who have a policy of not running a book on the units) price the Fund on an "offer basis"; whereas when there are net sellers the units are priced on a "bid basis". This gives rise to an unfortunate volatility in the price of the units which upsets me as much as I am sure it does you. I have raised this matter with my colleagues who have convinced me that short of taking a principal position in the units, there is no way of avoiding this situation. Rest assured though, that the underlying asset value is unaffected by these pricing policies. The units have been declining recently for the reasons I described earlier and because we have 50 per cent of our investments in South Africa which has been going through yet another of those bouts of political unrest which so upsets the market. **(155. 8/11/91)**

Julian marks the end of an era as he moves the Fund from James Capel to Mercury (SG Warburg).

It is with mixed feelings that I have to report that this will be the last time I shall be writing to you on this letterhead.

As my valued unitholders, I wanted you to be the first to know that "My Fund and I" are moving to Mercury Asset Management, the investment arm of Warburgs, who are busy beefing up their commitment to the mining sector and wanted to fill a gap in their range of unit trusts.

Obviously when you have been with an organisation for nearly a quarter of a century, to leave it is a sad occasion. I am grateful to Capels for their support over very many years in helping me to build up their presence in the mining market and subsequently to build this Fund. On the other hand, I am excited by the prospect of joining the largest Fund Management group in Europe and at the opportunities which are likely to present themselves in the wider context of the Warburg Group's mining interests.

In some respects the timing of the formation of this Fund was unfortunate. The gold price has fallen $100/oz since we started on April Fool's Day 1988. Luckily the gods have been kind to us, as the performance table demonstrates. The Fund is up 44 per cent since inception, which may or may not prove that the larger percentage a Fund Manager has of his own money in the Fund he manages, the more he needs to concentrate on what he is doing. The second moral seems to be that funds run by committee do not necessarily perform better even with the benefit of collective wisdom, than those run by individuals with a vested interest. I always tell people that no one looks after their money better than the person who earned it in the first place! (**159. 12/12/91**)

Julian alludes to the problem of capital gains tax following a stonking performance by the Fund.

Long-term holders of Mercury Gold and General Fund have a problem – don't worry, it's a nice problem to have, but a problem nonetheless.

Any fund which has appreciated by over 200 per cent in six months is likely to give the tax man ideas above his station. If you had bought say 10,000 units at the beginning of the year at 54p and were to sell them today at 154p, the tax man would grab up to 40p of your 100p profit! That would make it terribly painful to sell your units. Handing £4,000 to the government, however great its need, is not my idea of patriotism, so it's up to us to arrange things in such a way as to deny the tax man his pleasure and at the same time reduce the inherent risk of holding units as the price appreciates. Obviously the higher the units go the greater is the risk of holding them. But investors don't seem to see it that way. There are far more buyers now that the Fund has shown what it can do than there ever were at the end of last year when the units were so cheap. (**224. 8/7/93**)

While the UK Gold and General Fund cannot hold physical gold the International Fund can, and Julian explains why he has shifted some of his own money into the latter Fund.

As you know by now, I don't feel comfortable in a crowd. If I can't find reasonable value, I will tell you so and you can sell your units if you feel so inclined and pay your tax like a good'un. You will detect from this Newsletter that I think the time is right for us to shift down a gear as we approach the corner at the end of the back straight so to speak. Better to go rather slower round the bend than run the risk of losing our grip and ending up in the straw bales. The race is not over, but we are now sufficiently far ahead not to need to take unnecessary risks. Because of its ability to hold gold, the International Gold and General Fund is the less risky of the two funds, so I have switched part of my personal holding Gold and General Fund units into it, if that is of any interest to you. (**224.8/7/93**)

The Fund's star holding, Western Areas, rises more than 500 per cent in a year!

I am delighted to tell you that the share which has for many months been our largest single holding has risen 28 per cent in the last week alone, making it the star performer of the entire portfolio. We bought 6.9 per cent of the share capital of Western Areas in the dread days of 1992 when nobody wanted to be seen dead owning a gold share, particularly a marginal one. Our average cost was 59p per share. At its low point exactly a year ago, when the shares were selling for 25p, the entire company was only capitalised at £10 million! Now, one year later, some brokers are forecasting that the company will pay a dividend next year of 50p, putting the shares at today's price of 365p on a prospective yield of 13 per cent. It's not often that you own a company which looks set to pay a dividend amounting to twice its share price 18 months earlier. That is why I thought you might like to know that you own at least one. It also helps to explain the endless fascination of the mining market which so many investors seem to spurn. In fact, nine shares in our portfolio have each risen by more than 800 per cent in the last year.

Western Areas has come triumphantly through what amounts to a survival course in recent years. The northern part of its mine had to be closed because of the declining gold price and it had to give up its rights to South Deep, the exciting new mine on its southern border. Fortunately we were able to build up a major stake in South Deep when nobody wanted to know last year. A year ago South Deep's shares were selling for 33p. They now represent our third largest single holding and are currently priced at 357p – if you can get them. They are as rare as hens' teeth.

I mention this because Western Areas, if it goes on like this, will soon have used up all the tax losses which it accumulated during the bad years and thus will become eligible for tax. Because the South African tax regime is so harsh on mines which have no capital expenditure to offset against their revenues, the Mining Houses move heaven and earth effectively to make the government their partner in the financing of new mines. This can be done by offsetting the capital cost of starting up a new mine against the revenue of an existing mine, provided the two are contiguous and subject to the approval of the government mining engineer and receiver of revenue.

Western Areas has become South Deep's rich neighbour and you can bet your boots that the best brains are currently working out the most tax-effective way of financing the development of South Deep by using Western Areas' tax shield. It would not surprise me in the least if Western Areas and South Deep were shortly to announce their engagement.

South Deep has about five times the reserves of Western Areas, but Western Areas has the surface and shaft facilities that South Deep is already sharing. Far more important, Western Areas is now generating a considerable amount of cash which will be subject to tax unless they do something to shelter it. (**234. 7/10/93**)

Julian announces the launch of the Mercury World Mining Trust.

Now it can be revealed, as the papers say, why we have apparently been neglecting you these past three weeks. We tried to explain in our last Newsletter what we were up to, but the "boys in blue", those guardians of the law, obliged us to delete all reference to the launch of the Mercury World Mining Trust for reasons of compliance. Since it is now in the public domain that we are in the process of raising up to £500 million to start Britain's only investment trust to concentrate on mining, we can take this opportunity of thanking all those of you who are intending to support the new trust and apologising to those of you who missed getting the Newsletter.

Although there will almost inevitably be some overlap between the portfolio of the Mercury Gold and General Fund and that of the Mercury World Mining Trust, we trust you will view them as "complementary".

For some time, the Gold and General Fund has been almost fully invested in gold shares and has held only a minimal weighting in non-gold equities. This has been a very successful policy to date because, as you know, gold has been the first major metal to emerge from recession. It is our intention, however, to follow a much more broadly-based strategy with the Mercury World Mining Trust, and although initially "overweight" gold shares, the new Trust will be predominantly invested in base metals and diversified mining companies. Not all of the world's mining companies are in RTZ's enviable position of being at or near record share price highs. We hope that by launching the new Fund now, we will be providing those investors who are confined to investing in UK registered stocks with a choice, something they have not had since Hanson bid for Consolidated Gold Fields four or five years ago. The depressed state of the mining share market, which is suffering under the weight of very low metal prices, had much to do with the timing of the launch. (**238. 29/11/93**)

The Fund's size grows elevenfold in a year and the unit price is up 400 per cent, but Julian remains modest about the performance knowing that a reverse in gold shares will see admiring investors heading for the door.

This time last year the offered price of the units was 51.43p. Now, as you can see, they are about four times that. More importantly for us, the size of the Fund has grown from about £24 million this time last year, to £268 million today, a more than eleven fold increase. Whereas this time last year investors thought the gold price was in terminal decline and were selling their units, now it is more generally accepted that there is a place in a well-diversified portfolio for something that provides exposure to a metal which gives all the appearance of having bottomed.

One important reason why this Fund is attracting a steady flow of new money is that it has never made any pretence that it is possible for a gold fund to perform well when the gold price is falling. Our experience tells us that investors who think the gold price is going down, sell their units however highly they profess to rate the manager. One thing is certain, they never rate the manager as highly when the units are falling, as they do when the units are rising! Those who think that the gold price is going up, want to buy a unit trust that will give them the "biggest bang for their buck" if they are proved right. We flatter ourselves if we believe that people think so highly of our investment prowess that they will leave their money invested in this Fund even if they think the gold price has passed its sell-by date.

It has been our policy to try and give our unitholders what they want rather than what will provide us with a quiet life. That is why we are prepared to go out on a limb with a small proportion of your money in the full knowledge that we are not going to get it right every time and that if the gold price takes a nasty turn, some of the more faint-hearted of our unitholders will wish they had chosen a less aggressive Fund Manager.

Be that as it may, we at least try to leave you under no illusions. It is our view that we are close to, if not past the low point of the metal cycle. Base metals, broadly speaking, have tended, in the past, to triple from trough to peak. Although in the 1970's, gold more than matched this volatility, in recent years it has been very subdued. In the last metal cycle gold rose by only about one third as much as its base metal counterparts. This should not, however, put you off. Even if we use this reduced gold volatility as our guide and then assume that base metals will reach a new cyclical peak sometime in the next five years, (during which time all the world economies are hopefully going to be recovering at the same time), we see no reason why gold should not achieve a price of at least US$500/oz. (242. 17/1/94)

Provence

When Julian finally retired he spent a lot of time at the château he had bought in Provence, where he also owned a vineyard and practised as a potter – an activity he had taken up at school. He said little about this side of his life in the Newsletters but the charming piece below sums up his love for this hypnotic part of France.

The beauty of Provence stimulates Julian's imagination and he dreams of gold shares that yield what he has paid for them and more.

As I sit watching the restorative rays of the sun beat down on my frost-bitten vines,

I cannot help feeling a pang of jealousy for Peter Mayle whose widely read book "A year in Provence" makes those of us who can only snatch a week or two at a time here, wonder why we cannot all write best sellers in these idyllic surroundings.

My good friend Jean-Phillipe, the undiscovered potter from the next-door village who, in order to go on living there had to sell his soul for an automated production line, put it this way when he joined us for dinner the other night. We had walked rather unsteadily together to the bottom of the garden in the early hours of the morning. The frogs and cicadas had tired of our reminiscing and had turned in for the night. All we had for company were the stars which had descended so low that they seemed almost within reach. They do that in Provence.

"Mon ami" said Jean-Phillipe, with the turn of phrase of a true artist, "Nous sommes a la porte de Paradise."

"How do you know we are not already inside?" was my less imaginative reply.

The point is that Provence is good for the imagination.

Let's imagine, therefore, that gold was the only money in the world. If you wanted to buy shares in a gold mine you would have to pay for them with gold. You would not be pleased with your broker if he bought you a gold share whose earnings were less during its mine life than you paid for it in the first place.

I really do believe that gold is a form of money. I don't always succeed, but at least I try not to buy gold shares which will never earn enough profits to repay the capital (your capital!) I put into them. (137. 5/6/91)

Compliance

Julian found the attention of the burgeoning compliance function irritating; how he would view current compliance departments can only be guessed at. For Julian the unit holder always came first, and compliance concerns very often were to do with unwarranted suspicion and the need to tick boxes.

The "boys in blue" have a word with Julian about the Minorco bid for Cons Gold.

I have been asked by the Panel to remind you that Capels are advising Minorco. This I gladly do, but I hope you never have to accuse me of putting your interests second. Each week I tell you without fear or favour what I am doing with your money and why. I have no knowledge of what is going on in the minds of the combatants or their advisers. We have Chinese Walls to ensure that I do not. If I sometimes get it right, 25 years practice in the mining markets may have something to do with it not inside information. You know that. Others may not, so I am glad to put the record straight. My views on gold and gold shares are expressed solely to help you decide whether or not to stay with your investment in the fund. I do not, and will not tailor them to suit the interests of others, whether they be directors of mining companies or other interested parties. The fact that my opinions are sometimes contrary to conventional wisdom does not necessarily mean they are wrong, however. (**42. 7/3/89**)

Julian falls foul of the "boys in blue' again as Cons Gold bid fever hots up.

Following the publicity given to my scribblings last week in the Sunday papers, I was summoned to the Take-Over Panel on the 20th floor of The Stock Exchange and given a dressing down for giving you misleading information last week as to the number of Gold Fields shares which had changed hands since the 23rd March 1989. At the request of the Panel I must now endeavour to put the record straight. You may recall that I suggested that 8.4 per cent of Gold Fields' share capital had already changed hands and was likely to be offered to Minorco. I then incorrectly observed that Minorco had only to secure another 12.6 per cent to bag their prey.

I had arrived at that figure of 8.4 per cent by totting up the turnover figures for Gold Fields published by The Stock Exchange each day. What I had overlooked was that the published turnover figures include inter-market activity and are therefore misleading if used to determine the number of shares the public might have bought or sold in any one day. In fact I now understand that only about one quarter of the shares traded were actually bought by the public. The use of published figures which can be misleading was my fault and I therefore unreservedly apologise to you, to the Panel, the directors of Consolidated Gold Fields and their advisers, not to mention the Press. (**47. 19/4/89**)

Julian describes the compliance procedures relating to the publication of the Newsletter and harks nostalgically back to the early 70s when he started writing as a stockbroker.

I wrote my first mining Newsletter as head of James Capel's Mining Department in February 1971. Year after year Fund Managers, such as I am now, had to put up with my outpourings. From time to time they told me they were amused, sometimes they were informed, occasionally misled and intermittently upset but hopefully seldom bored For instance in a moment of pique many years ago, when they were going through a bad patch I irreverently referred to Charter Consolidated as the poor man's Thomas Tilling. Quite understandably they stopped dealing with us for a time but no one stopped me writing. By the time I left the mining department, the Newsletters were being sent to 750 money managers all over the world.

This is the 52nd edition of this particular publication which is sent to only 250 unitholders. No other Fund Manager writes to his unitholders once a week telling them what he is doing with their money. I enjoy writing to you. The average time it takes to compose this weekly letter is normally about three hours and it makes me think what I am doing at least once a week. That is good for me and therefore good for us as unitholders.

As you know, these are spontaneous scribblings and if I sometimes make a mistake in the rush to get the letter to you, I beg your forgiveness. Unfortunately, as you know, I overstepped the mark a few weeks ago and was hauled up before the Beak. Since that moment a new regime has been imposed.

The Newsletter has to be typed up and submitted to our Financial Control Officer. If he detects anything which could possibly be described as being in the slightest bit controversial it is his duty to pass the offending missive on to the Compliance Officer.

The Compliance Officer appends his comments and passes the letter on to the Corporate Finance Compliance Officer who makes doubly sure that nothing is said which might fall foul of the Authorities. The letter is then passed onto the Deputy Chairman who vets it to ensure that what I write to you is commercially sound.

At various stages of the proceedings I am called upon to make the necessary changes. The Newsletter is then amended to comply with everyone's requirements and re-submitted for final approval. Last week it took the best part of two days before everyone was satisfied. That is why you have been getting your Newsletters on Saturday mornings instead of on Wednesdays. When you get them at least you can be sure they are squeaky clean and sanitized.

Now of course I don't mind going to all this hassle if you find the Newsletter useful; but if you really don't mind whether you get it or not, my time would be better spent reading the James Capel Fund Managers Interim Compliance Manual. The Interim Compliance Manual is a quarter of an inch thick. The definitive Compliance Manual is awaited with trepidation! Therefore I crave your indulgence in filling in the attached form which is simply designed to let me know what you think. If you don't fill it in I will assume that you are already inundated with junk mail and you won't miss getting this. If I don't hear from you, we will remove your name from the circulation list and you won't be bothered any more. **(52. 23/5/89)**

Julian has another gentle dig at the "boys in blue".

Lastly, most of those who replied to last week's questionnaire seemed to want to continue to receive these missives despite the activities of the "boys in blue". Some

SOVEREIGNS AND THE SAVOY AND OTHER PET SUBJECTS

of your comments were hilarious and some were unprintable under the existing regulations. One I particularly liked went as follows:–

> There was an investor called Baring
> Whose efforts and skills were unsparing
> But they shouted (like mules)
> "He is breaking the rules –
> This scribbling is all much too daring."

As far as the newsletter is concerned ... thy will be done for each of you who filled in the form. For those who did not, this is the last you will be hearing from me until the next half yearly report is published. My apologies for imposing my views upon you uninvited. (**53. 25/5/89**)

Investment Technique

Julian's approach to broking was not without its cavalier side, but as a Fund Manager he became far more disciplined when it came to stock picking. Although he often found himself swimming against the tide, Julian's sometimes contrarian investment style was not based on simply doing what others were not doing, he simply found his own analysis of the market often pitted him against the crowd.

An early comment on timing in relation to share buying.

Many people in the investment world don't seem able to decide whether they come to work to collect share certificates or to collect money. If they work to collect share certificates, you would think that they would buy them on weak days, because they can get more of them that way. If they work to collect pound notes, you would think they would sell shares on strong days, because you can get more pound notes for shares when they have just gone up! If you think that is what happens in practice, you have got another think coming, but from what I have seen in the last week, the unitholders of the Gold and General Fund know exactly what they are collecting. Of course, when money comes in on weak days, it gives me a chance to buy more of the shares I like at favourable prices, so it helps us all. (**14. 19/7/88**)

Investing with the pack and its consequences.

Have you noticed that as soon as people get into a market place they behave instinctively, like shoals of fish, flocks of sheep or collections of gnus? They are happiest when following each other. Once they have decided which way they want to go, it is hard to divert them.

That is why at the risk of being over-simplistic, it is easy to see (especially with the advantage of hindsight) that markets go up until they stop going up and then down until they stop going down! So, to be a successful investor you have to be a trendie, going with the flow until the tide turns. The hard bit is knowing when to stop. When a market is high, there are many more reasons to buy it than sell it, otherwise it wouldn't be so high. Conversely, when a market is low there are many more reasons why it should fall further, than rise. That is why we all find it so hard to change tack. At tops and bottoms of markets, the reversal of the existing trend looks like a temporary aberration. All the reasons you were so bullish or bearish are engrained in your mind and it's hard to jettison them just because a trend line on a chart has been breached. (**16. 1/8/88**)

Julian once more returns to the subject of market timing and the worth in buying straw hats in winter when they're cheaper.

As we drift into the summer doldrums the mining brokers tell me it is harder and harder to come up with moneymaking ideas. I agree. Mining markets tend to be lifeless during the summer holidays when the only thing the metal-bashers are bronzing is their bodies.

It is, of course, at just such a time that you and I should be bargain-hunting. An Australian broker friend of mine, whose unstinting hospitality led him to an early grave, used to extol the virtues of buying straw hats in wintertime. I need hardly remind you that our summer coincides with their winter! There are plenty of straw hats about at the moment. It is not difficult to find value, merely difficult to find the money to buy it.

The problem is to prevent the straw hats we already own, from drifting with the rest. It does not help that at this time of the year the heat tends to sap the urge to buy more units. The bargains are likely, therefore, to remain on the shelf until you have returned from your summer holidays, unless the corporate raiders see this as their opportunity to pounce. It never ceases to amaze me that human beings really are so much happier when they are paying more for the things they want than they paid the last time they bought them. The fact that they can afford to buy less of them the second time round does not bother them in the least. They just like to see the price going up before they buy more.

They are just like us Fund Managers, who never seem to be able to make up our minds whether we are employed to collect share certificates or pound notes. When markets are high we all seem to collect share certificates and when markets are low we collect pound notes. It should be the other way round, shouldn't it? (**59. 26/7/89**)

The market is very seldom wrong.

When I first started in this game in 1967, there was a delightful old Partner of the firm called George Seebohm who had an uncanny knack of reading markets correctly. Like most of us of the old school of stockbroking, he would be the first to admit that detailed analysis did not come as second nature to him, yet he was one of the canniest investors I ever met.

Whenever I had a rush of blood to the head about a particular stock or market, he would invite me to lunch with him at the City Club and he would say, "Julian, don't overlook the fact that the market is very seldom wrong". I must tell you that over the years I have found that maxim worth remembering whenever I was tempted to make definitive statements about what should be where, regardless of what the market was indicating. (72. 30/11/89)

Judging the pain threshold in a falling market.

My previous experience tells me that markets do not bottom out until most investors have decided that such is the pain they have suffered that they will never, ever invest in equities again! That pain threshold is normally reached when markets have lost more than 60 per cent of their value. (121. 13/12/90)

Brokers

Julian always took a very firm line with stockbrokers, perhaps because he had been one himself for 20 years. Having established a carefully thought out "modus operandi" he expected that those who wanted to do business with the Fund should provide him with the information that he wanted, and in a form that fitted the operating parameters that he had laid down.

Julian is not persuaded by analysts' enthusiasm for gold shares, continuing to favour base metal shares.

Brokers' circulars which crossed my desk two short months ago, seldom gave any advice other than to sell the kind of stocks we were then buying. In order to justify these "Sell" recommendations, the mining analysts were calculating their earnings estimates on base metal prices which they are now having to revise upwards. I detect a growing level of discomfiture, as the June quarter reporting period draws nigh. The earnings are going to be much better than those predicted by the bears of base metal stocks. Needless to say, gold shares are much favoured by these Sages, but sadly for them, the precious metal indices have been lacklustre to say the least. I keep track of them, to make sure we are not missing anything. (**10. 7/6/88**)

Brokers' forecasts are too low for base metal prices, Julian argues, which is why they're missing the value in the sector.

It is interesting to watch the broker's circulars coming in and beholding how they gently change their metal price forecasts. Strange to relate, gold price estimates are being reduced all the time and hence the earnings projections of the gold companies. In contrast, the brokers are already increasing their 1989 forecasts for base metal prices. Their December projections are already starting to look too conservative. They see the base metal shares going up but they can't recommend them because, on their metal price forecasts, they look too expensive! As soon as they dare, they raise their metal forecasts just enough to justify recommending the shares. In no time the shares go up once again, putting them out of range. Sure enough they will be increasing their metal forecasts again before long. I can't wait!

What I am trying to do is to get the brokers to tell me two things, both perfectly reasonable. The first: what is the "right" price for the shares that they are recommending? The "right" price for a share is when you don't know whether to buy it or sell it. Having established that price I can then work out how much there is to go for if I take their advice. They don't seem to relish producing these figures. (**38. 31/1/89**)

Ever looking for brokers who give Fund Managers what they want, Julian highlights Ord Minnett's work in calculating historic real returns from leading miners.

But enough of this philosophising. I said last week I would share with you some of the excellent work done for me by some of our brokers. I have discovered that the broking fraternity is divided between those brokers who give their clients what they want and those who give their clients what they (the brokers) want! I know perfectly well what I want but, being not well endowed with the grey matter I like complicated things presented in a simple way which even I can understand.

Ord Minnett have hit the jackpot in this respect. They have come up with a diagram which depicts the real return offered by a number of leading mining companies, over their lives or 20 years, whichever is the shorter. The list is growing all the time. The metal prices I asked them to use are shown in the right-hand corner and can be altered at will. Brokers have discretion to use their metal price forecasts for the next 12 months only, otherwise they have to use mine.

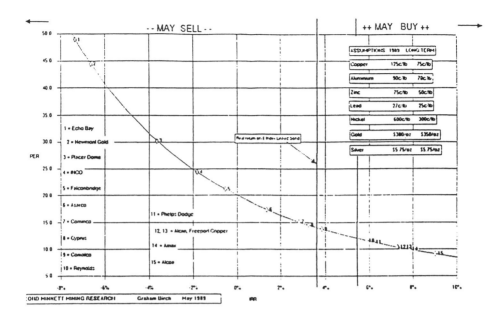

It seems to me that the very least you should expect to receive from your investments is the real rate of return of 3.6 per cent obtainable at no risk by lending your money to the government via a 20-year index-linked bond. This return is indicated on the chart by the left of the two heavy vertical lines. The right-hand vertical line is placed at a 50 per cent premium to that return, which seems reasonable compensation for the mining risk. The rest of the chart is self-explanatory. As the shares rise and fall in the market place they slide up and down the slippery slope and we buy and sell them accordingly. It seems to be working since our portfolio has been constructed using this methodology rather than by the use of PE ratios favoured by others. Did you realise that many gold shares sell on PE's of 25 or so when they have lives of less than half that? (**49. 2/5/89**)

Julian likens brokers to theatre impresarios.

It seems to me that brokers are a bit like impresarios. Do you remember a few years ago that many of London's theatres were dark? The impresarios, who had been putting on plays in order to interest each other, went cap in hand to Mrs Thatcher asking that theatre tickets should be exempted from VAT in order to make them more affordable. Instead of agreeing to their demands, Mrs Thatcher suggested that they might try putting on plays the public wanted to see. As soon as they started doing that, there were not enough theatres available to stage all the plays that the impresarios wanted to put on. (**110. 26/9/90**)

Other Musings

Julian takes on the role of Kipling crossed with Aesop as he spins a tale of South Africa.

Once upon a time, not so long ago, there lived in a game reserve in southern Africa, an elephant; a magnificent specimen who was king of all he surveyed. As with most proud rulers, he was not much concerned with the prowess of his rivals in other game reserves. True, he sometimes heard news of them via the bush telegraph, but he seldom came across them in person, for reasons we need not go into here.

When he did come across them, he was sometimes surprised, as we all are, at how much they had grown; but the fact that he lived in a reserve where hunting was banned gave him a reassuring feeling of security. So, relying on his age and experience, he felt able to guard himself and his herd from outside interference.

As the years rolled by, our hero was seen by game spotters to be getting rather portly and not so nimble on his feet as he used to be. Word got about the animal kingdom that you could flirt with some of his wives without running too much risk of getting his tusk up your backside.

Vultures and hyenas started to congregate on the fringes of his empire, waiting for some action. Not much happened since no one dared get caught in *flagrante delicto*. However, enough liberties were being taken to give the spotters the impression that it was only a matter of time before the elephant would be tormented to such an extent that he would be forced, either to relinquish some of his wives or take sufficiently violent action to remind everyone that he was still very much in command of his faculties.

Fortunately for you, space does not allow the continuation of this fable in this issue, but if you are interested to know how it all ends, don't sell your units! At least you have been appraised of the story, so far. (**13. 12/7/88**)

A colleague suffers injury from buying a corner shop with the financial return of a gold share.

On a lighter note, I was lunching with a "walking wounded" ex-colleague of mine who told me why his head was bandaged up. It transpired that he had recently informed his wife that he had bought the corner shop opposite their flat for £300,000. She had hit him on the head with the rolling pin, causing severe bruising when she heard that the shop was expected to make only £10,000 this year. His explanation that he worked in the gold share market, and that was the sort of price people paid for gold shares every day of the week, had clearly not impressed her! (**20. 6/9/88**)

A Christmas bottle of champagne is offered to the first unitholder who can translate a Latin inscription found on an ancient receptacle, and Julian manages to weave Minorco into the offer as well.

I am reminded of a letter which was written by a lower boy to the *Eton College Chronicle*, to the effect that when digging in his parents' garden during the school holidays, he had unearthed an ancient receptacle bearing a faded inscription. The only clue as to its origins was the inscription which he hoped might mean something to a classical scholar. The inscription read

"ITI SAPIS POTAN DATINO NE"

Classical tutors strained and strained but none could come up with a satisfactory translation. This prompts me to offer a bottle of champagne to the first holder of our units (outside James Capel) who can decipher the inscription. Two bottles if the unitholder is also a director of Minorco!

The fact that I find it difficult to interpret some of Minorco's recent moves is not meant to cast aspersions on their merits – merely on my ability fully to comprehend them. Perhaps with patience all will be revealed. In the meantime I wish you a merry Christmas. (**33. 20/12/88**)

Julian, according to Institutional Investor, still comes out among the leading mining analysts in the City although his stockbroking days are well behind him.

Last night I went to a wake. My own wake, or so it seemed to me. Irony of ironies, the Institutional Investor magazine held a cocktail reception at the Savoy of all places, to honour the members of the All British Research Team. Having sampled the opinions of the directors of research or heads of investments of 250 UK and US money management organisations, they selected the 130 best stockbroking analysts in their fields. I came second in gold, knocked off my perch by a thrusting 31-year-old called Jack Jones (no relation).

I would not mind if I had known I was competing, and I am sure the result would have been no different if I had known, but I gave up stockbroking last April to look after you lot! I am poacher turned gamekeeper but the memory obviously lingers on in the minds of the money managers like the scent of a ferret in a poacher's pocket. Next year I hope the Institutional Investor will ask me, in my capacity as a Fund Manager, who I think is the best mining analyst. If he is still at number one, I am going to vote for my old friend Alan Borer, who runs the TSB Natural Resources Fund. You all know it is my ambition, before I fade away altogether, to get this fund to outperform the TSB Natural

Resources Fund, the best-performing natural resources fund in the UK Since Fund Managers now seem eligible for the honours, I do not see why Baring should not vote for Borer.

They said about me, and I quote; "Julian Baring, winner in this category for three consecutive years, slips back into the second team – the result perhaps of the fact that he has been managing a gold fund since last April and has not produced much in the way of research." I am sure you would concur with that. But we have had a few laughs and anyhow investment is largely about ideas and you have not been starved of them in these weekly missives, have you?

In the blurb they referred to me as being the "father figure of the industry". When my younger brother was working at Capel's a few years ago, a clerk came up to him late one Friday afternoon and asked him whether his "father" was still in the office. I have not been allowed to forget that – and now we have this "father figure" bit – it's all too much! (**41. 28/2/89**)

The idea of lending long term to the government at 3.5 per cent amazes Julian – as it would have anyone at that time.

Just as there is a small chance that those who predict an acceleration of inflation might be proved right, so I think there is an equal chance that those who predict a severe recession or even a full-blown depression might be correct. We are covered for the first eventuality with our marginal gold shares but inadequately covered for the second. Hence the idea of investing some of our liquidity in War Loan or the like.

Hopefully neither forecast will be correct and the world will muddle through. In that case the main bulk of our portfolio will recover sharply. When it becomes clearer how things are likely to pan out, we can adjust the portfolio accordingly. Meanwhile, perhaps we should have some 3.5 per cent War Loan. Can you believe that anyone could have ever been persuaded to lend their money to the Government for 3.5 per cent per annum? 11.5 per cent currently offered does not seem so outrageous somehow. What do you think? I'd like to know.

I worked out the other day that the interest on £300 of War Loan would have been enough in 1950 to buy me a hot horlicks and a doughnut every school day for one year. Now the same £300 of War Loan would only provide the said snack for ten days. Lucky I'm on a diet! (**115. 31/10/90**)

Julian announces that 1996 will be his last year of running the Mercury mining department – but a wider role beckons.

You may have heard rumours of my impending retirement at the end of this year. Withdrawing from the day to day responsibilities of running the Mining Department – certainly: but retirement?! That word has connotations which don't fit at all with plans we have formulated, not just for my continued employment with Mercury Asset Management, but also for my ongoing involvement with the various mining funds we manage and with our investors and friends in the Mining Industry. If you had been working for 40 years, in an industry as exciting, fascinating and frustrating as the mining industry, you too would find it impossible to go cold turkey in order to tend your vines and make ceramics, however therapeutic those activities may be.

When I joined Mercury in 1991, I promised I would establish the finest Mining Team that could be assembled to look after your interests. That promise has been fulfilled. A Team of highly-qualified and experienced people are in place who know a great deal more about the industry than I do.

So no more admin. for me, no more reports, fewer committees, more travel, more face to face meetings with friends in the in dustry and clients. In fact, some clients will be seeing more not less of me in my new capacity. Less of the boring bits, more of the fun. We all remain strongly committed to the disciplined investment processes we have developed during my stewardship. Although my role will be changing I still intend to contribute to the investment process and I will make myself heard if I feel strongly about something. It's just too hard to break the habits of a lifetime! I hope my colleagues will spoil me by allowing me to write the occasional article for the Newsletter because I envisage that I will be travelling quite a bit next year and you always learn interesting new things at the slope face. (**364. 14/11/96**)

13. Julian's Wit and Wisdom

We have already come across a large number of examples of Julian's thought-provoking prognostications on the subject of mining share markets and other matters besides. Here is a further selection of his well-considered and often controversial views of the world of mining including the activities of other practitioners.

A familiar theme of Julian's - the selling of units at market bottoms.

When I was a broker I used to remind people running funds that mining shares never go up when the value of the metal they produce is going down. Judging by the recent performance of this Fund I have forgotten the facts of life – a clear sign of old age!

We all know that the more shares fall, the better the long-term value they offer. But bear markets tend to wear down our resolve and people are tempted to redeem their units which means that there is less cash with which to buy the improving value on offer. (**110. 26/9/90**)

With his mind on the grape harvest in Provence Julian points out the gold sector's recent fund raisings.

You may recall that before heading off to France to pick grapes I was writing to you about feeding ducks, pointing out that the bounce in the gold price, resulting from the Middle East situation gave the gold mining industry an opportunity to replenish its coffers.

At that time only American Barrick had tapped the market for $113m but I suggested it would not be long before others "followed-my-leader". Today the following companies are fund raising:–

Newmont Mining	$500 million
Amax Gold	$140 million
Amgold	$150 million
Western Areas	$70 million
Coeur d'Alene	$50 million
Poseildon Gold	$137 million
	$1047

Admitting the Fund's emphasis on general mining shares Julian promises a shift of emphasis at the right time.

If experience teaches one anything, it is that by the time the gold share market bottoms, most investors will have vowed never to buy a gold share again and people's backs will be turned on whatever value there is. My nightmare is that you too will have become fed up waiting for gold shares to perform and will sell your units at the very time that I need cash to buy bargains. Everyone teases me because this Fund is so much more general than gold. Please don't deny me the pleasure of converting it, when the time is ripe, into the James Capel Gold and General Fund. (**126. 7/2/91**)

Julian goes bargain hunting among South African marginals.

You have to buy shares when nobody wants them. This week I bought a quarter of a million Venterspost for £55,000. A year ago those same shares would have cost me £275,000. I know because I paid that much for them a year ago! Last week I bought a quarter of a million Libanon for £62,500. A year ago they would have cost £330,000. As far as I know both companies still have roughly the same amount of gold in the ground as they had a year ago. It's just valued differently, that's all.

One day you and I are going to wake up to find that gold in the ground is valuable after all. While the price is low the industry should be mining as little of it as possible. Why mine something valuable and sell it at a loss?

So long as the gold price is below the long-term cost of digging it out, gold is more valuable if left in the ground. (**127. 27/2/91**)

The headache of running a marginal gold mine is discussed.

Running a marginal mine must be rather like running a stockbroking firm. When the gold price is high the profit stream is nothing short of miraculous. Far-sighted projects which had to be put on the back burner during less prosperous times get put into effect. Costs start rising as more people are taken on in the belief that the more miners you employ the more production can be raised.

When times get bad again as they are in the gold mining industry some very difficult decisions have to be taken by people, some of whom have a tendency to think of the mining industry as a branch of the social services rather than as an engine of wealth creation. Do you close a loss making mine at very considerable further cost in terms of redundancies? Do you keep it ticking along at a reduced level but nonetheless continuing to build up losses until such time as a rising gold price bails you out? Or do you apply drastic surgery at some immediate cost in terms of redundancies, and accept the fact that by doing so you may cause the mine's life to be reduced?

Unprofitable sections of a mine which are abandoned can seldom be reopened. Talk about being caught between a rock and a hard place! (**130. 21/3/91**)

Further praise for Julian's assistant's investment technique.

Denise [Julian's assistant], whose mathematical prowess is even less well developed than my own, prefers to judge the quality of an investment by the colour of the Chief Executive's eyes or the cut of his cloth. Female intuition seems to be just as good an investment tool as any other so I am not knocking her methodology. Between us we seem to have consistently outperformed most of our peers, so our methods cannot be all bad. As far as you are concerned I suspect you couldn't care less how we do it so long as we do it. (**135. 15/5/91**)

What proportion of a portfolio should be in the Fund?

Professional investment advisers often ask me what proportion of their clients' portfolios they should invest in a specialised fund such as this. The answer I give is: not so much that if you turn out to have been wrong, your client will sack you; nor so little that if you turn out to be right, he won't even notice. (**142. 11/6/91**)

Gold as a one armed bandit.

From this you can tell that the price of gold is as unpredictable as a one-armed-bandit. All you can do is to buy it when it is down, sell it when it is high and the shares likewise. (**157. 22/11/91**)

Gold gets a drubbing from investors and analysts.

Conventional wisdom is a useful tool for determining investment strategies since it is almost always wrong. By the time wisdom has become conventional it is already reflected in the market price so you can do the opposite with impunity.

So what does conventional wisdom say now? The other night I had a visit from a Johannesburg broker who told me that gold would never rise again. Fancy a South African saying that! Talking down the gold price used to be a capital offence in South Africa, but in these days of enlightenment anything goes!

To say that the gold price will never rise again is indicative of an advanced form of "conventionalwisdomitis". Gold is no longer considered by the investment community to be a worthwhile component of a respectable investment portfolio and gold shares even less so. This has resulted in the FT Gold Mines Index falling, in real terms, to below the all-time low seen in 1971 when gold was still $35/oz. **(158. 29/11/91)**

The aim to raise gold production to the market approved level.

It may have occurred to you too that the price of a share often has less to do with its intrinsic worth than with the amount of money available to buy it!

One of the tricks of the trade, if you are a miner, is to produce enough ounces to qualify your company for the attention of the institutional investor. Institutional investors are quite happy to invest in your company if it qualifies, even if they have to pay a price for your shares which offers them little prospect of ever getting their money back (in other words they often accept a zero return or less). In contrast, they will eschew the smaller company even if it offers a real return of 10 per cent.

The answer, if you cannot increase your own production to 300,000 ounces, is to take over someone else whose production, when added to your own, gives you access to the charmed circle. **(164. 20/2/92)**

Apologies and explanations are offered for being in South African rather than Australian gold shares.

It is said that one should never apologise, never explain, but I do not think it does any harm to apologise if you get it wrong. "I'm terribly sorry, I made a mistake" can be quite disarming and the whole point of this Newsletter is to explain what I have been doing with your money!

Perhaps I should apologise that the Fund was not more weighted towards Australia, the best-performing market, rather than South Africa, the worst. Judging by the gold price received by the mining companies in each country, I was wrong for the right reasons! I won't apologise for that, but I would remind you that the reason why we are so heavily weighted towards South African shares is that the cost of buying an ounce of gold in the ground is far cheaper there than anywhere else in the world.

When the gold price is going through a weak patch, the less you have paid for each ounce in the ground, the less you stand to lose. If you doubt me, ask a property developer who paid too much for his land bank. (168. 19/03/92)

What is overlooked is that gold miners are obstinate creatures who value their jobs as much as the rest of us. Sure, they do silly things like selling gold they have not yet produced, thereby depressing the price, but at the same time we must admit that their minds are not all closed to new ideas. There was a time, for instance, when gold miners were in the business of producing ever-more ounces. Now some of them, under the enlightened leadership of Western Mining, have decided that in future they will turn their attention to producing more profits rather than more ounces! (**169. 26/3/92**)

Producing profits rather than ounces.

One of the potential elephant traps which await the unwary Fund Manager is the thorny question of reserves. When gold prices are depressed as they are at present, some mining companies become rather coy about their reserves, caught as they are, between the "Rock" of the SEC and the "Hard Place" of the market.

Obviously the value of a mine is the discounted profit that can be made over the life of its reserves. It is therefore very important that investors should be aware of the number of ounces which are payable at the current gold price – otherwise the rock in which the ounces are contained may only be good for road-making. (**172. 14/4/92**)

The market is seldom wrong.

One thing 25 years in this game has taught me is that the market is very seldom wrong. It is good at getting the balance right between risk and reward. The other thing I have learnt is that commentators are far smarter at explaining a move in the market than predicting it. (**178. 12/6/92**)

Going for liquidity rather than value.

As you know, we try to buy mining shares which offer investors more money back over the life of the mine than they invest in the first place. You would think that every investment should offer that prospect, but the perceived need to buy large capitalization, marketable stocks seems to be the overriding consideration in the minds of some institutional Fund Managers. Whether the company offers an acceptable rate of return, seems to be of secondary importance.

This "fact of life" virtually ensures that good value is most likely to be found in the smaller companies. The added attraction is that if ever a smaller company should become a larger company (and as such catch the eye of an institutional investor) it is at least possible that it, in turn, will become as overvalued as it was formerly undervalued. (188.18/9/92)

Market indices are always fully invested.

You have probably come across players in the investment game who appear to believe that the market should be judged by its performance against their predictions rather than that their predictions should be judged against the performance of the market. If they recommend something which loses you half your money, they will say the market is to blame, but if you double your money, you will not be allowed to forget who gave you such excellent advice. No doubt some of you will be thinking that I come into that category myself, but I have learnt from experience that the market is very seldom wrong.

We lesser mortals therefore, are content to be judged by that hard taskmaster, the market, as defined by the various indices by which it is measured. Our fascination with indices probably results from their maddeningly impersonal nature. They are oblivious to greed or fear and their future prosperity is not dependent on beating them, though the Fund Manager's often is. Accordingly, they are always fully invested at the bottom of the market since they have no perception of risk nor indeed reward for that matter. (227. 19/8/93)

Graham Birch touches on a common theme.

You are most unlikely to find the term "Stockmarket Force" in any physics textbook. However, it is wrong to assume that just because Sir Isaac Newton et al have neglected this area it is unimportant or that its effects cannot be felt. Stock-market forces are particularly potent in the mining industry. Commodity cycles create feast or famine cashflows for mining companies and most producers have little control over terminal market pricing. Because of the highly variable nature of the returns, banks and other "lenders of capital" are reluctant to finance early stage project development. This means that mining and exploration companies are a natural customer for the equity markets.

Mining companies' perceptions of what sort of risks the stockmarket wants to take on are thus very important shapers indeed of their strategic direction. (**248. 24/3/94**)

The Federal Reserve and the gold price.

As you know, I take the view that the gold price never goes up for the same reason twice. If it did, we would all be rich!

People will tell you that gold won't go up until inflation returns, but they never tell you whether inflation is caused by rising commodity prices or whether rising commodity prices cause inflation. It is said that Mr. Greenspan, the Governor of the Federal Reserve Bank, is keeping a watchful eye on gold as a barometer of inflation. There are those who go so far as to say that the Fed is keeping the lid on gold – the modem equivalent of imprisoning the messenger!

The suspicions of some Fed watchers are aroused by noting how cleverly the Fed relieved the plight of the international banking system by maintaining a huge differential between long- and short-term interest rates, thereby enabling the banks to rebuild their balance sheets at their customers' expense. It has been estimated that the subsidy to the US banks over the last two or three years (during the time of low interest rates policy) amounted to some US$350 billion, a cost which went almost unnoticed by the uncomplaining public. (**255. 20/5/94**)

The Fund for the first time starts to take platinum seriously.

We have never really been convinced that platinum's credentials as a precious metal are quite bona fide. This plus the relatively demanding ratings has meant that your Fund has never had significant exposure to platinum shares. This, for the reasons set out below, is now being rectified. Our coolness towards the metal has not stopped it outperfoming gold. Indeed the past few days have seen the platinum price move to a new all-time high in rand terms and a four-year high in dollars. The situation for palladium is even better – stimulated by the world's thirst for mobile phones (apparently the stuff is used in these gadgets). If only the gold price could do this well, we might all be feeling better off. Although broadly speaking the platinum price has been rising since 1991, the most recent surge was sparked off by a most exciting announcement by Engelhard.

Apparently, their metallurgists have found a way of drastically reducing city smog by coating car radiators with platinum. The effect in atmospheric terms is said to be broadly equivalent to strapping a tree to the bonnet of every car. The Californians could pounce on this technology as it holds out the prospect of clean air in LA. Where the Californians go others follow and there is a chance that this could be a major new source of platinum demand. We are told that each catalyst will use as much as five grammes of metal so every million cars sold would add 160,000 ounces to world demand (equivalent to a 3 per cent increase). The US auto market is about 10 million cars/year so if (a big if) this catches on then it adds up to a huge increase in consumption. If Europe adopts the system too, then platinum companies will really strike it rich. No wonder Engelhard is believed to have bought 100,000 ounces of metal ahead of its announcement. (**291. 11/4/95**)

Interpreting news in bull and bear markets.

It is a well-known market axiom that in bull markets every piece of news no matter how bad is interpreted as good news. In bear markets the stream of news, however good, is always treated negatively. Although we believe that things are about to change, the gold market is a little unusual in that it has been in neither a bear nor bull phase for quite a long while now. This gives people a great deal of freedom to reach completely opposite conclusions about the same news. (**300. 16/06/95**)

Quarter day portfolio performance statistics.

Having been torn off a strip in the *Guardian* for losing the Midas touch as far as the six-month performance of the Mercury World Mining Trust was concerned, I write to you in a contrite frame of mind, but with few permanent scars.

Fund Managers spend 361 days a year trying to find cheap shares or sectors which the market has overlooked. In other words we are constantly trying to demonstrate that the market is wrong.

Four times a year, on quarter days, our performance is compared with the market. The day before the quarter day, our portfolios contain shares which we perceive to offer better value than the market, but as far as the performance statistics are concerned, these are all the wrong stocks. If, as has just happened with the Mercury World Mining Trust, the shares in the portfolio subsequently start to outperform the market as more investors start to recognise their true value, that means nothing to the statisticians. As far as they are concerned we should have been in all the "wrong" stocks until valuation day and then switched into all the "right" stocks the day after. If you are running a £500 million Fund, that is easier said than done, even if we wanted to run your money that way. (**310. 23/8/95**)

The majority view is usually wrong.

As I pointed out at the conference the only thing I have learned during the last 30 years in investment is that when everyone thinks the same way, they are usually proved wrong. That is one of the great fascinations of the market. In 1980 everyone thought that gold was the greatest investment ever, even though the owner of an ounce of gold had never had so much purchasing power in history. Before the UK left the EMU, everyone said that an effective devaluation of the pound would lead to an increase in inflation. Before the financial rand was abolished, everyone thought the commercial rand would fall to the level of the financial rand.

The opposite occurred. The one thing that almost everyone in the gold mining industry is agreed upon is that it is a good thing to sell gold that has not yet been produced. That is why they are selling more and more of it. In an industry capitalised at US$66.34 billion as at 30th September 1995, the forward sales have now topped US$17 billion! You may think these are the outpourings of an angry young man who wants to change the world. You would be wrong about that too; they are the ramblings of an angry old man who is still trying to learn from experience. (**316. 5/10/95**)

The Fund as a geared play on gold.

A great many investors in the Gold and General Fund hold the units simply to gain gearing to a rising gold price. There is nothing wrong in this – indeed we have pointed out to you on numerous occasions that our investment strategy tends to favour those companies which do best when the gold price rises. We do this because we know that most investors share our view that gold is cheap at present and that they (like us!) hope to make money when the gold price rises. Although we are at all times careful with your money, we believe that you do not want us to structure the portfolio defensively so as to lose relatively less money when the gold price falls. If investors think that the gold price is going to fall then they simply redeem their units. (**318. 31/10/95**)

14.   Takeovers and M&A

While the mining sector has been the subject of much M&A activity over the years, this trend has been particularly strong for the last 15 years or so. In Julian's time of running Gold and General the dominant takeover story was the Minorco bid for Consolidated Gold Fields. This turned into a long and at times dirty battle for control, and in the end led not to Cons Gold falling into the mining hands of Minorco but into the building materials hands of Hanson Trust. This eventually broke up the historic UK-based mining conglomerate.

The Minorco bid for Consolidated Gold Fields, much forecast, finally arrives.

As Capels are brokers to Minorco, I have to be circumspect in my comments about the bid. It was interesting to watch the spectacle however, with the price bounding up well above the offer price to start with, as people bought in expectation of an improved offer. Later in the week, the price declined below the offer price as the gold price fell; white knights became harder and harder to identify, and potential slips between cup and lip made investors wary of the downside. By the end of the week a bird in the hand became worth one-and-a-bit in the bush. In other words the share price of Consolidated Gold Fields fell below Minorco's offer price.

I mention this not to appear smart but to point out what happens when someone drops a large boulder into a comparatively small pond. It has been pointed out that the market capitalization of all the companies in which Consolidated Gold Fields and Minorco have interests, amounts to no less than 10,000 million dollars! The Chief Executive of Minorco, Sir Michael Edwards, has said that if the bid is successful, all the group's investments will be subject to close scrutiny and those which do not fit in with the group's plans will be sold. In other words, a massive regrouping of the world's mining companies could be in the offing. The ripple effect of that would not be confined to these shores. Even if Minorco does not take control of Consolidated Gold Fields, they will no doubt buy another mining company. Their cash pile of $900 million is burning a hole in their pockets but holes in the ground are their real business.

I believe it is only a matter of time before someone bids for one of the mining companies in the USA The bid for Consolidated Gold Fields may be the catalyst. I have mentioned before that if one of our North American holdings is bid for, all the rest will rise in sympathy just as the UK companies in our portfolio did when Minorco dropped its boulder. This fund is tailor-made for that eventuality since it holds virtually all the leading North American mining companies. There can hardly be a neater way of participating in the action than by owning units in this Fund, a point which will not be lost on the professional advisors who receive these notes.

One thing is quite clear. There is a growing disparity between the way industry is viewing the economic outlook and the way investors see it. Investors do not like what they see, so the stock exchange value of companies declines as sellers predominate. This gives industrialists their opportunity to grow by acquisition. **(23. 27/9/88)**

Minorco's Cons Gold bid takes a wrong turn as it is referred to the UK Monopolies Commission.

When you think of the number of column inches that have been written about the lapsed bid by Minorco for Consolidated Gold Fields, it is hard to believe that the market may have failed to correctly assess the upside potential and downside risk for those two shares.

If you want to know what is the right price for a share in these circumstances, it is when you don't know whether to buy it or sell it. That's exactly what I feel about the Cons Gold share price at the moment as the market waits with bated breath for the Monopolies Commission to decide whether the UK's supplies of titanium and zircon are put at serious risk by the bid. Meanwhile it seems to me that our time might be better spent thinking what the move after next in this particular chess game is likely to be.

The gnus are still thinking about the next move, so if there are any bargains to be had, they are less likely to be in the shares of the combatants than in the shares of their next targets.

Minorco has said that if it is successful at taking over Consolidated Gold Fields, it will review their joint holdings and discard those which do not fit in with their long-term strategy. I liken this to feeding carp. The waters will be boiling as the fish thrash about trying to catch each tasty morsel thrown to them.

If, on the other hand, Minorco is frustrated in its attempt to buy Consolidated Gold Fields, it will be seen as a dangerous predator in its own right. In other words it will be looking for something else to buy.

In either case, instead of writing column inches on the fate of Consolidated Gold Fields, mining analysts will be burning the midnight oil trying to forecast the next ploy.

Holders of this Fund can lie back and enjoy it, since we have already positioned ourselves to take advantage of the move after next. We have all the most desirable mining companies displayed in our shop window. Every time you send me money, it is invested with the move after next in mind. While we are waiting, I am adopting a scattergun approach which is entirely suited to a Fund of this kind.

I hope in this way to provide a useful service to the latecomers to the party. Someone, after all, has to make stock available when the crowd decides it wants to buy. We have already bought, and can still buy, these shares at knockdown prices. Once the crowd focuses its attention on the goods displayed, I don't think the prices will stay at rock-bottom levels for long. We may as well buy them now and sell them to the latecomers. They may be so keen to get in that they won't care much about the price. (**26. 1/11/88**)

With Minorco's bid for Cons Gold lapsing, Julian buys Minorco. He believes the company is determined to remedy the perceived problem that it is a value trap for its many high quality assets …

Now that Minorco's bid for Consolidated Gold Fields has lapsed, I have bought some Minorco shares for the portfolio. We own most of the others already.

The reason I have done this is that I am now convinced that the directors of Minorco have started to look for the missing $1.5 billion. For many years I had my doubts whether they had noticed that it had disappeared! Recent events have convinced me at they were aware of it all the time and that they will now set about recovering it for the shareholders in a gritty and purposeful manner.

Perhaps I should explain that $1.5 billion is the difference between the value placed by the market on Minorco as a company and the total value of the investments which it owns. If the directors could find a way to eliminate the discount, they would increase the value of Minorco shares by about $6 a share. That is the equivalent of 50 per cent! They could thus add value to the shares without having to sink a single shaft or treat a single ton of ore. Indeed they would have to discover a pretty amazing mine to add that much to their share price in the normal course of their business. No, they don't need a mining engineer, a financial engineer will do nicely at this stage of the game.

What they need to do, and what they are starting to do to achieve this miracle, is to remove the layers of financial insulation which separates their profit and loss account from their operating companies' earnings. Take for example

Minorco's holding in Johnson Matthey. Johnson Matthey is held through Charter Consolidated. Charter itself sells at a sizeable discount to its assets and so in turn does Minorco. So the Minorco shareholders are getting a very watered down version of the real value of Johnson Matthey.

Consolidated Gold Fields has gold mining interests situated in the famous Carlin Gold Belt, Nevada. These are held through its 49 per cent holding in Newmont Mining. Unfortunately, Newmont Mining does not receive the full benefit from these gold mines since they are held through Newmont Gold. The value of Newmont Mining's holding in Newmont Gold exceeds the market capitalization of Newmont Mining and so "ad infinitum". By the time the earnings of these gold mines gets through to Minorco, which currently owns 29 per cent of Gold Fields, they are so watered down as to be hardly worth having.

Unwinding these complicated structures which entangle the profits of the producing companies in a web of cross-holdings is what the new look Minorco is all about. (**28. 15/11/88**)

… and he also buys Cons Gold.

Once Minorco's bid for Consolidated Gold Fields (CGF) had lapsed, there was nothing to prevent the Fund acquiring some shares in CGF. I grasped the opportunity since the market's understandable disappointment that the bid was to be referred to the Monopolies Commission had caused the shares to fall to more than £1 below the price Minorco had been prepared to pay. Perhaps naively, I found it hard to believe that the future supply of titanium and zirconium to the UK market was sufficiently threatened to be an insuperable obstacle to Minorco's ambitions.

I was fully aware when I bought them, that if Minorco was prevented from proceeding with its bid, the price of CGF was ready to fall even further, probably to slightly below the levels at which the CGF directors had sold their own shares on 29th December last year having exercised their options.

If they thought £9.23 was high enough for the shares then, when the gold price was £256/oz, today's gold price of £231/oz is hardly likely to have enhanced their true value. I mention the gold price in sterling in deference to Mr Agnew, the Chairman of CGF who likes to draw attention to the correlation between the price of CGF shares and the sterling gold price. I, too, have been following the ratio for a number of years, in fact ever since he first pointed it out to me! This is what the price of CGF divided by the sterling gold price, looks like:–

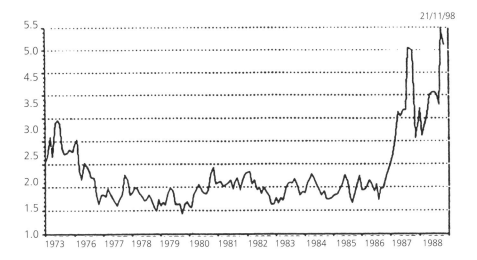

Two and a half years ago, when the shares of CGF were very out of fashion following an unfortunate episode with an investment they had made in a company with the unlikely name of Skytop Brewster, I remember banging the drum loudly in an attempt to draw investors' attention to the fact that CGF had seldom been cheaper relative to gold.

The drumbeats were picked up by the directors of American Barrick Resources. They built up a stake which resulted in CGF's shares changing from being historically cheap, to being historically expensive, relative to gold. They have remained expensive ever since because the market was thoroughly alerted to their takeover potential as a result of the Barrick episode.

The directors must have taken this into account when they exercised their options and sold their shares last year at £9.23. They must have thought at the time that the shares were not worth significantly more than £9.23, even with a takeover bid – a good enough reason, in anyone's book, to let a few go.

So when Minorco bid £13.06, it must have been difficult in the circumstances for them to fight it on the grounds of price. Since CGF's investments are mainly outside the United Kingdom, it must have come as something of a relief to them that the Powers that Be were persuaded to get the Monopolies Commission to look into the impact of the bid on the UK's potential supply of titanium and zirconium.

If the directors of CGF are to continue in office, the one thing they have to achieve above all others, is for the owners of their business to be denied the opportunity of deciding for themselves whether to sell their shares at the bid price. Far less risky from their standpoint is to have Big Brother decide that for us, unfettered as he undoubtedly is by vulgar commercial considerations.

It reminds me of the old adage "She did not marry him for his money, she just didn't know how else to get it." **(29. 22/11/88)**

Julian speculates as to whether any major break-up of Cons Gold – should Minorco's bid finally succeed – will have a buoying effect on the Financial Rand.

In summary, the bulk of the portfolio is in the areas where I perceive the least risk to lie. My money-making activities are focussed around the opportunities which are likely to arise from the Minorco bid for Consolidated Gold Fields and from the reorganisation of the Minorco group.

As you know, Minorco has expressed the firm intention, if its bid for Consolidated Gold Fields (CGF) is successful, of selling the South African interests of CGF. These investments are worth some R2.779 billion at current prices, so a reasonable man would surely be forgiven for thinking that the prospect of a sale of such magnitude would already be having a depressing influence on the financial rand.

Far from it, the financial rand has been relatively perky recently. It is certainly not behaving at all as if it was going to be hit with a wave of selling. Its behaviour may be partially explained by the fact that some 20 million shares of CGF are held in South Africa, mainly by companies in the CGF Group. The other reason is that there are hopes of peace breaking out in that troubled country.

In the unlikely event that all the South African holders decide to accept Minorco's bid, if it is reinstated, and remit the proceeds to South Africa; there would be a demand created for R1.74 billion financial rands.

So in summary, there could be R2.8 billion financial rands on offer and demand for R1.74 billion, leaving an overhang of R1 billion financial rands looking for a home. Don't hold me to these figures, they are only a guide. **(30. 29/11/88)**

Julian puzzles over why Cons Gold is going to such lengths to avoid being taken over, and suggests that shareholders sell now and buy the Fund, which should benefit from post-bid corporate and investment activity.

All the omens are that Lord Young will decide next week whether the shareholders of Consolidated Gold Fields are to be allowed to decide for themselves whether to accept Minorco's bid for their company or whether the decision is to be made on their behalf by the powers that be, egged on, if I dare use the expression, by the redoubtable Mr. Agnew, at a cost, we are told, of £50 million! What will they have to sell to pay for that?

The worry is that Gold Fields' tactics, which seem to be to go to any lengths to prevent themselves being taken over, may rebound on them. After all it is possible that we may be just as good judges of what is good for the country as the management of Gold Fields. Who knows, their efforts to influence the US President to stop the bid on account of Minorco's South African connections could easily rebound upon them. If the bid founders on that point, Gold Fields itself will be in danger of having to divest itself of its North American interests because of its own South African connections! Holding Gold Fields shares in hopes of a higher bid may be more dangerous than you think!

Whatever the rights and wrongs of this whole saga, I still maintain that the elegant way of playing it for Gold Fields' shareholders is to sell their shares in the market and buy this Fund before the bid, not after it. After all the Fund is stuffed full of companies which would benefit from the ripple effect of Minorco's attentions or its subsequent actions. The upside potential of the Fund could well exceed the upside potential of Gold Fields, inflated as it currently is by takeover hopes. The downside of the Fund in the event of the bid being disallowed is probably a good deal less than the downside risk in Gold Fields. The market is very good at assessing risk and reward when its mind is concentrated on a situation. It seems to me quite likely that the upside and downside on Gold Fields' shares is about equal, at 15 per cent. As I tried to show last week, I reckon that the upside on the Fund is considerably more than the downside.

The "Royals" and "Ladies in Waiting" in our portfolio are going from strength to strength and I am now having to top slice them to prevent them collectively representing more than 55 per cent of the portfolio – the maximum permissible under the rules.

One thought occurs to me in connection with the Gold Field's bid. More people will now probably opt to take Minorco paper to avoid having to pay capital gains tax on their Gold Field's shares. When the bid was launched there were plenty of losses for UK investors to set against their profits on Gold Fields. Now with the UK market behaving more like commodity shares than straight industrials, capital losses are getting increasingly hard to find! If I am right, this will be good news indeed for us, since one of the reasons Minorco shares are so neglected is that people fear that following the bid, there will be a lot of unwanted Minorco paper about to depress the price. Now it looks as if there may even be a shortage. Don't forget that a buoyant Minorco share price is good for De Beers and that in turn is good for Anamint. That in turn is good for Anglo American. We have them all to the maximum extent permissible. (**38. 31/1/89**)

Struggling to fend off Minorco, Cons Gold draws the attention of the UK's Department of Trade to the diamond monopoly which Minorco associate De Beers has built up in London – much to Julian's bemusement.

In the middle of last week, in an action which was reminiscent of Brian Clough's attempts to restrain the fans from running onto the pitch, Gold Fields drew the DTI's attention to a possible irregularity which had been overlooked for the best part of 60 years. They drew attention to the fact that the world's diamond business, which might be deemed to be a monopoly, was being conducted from London! Needless to say Gold Fields do not produce any diamonds, otherwise I expect they too would be using the services of the Central Selling Organisation, like the Russians, the Tanzanians, the Botswanians, the Australians, etc.

No sooner had it been announced what Gold Fields had done, than the brokers started ringing to tell me to sell our De Beers shares. De Beers is our second largest holding. (You can see last week was not a good one for me.) I told them that far from selling, I would rather buy any De Beers shares they persuaded their other clients to sell. Unfortunately they were unable to offer me a single share.

If De Beers is prevented from plying its trade in London as a result of Gold Fields' vigilance, I expect it will move elsewhere. Switzerland has been mentioned. On the other hand, if the DTI concludes that this particular monopoly is not detrimental to the public interest, it can do nothing but good to the value of our De Beers shares. After all De Beers were hardly likely themselves to ask the authorities if it was all right for them to continue running their business from here, in case the authorities said "no". If someone else asks the question and the authorities are put in a position of having to say yes, it seems to me that the upside on De Beers is far greater than the downside if they say no. They could hardly be cheaper than they are as I have explained in previous letters.

I asked my wife what she thought, and she said that as long as no one did anything to reduce the value of her engagement ring then as far as she was concerned we men could go on playing our little games. Mr Agnew, who recently explained to the annual general meeting of Gold Fields that he had sold his Gold Fields shares at £9.50 because he had three wives to support, should know better than most the cost of incurring the wrath of the female of the species. After all, they are the ones that own the diamonds. The girls have been quite happy so far to leave De Beers to protect the value of their jewellery. (**39.** 7/2/89)

Julian begins to worry that some investors are trying to pressure Minorco into making a silly bid for Cons Gold.

Let's turn to more serious matters. I don't like the way the greedier punters are trying to rumble Minorco into making a silly bid for Gold Fields. What frightens me is that Minorco might be persuaded to pay too much and then have difficulty in finding buyers for the bits. Investors don't understand how to value mining shares as well as mining companies do and it is mining companies, not investors, who are going to have to buy the bits. I am getting frightened that these potential buyers may be backward in coming forward if the price they are being asked to pay is set too high. We certainly don't want to be left holding Minorco if they get landed with overvalued assets. Gold mining companies are always telling us Fund Managers that the market is overvaluing every gold company bar themselves. It is of course gold mining companies that Minorco proposes to sell. You can't stop the gnus being silly with their money but you can get out of the way when you see them coming and when you know they are not looking where they are going.

I am also scared about what would happen if Minorco walks away and leaves Gold Fields stranded on some 20 times earnings. It is either going to make RTZ look very cheap on considerably less than ten times earnings, or Gold Fields particularly vulnerable on 20 times.

If the institutions hold out for an unrealistically high price you and I are going to make for the exits. I don't want the whole edifice falling down round our ears. It is probably yet another sign of old age, but the stakes in this particular poker game are getting dangerously high. I'll keep you informed if I decide to leave the party, but rest assured I am not doing this job in order to earn medals for bravery armed with your money. (**41. 28/2/89**)

He also begins to worry that in the aftermath of a successful bid by Minorco a break-up of Cons Gold will have negative implications for the gold share sector in particular, and about Cons Gold and its premium rating if Minorco withdraws.

Suddenly the market seems to be taking on board that the battle being fought out between Minorco and Consolidated Gold Fields is not safe for widows or orphans – or for unitholders of this Fund, who don't like taking undue risks with their savings. The price of Cons Gold shares has sunk down close to the level of Minorco's bid, as if to suggest that the punters are losing faith in the prospect of a higher bid. I am grateful for that, since I believe the last thing Minorco should do is to be rumbled into paying up for fear of finding itself unable to off-load the discards at a reasonable price. You may have noticed how "big" people talk when they know there is no immediate danger of having to reach for their cheque books!

What worries me is that if and when the crunch comes and Minorco's bid goes unconditional, the "big talkers" will read Minorco as a forced seller of gold shares and start "umming and aahing" about the gold price. Unitholders will be called to prayer at that time to beg the Almighty to make the gold price go up while Minorco is unloading.

Meanwhile the "ripple effect" is starting to work wonders for the price of our units. The encouraging thing is that the great majority of people appear to be waiting for their cheques from Minorco before deciding what to do with the money. Someone has got to be in a position, when they get it, to provide them with the stocks they will require. Hopefully we will be in that position.

Of course the other side of the coin is what the holders of Gold Fields will do if, for any reason, Minorco is obliged to withdraw. They will be holding shares in a company selling on 16–18 times earnings when the next most expensive mining share in the UK is RTZ selling on a prospective multiple of nine times. The Gold Field's directors are rumoured to be down at Charlie Atlas's gym improving their weightlifting capabilities, but it's hard to see what anyone, not gifted with the power of levitation, could do to keep the shares at their present level. Thank heavens we don't have to worry about that. We don't have any. (**42. 7/3/89**)

The American courts rule against the Minorco bid but Minorco continues to hang on.

I thought you wouldn't notice if I took advantage of the Easter holiday to escape to the pleasures of Provence. Those of you who know exactly where I have been will understand my motives. And to anticipate your next question, it has never looked better! The Provencal peace was interrupted by the London broking fraternity telephoning with blow-by-blow commentaries on the ongoing Minorco/Gold Fields saga.

I told you before I left, that that situation was much more dangerous to your financial health than you probably thought it was! I said that if anything looked like preventing Minorco from going ahead with its bid, Gold Fields' shares would look very expensive, especially relative to RTZ. Just before I left, it looked as if the market was trying to talk Minorco into paying up for Gold Fields so I sold our Minorco shares as I warned you I would in my letter of the 28th February.

What happened is now history. The American courts prevented the bid from proceeding, so Gold Fields' shares fell the best part of £2 to £12.70. Minorco shares held up well since the need to pay up had obviously diminished. This enabled me to exchange our holding of Minorco at $12.75 for Gold Fields at £12.88.

At the time of writing Minorco has said it will persist. At the price I paid, a buyer of Gold Fields would get back into Minorco at a sizeable discount by accepting Minorco paper rather than cash. In a nutshell it would be like buying

Minorco for £5.50 having sold them at £7.50. As you know, I think Minorco paper is extraordinarily attractive. I salivate at the thought of owning a sizable stake in a company which most institutions are said not to own, or want to own. My belief is that the present management of Minorco is quite capable of producing the sort of earnings growth that will, in due course, convince the institutions of their shortsightedness in not giving Minorco the benefit of the doubt. In the end they will all change their minds at much the same time, just as they did recently about De Beers. I certainly don't want to be out of the stock when that happens, so if Minorco bids again I will gladly take their unfashionable paper and others can have their cash.

I find it interesting that much of the fuss about Minorco seems to be on account of their South African connections. Our revered leader, Mrs Thatcher, is at this very moment visiting southern Africa and telling much the same audience that she has detected the modern equivalent of the wind of change that SuperMac let it be known had started to blow all those years ago. She is even inviting South African leaders to tea at No.10 on the grounds that Jaw, Jaw is better than War, War. I do like contrarian! Just think how much our Anglo Americans, De Beers, Gencors and FSCOM bonds will fetch if they all become respectable investments again as a result of the changes which are now taking place in southern Africa, largely unnoticed by the foreign investment community! (45. 30/3/89)

Julian likens himself to Bertie Wooster's stunned mullet as Minorco raises its bid for Cons Gold.

Whenever Bertie Wooster was on the receiving end of an unwelcome surprise, which seemed to occur with some regularity, he was described by PG Wodehouse as having taken on the appearance of a stunned mullet. I can tell you that when Minorco increased its bid for Consolidated Gold Fields by £1.50 a share on Monday, and the shares of Consolidated Gold Fields actually fell 60p on the news to £13.30, your correspondent, if placed on a fishmonger's slab, would have been indistinguishable from a dead one!

When the market behaves in a way which is totally different to what you expect, you can't help wondering whether you really are the only one in step. Let's look at what happened. As I feared, Minorco paid up for Consolidated Gold Fields. This reduced Minorco's asset value from $20.50 to $15.40 a share. If that is not generosity almost to a fault, I do not know what is.

Assuming that Minorco will eventually sell at a 30 per cent discount to its assets, the price of Minorco cum Gold Fields is likely to be about $10.75 or £6.30. This is 15 per cent below the current level. However holders of Gold Field's shares like us can accept Minorco's bid and thereby effectively acquire Minorco shares at $5.25

or £3.10. That level represents a 66 per cent discount to Minorco's asset value! The value of Minorco's existing investment portfolio of Englehard, Inspiration and Charter would be £4.77 per share on the increased capital. We will, of course, be accepting Minorco's paper and enjoying the re-rating when it comes.

Since the American courts became involved on the 23rd March 1989, Gold Fields shares have traded well below the value of the Minorco bid because the market knows what will happen to Gold Fields' shares if its shareholders are prevented by the court from deciding for themselves whether to accept the bid on its merits. Between then and Tuesday 11th April, 8.4 per cent of Gold Fields shares have changed hands. All those who have bought them including this fund are being offered £15.50 per share by Minorco. Either we accept £15.50 and hope that the US courts can be persuaded that the Anglo American Group could not corner the gold market even if it wanted to, or we suffer a fall in our shares to £12 or below. I am sure all those who bought since 23rd March did so with the intention of accepting Minorco's bid. So far, holders of 8.4 per cent of the company's shares are in that position. In order to ensure that Minorco gets over 51 per cent acceptances, only a further 12.6 per cent of the company's shares have got to change hands. That is the equivalent of 27 million shares or 2.4 million shares a day for the remaining 12 working days of the offer. By no means an impossible target.

Of course those who have not traded Gold Field's shares recently will be equally tempted to accept £15.50 from Minorco, rather than risk seeing their shares fall to £12 or less in the market. So if it all looks so good, why have the shares gone down 60p when the offer has been increased by £1.50? The reason seems to be related to people's perceptions of the American legal system. I cannot share their pessimism in this case. Surely the Judge will see that justice is done. However if the worst came to the worst and the Courts decided against Minorco, it would simply open the door for someone else whose paper may be more acceptable to the institutional shareholders. (**46. 11/4/89**)

Minorco's pursuit of Cons Gold ends with defeat in the US courts, so it's back to the drawing board to unlock Minorco's value.

I find that running a portfolio is awfully like playing snakes and ladders. Sometimes you can't help thinking a child of six would be just as good at it! Those of you who follow the price of our units daily will know that two days before the American Judge refused to be moved, our Fund reached the top of the highest ladder encountered so far at 69.34p; a 38.6 per cent improvement on the 54p launch price of some 13 months earlier. At the time of writing we are probably about to slide down a short snake marked Gold Fields. Those of you who were looking for a setback to top up may now get your chance.

Jim Slater used to say "How can we turn a disadvantage into an advantage?" That, I hope, is what the directors of Minorco are saying to themselves this morning. I can't help wondering whether they would have gone to all this trouble and expense if they had originally thought what they wanted to buy would be whittled down to two small North American gold mines and a UK aggregate company, albeit the best one. Who knows, if Mrs Thatcher has her way and South Africa can be brought back on side by the gentle persuasion of the Downing Street carrot rather than Washington stick, in a few years time South African investors will be welcomed worldwide with open arms. As things now stand Minorco own no more or less of Gold Fields than they did when they started. By sitting tight with what they have got, they may not be worse off in the end.

Being something of a contrarian, my disappointment with the outcome was tinged with a feeling of relief. The Judge had concluded that the Anglo American Group could not be trusted not to close down Newmont's mines and so force up the price of gold and make the South African mines more profitable! You can't help admiring Gold Fields' and Newmont's powers of persuasion over the Court in this matter, just as you can't help admiring Shearson's clever assessment of the market's likely valuation of Newmont's North American assets: a valuation which could not be attacked by Minorco without undermining the value of the very investment they most wanted to sell if the bid succeeded.

In the event, this valuable package of gold mining interests was spurned by the only people who mattered, namely the North American mining companies who might have been expected to show an interest in buying them – but apparently not at current prices. Game, set and match, Shearsons!

The explanation for this apparent dichotomy lies in the fact that unsophisticated investors look upon gold shares as collectables, whereas mining companies cannot afford the luxury of buying mines which offer no prospect of giving a real return on the money used to buy them. The problem facing Minorco was that collectors have little appetite for collecting gold shares at the moment, yet at current levels the shares do not provide the returns needed to attract other mining companies. I can see trouble coming, can't you?

If Minorco had acquired Gold Fields on the agreed basis they would by now be entering a nightmare period of having to dispose of gold assets into a falling market within a 12-month time frame. Investors, who are fickle creatures, would have soon got a whiff of a forced seller. Mining company buyers would have been conspicuous by their absence. You can see why I sold our Minorco stake when it looked as if they were going to pay up. Minorco may not have liked owning a large holding in a company in which they had no control over the cashflow. As it turned out they might have been even worse placed if the judgement had gone the other way – we will never know. The whole process took much longer than anyone could have envisaged when they started. Now there is time to go back to the drawing board and consider whether there is not an even better way of spending the cash mountain and finding the "missing billions". (**51. 16/5/89**)

Hanson Trust strikes and wins the bid for Cons Gold.

There I was sitting in my "cave" in Correns, Provence, experiencing what can only be described as an underwhelming desire to put pen to paper, when an urgent message came in from the Corporate Finance Compliance Officer, reminding me of my obligations to him in the event of the underwhelming desire showing signs of abating.

Well, to be quite truthful with you, I had virtually decided not to scribble on holiday, but the more I thought about the Corporate Finance Compliance Officer and his red pencil the more I came to realise what was expected of me. What finally spurred me into action was the arrival of Friday's *Times* in which it was reported that Mr Martin Taylor, a director of Hanson Trust, when asked when Hanson first took an interest in Cons Gold said, "You have to be a caveman not to have seen Cons Gold as a bid situation as the Minorco development unfolded."

Well, as the self-appointed spokesman for cavemen I have to tell you that I too had heard rumours that Hanson was going to bid for Cons Gold but had dismissed them as symptomatic of the silly season on the grounds that Hanson would surely be reluctant to become enmeshed with Lowa Falongan politics, if not with the American courts. Furthermore I did not really believe that Minorco would want to be seen selling Cons Gold in June for less than it had been prepared to buy it for in May.

For these reasons the caveman's Fund is unrepresented in the shares of Cons Gold, Minorco and Newmont Mining, the main beneficiaries of Hanson's attentions! Sometimes I think we would be better off if we had a real live caveman running our affairs!!

All is not lost, however; we had recently been adding to our holdings in Anglo American, RTZ and English China Clays. Charter Consolidated, Johnson Matthey, Englehard and Renison were already among our larger holdings and all these benefited from the ripple effect of the bid. Furthermore Minorco will soon have £1.5 billion in the treasure chest with which to pursue its ambitions to become a "hands on" international mining company. Let's hope they decide to buy one of our "Royals" or "Ladies in Waiting", in other words one of the companies which we think offer the best long-term value in the mining field.

Of course the Minorco directors are motivated by the desire to find for their shareholders the "missing millions" which comprise the discount at which Minorco sells to its assets. Their bid for Cons Gold was originally designed to unlock some of this value, but the Hanson bid achieves much the same result and will enable Minorco to continue with the programme of rationalisation which was frustrated by the American courts.

If anyone had any doubts whether Minorco would be prepared to sell assets in order to unlock the discount, these doubts must now be dispelled. Perhaps the Hanson formula will soon be applied to Charter Consolidated.

The logic of the current situation would appear to be that if the market won't give a decent rating to Minorco because of its Lowa Falongan parentage, its shareholders, the principal two being Anglo and De Beers, would be no worse off doing their own overseas diversification. At least they would have 100 cents in every dollar working for them instead of the 75 cents they now get via Minorco. Recent events show that the directors are not averse to cash which, in extremes, can always be returned to the shareholders.

It seems to me that Minorco's decisive action over the Hanson bid for Cons Gold has cleared the log jam surrounding Minorco's longer-term ambitions. So although the shares have been substantially in the news, thus reducing the discount, I can't help thinking they should be represented in our portfolio. You can therefore expect that at some suitable moment I will swallow my pride and buy some. If Minorco is going to make a sizeable acquisition, there will no doubt be opportunities to do so. Meanwhile ... back to the wine making! (**56. 27/6/89**)

Hanson begins the break-up of Cons Gold, starting with Newmont Mining.

Readers will know that it has been a constant refrain in these weekly letters that there is nothing magic about mining gold – as opposed to mining base metals. Mining men could not care less what they mine as long as they can do so at sufficient profit to keep themselves gainfully employed and their shareholders happy.

It is the investing public who invest gold mines with almost mystical qualities. It does not seem to worry them that there is little prospect of their favourite gold mining companies earning enough during their remaining lives to recoup the cost of buying them in the first place. It is as if people who buy gold shares think they know something about the future behaviour of gold which has escaped the notice of people who buy the metal itself. In my experience there is no evidence whatsoever that they ever do, or ever will. After all, why should they?

Oh to be a fly on Lord Hanson's wall as he negotiates with the gold mining companies who come to see him hoping to buy his stake in Newmont Mining! No doubt he will be reminding them of what they know already, namely that the Carlin Gold Belt is the best bit of gold real estate outside South Africa and that the best real estate does not come cheap.

Oh to be a fly on the wall of the gold mining companies when they approach their bankers for funds to make the acquisition. Finally I would like to be a fly on the wall when the Finance Directors of the bidding companies point out what could happen to their own earnings if they pay too much, in order to own the prize they are all seeking. Not only do they have to get a sufficient return to repay their bankers, but they need to have enough left over to reward their shareholders in whose name, after all, they are taking the ultimate risk. If I suggested to you that a real return of 10 per cent should be adequate to recompense all concerned, it would tie in quite closely with the return CRA says it looks for when it invests its shareholder's money in new projects. Is a lesser return realistic when there is so much to lose if things go wrong?

We have been doing some calculations which may help to place a fair valuation on Newmont Gold, by far the most important investment of Newmont Mining. Newmont Mining, you will recall, is the key which unlocks the value of Hanson's bid for Cons Gold. What we have done is to work out what price Newmont Gold should stand at in order to provide another mining company with a 10 per cent real return, using a long-term gold price of $350/oz. The answer comes to $12.82 compared with today's price of Newmont Gold of $37! We have calculated that, taking gold at $350/oz, the sustainable annual net profit per ounce is $87.5 or $157.5 million, on future production of 1.8 million ounces a year. In the first six months of 1989, Newmont Gold earned $44 million on production of 643,000 ounces, an after tax profit of $69/oz.

You may be interested to know that in order for Phelps Dodge to earn $157.5 million p.a., the copper price would only have to average 82.5 cents/lb which is nearly 40 per cent lower than it is today, whereas, of course, the gold price needed for Newmont Gold to earn the same amount of money is only 4 per cent lower than it is today. (**64. 22/9/89**)

Julian gets involved in a gold trust launched to replace Cons Gold holdings.

For the past week or so I have been helping to market a new gold investment trust being launched by Capels and Flemings. The idea behind the Trust is that a UK quoted replacement for their holdings in Consolidated Gold Fields could well appeal to the institutions. The marketing coincided with the recent drop in the gold price. Despite the fact that gold and gold shares have fallen severely and are now closer to the bargain basement than they were in January, the institutions almost to a man, have now become very bearish, usually a reliable sign that we are close to a low. Come back private clients, all is forgiven! Private clients don't care about quarterly performance. (**89. 4/4/90**)

Gold Fields (of South Africa) begins a corporate rationalisation of its gold mines, much to Julian's chagrin – leading him to muse on the attractions of these gold mine marginals to American Barrick.

Finally, the terms for Kloof's acquisition of our holdings of Libanon and Venterspost have been published. They are nine Kloof for every 100 Libanon shares and six Kloof for every 100 Venterspost. In the last month or so Libanon has risen 28 per cent to 32p and Venterspost by 57 per cent to 22p reflecting this bid.

I do not wish to appear ungrateful but, these two companies between them have 6.5 million ounces of gold in the ground which Kloof shareholders are buying for US$45 million, or for US$7 per ounce, causing them a dilution of a mere 5 per cent. The will save US$25 million in capital costs for new pumps and US$18 million per annum thereafter in operating those pumps, to say nothing of the tax losses carried by these companies. Kloof has some 29 million ounces of gold in the ground so it is increasing its gold in the ground by 22 per cent. What a bargain for those who profess to have faith in a rising gold price!

If only I could persuade American Barrick or someone of that ilk to counter-bid. By doing so they would increase their gold in the ground by 24 per cent for a dilution of a mere 1.1 per cent in their capital, and they could use their forward sales to make both mines profitable from the word go.

I say "if only" because if they did counter-bid, Kloof, or its parent, Gold Fields of South Africa, would have to pay up or face losing two mines from their stable in one hit. That would never do!

Foreign mining companies are now quite prepared to do deals in the former Soviet Union but they are not prepared to pay even a silly price for South African assets so long as that country's political future is unsettled. That is why we will probably have to make do with what we have been offered. Our holdings of 4.1 per cent of Libanon and 5.8 per cent of Venterspost are just not large enough to carry much clout, but even so I am seriously considering voting against the resolutions just to show we care. (**182. 30/7/92**)

More corporate activity in the South African gold mining industry in both the Gold Fields and Randgold groups.

In another move, Gold Fields agreed to sell its small unprofitable mine, Doornfontein, to Blyvoors, having at last come to the conclusion that it would not be getting its management fee for much longer if the Doornfontein mine went bust. Gold Fields' management skills would be far better occupied improving the financial returns of its major holdings in Driefontein and Kloof, to say nothing of Northam, its ailing platinum mine. Is it too much to hope that logic will be allowed to prevail and that Gold Fields will now agree to allow the merger of its Deelkraal mine, in which we have a sizeable shareholding against all conventional wisdom, with the neighbouring Elandsrand mine? No, this dull gold price is forcing reality on not just the Mineworkers Union but also on the mine owners.

Meanwhile, there are some encouraging signs that the changes Randgold instituted in its management structures at our behest are starting to bear fruit. This is most important since the rest of the industry is watching with bated breath to see if Randgold can succeed in turning round what was generally seen as a rat-bag of loss making mines. The jury is still out, but one of their mines, Harmony, has now returned to the dividend list! Blyvoors has acquired Doornfontein, giving both the chance of a new lease of life. And Durban Deep which they have now amalgamated with neighbouring Rand Leases, is in severe danger of making a profit! Only ERPM is keeping everyone awake at night worrying whether it can survive. The management of each of these mines know their salvation lies in their own hands. If they fail, there go their incentive bonuses! If they succeed, they can look forward to a comfortable future. In the effort to survive, the decks have been cleared. Gone or going, are the little luxuries of life. Gone, literally, is Head Office. Overheads have been cut to the barest necessities, even subscriptions to the World Gold Council have been cancelled! (**308. 10/8/95**)

15. Epilogue – the New Millennium

When Julian Baring announced that he was stepping down from the day-to-day running of the Gold and General fund in late 1996 it was the end of an era, although he remained active in promoting Mercury's suite of mining funds and contributing to the Newsletter for a couple more years. However, Julian had planned carefully for the time when he would take a back seat. As he said then, "When I joined Mercury in 1991, I promised I would establish the finest Mining Team that could be assembled to look after your interests. That promise has been fulfilled. A team of highly qualified and experienced people are in place who know a great deal more about the industry than I do."

A year later Merrill Lynch bought Mercury Asset Management, and in 2006 what then had become Merrill Lynch Asset Management was acquired by Black Rock, the largest Fund Management group in the world. Many of the team that Julian had assembled continue to work for the Black Rock commodity equity section which runs a number of mining and natural resource funds, with the Gold and General Fund and the World Mining Trust still very much to the fore. The team has remained remarkably stable over the years with Evy Hambro and Richard Davis having clocked up in the region of 20 years managing the Funds. Of the other early assistants to Julian, David Baker and Trevor Steel left to set up their own Fund Management group in 2001 and Geoff Campbell left a year later to return to the industry as a director of DRD Gold. Graham Birch, who had taken over the mantle from Julian as overall head of the Fund Management Team at Mercury, effectively retired from Black Rock in 2009.

In certain areas the team continued to support some of Julian's old pet issues, particularly gold hedging, but inevitably it also had its own furrows to plough. One of those related to Gold and General's traditional emphasis within the portfolio on South African gold shares. The meteoric rise in the gold price in 1980 to over $800 ignited a surge in gold exploration around the world, much of it away from South Africa – at that time still the largest gold producer. The process of gold exploration and then mine development was a long one and it was not until the mid 1980s that production started to rise, a trend that was to accelerate during the 1990s. Throughout this period South African production *fell sharply, from 22 million ounces in 1980 to 14 million ounces in 2000, a trend that has continued to this day. It was Julian's belief that following the first universal elections in South Africa in 1994 South African gold shares, then largely valued on the basis of their dividend yields, would begin to attract general foreign investor interest, thereby pushing up their ratings. At the same time he expected that direct foreign interest in investing in South African mining development would increase rapidly.*

In the event it was one of the few big theories that failed to go Julian's way as corporate mergers reduced the number of South African gold stocks available, and persistently low margins reduced output and profitability. This created both a problem and an opportunity for Graham Birch and his colleagues – Gold and General's historic bias towards South Africa as far as gold shares were concerned would have to change. This trend has continued since the 1990s, when South Africa was 50 per cent of the portfolio, until today when it is barely 3 per cent.

The Fund spreads its wings

For most of the period since President Nixon closed the Gold Window in 1971 and ushered in the modern era of gold, Fund Managers running mining sector money travelled to South Africa to assess trends in the gold mining industry, and Julian made a number of such trips. But the expanding mining team at Mercury increasingly found themselves in some strange places as the South African industry declined and new opportunities opened up elsewhere. Indeed, in 1991 Julian had himself joined a Canadian broker's trip to the US.

Last week I visited a number of gold mines in Nevada, courtesy of Bunting Warburg. Since the Bunting Warburg tour included some of the most highly esteemed gold mining companies like American Barrick and Newmont Gold, which I like but have never been able to afford, I could not resist the opportunity to take up their kind invitation. As a wine producer, I tried not to regard the visit they arranged to the Napa Valley at the end of our tour as an additional incentive to leave these shores. As it is I am glad I went since the tour was one of the best organised series of mine visits in which I have participated. (**153. 16/10/91**)

In 1993 Julian was in Ghana for the opening of the Iduapriem gold mine and in 1994 he attended the Gold Conference in Kalgoorlie, where he recalled amongst other things his earlier Ghanaian visit.

You will have long forgotten that in Newsletter 208 of 25th February 1993 I tried to describe the opening of a gold mine in Ghana which you and I, as unitholders in this Fund, had helped to finance. The mine was the Iduapriem Mine of Golden Shamrock, a small and successful Australian company, the shares of which have risen 200 per cent since we bought them.

The main reason why I made such a song and dance about it was to alert Australian investors who had become so preoccupied with what was going on in their own backyard that they failed to hear the jungle drums' message. The message was that a small team of Australian miners had done something important in the steamy rain forests of Africa.

Having just attended the second Gold Conference in Kalgoorlie I can now understand why the message never got through. There is so much prospecting activity going on in Western Australia that it is not at all surprising that all eyes and ears are focused on the sand-covered outback.

The only throbbing sensation to be felt in Kalgoorlie last week was in the heads of the delegates the morning after the night before. With so many prospecting successes to celebrate during the last year, it would be churlish to criticise an occasional bout of over-indulgence. I remember making a solemn pact with some British "journos" as they are affectionately known in Australia – that I wouldn't tell tales, if they didn't!

So much prospecting activity made me wonder why a section of the mining community felt so hard done by. A number of the speakers warned that unless part of the legislation under which the mining industry had to operate, particularly with regard to aboriginal land rights, was not modified in their favour the industry would soon be forced to follow the example of its American counterpart and concentrate its efforts off-shore. None suggested that South Africa might be the place to go. Perhaps if South Africa adopted the Australian mining laws, there would be as much prospecting activity there as there is in Australia with all that would entail for employment and foreign investment. **(247. 17/3/94)**

By the time Julian retired in the late 1990s the managers of the Gold and General Fund were ranging far and wide in pursuit of new gold companies to replace the fading giants of South Africa. As an example, for many years the Fund's largest holding was Buenaventura, whose main interest was the Yanacocha gold mine in Peru, one of the largest in the world with annual production running at over 3 million ounces in the mid 1990s. Today output is barely half that level and Buenaventura no longer features in Gold and General's portfolio. One of the early visits to Peru and South America was by Graham Birch in March 1995 with the Yanacocha mine the first port of call.

Anyone who as a child remembers digging for gold in the garden will know that gold deposits are located where the Almighty put them and not necessarily where we would want them to be! Visiting gold deposits therefore almost always involves arduous journeys to far flung "difficult to get to" places, well off the beaten track. With this in mind, you should not be surprised therefore to hear that this week's newsletter comes not from London but from Cajamarca, Peru.

> Cajamarca is a medium sized town about 800 km north of Lima. Set at an altitude of 2,000 metres, Cajamarca is famous for its mountains, cows, milk, cheese and hot springs. As the aircraft makes its final approach you could almost imagine that you were about to land in Switzerland. The illusion is shattered once on the ground. Despite the beautiful setting, Cajamarca is clearly not a "first world" town. The muddy pot-holed streets are lined with peasants selling all manner of local produce. Barefoot children rush up to your car as soon as you park vying for the privilege of guarding it while you are gone – in exchange for loose change. The buildings are shabby and in need of attention.

It would be easy to write off Cajamarca as just one more Andean town struggling for survival. Yet this would be wrong. If you were observant you might notice in Cajamarca a few smart new 4WD jeeps cruising around. You might discover that the best hotels and restaurants are fully booked. You might hear English being spoken in the bars, by hairy men wearing Newmont or Barrick baseball caps. This is because Cajamarca is fast turning into one of the world's top gold mining towns. Most importantly, Cajamarca is the base for Minera Yanacocha, a gold mining joint venture between Newmont (38 per cent), Buenaventura (32.3 per cent), BRGM (24.7 per cent) and IFC (5 per cent). Your Fund has significant investments in the first two of these companies, so when Buenaventura offered me the chance of visiting the mine I jumped at it. (**287. 8/3/95**)

With the sale of UK reserve gold by the Labour Government, starting in 1999 and ending in 2002 (of which more later), the bottom of the long gold bear market was signalled and the Gold and General team began the process of looking for new investment opportunities, as interest in the yellow metal started to increase. Two of the areas that caught the team's eye were Russia and China, the latter now the largest producer in the world.

Richard Davis made the team's first visit to Russia in 1999 to check out the Fund's then sole Russian gold holding, Buryatzoloto in Siberia, and its Zun-Holba mine.

The Fund's holding in Buryatzoloto was initiated in 1996 following the company's privatisation in 1994. Since then Buryatzoloto has invested more than US$25m on upgrading its mines. The trip to Zun-Holba confirmed our prejudices – that the company's management is capable of meeting its targets. Indeed, Buryatzoloto's achievement is all the more commendable in light of the financial crisis affecting the country, and of course, the tragedy of last year's helicopter crash.

Helped by a weaker rouble, and the commissioning of the new CIP plant, Buryatzoloto reported an impressive set of results for the first quarter of 1999. The company earned US$1.18 million, which may not sound much, but annualising its quarterly profits puts the stock on an attractive PE of 2.3 times. We won't be selling the stock at these prices, and look forward to reaping the benefits of the investment in due course.

The level of hospitality at Zun-Holba seems to have even surpassed what would have been expected in the more traditional stamping ground of South Africa.

Salt mines and gulags – for many people these enduring images of Siberia are not exactly inviting. But the hospitality of our hosts was as warm as a Siberian winter is cold. In the evening, we attended a traditional Buryat feast on the banks of an icy mountain lake. The dinner featured several local delicacies, including different types of fishes, some of which were natives of Lake Baikal. In typical Russian fashion, numerous toasts were made during the meal, all of which were accompanied by the ubiquitous shot of vodka. The toasts were closely monitored by the Buryats to ensure that abstinence was not an option. (**437. 25/6/99**)

Three years later (in 2002) the Team reviewed the Fund's spreading wings in the end of year Newsletter.

On the "plus" side of the equation, we have added over twenty new names to the portfolio. This is partly to compensate for the consolidation going on in the industry, partly to spread our risks as the Fund has grown and partly to increase exposure to the "up-and-coming" stocks in the gold sector. When looking at all of these new holdings in the Fund several key themes emerge:

Russian exposure. Investors may recall our earlier foray into Russia (via the ill-fated Star Mining) and wonder if we are mad to add to holdings. In fact we've never been away from Russia and have always had a position in the emerging producer Buryatzoloto. In 2002 we added to our holding in this company by building up a stake in High River Gold – Buryatzoloto's parent. In addition we subscribed for the flotation of two promising AIM listed Russian gold mining companies Peter Hambro Mining and Highland Gold. Our interest in Russia stems from the fact that it appears to have the highest growth potential of any gold mining region of the world that we know of. In our view the value of this growth potential in the context of a shrinking global gold industry outweighs the rather obvious risks embedded in the equities. The real problem in Russia is a shortage of suitable investment opportunities hence our exposure to the region is only just over three per cent of the Fund.

Chinese exposure. Until very recently it was impossible to gain exposure to Chinese gold. However, like Russia, there is great latent potential. Although insignificant to the Fund (<1 per cent), we now have two holdings, Sinogold and Southwestern Gold.

Exposure to "up-and-coming" small producers. With a higher gold price, the small miners (<250,000oz/yr) have a more favourable environment in which to grow both from an operational and a capital markets perspective. Following on from the industry consolidation, smaller companies have opportunities to acquire assets which are surplus to the requirements of the mega-gold miners. Furthermore, there is a clear pick-up in greenfield exploration. Examples of such companies are EAGC (merging with Bema), Eldorado Gold (producer in Brazil, developer in Turkey), Thistle Mining (operator in the Free State), Bendigo (re-developing the Bendigo gold field in Victoria), Croesus (bought some of WMC's gold mines), Kingsgate (developed a gold mine in Thailand), Oxiana (developing a gold mine in Laos), Afrikander Lease (developing a gold mine in South Africa). Altogether these companies add up to just under 4 per cent of the Fund a figure which will hopefully grow. (**482. 19/12/02**)

In October 2004 Richard Davis was back in Russia to attend the tenth anniversary of the opening of the Pokrovskoye gold mine in the Amur region, then the main asset of Peter Hambro Mining (now Petropavlovsk PLC). The level of hospitality seems not to have flagged since the Siberian visit five years before but in the interim Gold and General's exposure to Russia had expanded to half a dozen stocks, representing around 11 per cent of the portfolio by value; the category also includes stocks with operations in the republics of the former Soviet Union.

"Last month I was invited to Russia to celebrate the 10th anniversary of the Pokrovskoye gold mine. The mine is the key asset of Peter Hambro Mining plc (PHM) and is located in the Amur region in the far eastern part of the Russian Federation. To get there we first travelled to Moscow and then to Blagoveshchensk, an eight-hour flight more or less due east of Russia's capital. From Blagoveshchensk, which means "Good News", we travelled northwest for 320 km through the seemingly endless forests of larch, fir and birch to Pokrovskoye.

Following an inspection of the plant, we joined the mine's workforce in the celebrations. The festivities were splendid, befitting the company's considerable achievements since raising venture capital to fund the feasibility study on the mine a decade ago. The mine staged a concert, which included acts by a number of famous (in Russia) singers, dancers and musicians. There was also a magician who was quite useful at making things "disappear". Fortunately for the shareholders he didn't come with us to the gold room. Later, our hosts laid on a banquet, where the presence of several top ranking officials was testament to the importance of the mine to the Amur economy, as was the number of vodka-charged toasts.

We also visited Pioneer, PHM's next cab off the rank, which is located 40km from Pokrovskoye and is shaping up to be a high quality orebody. This year, Pokrovskoye will drive PHM's production to over 200,000 ounces at an enviable cash cost of US$105/oz – although based on the impressive results for the six-month period to June this could be conservative. In 2003, Russia was the fifth-largest gold producer, after China, with 182 tonnes. It has been estimated that by 2008, production could rise to as much as 265 tonnes with PHM contributing to this growth. At this level, Russia would challenge Australia as the world's second-largest producer. By contrast, output from many of the other major producing nations is in decline. Operating costs are also lower. Troika Dialog, the Russian broker, estimates total cash costs for Russian producers in 2003 were US$173/oz, while costs for other global producers were north of US$200/oz. Russia also has a huge, largely untapped resource base, estimated at between 26,000 and 35,000 tonnes with reserves up to 15,000 tonnes second only to South Africa. **(494. 1/11/04)**

Earlier that year team newcomer Catherine May had been dispatched to Kyrgyzstan to visit Canadian miner Centerra's Kumtor gold mine, a 4 per cent portfolio holding. Catherine was less fortunate than Richard in that hospitality was the least of her problems.

When told that I was to visit the Kumtor gold mine in Kyrgyzstan, my initial reaction was one of trepidation. But in the name of research, I swallowed my fear and ventured where no team-member had ever gone before. Kumtor is situated in northeastern Kyrgyzstan, near the Chinese border. At an elevation of over 4,000 metres, the air tends to be a little thin, so prior to making our ascent we were given a medical and warned about the dangers of altitude sickness. Sitting there at 8 o'clock in the morning suffering the effects of some dodgy food in Uzbekistan, the doctor described the symptoms of altitude sickness. As he went through the list I began to panic; nausea, dry mouth, headaches, drowsiness ... I had them all and we hadn't even started our ascent! Packed with every type of medicine, we headed off on the six-hour drive, past the crystal clear waters of Lake Issyk-Kul (the world's second-largest mountain lake) and up through the mountains to Kumtor. As we approached the mine, the sight was awe-inspiring. Set between two glaciers, surrounded by snow-capped peaks and carved out of the side of the mountain, Kumtor's open-pit was the stuff of legends. After a tour of the mine, the processing plant and front row seats at the day's gold pour, I was giddy with wonder – or maybe it was just the lack of oxygen. (**494.1/11/04**)

In April of 2004 Graham Birch visited China, where the Fund had built up holdings in three direct Chinese gold plays. Whether the hospitality that his colleagues received in Russia was repeated in China Graham does not relate!

Zijin Mining (3.2 per cent) is a new entrant to the Fund's "top 10" and out of the three "real Chinese" gold companies in our Fund it is the one which has the most aggressive growth profile. The picture below shows the Zijinshan gold mine in Fujian province – which we visited in April. This is Zijin's flagship operation and it is the largest open-pit gold mine in China. Zijin has four operating mines in "growth mode" and 2004 will see a ramp up of production at the Shuiyindong mine in Guizhou province. This mine is next to Sinogold's Jinfeng project – scheduled to enter production in early 2006. Zijin is in a superb position to grow in the fragmented Chinese gold mining industry. There are some 1,500 gold mines in China – many of which have not been properly explored and have only limited access to capital. We expect Zijin to be a consolidator and in April, Zijin said "We expect to report a batch of new gold and copper mine acquisitions in our interim report." With 2003 output of 345,000 ounces, we expect Zijin to be catapulted into the FT Gold Mines Index at the next review. (**492. 28/5/04**)

Writing at the end of 2003 (ahead of Graham Birch's visit) the Gold and General gold team, including Richard Davis and Evy Hambro, flagged their growing interest in China both as a gold producer and as an emerging source of quoted gold stocks. The comments are very prescient and so very much in the tradition of Julian Baring.

It's a little known fact that China is the world's fourth-largest gold producer – behind only South Africa, the USA and Australia. Yet most gold mining analysts know almost nothing about the Chinese gold mining industry and still less about the leading companies in the nascent Chinese gold mining sector. The reasons for this profound ignorance relate to the poor development of the Chinese capital markets. Until mid 2003 there were no Chinese quoted gold stocks and few ways in which our gold Funds could participate in this part of the world.

Given that lean mean workers in China, say, are putting in longer harder hours than fat happy workers in France or Germany, it should not be surprising that manufacturers are switching production to China and that China's economy is growing at a far faster rate. Per capita GDP is improving and therefore stimulating domestic demand for many ordinary day-to-day items. As people get richer they have more disposable income to deploy on non-essential items like gold jewellery. According to Gold Fields Mineral Services, China's jewellery industry consumed 194 tonnes of gold in 2003 – equivalent to a mere 0.15 grammes per capita (worth about $1.9 per person). This is a lot lower than comparable emerging markets. In our view as China's per capita GDP rises, this gold consumption has the potential to rise exponentially. If it does, then China could become a net importer of gold – despite the fact that it is the world's fourth-largest producer. (2003 mine output was about 210 tonnes). China seems to want to encourage this process and has recently proposed eliminating the 5 per cent sales tax on gold jewellery sales – a move which further de-regulates the market and can only have the effect of stimulating demand. (**490. 17/12/03**)

A few months after the Chinese visit Graham Birch once more drew attention to the rising importance of the expansion of the Chinese gold mining industry, where the Fund's exposure was increasing.

"Although few gold funds paid much attention at the time, one of the most important events to occur in the gold share market last year may well have been the birth of the Chinese gold sector. Three domestic miners; Zhongjin, Shandong and Zijin were listed in 2003 and all of them got off to a good start in the market; China has therefore "arrived" in the global gold equity sector, although this fact has yet to be recognised by the FT Gold Mines Index. The creation of listed Chinese gold miners is well overdue. China is the fourth largest gold producer in the world (producing over 200 tonnes per annum). Only South Africa, the USA and Australia produce more gold than China. Furthermore, China is playing an increasing role on the demand side too, with consumption of around 220 tonnes/year. For the Fund, therefore, we believe it is vital that we have at least some exposure to what promises to be a fascinating segment of the marketplace." (**493. 23/7/04**

Company	Listed	per cent fund	New Mines?	Profit trend	Div Yield
Newcrest	Australia	8.2	•••	+++	0.5 per cent
Harmony	S Africa	8.1	••	+	1.1 per cent
Placer Dome	Canada	7.8	••	+	0.7 per cent
AngloGold Ashanti	S Africa	6.5	•	+	3.6 per cent
Buenaventura	Peru	6.0	•	+	1.5 per cent
Gold Fields	S Africa	5.2	••	++	1.4 per cent
Newmont	USA	5.0	••	+	0.7 per cent
Lihir	PNG	3.4	None	Same	None
Fujian Zijin	China	3.2	••	+	3.1 per cent
Penoles	Mexico	2.8	•	++	0.6 per cent
Total		56.2			

Source: MLIM

In July 2013 the portfolio looked like this:–

Company	Listed	Main operations	per cent fund
Randgold Resources	UK	West/Central Africa	8.6
Franco Nevada	Canada	North America, Australia, Africa	8.0
Goldcorp	Canada	North/Central/South America, Mexico	7.6
Fresnillo	UK	Mexico	6.1
Eldorado Gold	Canada	Turkey, Greece, China, Brazil	5.8
Newcrest Mining	Australia	Australia, PNG	4.7
New Gold	Canada	North America, Australia, Mexico	3.9
Yamana Gold	Canada	Brazil	3.5
Industrias Penoles	Mexico	Mexico	3.0
Polyus Gold	UK	Russia	2.8
Total			54.0

The 2013 portfolio had only one stock in common – Penoles – with the 2004 portfolio, and the South African content had fallen away to just 3 per cent, having been over 20 per cent, with none of the holdings in the top ten stocks. The other thing to note is that many of the Fund's holdings are listed/incorporated in quite different countries from where they actually operate, partly as a result of the revival in London's role in financing mining projects.

Recurring themes

While the Fund changed materially over the years following Julian Baring's retirement, the new and then changing team remained true to a number of Julian's key Newsletter themes. In August 2005 (the 500th edition of the Newsletter) Graham Birch summarised what he called the "recurring themes".

RECURRING THEME #1 – HEDGING

Over the years there have been several themes which have cropped up again and again. Chief amongst these has been hedging of gold by mining companies – a practice that we always opposed. At a basic level we felt that hedging creates an underlying conflict of interest between shareholders of a company (who want gold exposure) and executives (who prefer a quiet life). Julian used to call this the "School Fees Syndrome"; as shareholders we are best able to pay our school fees if gold rises, whereas by hedging the executives can pay their school fees regardless of price. We also felt that hedging sent a bad signal to the market as to what gold producers really felt about the price trend of their main product. If the producers felt that the price was going to fall then why would investors or Central Banks want to hold the stuff? Furthermore, the very act of hedging resulted in gold which had not yet been produced being sold into the spot market with a corresponding negative impact on prices.

RECURRING THEME #2 – WHAT YOU PAY & WHAT YOU GET

While some investors seem to look at gold shares as if they are casino chips we try to look at them as investments. In order for the investment to be a good one then the returns must exceed the price paid. As buying a gold share is tantamount to buying gold which has not yet been mined the most important variables are therefore the number of ounces in the ground, the cost of getting them out and the prevailing gold price. In order for this Fund to prosper, we need to make sure that what we are paying for the ounces is less than the profit margin achievable by mining them. This is so obvious that it is amazing that most gold share buyers don't bother to do the sums and prefer instead to look at production growth rates or sensitivity to gold price.

Recurring Theme #3 – Lobster Pots

Some readers may recall Eike Batista, the flamboyant CEO of the gold miner TVX (since merged with Kinross). It was he who first coined the expression "Blah Blah ounces" to describe gold resources which are even more uncertain than "possible" resources never mind the better defined "proven & probable" reserves. He also described to us a category of reserves that he called "Soon To Be Discovered" or STBD gold. Batista knew that at certain stages of the cycle, investors get so enthusiastic about exploration that they will pay more <u>per ounce</u> for the exciting STBD gold than for the dull proven/probable. Companies with vast amounts of STBD gold abound on markets like AIM or the Canadian Ventures Exchange. The brokers who deal in such stocks can always help us to "build a position" by arranging private placements. This makes the stocks easy to get into but when it comes to getting out of them the brokers are rarely so helpful – especially if the drilling proved unsuccessful. We christened these easy to enter/hard to exit stocks "Lobster Pots" for obvious reasons. While investors in the Fund may not appreciate it, we have saved a fortune by not putting much of your capital into lobster pots like Bre-X.

Recurring Theme #4 – Politics and Geography

The Newsletters have not shied away from politics. We will criticise any government policies which appear to take money out of the Fund's pocket and place it into somebody else's. The biggest such changes over the span of these Newsletters have taken place in South Africa where miners have had to adapt to a changing political environment involving BEE and nationalisation of mineral rights. Soon they will face royalties. We have made our views known on such matters both verbally and in print. Other countries too have shown periodic hostility to the mining sector and in truth the industry is a sitting duck as a mine can't "up sticks" and go. Shareholders though can do just that, and if governments believe that bad legislation can be enacted without capital providers noticing they are mistaken.

Recurring Theme #5 – The Gold Price

It's no surprise that the topic which recurred most in these 500 Newsletters was the gold price itself. Unfortunately much of this commentary was wrong – we were too bullish. For years we watched aghast as hedge funds shorted, miners hedged, Central Banks dumped and super-bears like Andy Smith predicted ever lower prices. We didn't believe that gold in real terms would go as low as it did and that having done so it could stay depressed for long. This over-optimism though probably didn't hurt your Fund returns too adversely. In constructing the portfolio we try not to lose sight of the fact that the price of gold might not go up and indeed might fall. This makes our job hard – the need to balance risk and reward.

We have to ensure that there is enough gold exposure to satisfy expectations but not so much that a price fall could wipe out the Fund. We also have to try and deliver an acceptable long-term rate of return. (**500. 29/8/05**)

The gold price, gold shares and Beta

In 2003 Evy Hambro explained the Fund's strategy with regard to balancing portfolio returns and risk – the Beta of the portfolio.

Over the years we have spent many hours explaining our trade to investors. The key message has always been based on the merits of gold exposure in a portfolio. The typical themes of portfolio diversification, lack of correlation, safe haven asset class, etc. are commonplace when talking about "What gold can do for you". Those who have listened to us extol these rare qualities might well be patting themselves on the back right now given the performance of gold, and the Fund, during the last few years.

As well as lessons on gold bullion we have also tried to educate people on the drivers for gold equities. Many of the characteristics associated with bullion mentioned above run true for gold shares, after all they are exposed to the underlying gold price via the revenue line (assuming management has not speculated on the gold price via the derivatives market). The following chart highlights the traditional relationship between the price of gold and the valuations applied to gold shares by the stock market.

The correlation between the two variables is probably one of the best positive relationships of any two financial variables. After all when gold rises gold producers should make more money!

With the evolution of financial markets investors and bankers have sought out ever more complex ways of trying to reduce risk and optimise return. Often the clever people behind this work are known as "rocket scientists" due to their understanding of mathematics way beyond that required by most people other than rocket scientists themselves.

When breaking down such relationships into component parts they often manage to boggle the minds of mere mortals with reams of numeric information. In an effort to try and prevent this from happening some clever people thought it best to classify the data into something more friendly. Why they chose the ancient Greek alphabet no one knows.

Anyway to cut a long story short one of the aims we have as managers of the Fund is to try and deliver the best possible returns from investing in the gold sector. We do this by trying to build as much risk adjusted gold exposure as possible into the portfolio i.e. gold exposure at the right price. This relationship between the gold price and the Fund is known as the Beta of the portfolio i.e. the amount the Fund is expected to change by in value terms for a given change in the underlying gold price. Obviously we are limited in this process by the fact that we do not use derivatives or gold bullion in the process.

During the last few years we are proud to have achieved a highly cost effective gold Beta for the Fund. This can be seen in the table below. It shows the change in the value of the Fund compared with the gold price and the FT Gold Mines Index (the Benchmark).

	6 Mths*	1 Year*	3 Yrs*	5 Yrs*
MLG&G	14.4 per cent	101.5 per cent	121.5 per cent	171.9 per cent
Benchmark	5.1 per cent	54.2 per cent	37.7 per cent	20.8 per cent
Gold Bullion	8.0 per cent	24.0 per cent	18.0 per cent	18.7 per cent

* % change in US$ to end December 2002. Fund Price on bid to bid basis. Source: Datastream

What is noticeable from the most recent data is how the Beta has slipped both for the Fund and for gold equities. The loss of Beta in the Fund can in part be explained by the loss of Beta for gold shares and given this change it is remarkable how well the Fund has performed.

In the last Newsletter we highlighted some of the new holdings in the Fund. A common characteristic of these companies was the high levels of Gold Beta they enjoyed as well as the compelling investment rationale.

All in all we are very comfortable with the allocation of the Fund. The relative value that is available in the gold equity sector today is fully reflected in the Fund and should Beta come back from holiday anytime soon the Fund should be a big beneficiary. (483. 8/2/03)

The Fund has a swing at Gordon Brown

In the next section we hear the Team's view on South African politics but in April 2007 Graham Birch had a swing at a target much nearer to home, Chancellor Gordon Brown, following a Freedom of Information battle with the UK Treasury.

The sound of loudly flapping wings was to be heard in Downing Street this month as the chickens came home to roost at the home of Gordon Brown – Chancellor of the Exchequer for the past ten years. Poor old Gordon Brown has been getting "flak" recently for his decision around a decade ago to impose a "stealth tax" on the pension pots of Britain's savers by scrapping tax relief on dividends. Now, as the cumulative effect of this policy bites hard, people are beginning to feel impoverished and are looking for a scapegoat. After a long battle the Treasury has finally capitulated to the Freedom of Information Act and published the contemporary notes on the decision. It would seem that many of Gordon's advisers anticipated that impoverishment might be the end result and warned the government of this. Nonetheless, Gordon remains unrepentant despite the fact that from the vantage point of history his decision looks awful.

Of course long-term holders of the Gold and General will know that another of Gordon's early mistakes (1999) was to sell roughly half of Britain's gold reserves – equivalent to about 400 tonnes. So keen was Gordon to dump the gold onto an already depressed market that he successfully "rang the bell" for the bottom of one of the longest bear phases in gold history – the nadir coming on one Spring morning in 2001 when the UK sold some 804,000 ounces of the citizen's gold for a measly US$254/oz – representing a 22-year low in the market price. The trough in the gold price between May 1999 and the sale completion in 2001 is now referred to in the gold trade as "Brown's Bottom".

In the case of the gold sale we don't need to invoke the Freedom of Information Act to discover the advice that was given to Brown. It was common knowledge at the time that the Bank of England opposed the sale. Furthermore the press was full of hostility and delegations from gold producing countries were swiftly dispatched to London to complain at the social impact that the sale might have on communities in places such as South Africa. There were plenty of critics to listen to but none of this cut any ice with Brown and the sale went ahead.

Obviously this gold would be worth a lot more today (circa U$5 billion more), and the government's strategy of switching out of gold and into US dollars, Euros and Yen on a 40:40:20 ratio has been unsuccessful from a portfolio management perspective. Apology from Brown? Not a bit of it – in fact from time to time over the years he has even called upon the IMF to follow his lead and implement a gold disposal programme of its own. Thus far the IMF has declined to follow his advice and has a stronger balance sheet as a consequence. (**10/4/07**)

The future of South Africa

The issue of politics in South Africa has been a theme of the Newsletter since the inception of the Fund in 1988, just before FW de Klerk became President and changed the face of South African politics forever. Julian Baring tried to take the optimistic view as the new political dispensation in South Africa was rolled out, but the medium-term reality was more worrying, as Evy Hambro wrote in August 2002.

For many years now investors in South Africa's mining sector have been coming to terms with the likely rationalisation of the country's imperialistic mining code. This outdated and old-fashioned legislation has stood still for decades despite most other countries refining their own codes to keep up with the subtleties of modern day business. In addition, to meet the objectives of the constitution of the New South Africa, the mineral wealth of the country has to be opened up to all rather than remain concentrated in the hands of a few. These objectives were combined into what became known as the "use it or lose it" framework. As a whole the concept was accepted by the country's mining companies but recent developments in the path to achieving this goal have alarmed those exposed to this sector.

Last year the South African Department of Minerals and Energy Affairs (SADMEA) issued a draft of the proposed new Minerals and Petroleum Resources Development Bill. This "first position" document caused much consternation amongst the leaders of the mining sector. The main point of contention was the amount of discretion afforded to the Minister when awarding mining licences, and the lack of a framework for recourse for those who felt aggrieved by the Minister's final decision. However over the following months management from the mining sector met with the Minister and negotiated a compromise which alleviated many of the concerns shared by all stakeholders. Merrill Lynch participated in this process as Graham Birch was asked by the South African Government to outline the view of foreign investors at a meeting in London.

Earlier this year the Government released the final version of the Minerals Bill. To the surprise of the market a number of the modifications that were agreed in 2001 were not incorporated into the final version. As you can imagine this does not boost the investment case for South Africa, nor does it set a good precedent for future good faith agreements. However the silver lining was that the financial impact did not seem that damaging since the Government gave the impression that security of tenure for existing operations was sound. The implementation framework of the Bill would be left to the minerals Charter!

On Friday July 26th South Africa's Mining Web, a leading internet newspaper, reported details of a draft minerals Charter leaked to them. There were two main points:

1) **Licensing:**
   a) Applicants for a mining licence should have a black economic empowerment (BEE) partner with at least 30 per cent equity in an existing operation
   b) Applicants for a new mining license (i.e. for a new project) should have a BEE partner with at least 51 per cent equity in a new operation
   c) Should the applicant be unable to find a suitable partner, government should intervene through vehicles such as the IDC or the Development Bank so that such shares can be warehoused within these organisations

2) **Ownership and Joint Ventures:**
   a) Government and industry undertake to negotiate the transfer of ownership of at least 51 per cent of mining industry assets to Historically Disadvantaged South Africans (HDSAs) within the next ten years
   b) Assets fit into two categories. Class one are those assets that have significant reliable markets and revenue, are in abundance and their ores are easily beneficiated. Class two are those considered risky and marginal ventures owing to geological factors, or because they have unreliable markets, or because they have assets that are too small to make a significant impact. This class is not considered as real empowerment.

As you can imagine the impact of such demands, although in draft form, was stunning. Previously the government had given the impression to investors that security of tenure for existing operations was guaranteed. Should the Charter become law then this would seem to be no longer the case. In addition the question arises about payment of compensation for the loss of the asset. At present the amount of money required to acquire such large stakes in existing and future assets would run into many tens of billions of dollars. The BEE's that exist today do not have access to large sums of capital and more importantly nor does the South African Government. Investors therefore jumped to the immediate worry that part or all of the stakes would be transferred without suitable compensation!

The controversy surrounding the implementation of the Minerals Bill and its accompanying Charter has increased our perception of South Africa's political risk and become very damaging to investor sentiment generally. In the past we have made submissions to SADMEA which were broadly supportive of the principle of black empowerment. However we also stated that there was no support for asset transfer without satisfactory compensation. We now feel that unless the issue is resolved swiftly and satisfactorily this situation is likely to have a lasting impact on our willingness to remain invested or make further investments in the country.

It is likely that what lies ahead is many months of negotiations between all the mining industry stakeholders and government in the creation of acceptable terms for meeting the objectives of the Minerals Bill. In the meantime we will continue to monitor the situation carefully and make sure that the Fund's exposure to South Africa is concentrated in risk adjusted value-based opportunities which are likely to be least affected by a negative Minerals Bill outcome. (478. 9/8/02)

A few months later the South African Government produced its new Minerals Charter, centring on the issue of black empowerment and the route to be taken to increase black participation in the mining industry. Graham Birch was firm but fair in his assessment of the Charter, and uncharacteristically lyrical.

"Oh but my joy of today is that we can all be proud to say to be young, gifted and black is where it's at."

Those of a certain age will recall the above lyrics belted out by Aretha Franklin in 1972. Now, 30 years on, it's coming true at least so far as black South Africans are concerned. The new Minerals Charter – unveiled by the government – sets out a road map for increasing black ownership of the mining industry. There is no doubt that this will create enormous opportunities for young, gifted black entrepreneurs – although hopefully the word "gifted" should be an adjective rather than a verb.

Terms of the Charter in a Nutshell
- 15 per cent equity target for Black Empowerment Groups (BEEs) within 5 years and 26 per cent within 10 years. This represents a softening of the original Government stance (30 per cent).
- The requirement for BEE groups to hold 51 per cent of new projects has been dropped.
- Where participation exceeds 26 per cent at one operation, the "extra" counts as a credit.
- Scorecard approach: beneficiation, procurement and skills training can be credits.
- Equity transfers at "fair market prices".
- No nationalisation.
- Industry to help secure R100 billion of funding (probably in the form of loan guarantees).

The Charter runs to ten pages and is "long" on concept and "short" on detail – so it's clearly going to have to rely on goodwill.

It's hard to know whether history is going to smile on this piece of legislation. Our sense is that there will be a swag of "unintended" consequences. With South Africa making up 40 per cent of the portfolio, the Charter is "big news". A sceptic might argue that over the next decade we will therefore suffer erosion of value as companies transfer 26 per cent of assets to BEE groups. The worst-case scenario is therefore a "give-away" of 10.4 per cent of portfolio value over 10 years or put simply 1 per cent per annum. This assessment is too pessimistic. That's because some of the companies in our portfolio have already done a lot of empowerment deals and are well on the way to hitting the initial 15 per cent (5-year) target already. Some of our investments are classified as black empowerment companies and are thus immune from the Charter.

At the end of this month we are having a meeting with the South African Minister of Mines. We will be telling her the following;

- The new Charter is flawed but workable.
- Goodwill will be needed to make it work.
- A period of calm is needed in which confidence in government policy is rebuilt.
- That the returns we seek from investment in South Africa are now higher than before.
- That the mining industry exists within a global context as well as a local one.
- That proceeds from asset sales to BEE vehicles, must be remittable to investors.
- That if, as we hope, the uncertainty dies down we will not need to take action at this stage regarding our South African exposure.

The South African Charter fiasco serves as a timely reminder that diversifying geographic risks has become more important than ever. It takes much longer for a country to build a reputation as a good destination for investment than it does to destroy it. Hopefully the lessons are learned. (**480. 15/10/02**)

In July 2003, concerned by economic developments in South Africa, Graham Birch decided to visit Johannesburg and try and beard the lion in his den.

One of the factors which has hobbled this Fund's performance in 2003 has been our exposure to South Africa. There was a horrible few weeks between late January and early April in which the gold price fell and the rand strengthened. This hit earnings of the gold miners hard and in the midst of the period, the South African Treasury unveiled its proposed minerals royalty regime. We hate to perform poorly, and this series of events stung me into action and provoked me to bring forward travel plans and hop on to a plane bound for Johannesburg.

The main purpose of the trip was to visit some of our biggest investments and "take their temperature". Additionally, however, I paid a long overdue visit to the South African Treasury – we've got less exposure to this country than we used to have and I wanted to tell the government why this is the case. Now it would not be fair to give away too much information on what was, after all, a private meeting. However you will not be surprised to hear that, amongst others, I made the following points:

- We believe that political risk in South Africa has risen.
- The royalty bill is an aggressive tax in that it takes no account of ability to pay and effectively adds to a company's "fixed" costs.
- I told the Treasury that the cumulative effect of the past 18 months of changes would lead to long-term damage to the industry.

Although I appreciated the opportunity to meet with the Treasury and discuss our concerns, I did not come away feeling particularly reassured. It would seem that in formulating its proposals, the Treasury paid little heed to the policies of the Ministry of Mines. As a result there are too few threads of continuity running through government minerals policies. Ironically the biggest losers from this lack of dialogue are probably the Black Economic Empowerment (BEE) companies (BEE is masterminded by the Mines Department). Most BEE companies will be asset rich/cashflow poor and by letting the Treasury take the first bite of the cash cherry, the Royalty Bill will make it much more difficult to fund BEE initiatives as free cashflow will be reduced – especially for new mines. (**487. 15/7/03**)

The Christmas Box, Compliance (the "boys in blue') and hedging

In December 2003 the Newsletter team of Graham Birch, Richard Davis and Evy Hambro were in nostalgic mode remembering Julian's old Christmas Box strategy, by now a Compliance Department 'no-no', as was the buying of physical gold, and they also considered again the issue of hedging. In the case of gold buying the Fund had finally been able to find a bullion vehicle that got round the rules and Barrick Gold had unexpectedly announced an end to its hedging; two bits of news that more than made up for the inability of the team to create a Christmas Box of mining shares for readers.

The late Julian Baring used to tell clients every year that if you bought a basket of gold shares on his birthday (9th December) and sold them at the end of the following January you could use the profits to pay for all your Christmas excesses. He called this the "Christmas Box". Of course in this day and age MLIM's Compliance Department would never permit such an assertion and would undoubtedly go into a "flat spin" if we ever made such an unverifiable "forward looking statement" in print. Compliance love to wield their "blue pencil" and seem to delight in striking out anything in this Newsletter that implies people might actually make some money in the future.

Compliance are also good at upholding the fund management rules and regulations. While most of the time we are grateful to them for this service, there are times when it has led to frustration. For example, one of the things that we've always wanted to do in the Fund is own physical gold. After all, a fund which has gold in its name ought to be able to own the real thing. Unfortunately, despite considerable pleading and pestering on our part, the powers that be have always forbidden it. The UCITS ("Undertakings for Collective Investment in Transferable Securities") rules which govern the Fund, expressly forbid the ownership of metallic gold or certificates which represent it.

We've always thought that this prohibition was bonkers and we never understood the thinking behind it: indeed we wonder whether any of the regulators involved could tell you either – the rationale for the decision may have been forgotten. Now however those clever chaps at the World Gold Council have devised a structure which meets the requirements of the UCITS rule. Effectively they have created an exchange traded fund – Gold Bullion Securities "GBS" – which has one sole asset, namely physical gold. With GBS, every share you buy is backed up by 0.1 ounce of gold. The shares trade on the London Stock Exchange and anyone can buy them. They are unlikely to go to a discount to their see-through value as gold bullion dealers can arbitrage them (although we cannot). We've waited a long time for a UCITS compliant gold vehicle and you won't be surprised to learn that we were first in the queue and have bought 850,000 shares for the Fund – equivalent to about 4.5 per cent of the Fund's assets.

Another event that reminded us of Julian recently was Barrick's abrupt decsion to quit hedging gold. Regular readers will doubtless remember the crusade against hedging waged in the pages of this Newsletter over the years. The main protagonists were Mercury/MLIM on one side and Barrick/AngloGold on the other. In particular Barrick's Peter Monk was passionately in favour of locking in the gold price and he firmly restated this deeply entrenched view at Euromoney's gold seminar in London on 20th November 2003. Imagine our surprise when a partial retraction of Munk's speech was made by Barrick the very next day and then on 2nd December Barrick issued a full statement of clarification making the following key point:

"Barrick announces that hedging is no longer necessary for the Company and intends to bring it down to zero over time."

Of perhaps even more importance was a further written observation in Q&A:

Question: "If the gold price goes to $500 per ounce, are you saying that you will not sell forward any gold?"

Answer: "Yes. We are committed to shareholder value and want to eliminate the discount that the market ascribes to hedging."

It seems perfectly clear to us that Barrick has had a "Road to Damascus" conversion. Given that Barrick's hedge book is underwater we have to assume that they will be delivering into the contracts (relatively painless) rather than buying them back. If this is the case then Barrick's 500 tonne hedge book will probably provide underlying support for the gold market for quite some time to come. Furthermore, AngloGold too is likely to be further reducing its hedge book in the light of the Ashanti transaction. Taking no action would lead to an overly hedged situation. All in all de-hedging is likely to remain a positive force through 2004. **(490. 18/12/03)**

Takeovers

One of Julian's earlier conundrums was what to do during the classic battle for Consolidated Gold Fields (CGF) in 1988, as we've seen, when Minorco, not for the first time as it turned out, laid siege to CGF. Since the start of the long bull market in mining shares at the start of the new millennium there have been a considerable number of "corporate actions" in the mining sector, some of which have involved Fund holdings. Perhaps the one that caused the most problems for the Fund was Harmony's bid for Gold Fields where it held a combined 11 per cent stake. The bid also included a side deal with Iamgold where the Fund had a near 2 per cent holding. Graham Birch goes through the pros and cons.

Most investors in the Fund will be aware of the hostile battle unfolding between Harmony and Gold Fields. The key facts are as follows:

- Harmony is offering 1.275 shares for every Gold Fields share. In order to do this Harmony must first receive shareholder approval to enlarge its share capital.
- There is a controversial two stage bidding process. The first stage is a tender offer for 34.5 per cent of Gold Fields. This will be followed by a full merger offer. Norilsk has pledged to sell its 20 per cent stake in Gold Fields to Harmony as part of stage two.
- The full merger is conditional on Gold Fields abandoning its deal with the Canadian company Iamgold. This deal would have seen Gold Fields injecting its international assets into Iamgold in exchange for equity.

We've been bombarded with calls from investment bankers about our views on the battle. We have spent hours locked in meetings with Harmony and Gold Fields, listening to their views on the best way to deliver "value" in South Africa. Having heard all sides of the argument we can now come down off the fence with our own views.

The story of Harmony's hostile bid for Gold Fields broke over the weekend of 16th/17th October. Our initial reaction was that this merger would do more harm than good for our funds and we were swiftly proved right. By close of business on the 18th October all three companies affected (Gold Fields, Harmony and Iamgold) were trading down from their levels of the previous week. Subsequent movements in the stock market have done nothing to change this initial verdict.

The share price falls have, in absolute terms, sliced 1 per cent off the value of the Fund – and have contributed to underperformance against the FT Gold Mines Index. Even more frustrating is that this fall in value has come against the background of a rising gold market. Since 15th October gold bullion has risen to a new 16-year high of $434/oz and the FT Gold Mines Index is up by 7.2 per cent. Put simply therefore, if this bid had not taken place and the affected companies had risen in line with the Index – instead of falling – then the Fund would be better off by 2 per cent. Making money in the gold share market is never easy and it is annoying to say the least when the "value" in the Fund sprouts wings and disappears off to "money heaven" like this.

Harmony would like to convince shareholders that we will recover this lost value by nodding through the transaction and waiting for a re-rating. The main thrust of Harmony's bid is to move the company "up the food chain" by merging with a better financed company with more robust operations. The strong rand has seriously eroded the profitability of all the South African mining companies but as a high-cost operator Harmony has been pushed into a loss making situation. Harmony is therefore stretched financially and the merger with Gold Fields provides an opportunistic exit from the quagmire. The counterargument from Gold Fields quite reasonably poses the question as to why Gold Fields has to be taken over in order to solve Harmony's problems!

We have known the executives of Harmony and Gold Fields for years. We like them personally and respect their accomplishments. It is awkward for us to be put in a position where we have to help choose who will be making that "long walk back to the pavilion". However our duty is to the Fund and it doesn't matter what our personal views might be on the individuals involved. Allan Gray, Harmony's largest institutional shareholder has come out and said that it supports Harmony's plans. We understand that of the three companies involved Allan Gray only holds Harmony. If we were in the same position (holding only Harmony) we too would be inclined to vote in favour of Harmony's proposals. However for our Fund the choice is complicated by our ownership of all three stocks. On balance we have decided that it would be better for our portfolio if the merger were to fail. The benefits from this might be as follows:

- Harmony and Gold Fields preserved as distinct entities – keeping portfolio flexibility.
- Short positions in Harmony established to benefit from the merger arbitrage unwound. This might lead to a share price rally.
- We are strongly in favour of the Iamgold transaction – which might be resuscitated leading to a rally in the stock.
- While Gold Fields shares might weaken initially, the stock would remain "in play" as it would still have a dissident 20 per cent shareholder. Furthermore, the management at Gold Fields would strive to achieve some of the cost savings outlined by Harmony.
- Value transfer from Gold Fields to Harmony implied in the merger ratio reversed.

The danger for the Fund is that any rally in Harmony might be shortlived. Gold Fields' defence highlighted Harmony's weak financial position in the strong rand environment and this could undermine the shares in the medium term. The weak link in Harmony's merger proposal is the EGM on 12th November and by the time you read this the outcome will probably be known. If Harmony shareholders have rejected the vote to enlarge share capital then the merger cannot proceed. With a heavy heart we have therefore voted against Harmony's EGM proposals – although this should not be seen as a vote of "no confidence" in management.

If Harmony succeeds in gaining approval for enlargement of capital at its EGM, then in all likelihood it will be successful in its tender offer and bid. This would leave Iamgold as a "jilted bride" at the altar in which case our holding in this company is too high. Our holding in the combined Harmony/Gold Fields would add up to over 10 per cent of the portfolio – a level which is above "UCITS" fund rules. We would have to reduce the position – another aggravating aspect of this transaction.

The worst outcome might be a "partial" success with Harmony securing a sizeable minority of Gold Fields. While this would strengthen Harmony's balance sheet, it would leave the companies locked in combat and would be messy. In these circumstances we would agitate for the two companies to negotiate a friendly deal – it must surely be possible to structure an arrangement which gives all the parties what they want. (495. 11/11/04)

In the end Harmony's bid failed, foundering on the fact that this was in essence a reverse takeover of a strong company by a weak one. However, it presented the Fund with a real headache as Gold and General had substantial holdings in both Harmony and Gold Fields, companies which it saw as offering quite different qualities of exposure to the gold sector (Harmony being a highly leveraged play and Gold Fields being a relatively low-cost, financially conservative play). The merger also challenged the principle of portfolio diversity which had been one of the major drivers of the Fund since its inception.

The Fund and its future

The Gold and General Unit Trust Fund, then under the James Capel banner, was launched on 8th April 1988 at a price of 50p per income unit. It peaked above 1600p in the second half of 2011 and in the summer of 2013 was priced around 800p. The price performance has been very much steadier than anyone might have imagined, bearing in mind the volatile nature of the gold and mining share sectors, and the percentage appreciation in the price of the units has for instance more than matched the appreciation in house prices in London – perhaps the most vibrant property market in the developed world, and seen by some as a licence to print money.

Whether the Fund can repeat the performance of its first 25 years on the journey to its 50th anniversary is obviously a moot point but one would not bet against it. Over its 25-year life, both during the Julian Baring era and afterwards, the Fund has successfully mixed basic, almost immutable, principles with forward thinking flexibility, a strategy that has done unitholders proud over the years.

It is perhaps appropriate to end with the very generous tribute paid to Julian Baring on his death in September 2000 by Graham Birch.

The Gold Guru

I well remember the first time I spoke to Julian. It was soon after he launched the Fund – then known as the James Capel Gold and General Fund – back in 1988. I was a young stockbroker with Kleinworts at the time, and quite inexperienced. The phone rang and it was Julian on the other end asking for information on some research I had written. I was immediately sent into a total panic. Here was the world's #1 gold guru with decades of experience asking a mere whippersnapper for advice. Julian wanted my top stock pick and I suggested Freeport Copper – which was in the midst of its IPO. Freeport had just found Grasberg and was, to my mind, undervalued.

359

To my utter astonishment, Julian then gave me an order to buy some Freeport for the new Fund. A day or two later I phoned Julian with the good news that the stock had risen 20 per cent. "Good news" he thundered – "that's terrible news because I want to buy some more." I tried to "hose him down" but he insisted and we bought more. Over the subsequent days and weeks he kept on increasing his position and I kept on trying to put him off. He was right of course, and over the subsequent five years the Freeport shares rose ten-fold. So began a friendship between us and in the process I had learned my first lesson from Julian – "Don't be a Whimp!"

Since then of course I have learned many more things from Julian. One important lesson that he taught all of us in the Mercury Mining Team is not to think like "gnus". Julian drummed into us that markets go up until they stop going up and then go down until they stop going down. When a market is high there are more reasons to buy it than sell it, otherwise it wouldn't be so high. The opposite applies when markets are low. At tops and bottoms, the reversal of the existing trend always looks like an aberration. The "gnus" find it hard to jettison their ingrained ideas just because a trend line has been breached. Julian's way to analyse markets took little account of "gnu" sentiment. Instead he believed that the level of an index or share should be proportionate to the underlying earnings power. When the "ducks were quacking" and gold shares were hot, we were taught that it was better to "feed a duck than become a duck". This saved the Fund's investors enormous sums of money at various times – especially in the Bre-X led exploration boom when any company able to spell the word "gold" could tap the market for cash.

Stockbrokers and Miners

Having been a highly rated stockbroker himself, Julian felt that he knew how to handle such people. It is a fact that stockbrokers divide into two groups; those who enjoyed sparring with Julian and those who were terrified of him. Julian would never tolerate "muddled thinking". Brokers who phoned up peddling a poorly thought out story would be dealt with mercilessly – "you just haven't got all your ducks in a row" was a much-heard expression. If research was particularly bad then Julian would take the telephone receiver, put it in the bin, rustle the paper around and then ask the luckless broker, "Did you hear that sound? It's the sound of your research being put in the bin!" I can only imagine what some of today's highly paid prima-donna analysts would think of such treatment.

Of course Julian also prized and rewarded good work; those brokers who understood gold found that working with Julian could be profitable in more ways than just commission income. Very often Julian's ability to think laterally helped refine and improve money-making strategies to such an extent that sow's ears really did turn into silk purses.

Mining companies too frequently felt the full force of his intellect. Time and again we would watch in awe during a company meeting while Julian, with the efficiency of a barrister, exposed weaknesses in their corporate strategies. Very often, the executives concerned would not even realise that they had fallen into one of Julian's "elephant traps" until it was far too late. Although many mining companies disagreed with Julian on various topics – especially gold hedging – most had the highest respect for his views and will miss his commentary. Not one executive – even after a mauling – could ever have the slightest doubt that Julian's sole mission was to further the interests of the mining industry and help the gold price.

In some instances, Julian's influence went far beyond that normally expected of a Fund Manager. Harmony Gold for example – one of the largest holdings in our Fund and one of the best performing companies in the gold sector – might not exist today were it not for Julian's determination to prevent it being strangled by the dead hand of Randgold (as it was then). Julian saw that by liberating assets like Harmony, and encouraging new management to be forward looking, instead of backward looking, progress (and money) could be made.

Savoy Dinners

When it came to gold bullion, Julian always believed that it was the affordability of gold rather than its exact price that mattered the most. He liked to look at this in many different ways, i.e. gold price adjusted for inflation or the number of hours an average person needed to work to earn enough to buy an ounce of gold. His favourite way of getting this message across though was to monitor how many gold sovereigns it took to buy a set dinner for two at the Savoy. The beauty of this approach was that he (and we if lucky) had to periodically test the fare in order to update the ratio. The Savoy dinners ratio became a Julian Baring hallmark.

We have learned the lessons

None of us on the Team, myself, David Baker, Trevor Steel, Evy Hambro, Richard Davis, Robin Batchelor and Maria Dinallo, would be working together were it not for Julian. We will sorely miss his drive, enthusiasm, creativity and lateral thinking.

We will never forget the lessons we have learned from him. He was a good friend and his untimely loss will be felt by us all far into the future. (**456. 7/9/00**)

While paying tribute to Julian Baring's enormous contribution to Gold and General the Team that succeeded him was also very aware that markets, particularly volatile ones such as gold and mining, change materially over time and the Fund had to reflect that. The fall from grace of South Africa is a particular case in point. However, many of the basic themes that exercised Julian also exercised Graham Birch, and continue to be relevant for today's BlackRock mining team.

Index